The Mammoth Book of

IQ PUZZLES

About the Authors

Philip Carter is a Justice of the Peace and an Estimator from Yorkshire. He is Puzzle Editor of *Enigmasig*, the monthly newsletter of the British Mensa Puzzle Special Interest group.

Ken Russell is a London surveyor and is Puzzle Editor of *British Mensa*, a magazine sent to its 43,000 British members monthly.

The Mammoth Book of

IQ PUZZLES

The complete collection of

IQ Powerplay
IQ Hotshot
IQ Countdown
IQ Firepower

PHILIP CARTER & KEN RUSSELL

Robinson
LONDON

Robinson Publishing
7 Kensington Church Court
London W8 4SP

This collected edition first published in the UK
by Robinson Publishing, 1996
First published as *IQ Powerplay* (1994), *IQ Hotshot* (1994),
IQ Countdown (1995), and *IQ Firepower* (1995)

A copy of the British Library Cataloguing in Publication data is available from the British Library
ISBN 1-85487-449-7

Printed and bound in the EC
10 9 8 7 6 5 4 3 2 1

About Mensa

Mensa is a social club for which membership is accepted from all persons with an IQ (Intelligence Quotient) of 148 or above on the CATTELL scale of intelligence. This represents the top 2% of the population. Therefore one person in 50 is capable of passing the entrance test, which consists of a series of intelligence tests.

Mensa is the Latin word for *table*. We are a round-table society where all persons are of equal standing. There are three aims: social contact among intelligent people; research in psychology; and the identification and fostering of intelligence.

Mensa is an international society with 110,000 members of all occupations: clerks, doctors, lawyers, police officers, industrial workers, teachers, nurses, and many more.

Enquiries to:
MENSA FREEPOST
Wolverhampton WV2 1BR
England

MENSA INTERNATIONAL
15 The Ivories,
6-8 Northampton Street,
London N1 2HV
England

Acknowledgements

We are indebted to our wives, both named Barbara, for checking and typing the manuscript, and for their encouragement in our various projects.

Preface to this edition

This volume includes four complete collections of IQ puzzles. Each collection is separately titled, and is followed by its own solutions and each puzzle has been given a differently numbered solution - i.e. they are not in sequence, so that when you look at the solution for puzzle 1, you will not accidentally see the answer for puzzle 2 on the same page.

IQ Powerplay

1 'X' Puzzle

Find 22 words in the grid, each must have at least one X in it. Words may be in any direction but always in a straight line.

D	I	O	L	Y	X	X
E	X	A	M	E	Y	I
X	A	L	S	L	L	P
T	I	Y	E	X	E	H
E	E	N	X	O	M	O
R	E	X	A	C	T	I
X	Y	P	T	U	X	D

(Solution 4)

2 Warehouse

A warehouse has to be built at one of the mile points along a road so that its weekly delivery miles are kept to a minimum.

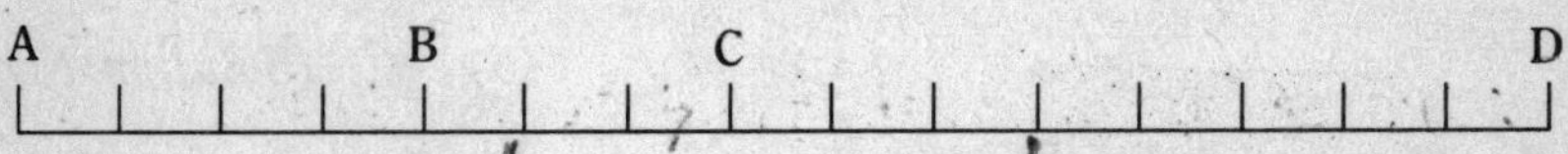

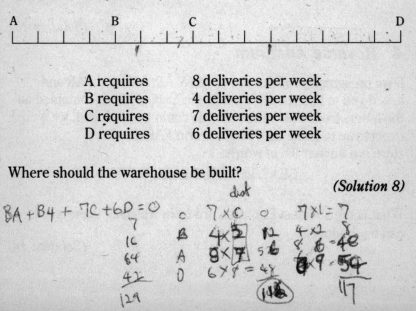

A requires	8 deliveries per week
B requires	4 deliveries per week
C requires	7 deliveries per week
D requires	6 deliveries per week

Where should the warehouse be built?

(Solution 8)

3 Alphabet Crossword

Complete the grid by using all 26 letters of the alphabet.

A B C D E F G H I J K L M
N O P Q R S T U V W X Y Z

	■	K	■	S		U	I	
A	C		E	■		■		■
	■	A	■		I		E	D
E			S	■		■		■
R	■	I	N		E	R	■	G
■		■		■	R	A	I	
F	A		R		■		■	O
■	V	■		■		E	R	
	E	B	R		■		■	E

(Solution 11)

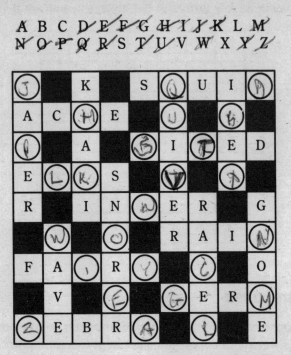

4 Reverse Anagram

If we presented you with the words MAR, AM, and FAR and asked you to find the shortest English word which contained all the letters from which these words could be produced, we would expect you to come up with the world FARM.
Here is a further list of words:

BEAT, ROUTE, BRAIN, MINT

What is the shortest English word from which all these words can be produced?

(Solution 16)

5 No Blanks

The blank squares have been removed from this crossword. Letters have been inserted in their place. You have to find the blank squares.

S	C	A	L	A	R	A	R	E	M	A	N	D
E	R	R	I	C	E	P	A	P	E	R	E	I
M	I	T	T	E	N	A	M	E	T	R	E	S
I	O	I	O	R	E	V	U	E	O	I	D	I
C	A	S	T	A	W	A	S	L	O	V	E	N
O	L	T	E	G	A	T	E	H	O	E	D	V
N	O	O	N	E	W	I	F	E	Z	S	R	E
D	O	C	O	T	E	M	I	N	E	T	I	S
U	P	O	N	P	L	A	C	E	S	O	F	T
C	A	V	E	D	O	N	O	R	T	I	T	M
T	R	E	P	A	N	O	M	E	A	L	I	E
O	E	R	E	M	E	D	I	A	T	E	E	N
R	O	T	T	E	R	O	C	R	E	D	I	T

(Solution 21)

6 Reserves

In a game of 36 players that lasts just 15 minutes, there are four reserves. The reserves alternate equally with each player, therefore, all 40 players are on the pitch for the same length of time. For how long?

(Solution 23)

7 *Anagrammed Synonyms*

In each of the following, study the list of three words. Your task is to find two of the three words which can be paired to form an anagram of one word which is a synonym of the word remaining. For example:

LEG - MEEK - NET

The words LEG and NET are an anagram of GENTLE, which is a synonym of the word remaining, MEEK.

1. BIDS - SEE - TOO
2. VEERED - WEAK - TAN
3. SIT - HIND - POORER
4. OUT - KISS - SCALE
5. POST - SLAP - AIDE
6. TREE - ART - EBB
7. WHET - MUTE - TAILS
8. DRAIN - ONCE - ACT
9. SIN - EAT - GET
10. SANE - VICE - SKEW

(Solution 27)

8 *1984*

The digits 0, 1, 2, 3, 4, 5, 6, 7, 8, 9 can be arranged into an addition sum to add up to almost any total, except that nobody has yet found a way to add up to 1984.
However 9 digits can equal 1984 by an addition sum. Which digit is omitted?

(Solution 32)

9 Round the Hexagons

Can you work out what should be the contents of the bottom hexagon?

(Solution 36)

10 Hexagon

Fit the following words into the six spaces encircling the appropriate number on the diagram so that each word correctly interlinks with the two words on either side (you will see that each word has two consecutive letters in common with the word on its side). (NOTE: to arrive at the correct solution some words will have to be entered clockwise and some anti-clockwise.)

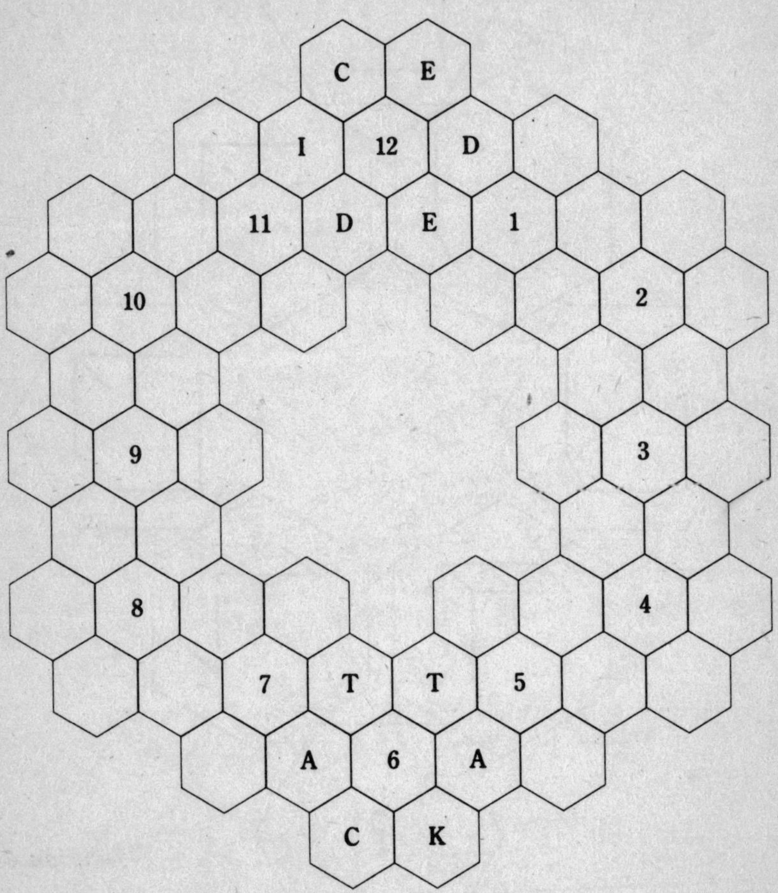

ADROIT - DEFERS - GERUND - ROTATE - REMARK - TAGGED - ~~ATTACK~~ - ~~DECIDE~~ - URGENT - MALADY - WIDENS - DIVIDE

(Solution 40)

11 Circles

Which of these fit into the blank circle to carry on a logical sequence?

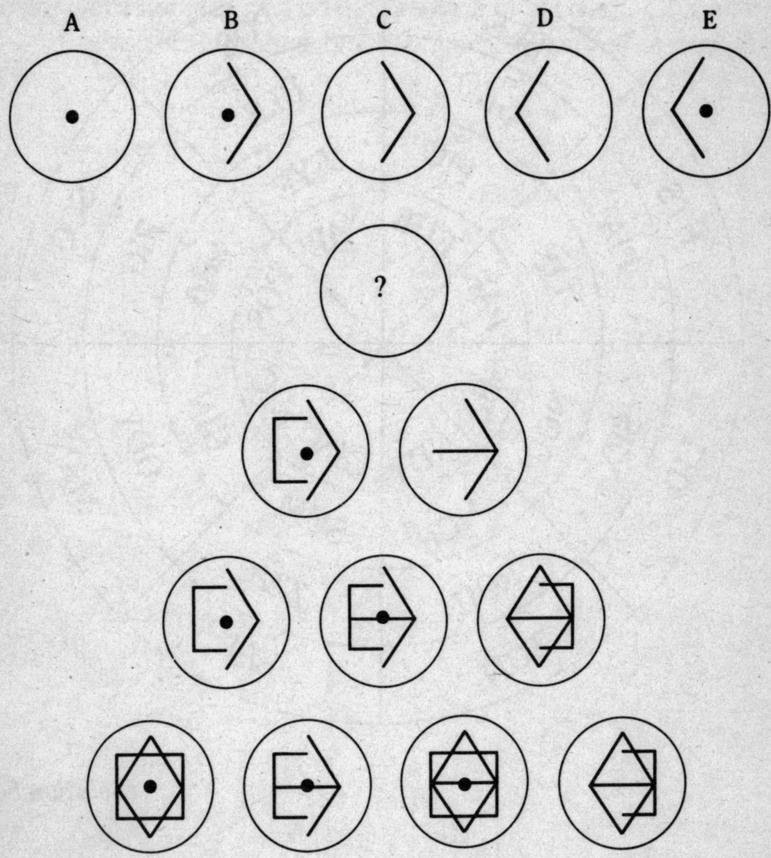

(Solution 44)

12 Target Crossword

Find sixteen 6-letter words by pairing up the thirty-two 3-letter bits.

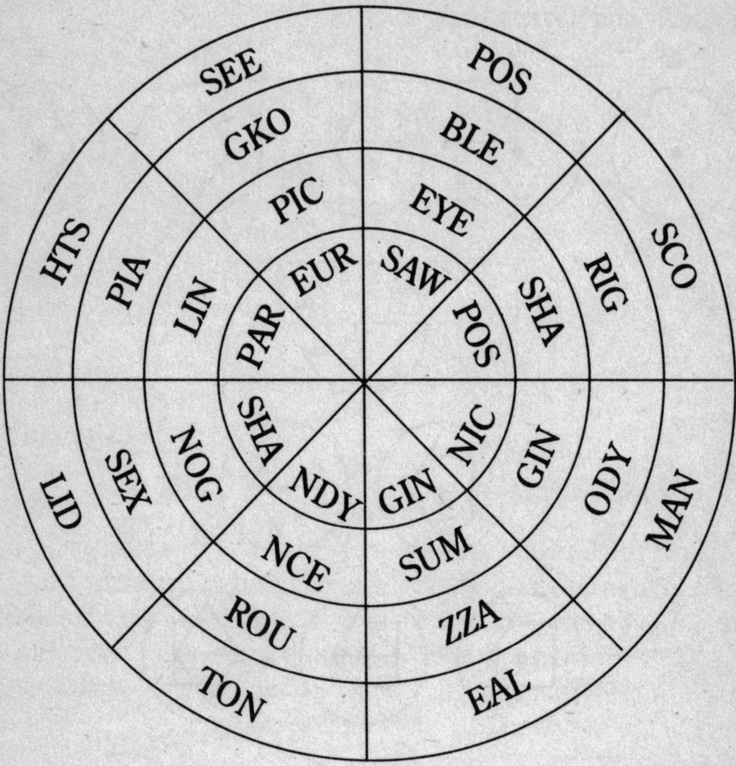

(Solution 50)

13 Sequence

What number comes next in this sequence?
101, 65, 131, 116, 131, 1021, ?

(Solution 54)

14 No Repeat Letters

The grid below contains 25 different letters of the alphabet. What is the longest word which can be found by starting anywhere and working from square to square horizontally, vertically or diagonally and not repeating a letter?

J	N	B	D	I
X	E	R	V	G
P	O	C	U	Q
S	K	T	W	L
Y	H	M	A	F

(Solution 58)

15 Word Circle

Complete the fifteen words below, so that two letters are common to each word. That is, reading across, the same two letters that end the first word also start the second word, and the two letters which end the second also start the third word, etc. The two letters that end the fifteenth word also are the first two letters of the first word, to complete the circle.

. . AR . .	. . EE . .	. . NA . .	. . NU . .
. . SU . .	. . TT . .	. . GA . .	. . PH . .
. . MI . .	. . BU . .	. . VI . .	. . EL . .
. . ND . .	. . IG . .	. . FE . .	

(Solution 61)

16 Missing Square

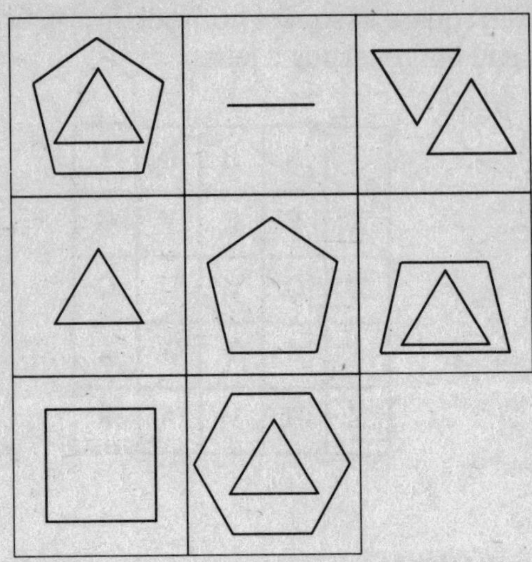

Which of the following is the missing square?

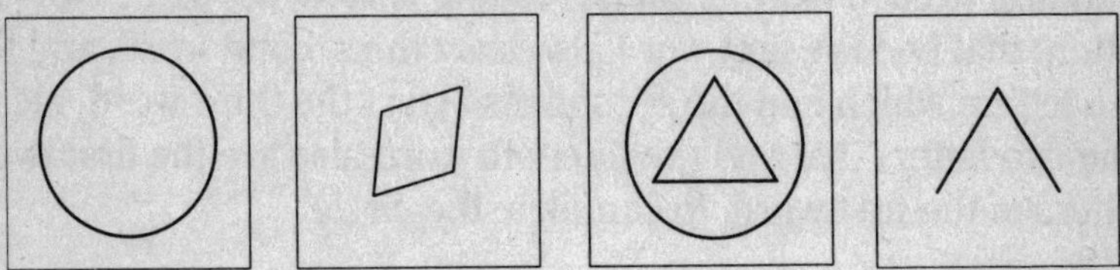

A B C D

(Solution 66)

17 Logic

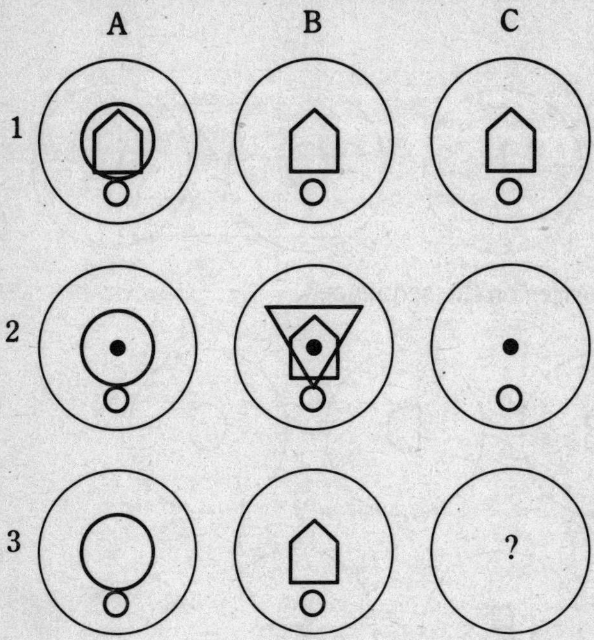

Logically which circle below fits the above pattern?

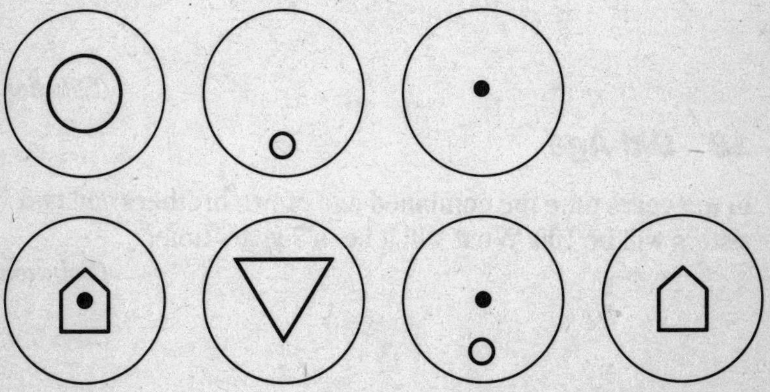

(Solution 70)

18 Sequence

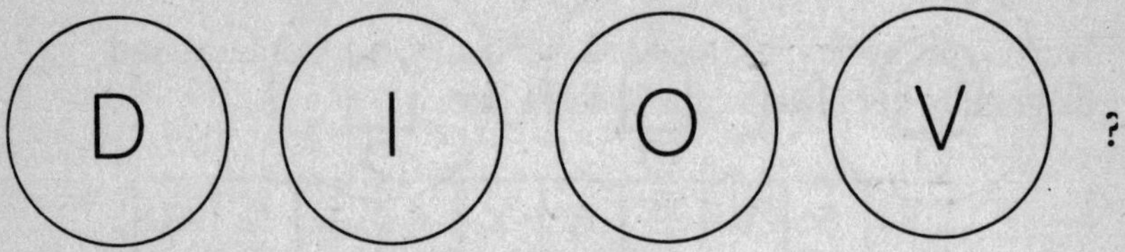

Which option carries on the sequence?

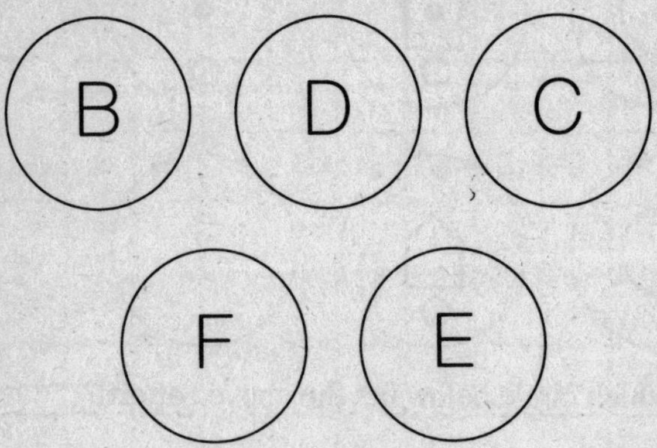

(Solution 79)

19 Old Age

In ten years time the combined age of two brothers and two sisters will be 100. What will it be in 7 years time?

(Solution 74)

20 Word Search

Find 20 words to do with
DRINKS

Words run backward, forward, vertically, horizontally, and diagonally but always in a straight line.

E	S	U	E	R	T	R	A	H	C
N	E	Y	V	E	Z	L	O	A	O
I	R	N	A	Z	C	C	P	X	I
D	E	W	I	O	K	P	K	N	N
A	G	F	H	D	U	C	I	A	T
N	A	O	G	C	A	T	H	E	R
E	L	O	C	R	R	C	L	O	E
R	R	I	R	A	G	M	S	E	A
G	N	A	M	O	I	E	L	U	U
O	R	A	N	G	E	A	D	E	M

(Solution 83)

21 Letters Sequence

Which two letters come next in the following sequence?

TO, NE, US, RN, ER, RS, ?

(Solution 87)

22 Bracket Word

Place two letters in each bracket so that these finish the word on the left and start the word on the right. The letters in the brackets, read downwards in pairs, will spell out a 10-letter word.

ME (..) AS
UN (..) UT
SA (..) NE
MO (..) IN
LE (..) GO

(Solution 91)

23 Odd One Out

Which is the odd one out?

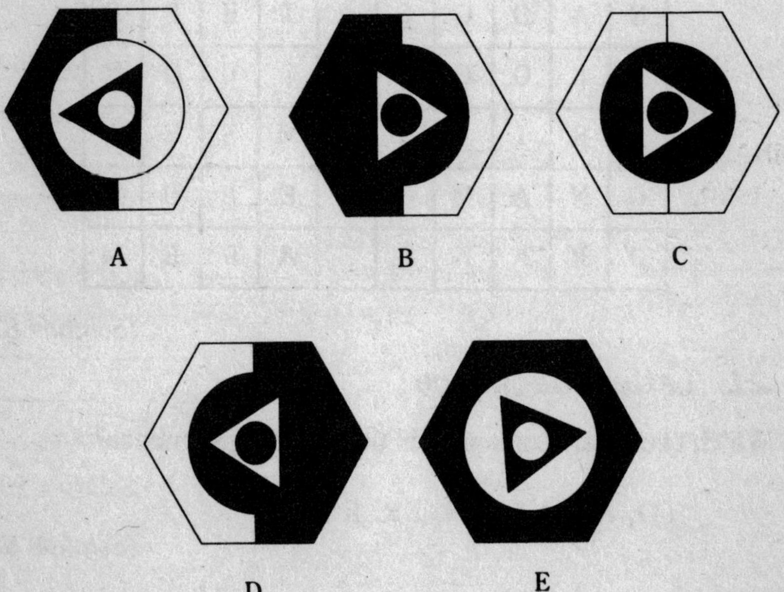

(Solution 95)

24 Word Power

In column (A) is a list of words. The problem is to rearrange them so that their initial letters spell out a quotation. To make the task easier, refer to the definition in column (B) and put the correct word with that definition in the answer column (C). When all the words have been correctly placed in column (C), the quotation will then appear reading down the initial letters.

(A) Words	(B) Definitions	(C) Answers
KOHL	Unearthly, weird	________
ESCULENT	A rare word for edict	________
TOLU	Refreshment with food and drink	________
GERUND	Uproot	________
ELDRICH	A cosmetic powder	________
VICARIOUS	With great strength	________
UKASE	Penniless	________
INANITION	Delegated	________
AMAIN	Edible	________
ODALISK	A noun formed from a verb ending -ing	________
REFECTION	Female slave in a harem	________
IMPECUNIOUS	A female swan	________
EXTIRPATE	Exhaustion	________
TERMAGANT	An aromatic balsam	________

(Solution 99)

25 Greek Cross to Square Puzzle

Draw two lines which will dissect the Greek Cross into four congruent (same size and shape) pieces which can then be arranged to form a square.

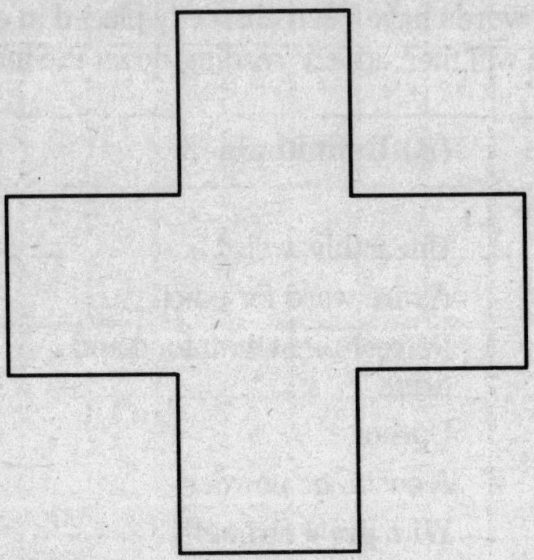

(Solution 103)

26 Appropriate Anagrams

Find the appropriate anagrams of these words and phrases.

PARADISE REGAINED
SAINT ELMO'S FIRE
SAUCINESS
SEMOLINA
TOTAL ABSTAINERS
WAITRESS
THERAPEUTICS
THE MONA LISA
MEDICAL CONSULTATIONS
A SENTENCE OF DEATH

(Solution 107)

27 Jumble

Commencing always with the centre letter V spell out eight 11-letter words travelling in any direction (but each letter can only be used once).

I	T	Y	E	R	I	S	L	Y
L	C	U	T	A	O	U	Y	L
I	I	L	A	C	X	A	U	S
T	M	R	E	I	E	T	I	O
P	A	S	E	**V**	A	C	I	A
I	H	R	I	E	E	C	N	T
Y	S	C	E	R	N	N	T	I
O	E	O	S	U	T	A	I	O
R	E	M	N	O	I	T	L	N

(Solution 111)

28 Four Integers

ABCD represents four integers such that the following arrangements are square numbers. What integer does each letter represent?

CABA
DCBA
DACB

(Solution 114)

29 Symbols

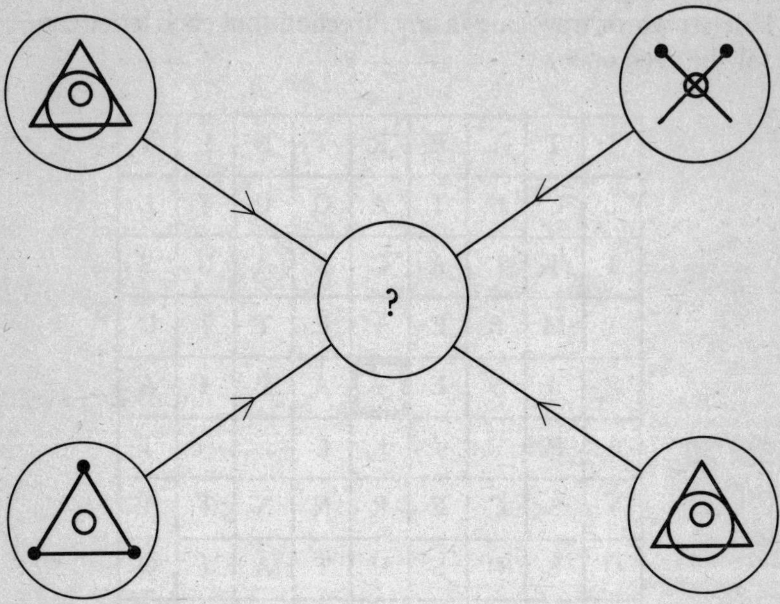

Each line and symbol which appears in the four outer circles, is transferred to the centre circle according to these rules.

If a line or symbol occurs in the outer circles:

Once	it is	transferred
Twice	it is	possibly transferred
3 times	it is	transferred
4 times	it is	not transferred

Which of the circles A, B, C, D or E, shown opposite should appear at the centre of the diagram?

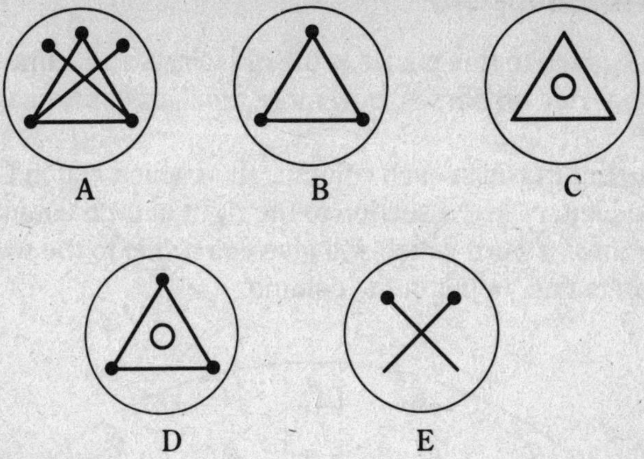

(Solution 116)

30 Cheeses

6 cheeses of different sizes are placed on stool A.
How many moves will it take to move the cheeses one by one to stool C?
A cheese must not be placed on a cheese smaller than itself.

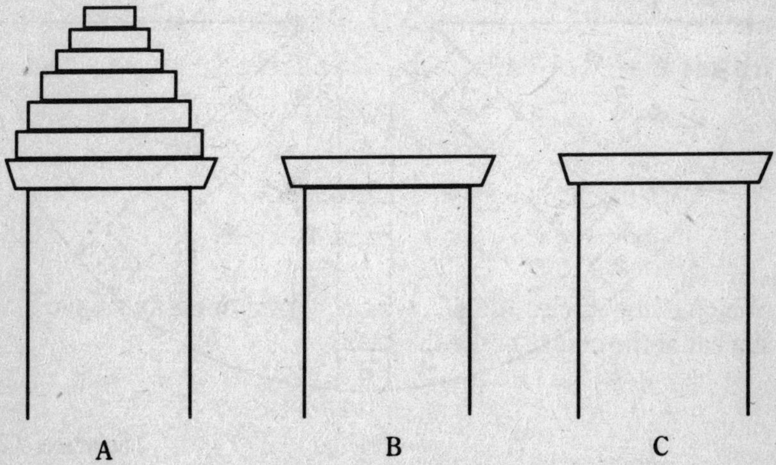

(Solution 118)

31 The Gallopers

The name given to this puzzle is the old fairground name for the roundabout ride on horses, now more familiarly known as the carousel.

Complete the words in each column, all of which end in G. The scrambled letters in the section to the right of each column are an anagram of a word which will give you a clue to the word you are trying to find, to put in the column.

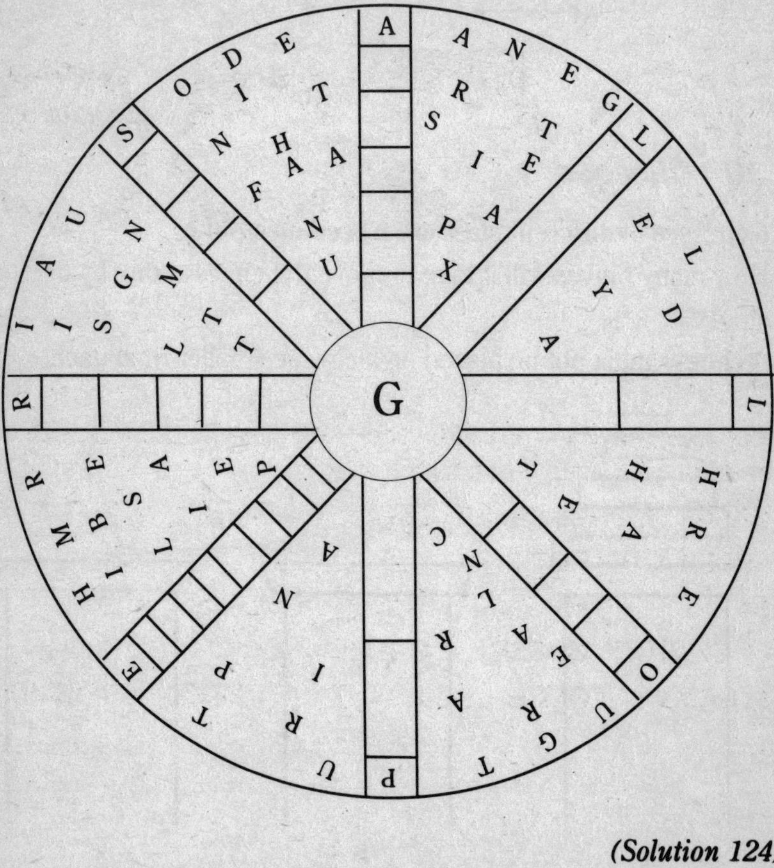

(Solution 124)

32 Analogy

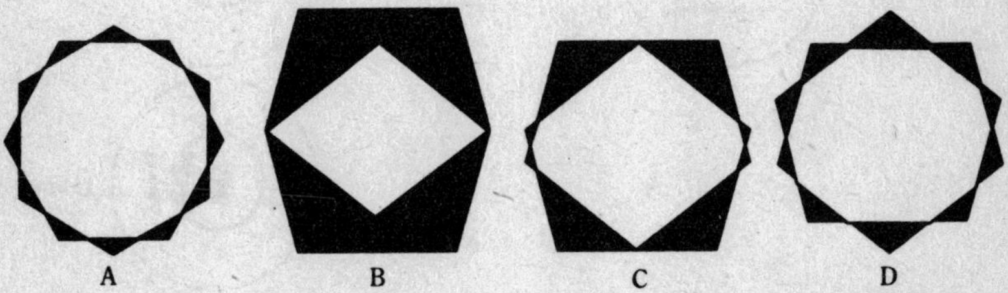

(Solution 129)

33 Birds

The twenty five words can be paired up to make 12 birds with one word left over. Which is the word?

GREBE	WARBLER	DOVE	WATER	PIGEON
CARRIER	PEACOCK	HAWK	PETREL	SNOW
NIGHT	MUSCOVY	WILLOW	BLACK	OUSEL
COCKATOO	HOUSE	GOOSE	OWL	MARTIN
STORMY	DUCK	TAWNY	TURTLE	CRESTED

(Solution 133)

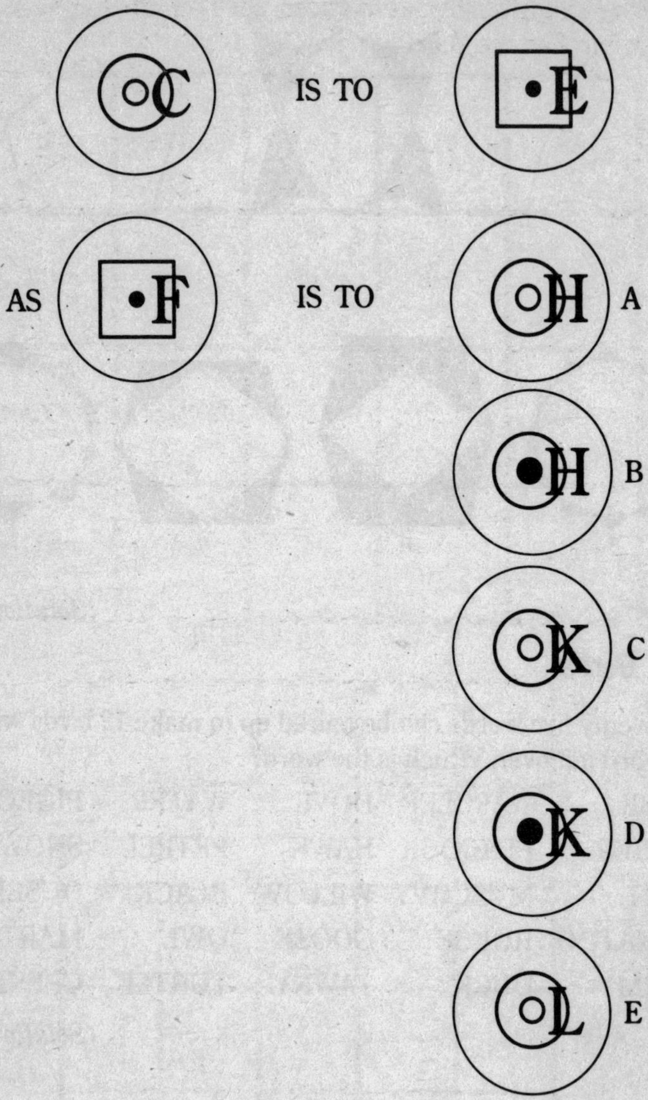

(Solution 121)

35 Knight

Using the knight's move as in chess, spell out the message. You have to find the starting point.

AS	IT	OWN	PEOPLE'S	ARE
BUT	OTHER	ARE	HARD	OUR
FIND	SILLY	BELIEVE	PROBABLY	THOUGHTS
THAT	THEY	WE	AS	TO

	x		x	
x				x
		Knight		
x				x
	x		x	

(Solution 135)

36 Series

Write down the tenth term of

6, 18, 54, …

And find a formula for quickly working out the answer.

(Solution 138)

37 Division

Divide the grid into four equal parts, each of which should be the same shape and contain the same 9 letters which can be arranged into a 9-letter word.

N	T	G	E	O	O
N	U	Y	N	S	S
Y	U	R	R	Y	E
R	G	O	S	U	G
E	Y	S	O	T	U
T	G	E	T	R	N

(Solution 142)

38 Three Animals

Use all the letters in the sentence below once each only to spell out the names of three animals.

ALL HERE NAME A POT PLANT

(Solution 146)

39 Equilateral Triangle

Draw in the largest possible equilateral triangle so that it does not touch another triangle and does not overlap the side of the grid.

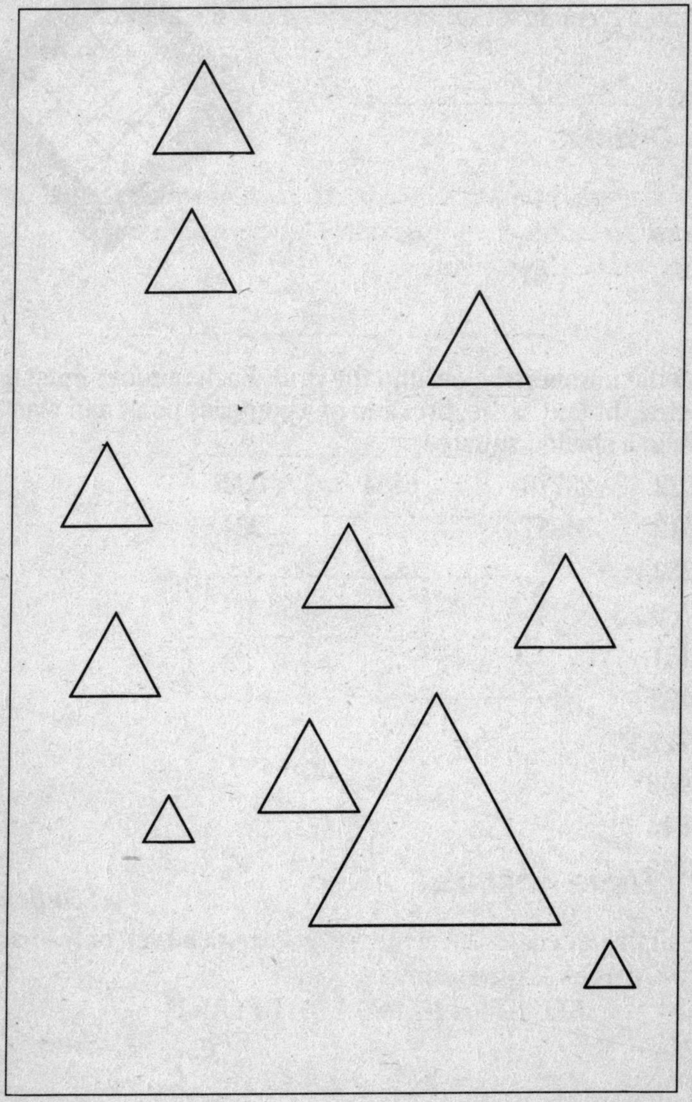

(Solution 151)

40 Directional Numbers

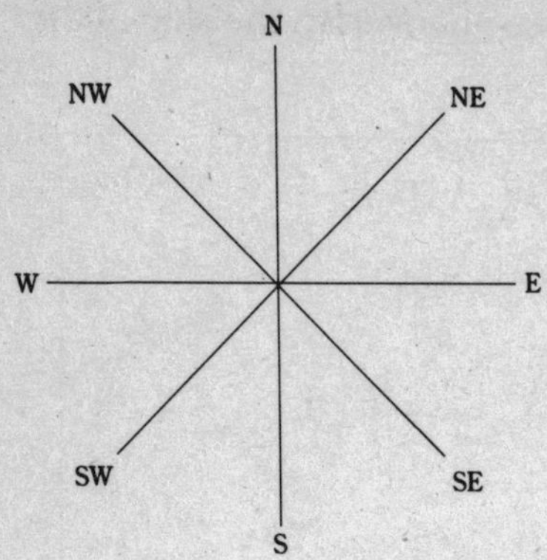

Fit all the numbers below into the grid. Each number must travel in a straight line in the direction of a compass point and start and finish in a shaded square.

217932	28778	6884	632
482912	34981		984
834252			
911763			
864131			
882122			
982711			
276966			
417644			
924492			

(Solution 157)

41 *Find a Word*

Trace out a 13-letter word by travelling along the lines. You need to find the starting letter and must not cross a letter twice.

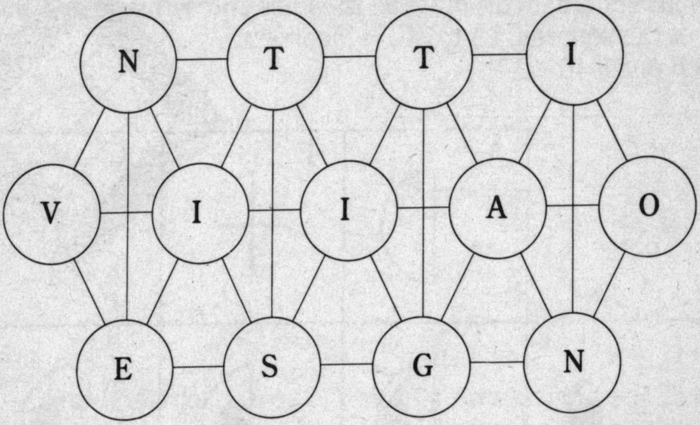

(Solution 1)

42 *Synonym Circles*

Read clockwise to find two 8-letter words which are synonyms. You have to find the starting point and provide the missing letters.

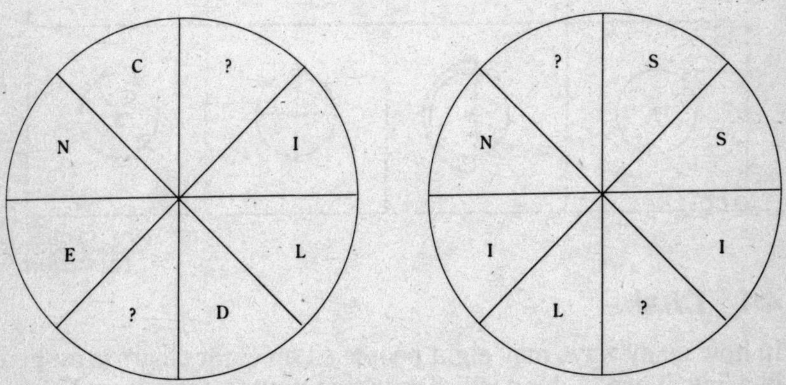

(Solution 5)

43 Grid

Each of the nine squares marked 1A to 3C should incorporate all the lines and symbols which are shown in the squares A, B or C and 1, 2 or 3, directly to the left and directly above.
Thus 2B should incorporate all the lines and symbols in 2 and B.
One of the squares, 1A to 3C, is incorrect.
Which one is it?

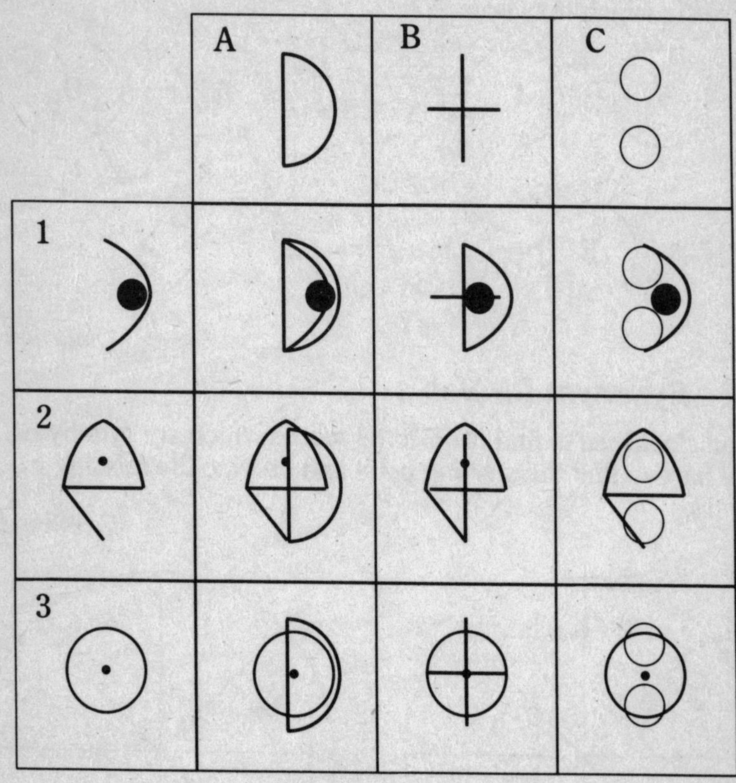

(Solution 9)

44 Chairs

In how many ways may eight people sit on eight chairs arranged in a line, if two of them insist on sitting next to each other?

(Solution 13)

45 Double-Bigrams

A bigram is any sequence of two consecutive letters in a word, for instance IG in the word BIGRAM, and a double-bigram is such a sequence which occurs twice in succession, such as IGIG in the word WHIRLIGIG.

Below we list several double-bigrams. Can you complete the words in which they occur?

••• POPO •••••
••• LOLO ••
••• ENEN •••
••• VIVI ••
•• LALA •••
•• TITI ••
•• BIBI ••
••• WAWA •
•• OTOT •••
•• ODOD ••••••
• NINI ••••••
••• ININ •
••• DIDI ••
• ATAT ••••

(Solution 17)

46 Number

What number is missing from the grid?

8	12	6
3	20	6
3	9	?

(Solution 20)

47 Matrix

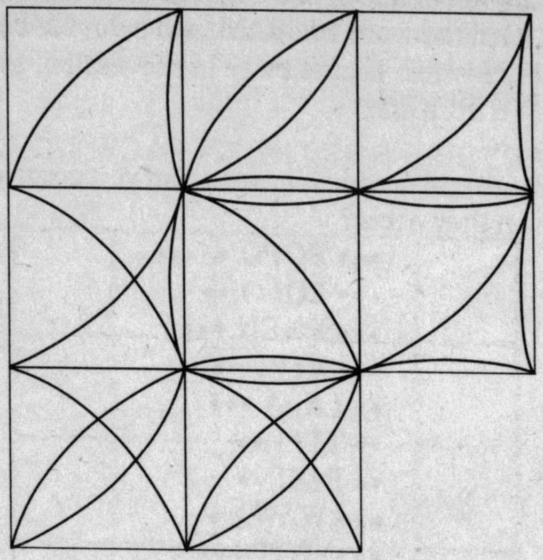

Look along each horizontal line and down each vertical line and choose the missing square from the options below.

A

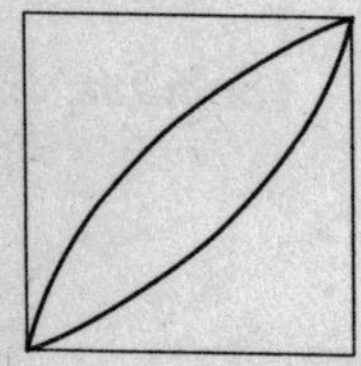

B

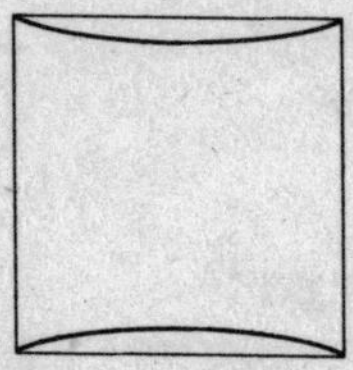

C

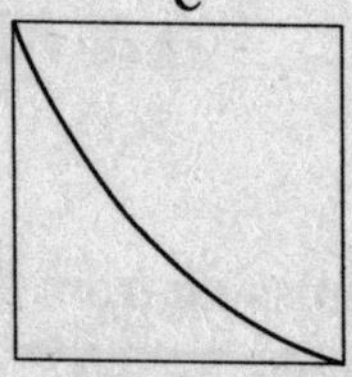

D

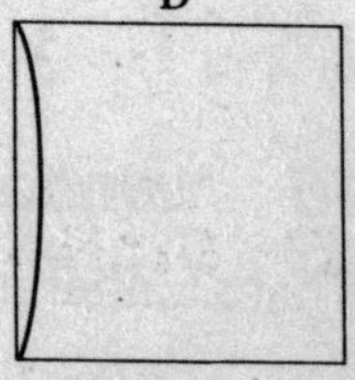

E

F

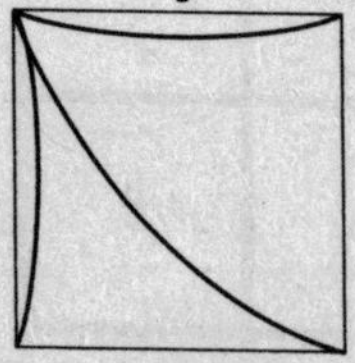

G

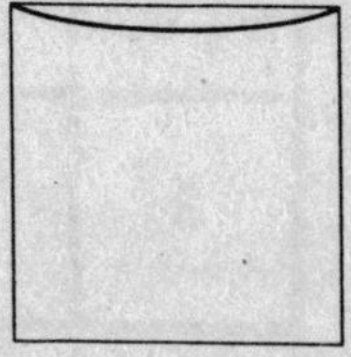

H

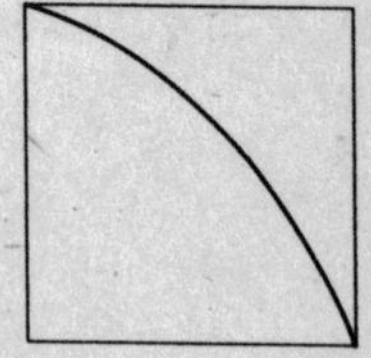

(Solution 25)

48 Anagrammed Magic Square

Using all 25 letters of the sentence below once each only, form five 5-letter words which when placed correctly in the grid will form a magic word square where the same five words can be read both horizontally and vertically.

CARTER'S NORTHERN FACE SAFEST

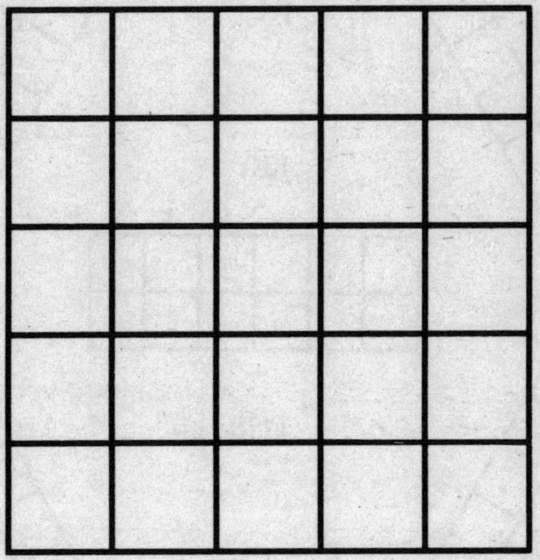

(Solution 29)

49 Stations

If there are 8 stations between towns A and B. How many different single tickets must be printed so that one may book from any station to any other?

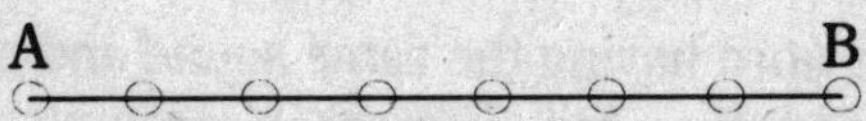

(Solution 33)

50 Hexagram

Solve the six anagrams of FISH. Transfer the six arrowed letters to the key box and solve this anagram to discover a key seventh.

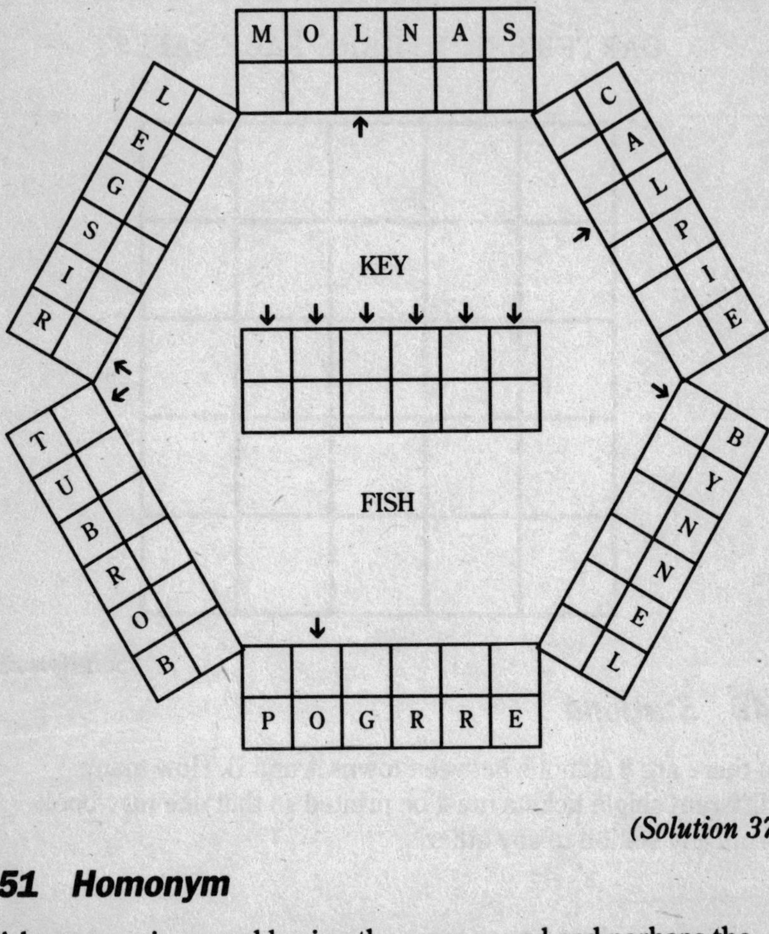

(Solution 37)

51 Homonym

A homonym is a word having the same sound and perhaps the same spelling as another, but different in meaning. For example, Cleave and Cleave or Sun and Son. The words I and Eye are examples of a pair of homonyms in which none of the letters in one word appear in the other. Can you find another pair of homonyms which have this feature?

(Solution 41)

52 Circles

Which of these fit into the blank circle to carry on a logical sequence?

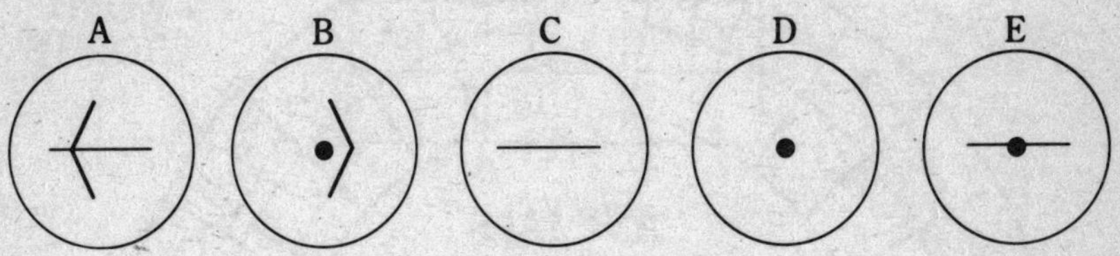

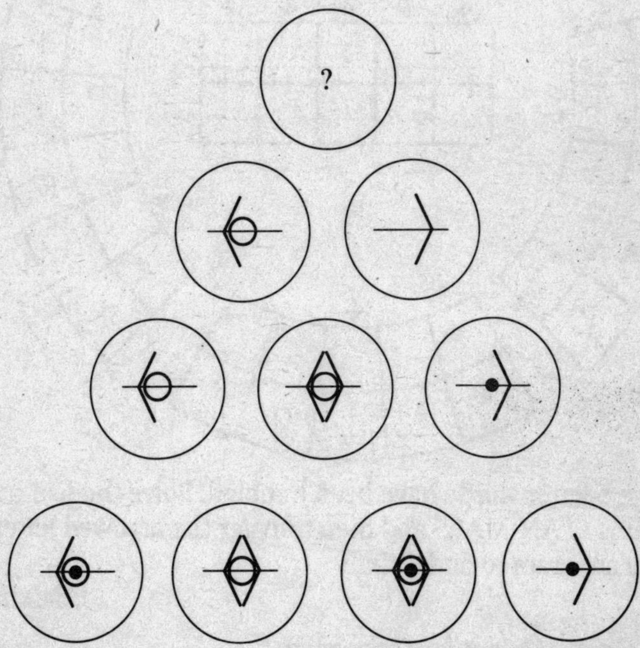

(Solution 46)

53 Pentagram

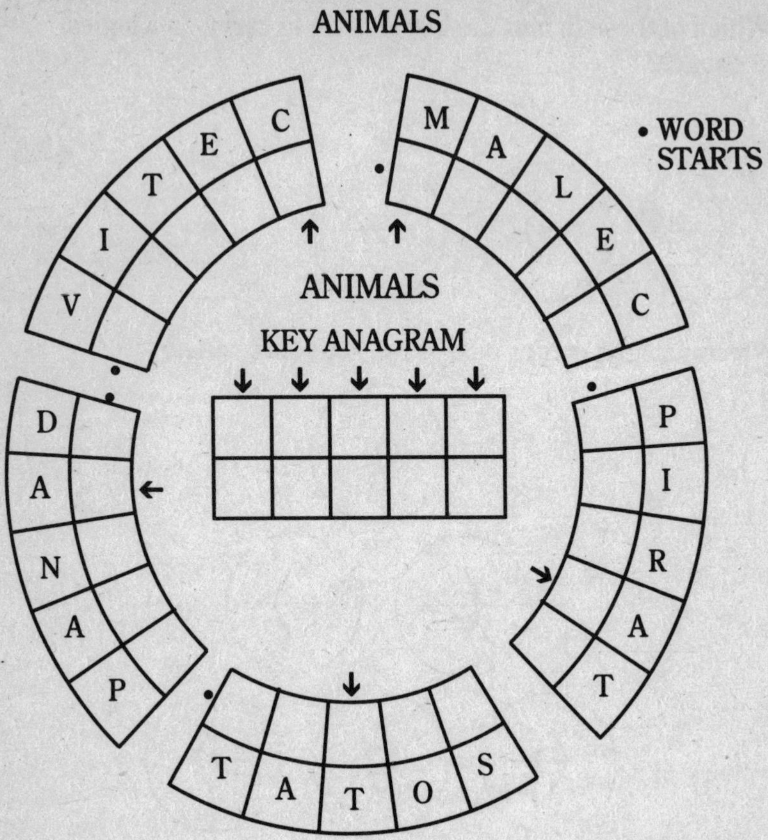

The five 5-letter words have been jumbled. Solve the five anagrams of ANIMALS and then transfer the arrowed letters to the key anagram to find a sixth.

(Solution 48)

54 Something in Common

What do the answers to the following clues all have in common?

A small container	A European monetary currency
To enter abruptly	An inside covering
To strike smartly	To walk long and far
Easily damaged	Broker

(Solution 51)

55 Octagons

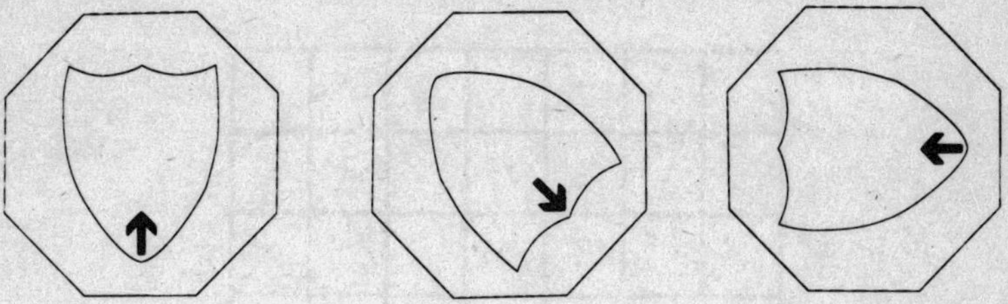

Which octagon comes next in the above sequence?

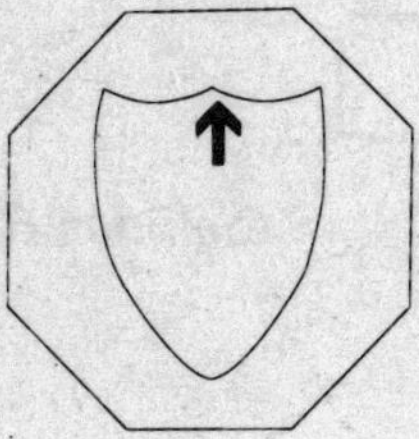

A

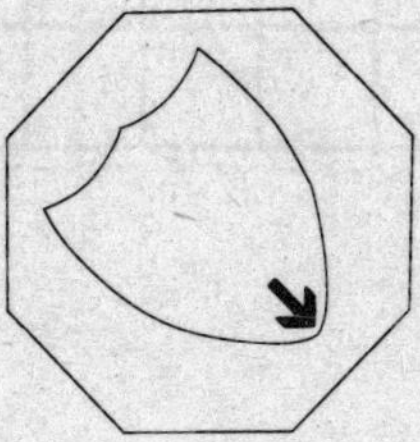

B

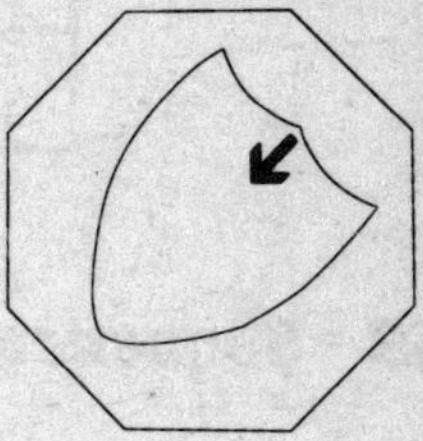

C

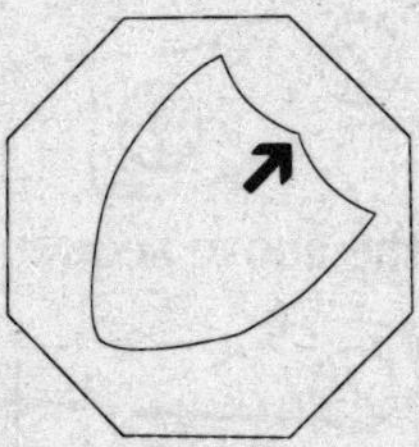

D

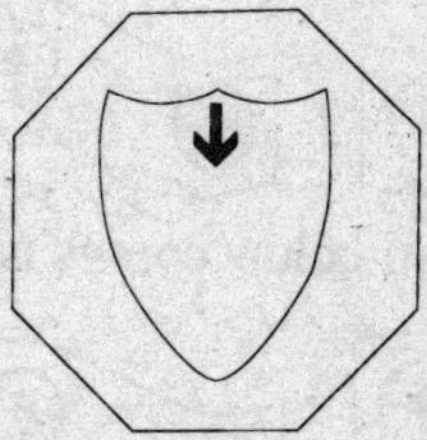

E

(Solution 55)

56 Cards

Permutation = Arrangements
How many 4-card permutations can you make in a pack of 52 playing cards?

(Solution 59)

57 Number Logic

Where, logically, would you place the number 1 in this grid?

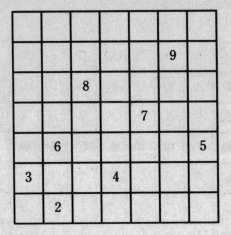

					9	
		8				
				7		
	6					5
3			4			
	2					

(Solution 63)

58 Sequence

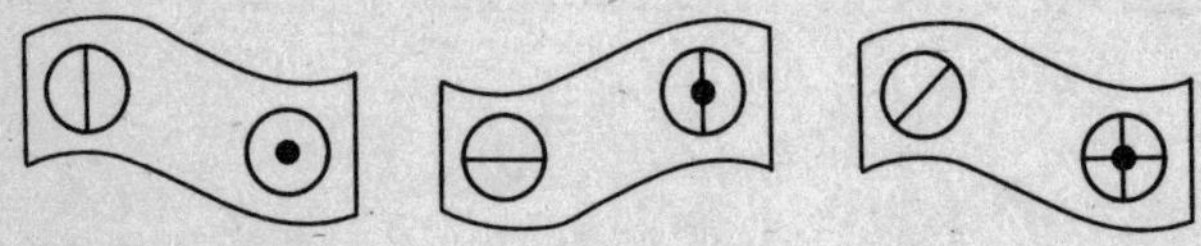

Which option below comes next in the above sequence?

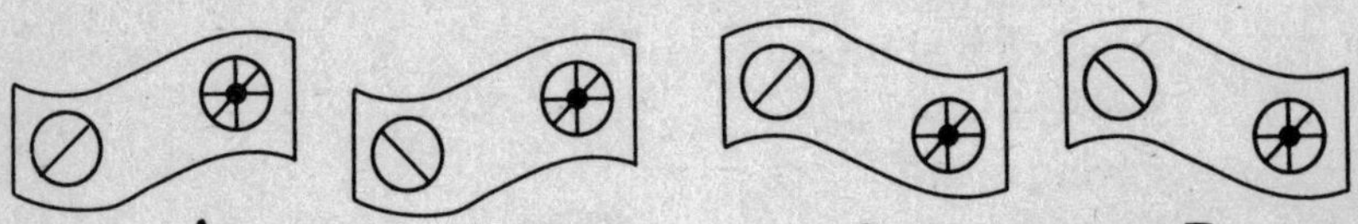

A B C D

(Solution 67)

59 Word Power

The answers are all 9-letter words and will be found in the grid one letter on each line in order.

C	G	P	R	M	D	F	M	O
B	A	E	U	E	A	U	L	A
S	C	S	J	A	B	N	R	L
E	L	G	T	K	U	I	A	S
C	A	S	U	I	Y	J	E	M
C	V	U	F	T	L	T	B	T
H	A	E	O	A	O	I	O	E
O	U	O	E	E	N	N	N	N
T	T	N	R	A	P	E	R	T

CLUES

1 To go stealthily
2 A soldier armed with hand fire-arms
3 Small ribbed melon
4 Seducer
5 Paving stone
6 Dried hemp
7 Reclining
8 Argument against
9 To gad about

(Solution 71)

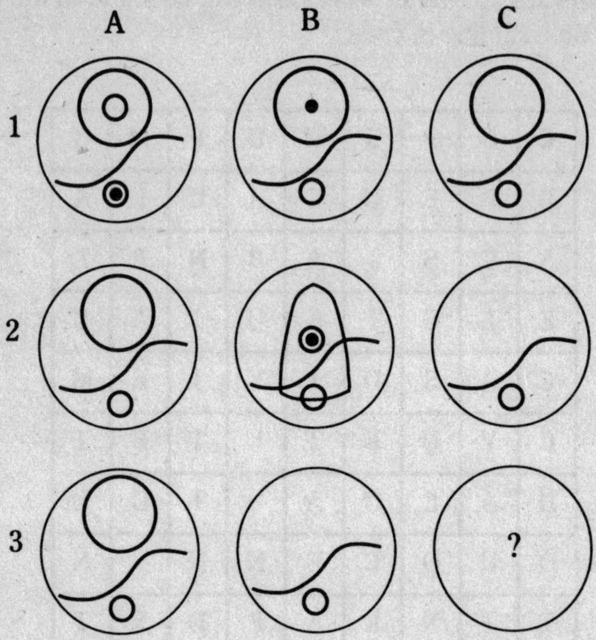

Logically which circle below fits into the above pattern?

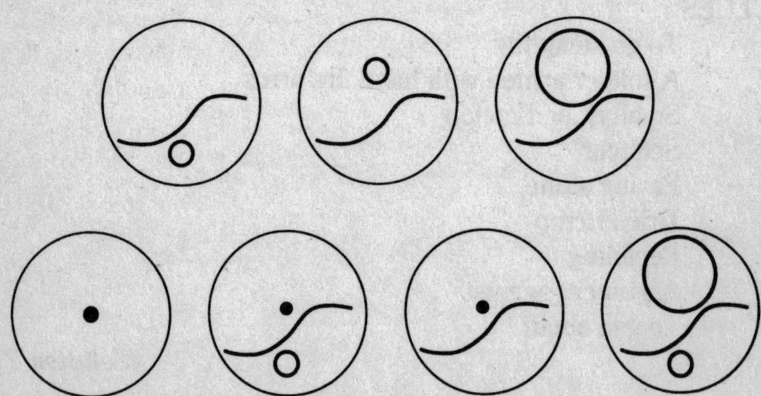

(Solution 75)

61 Pyramid

Spell out the 15-letter word by going into the pyramid one room at a time. Go into each room once only. You may go into the passage as many times as you wish.

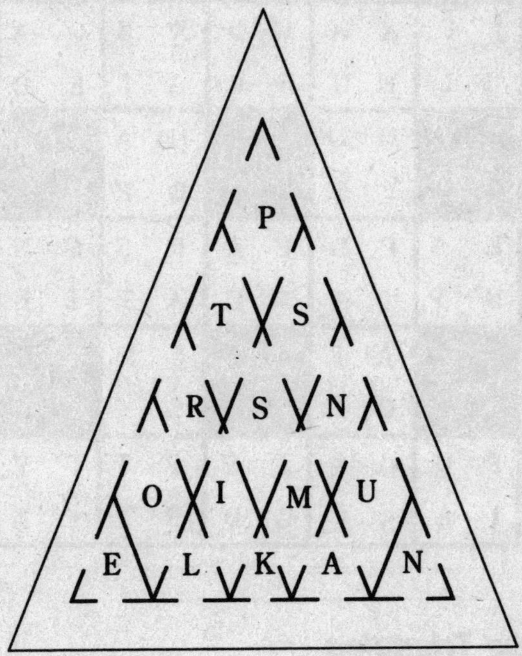

(Solution 78)

62 Sequence

ANDY, AMY, DES, DEAN, RUTH, RAY

What name below completes the above sequence?

TERRY, JANE, ALEC, BETH, TRUDY

(Solution 80)

63 Clueless Crossword

In each square there are four letters. Your task is to cross out three of each four, leaving one letter in each square, so that the crossword is made up in the usual way with good English interlocking words.

F P Q T	J C U L	H A N U	M O E R	R B A T	O A E D	R S F L
P U L E		N O P E		U A E R		A L E O
L E I A	E A N P	P D G A	E A N K	R S A T	O N I E	L K I M
E O T B		A E O N		E M S N		I A C E
K D P E	R U I A	D R S E	E S A D	P I R T	I E C N	D C K G

(Solution 84)

64 Three Triangles

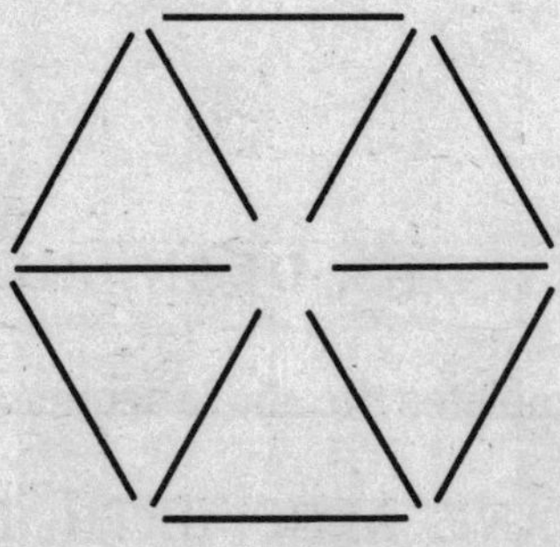

Move the position of four matches only to make three equilateral triangles.

(Solution 88)

65 Alternative Crossword

In the upper grid, the crossword letters have been replaced by numbers. Select the correct letter for each number from the three alternatives given, and enter the letter into the grid on this page, to make a crossword.

2	6	5	5		1	3	6	7
4		6	7	5	6	7		6
3	7		2	3	2		5	2
6	3	7		5		6	5	2
	2	2	1	3	2	2	2	
3	2	5		5		2	2	8
7	7		5	7	1		7	5
5		7	3	5	2	2		6
7	5	5	4		3	5	5	2

1	A B C
2	D E F
3	G H I
4	J K L
5	M N O
6	P Q R
7	S T U
8	V W X
9	Y Z

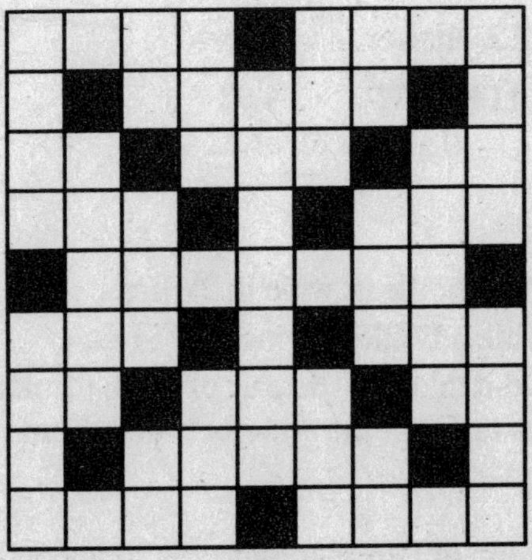

(Solution 93)

66 Circles

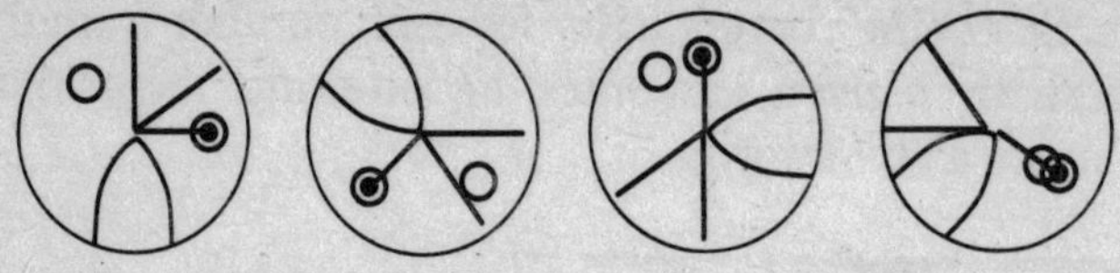

Which circle continues the sequence?

A B C D E

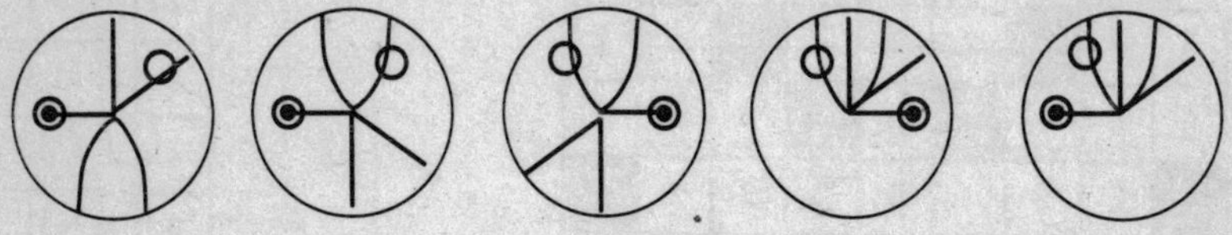

(Solution 96)

67 Square Roots

Does the number

Note
Integers = whole number

6 2 4 9 7 3 2 3

have a square root composed of integers?

i.e. $\sqrt{144} = 12$, answer in integers

$\sqrt{141} = 11.874342 \ldots\ldots \rightarrow 00$

(Solution 100)

68 Wine

A man can drink a bottle of wine in $2\frac{1}{2}$ hrs.
His wife can drink a bottle of wine in $1\frac{1}{2}$ hrs.
How long would it take for the pair of them drinking at their respective rates to finish the wine between them?

(Solution 104)

69 Alternative Crossword

In the upper grid, the crossword letters have been replaced by numbers. Select the correct letter for each number from the three alternatives given, and enter the letter into the blank grid to make a crossword.

7	8	1	3	2
3	1	6	2	5
5	8	5	4	5
6	2	5	3	7
7	6	1	2	2

1	A	B	C
2	D	E	F
3	G	H	I
4	J	K	L
5	M	N	O
6	P	Q	R
7	S	T	U
8	V	W	X
9	Y	Z	–

(Solution 108)

70 *Anagrammed Phrases*

All the following are anagrams of well-known phrases. For example, SO NOTE HOLE = ON THE LOOSE.

1. SINGLE GLIDE LOSE PET
2. HUG TIGHT VETO POSE
3. BOTH ONES GET QUIET
4. HALF YELLOW ANT
5. YES LOOP A SAND FLAT

(Solution 112)

71 *Work it Out*

What number should replace the question mark?

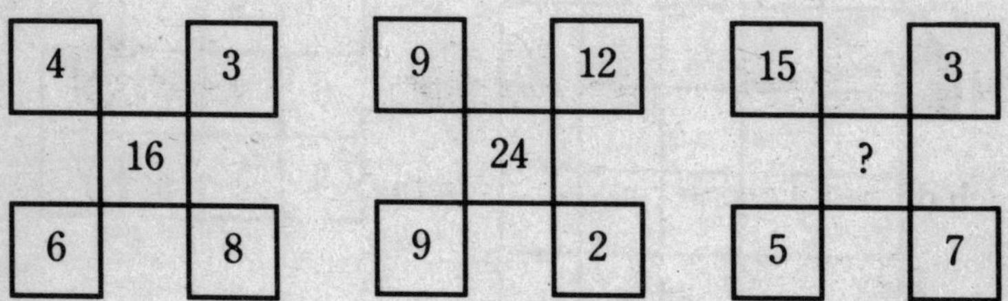

(Solution 117)

72 Cryptogram

This is a straight substitution cryptogram where each letter of the alphabet has been substituted for another.

CLUNK CK AZQC UX CLUNNKZ LUMYN,
CYKZ CK XKK UN CLUNNKZ CLUNK;
PSN CYKZ CK XKK UN CLUNNKZ CLUMYN,
CK AZQC 'NUX ZQN NYKZ CLUNNKZ LUMYN;
TQL CLUNK NQ YDFK UN CLUNNKZ LUMYN,
GSXN ZQN PK CLUNNKZ LUMYN ZQL CLUMYN;
ZQL BKN XYQSJV UN PK CLUNNKZ LUNK,
PSN CLUNK – TQL XQ 'NUX CLUNNKZ LUMYN.

(Solution 122)

73 Sequence

Which of the following comes next in the above sequence?

A B C D

(Solution 126)

74 Sequence

RAYON, EPAULET, WORTH, ?

What word below continues the above sequence?
ITINERARY, ROMANCED, CARDIGAN, REEF, CHANCE.

(Solution 130)

75 Threes

Can you group these into sets of three?

- ROOKS	- WHALES	- PIGS
- MACHINE GUNS	- ACTORS	- HIPPOPOTAMUSES
- SCOUTS	- OXEN	- WASPS
- HYENAS	- SEALS	- SWINE
- PEAS	- BABOONS	- MICE
- WOLVES	- PENGUINS	- CIGARETTES

(Solution 136)

76 Common

What do these words have in common?

1	BIBBER
2	PRACTICAL
3	BADLY
4	BARCELONA
5	RAGGED
6	EDITOR
7	TWENTY
8	ACROSS

(Solution 139)

77 Scales

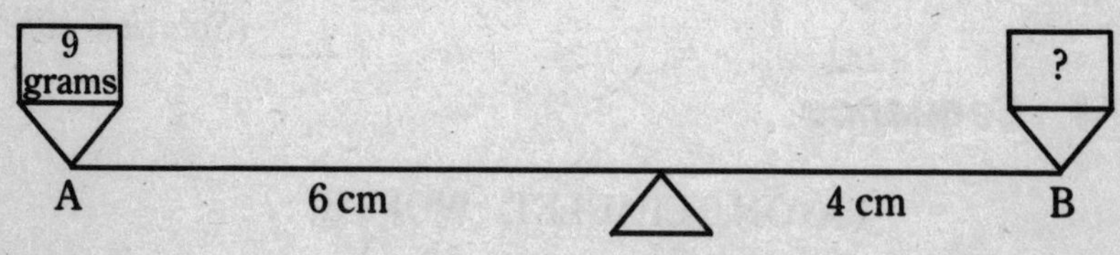

What value weight should be placed on the scales at B to balance the scales?

(Solution 143)

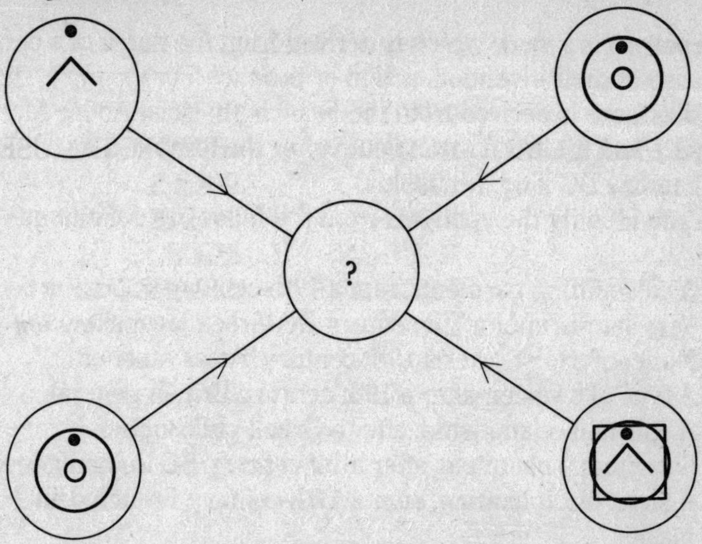

Each line and symbol which appears in the four outer circles, is transferred to the centre circle according to these rules.

If a line or symbol occurs in the outer circle:

once	it is transferred
twice	it is possibly transferred
3 times	it is transferred
4 times	it is not transferred

Which of the circles A, B, C, D or E, shown below should appear at the centre of the diagram?

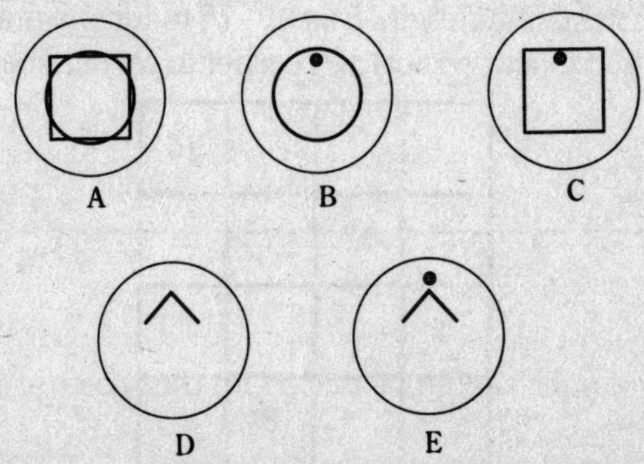

(Solution 147)

79 Eponyms

An eponym is a word which is derived from the name of a person because of their invention, action or product. For example, the word ampere is derived from the French physicist André Marie Ampère and the word mausoleum after the tomb of a 4th-century BC king, Mausolus.
Can you identify the eponyms from the following definitions?

1. A close-fitting garment, from a 19th-century trapeze artist.
2. Very harsh, after a 7th-century BC Greek lawmaker.
3. Nonconformist, after a 19th-century Texas rancher.
4. A type of sweater, after a 19th-century British general.
5. A spiritual relationship, after a Greek philosopher.
6. Sumptuous banquets, after a 1st-century BC Roman general.
7. A strict disciplinarian, after a 17th-century French drill master.
8. Dull-witted, after attempts to ridicule followers of an 11-12th-century Scottish theologian.
9. Spellbind or enchant, after an 18-19th-century German physician.
10. Crafty or deceitful, after a 15-16th-century Florentine statesman.

(Solution 152)

80 Magic '34'

Arrange the remaining digits from 1 - 16 to form a magic square where each horizontal, vertical and corner to corner line totals 34.

			16
	12		
4			
		8	

(Solution 2)

81 Square Numbers

Each horizontal and vertical line contains the digits of a four-figure square number. All digits are in the correct order but not necessarily adjacent. All digits are used only once.

4	4	9	4	8	1	9	2
1	1	6	2	8	1	3	2
2	7	8	9	5	4	1	6
3	9	6	3	0	4	1	0
6	2	0	0	9	4	4	1
5	6	3	0	2	2	3	5
5	4	1	4	7	7	6	6
6	3	1	3	9	4	6	9

(Solution 6)

82 Middle Letters

Find the complete words that contain these middle letters.

SSB*
ISERL
ZZYW*
NGIP
NKEYD
USTJ*
RFETC
TEDDF
ISYC*
PPLEG*

* These words are hyphenated

(Solution 10)

83 Sequence

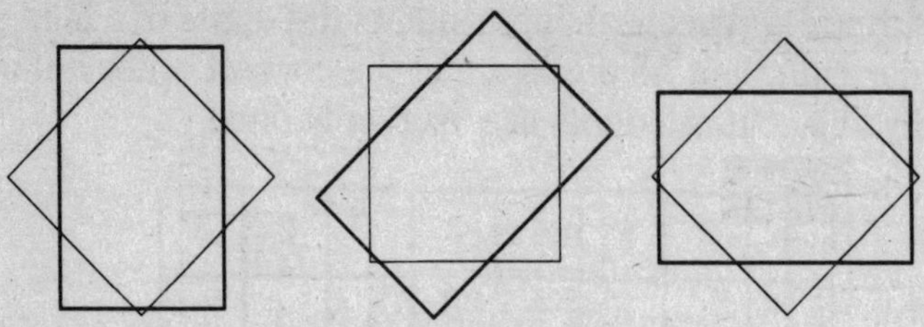

Which of the options below continues the above sequence?

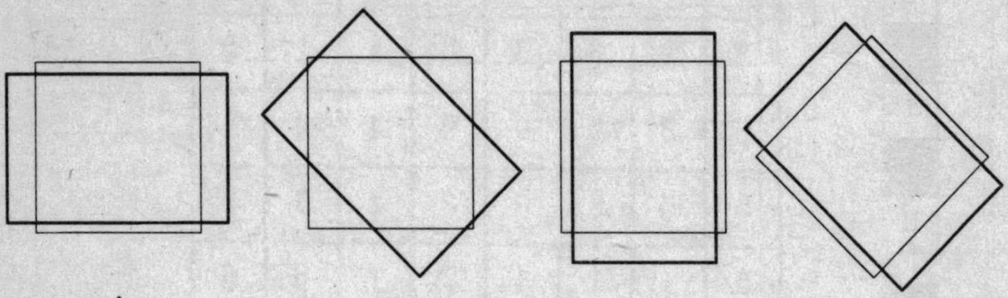

A B C D

(Solution 14)

84 Baby

How heavy was the baby at birth, asked the mother?

The nurse replied 12.96 lbs, divided by $\frac{1}{4}$ of his own weight.

How much did the baby weigh?

(Solution 18)

85 Names

What have the following names got in common?

STAN, TINA, MARK, DAN

(Solution 22)

Place the pieces in the grid in order to complete the crossword.

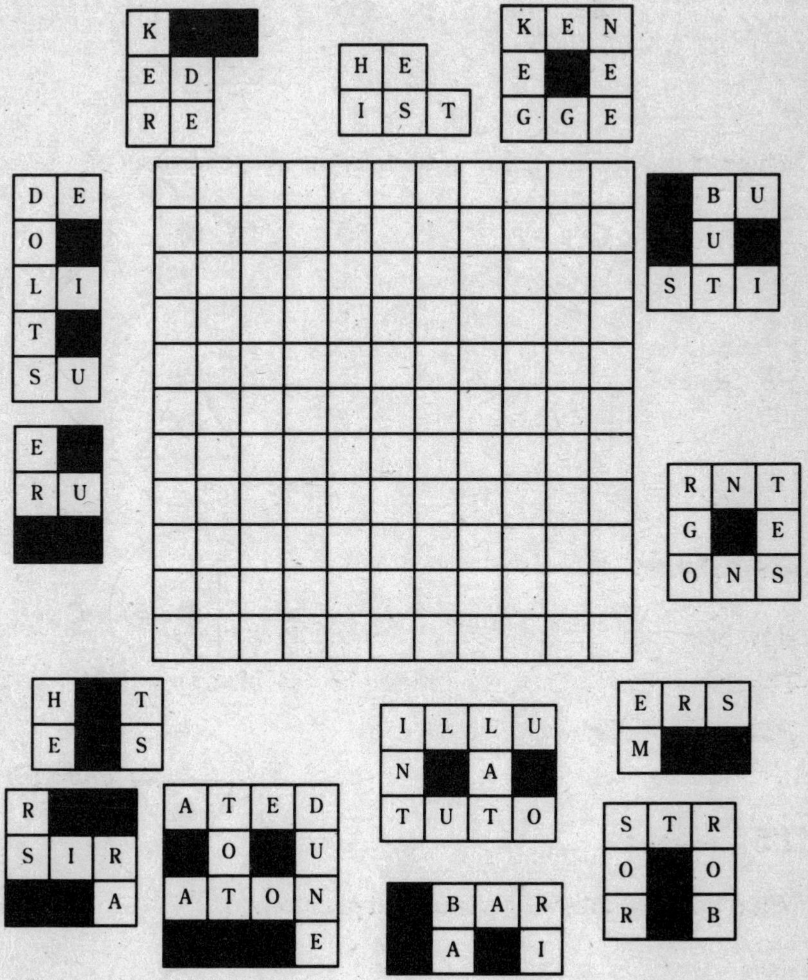

(Solution 26)

87 Comparison

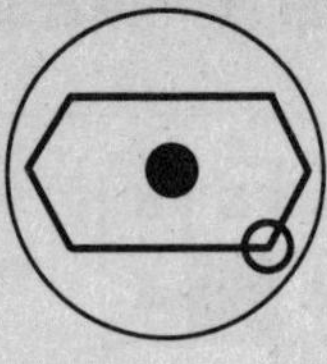

IS TO

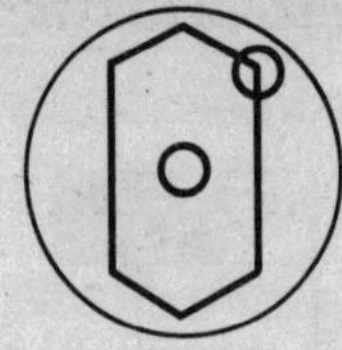

AS

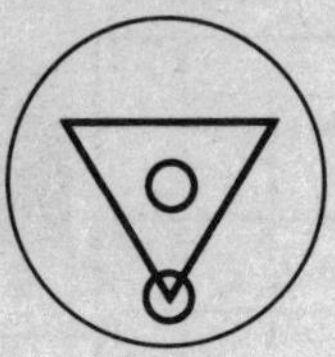

IS TO

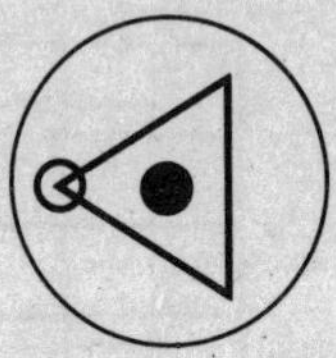

A

B

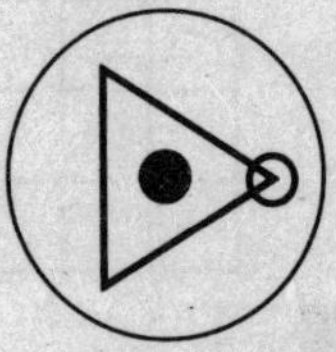

C

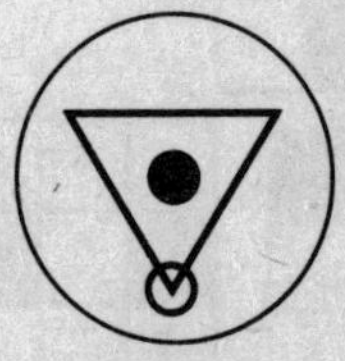

D

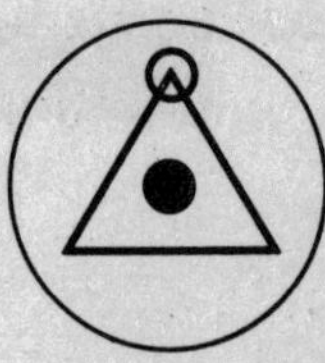

E

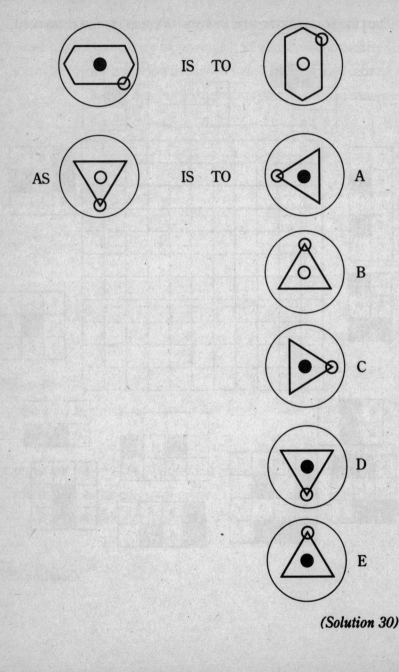

(Solution 30)

88 The Puzzling Puzzle

Start at the middle square and work from square to square horizontally, vertically or diagonally to spell out six puzzling words. Every square must be visited once each only and every square is used. Finish at the top right-hand square.

U	N	O	S	M	E	T	→
N	C	T	E	Y	R	N	
R	D	Y	R	M	I	E	
N	U	M	*	W	D	L	
I	E	D	O	E	B	M	
M	G	A	R	X	O	E	
A	P	A	P	R	L	B	

(Solution 34)

89 Bath

You are trying to fill a bath with both taps full on, but have accidentally left out the plug. Normally the hot water tap takes 8 minutes to fill the bath and the cold water tap takes 10 minutes. However, the water empties out through the plug hole in 5 minutes. How long will it take for the bath to fill?

(Solution 38)

90 Circles

What should be the contents of the circle with the question mark?

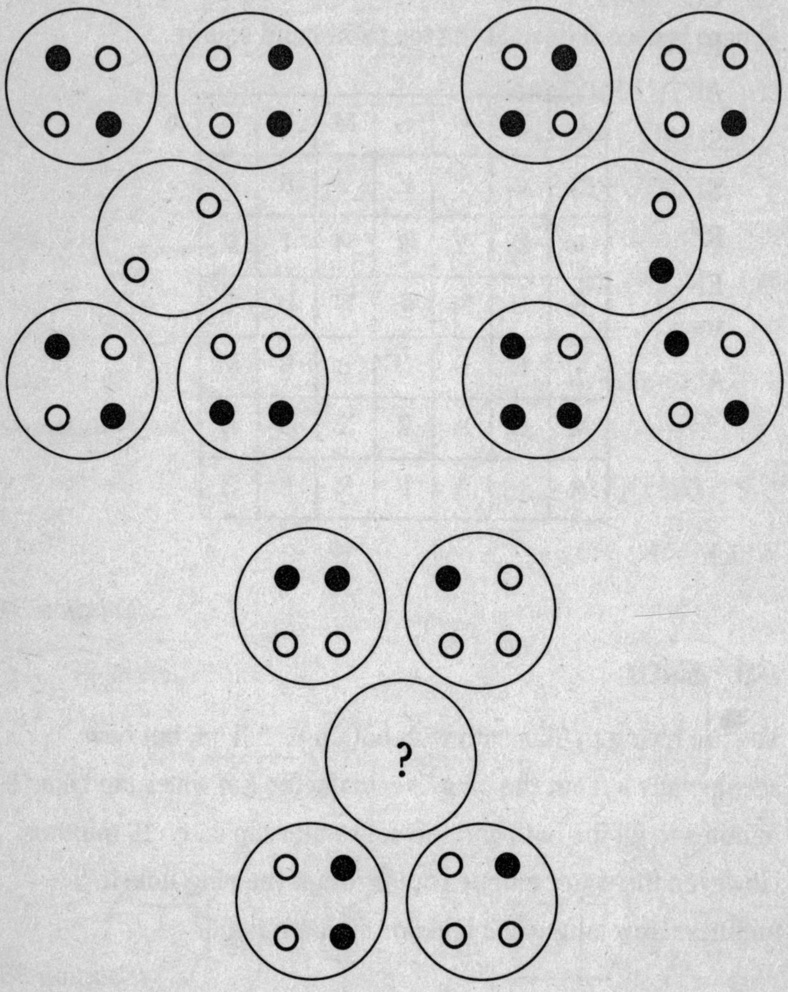

(Solution 43)

91 Fish

Change one letter of each answer to obtain the name of a fish.

		ANSWER	FISH
1.	CORRECT	-------	*-----
2.	KINE	-------	-*----
3.	ARTILLERYMAN	-------	------*
4.	SMALL CHILD	-------	*-----
5.	STUPID PERSON	--------	*-------
6.	RESENTMENT	-------	*-----
7.	ENGINEER	-------	*-----
8.	VISION	-----	*----
9.	AMMUNITION	-------	*-----

(Solution 47)

92 Odd One Out

Which is the odd one?

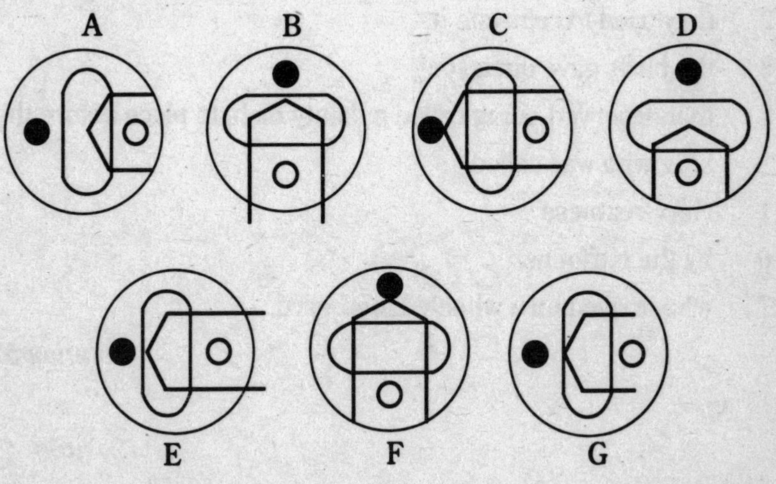

(Solution 52)

93 Nursery Rhyme Crossword

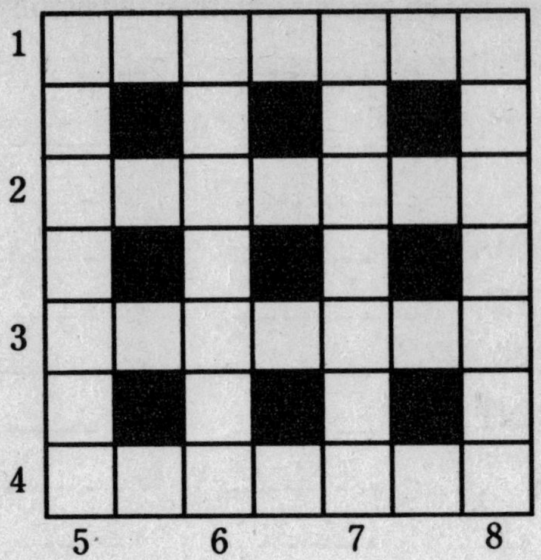

In the narrative are eight clues. Find them, solve them, and then place the answers in the grid.

4 The longed for number, four and twenty blackbirds,

3 were dealt with, by being baked in a pie

2 they tried to reinstate it,

8 the birds gave out a song

5 that deserved being called a dainty dish, to place before the king who was called

1 His Greatness

6 by the buffoons

7 who arrived on a wheeled footboard.

(Solution 57)

94 Network

Find the starting point and travel along the connecting lines in a continuous path to adjacent circles to spell out a fourteen-letter word. Every circle must be visited once only.

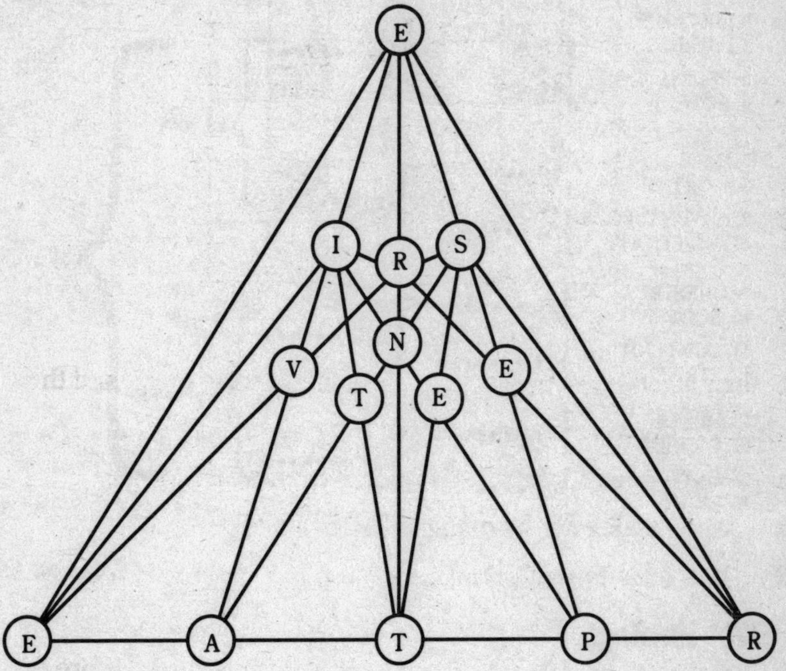

(Solution 60)

95 Find Another Word

BELOW, ORE, ROWER

Which word below goes with the three words above?

BOAT, LONG, SHORE, CARRY, WIND

(Solution 64)

96 Connections

Each pair of words, by meaning or association, leads to another word. Find the missing words 18-30. The number of letters in the missing words are indicated by the dots.

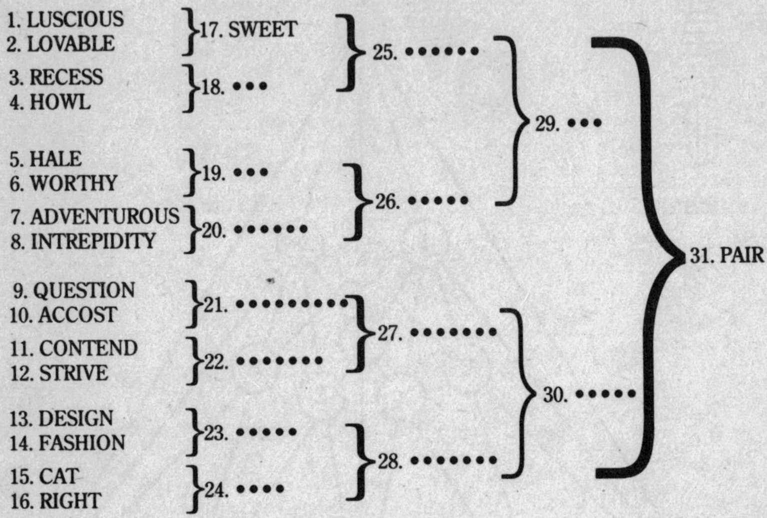

(Solution 69)

97 Ending

Find a 3-letter word which when placed on the end of these words make new words.

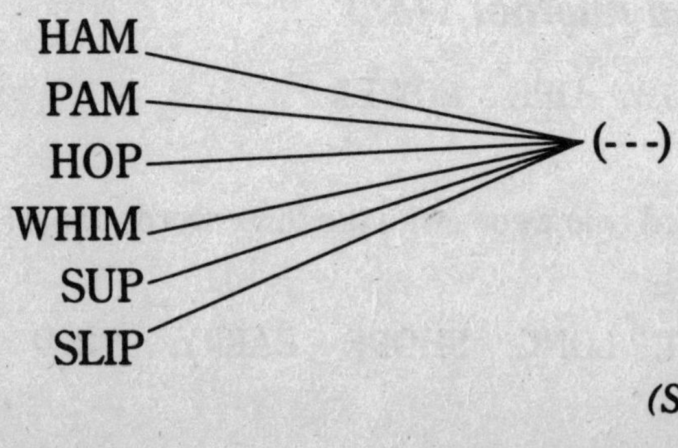

(Solution 72)

Which option below continues the above sequence?

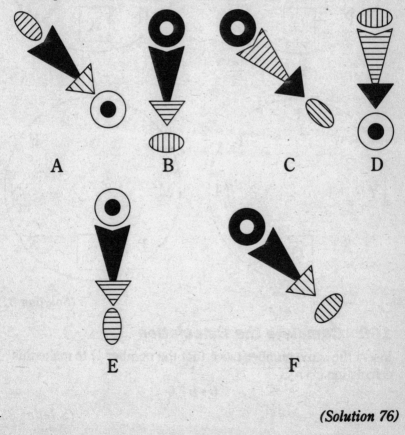

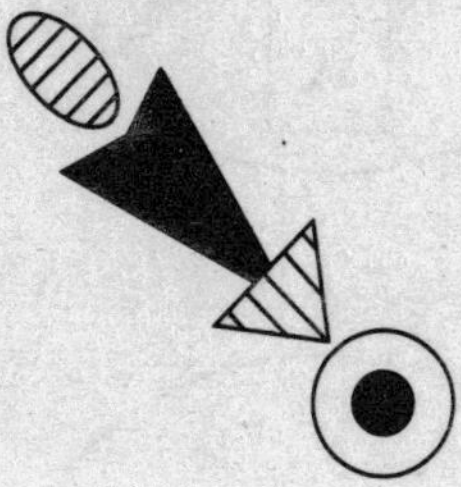

A

B

C

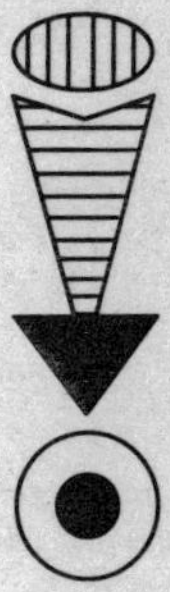

D

E

F

(Solution 76)

99 Safe

In order to open the safe, you have to rotate the wheels to find a 4-letter word.

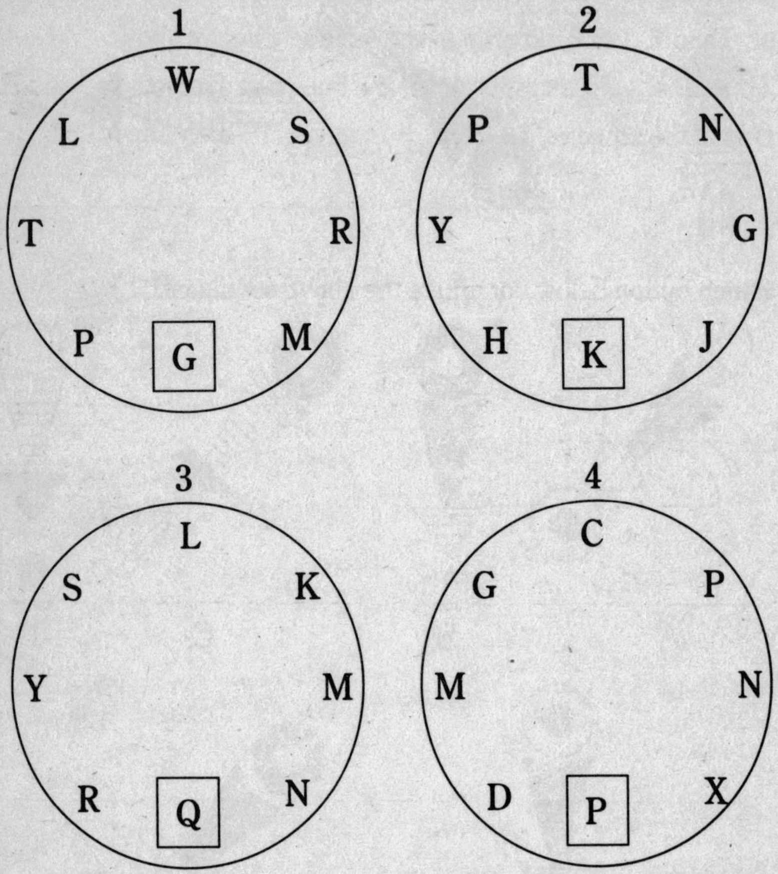

(Solution 81)

100 Complete the Calculation

Insert the same number twice (not the number 1) to make this calculation correct.

$$6 \div 6 = 6$$

(Solution 85)

101 Grid

Each of the nine squares 1A to 3C should incorporate all the lines and symbols which are shown in the outer squares marked A, B or C and 1, 2 or 3, directly to the left and directly above.

Thus 2B should incorporate all the lines and symbols in 2 and B.

One of the squares, 1A to 3C, is incorrect. Which one is it?

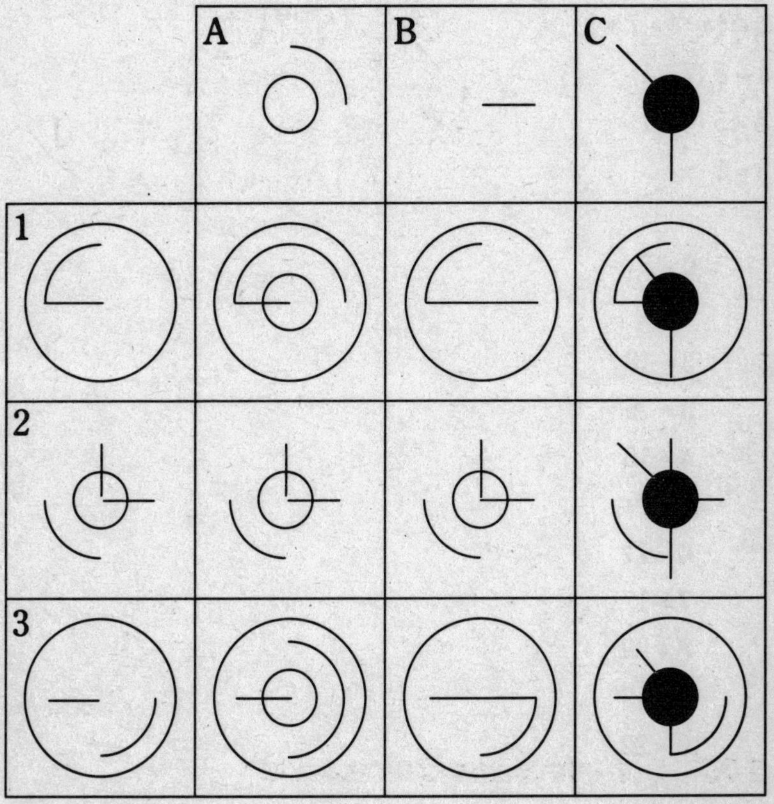

(Solution 89)

Insert the numbers 0 - 10 in the circles opposite, so that for any particular circle the sum of the numbers in the circles connected directly to it equals the value corresponding to the number in that circle, as given in the list.

Example:

1 = 14 (4 + 7 + 3)

4 = 8 (7 + 1)

7 = 5 (4 + 1)

3 = 1

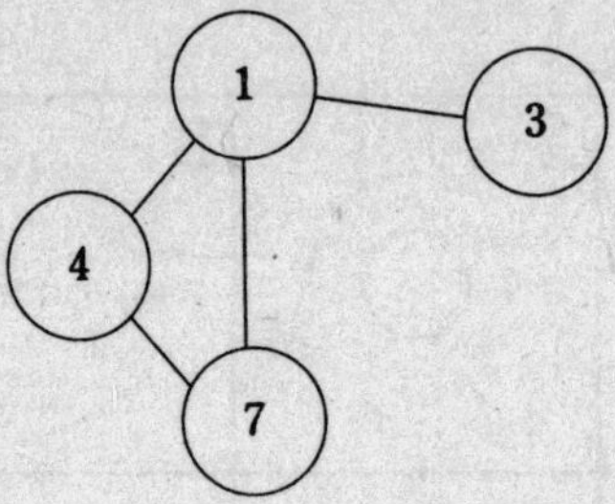

0 = 8

1 = 4

2 = 18

3 = 25

4 = 16

5 = 7

6 = 11

7 = 17

8 = 29

9 = 13

10 = 22

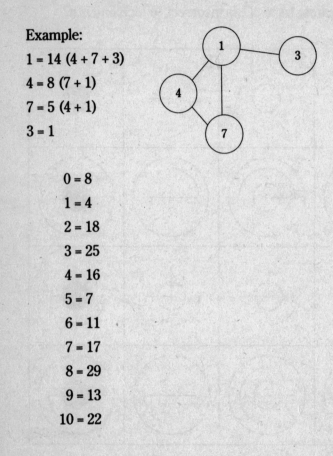

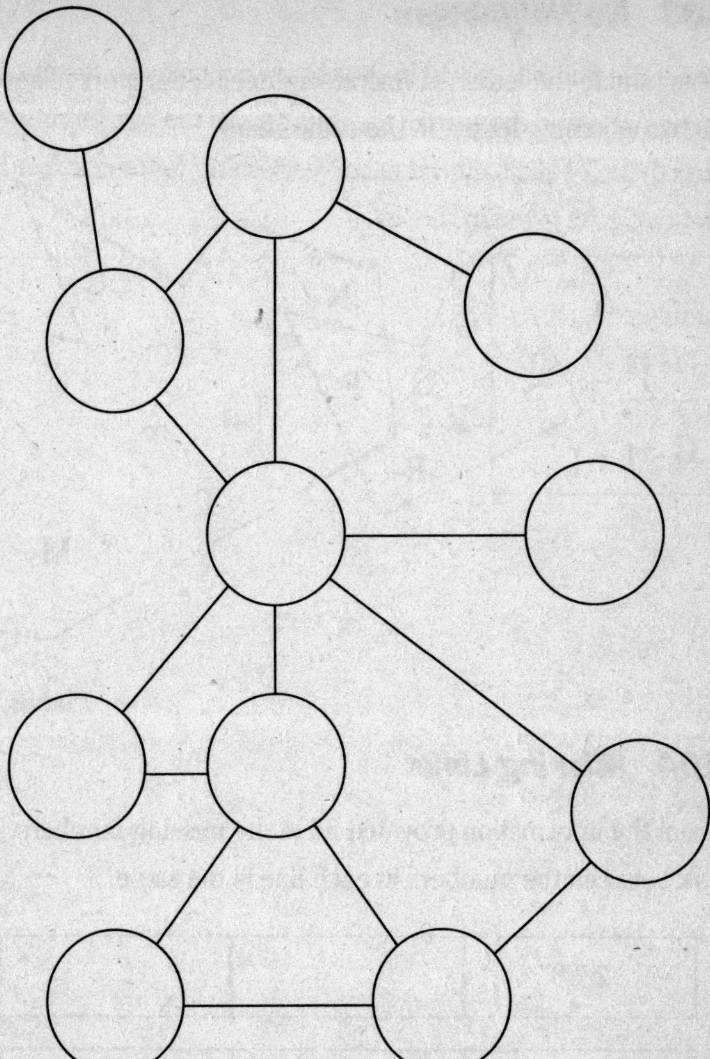

(Solution 98)

103 No Neighbours

Unscramble the letters to find an eighteen-letter word. There are no two adjoining letters in the same shape.

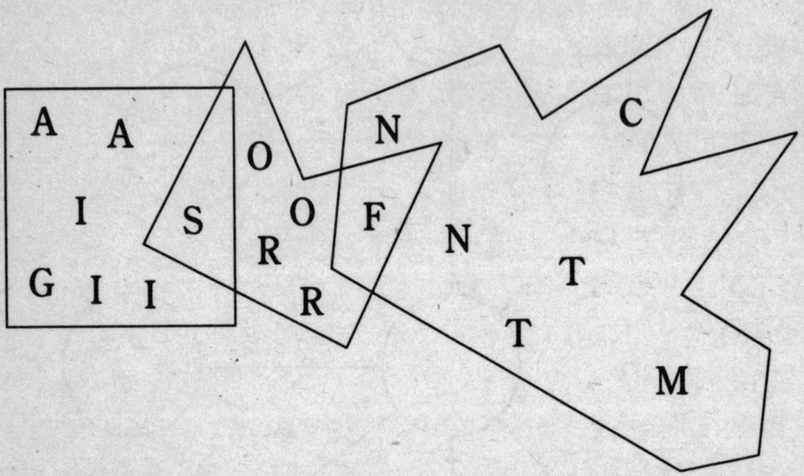

(Solution 92)

104 Missing Links

From the information provided fill in the missing numbers. The link between the numbers in each line is the same.

2798		
4389	3827	
4051		800

(Solution 101)

105 Occupations

These 36 three-letter bits can be grouped up to form 12 nine-letter words which are all occupations.

PRO	KER	BAL	NOT
ATH	PUP	KEE	OST
HYP	EOP	MAJ	HER
EER	ZOO	IST	ORD
IST	PLO	PET	GON
GEO	LOG	PER	UGH
OMO	FES	POO	NER
ROP	EMA	SOR	IST
MAN	HAR	IER	DOL

(Solution 106)

106 Sea Level

If you were standing on top of a 50 ft high cliff, how far would you be able to see out to sea?

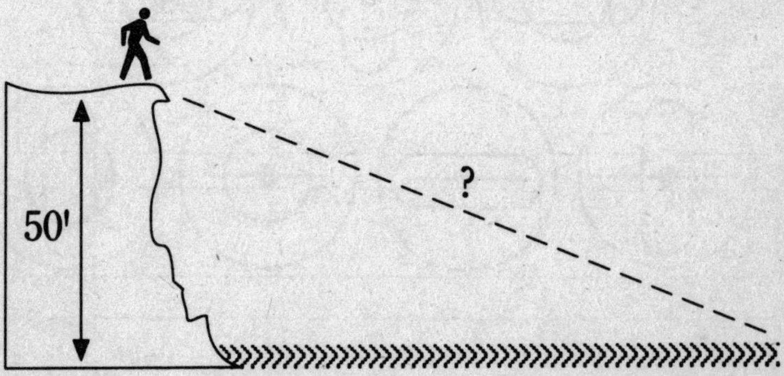

(Solution 109)

107 Logic

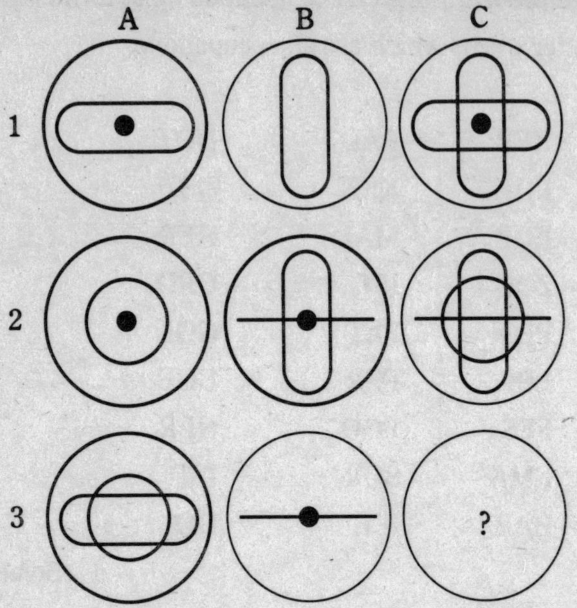

Logically which circle below fits into the above pattern?

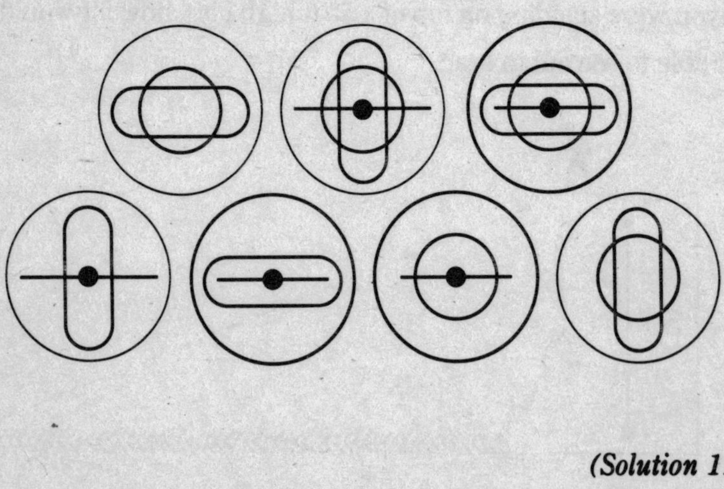

(Solution 113)

108 *Quotation*

Re-arrange the words to form a quotation by Irene Peter.

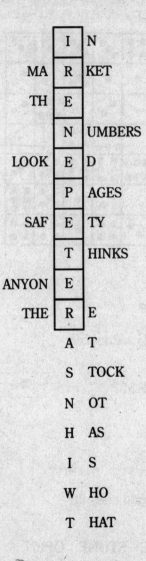

	I	N
MA	R	KET
TH	E	
	N	UMBERS
LOOK	E	D
	P	AGES
SAF	E	TY
	T	HINKS
ANYON	E	
THE	R	E
	A	T
	S	TOCK
	N	OT
	H	AS
	I	S
	W	HO
	T	HAT

(Solution 120)

109 Dominoes

Draw in the lines of the 28 dominoes, which are from 0-0 to 6-6.

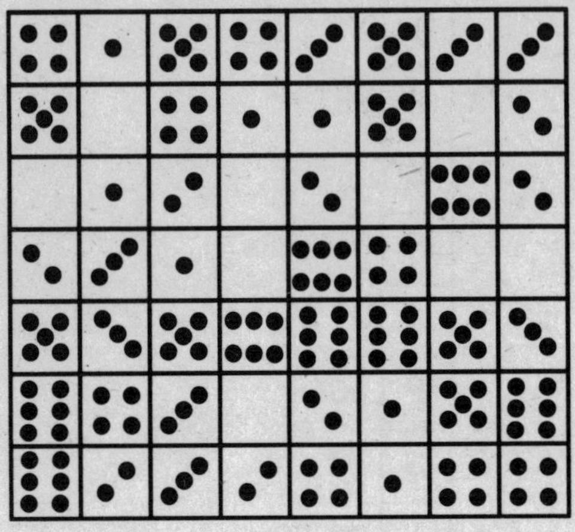

(Solution 123)

110 Letter Sequence

What letter comes next in this sequence?

T E N T D T T S F M ?

(Solution 127)

111 Odd One Out

Which of these words is the odd one out?

TEN ONE STONE OPEN
TENT TOE OFTEN SON

(Solution 131)

112 Missing Number

What number should replace the question mark?

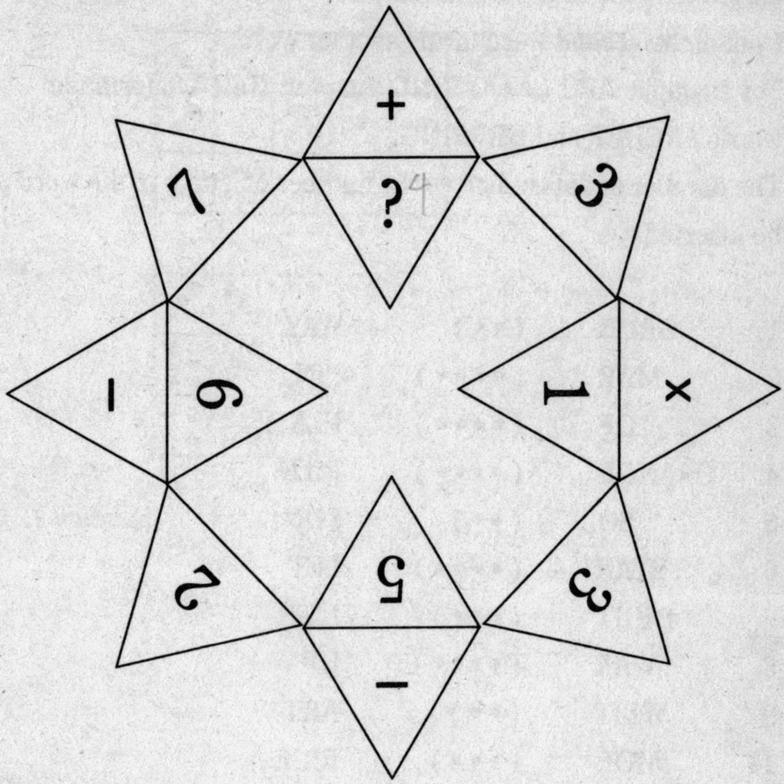

(Solution 134)

113 Middle Words

In each of the following insert a word in the bracket which when tacked onto the first word forms a new word and when placed in front of the second word forms another word.

For example: ARC (•••) RING. Answer: HER – to form the words ARCHER and HERRING.

The number of dots indicates the number of letters in the word to be inserted.

1	GRUB	(••)	WAY
2	MAR	(••••)	PIN
3	OF	(••••)	PLATE
4	ORANGE	(••••)	PILE
5	SO	(••)	SON
6	STAR	(••••)	LET
7	DIGIT	(•••)	LIER
8	WAR	(••••)	UP
9	WRIT	(••)	ART
10	MOB	(•••)	RICE

(Solution 140)

114 Track Word

Work round the track to find a 15-letter word. You have to provide the missing letters and find the starting point. The word might appear reading clockwise or anti-clockwise, and the overlapping letter appears twice.

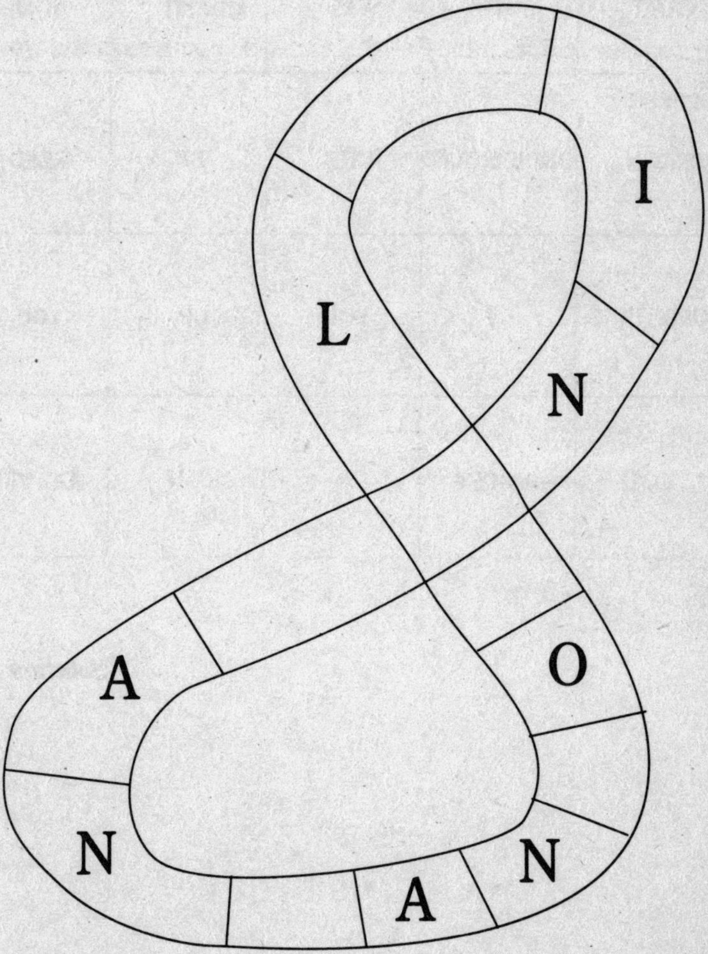

(Solution 144)

115 Quotation

Re-arrange the words to read out a quotation by Will Rogers.

CAN'T	IT	WAS	MINUTE	SURE
DRAWN	UNDERSTAND	THE	BE	READ
SOMETHING	BY	YOU	UP	YOU
YOU	ALMOST	A	CAN	LAWYER

(Solution 148)

Which option below continues the above sequence?

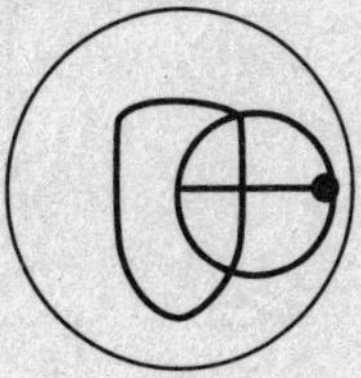

A

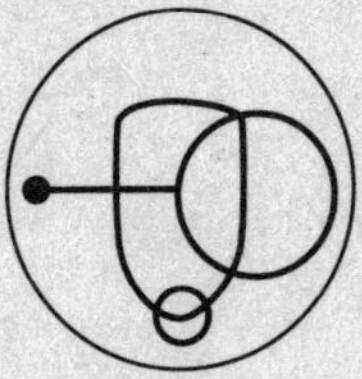

B

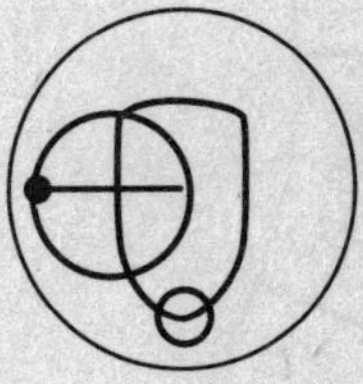

C

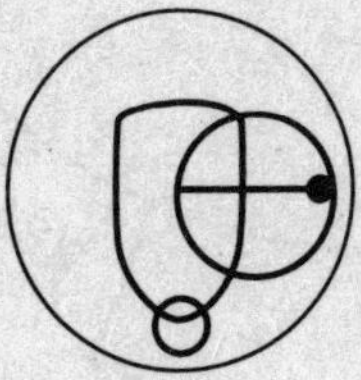

D

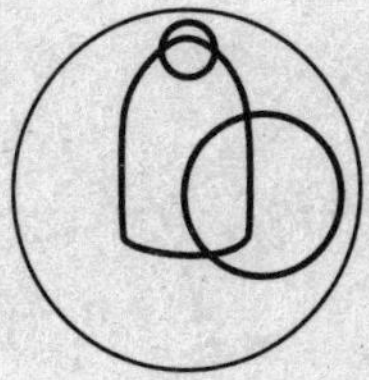

E

(Solution 153)

117 Quotation by Mark Twain

Find the quotation. Start at I.

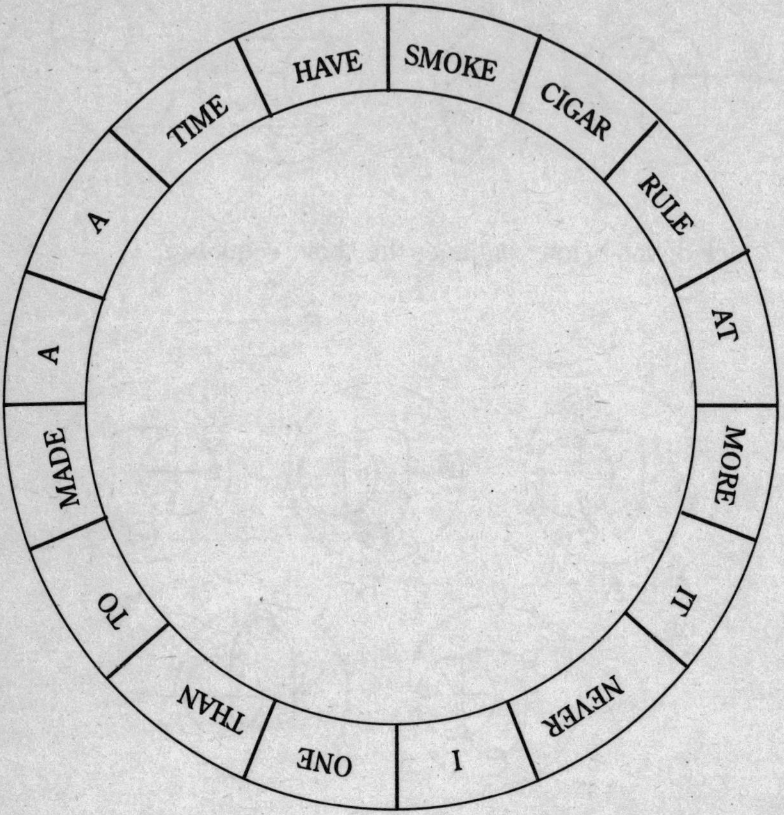

(Solution 156)

118 Spots

When spots are placed on the circumference and then joined, regions will be formed.

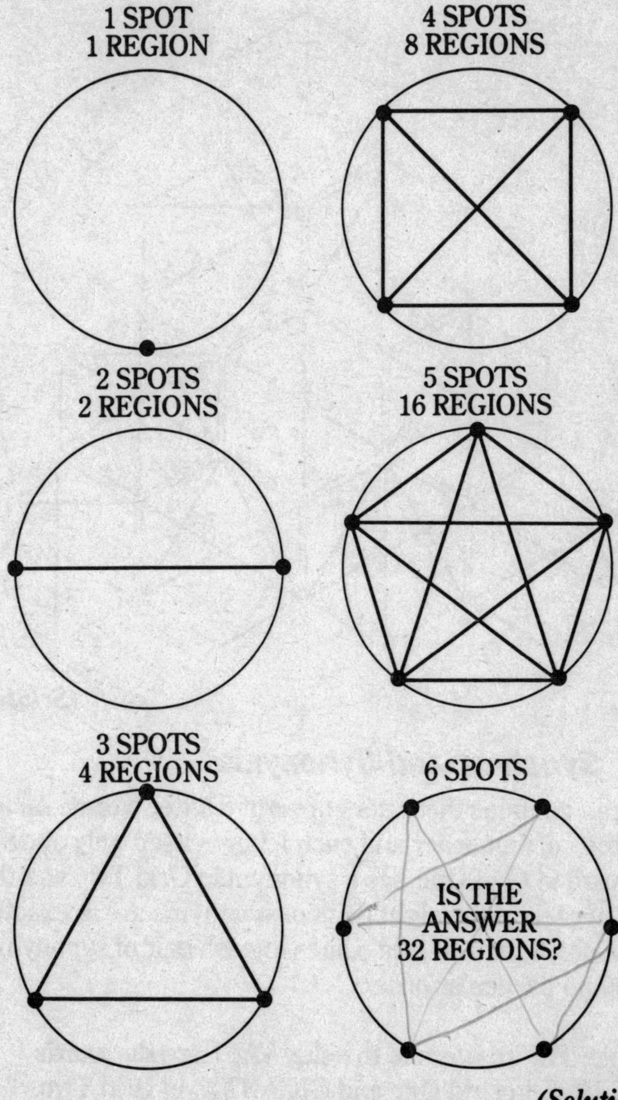

(Solution 160)

119 The Hexagonal Pyramid

Work out the contents of the top hexagon.

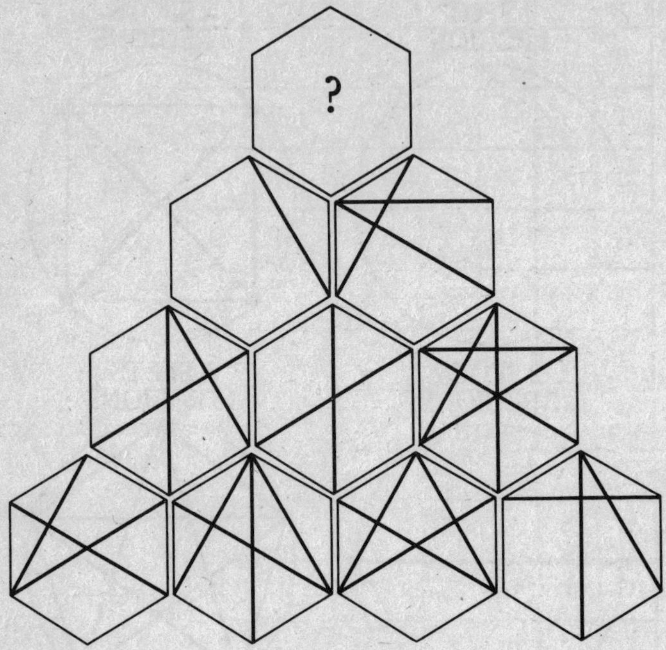

(Solution 158)

120 Synchronized Synonyms

Each grid contains the letters of eight 8-letter words. All letters are in the correct order and each letter is used only once. Each word in Grid One has a synonym in Grid Two and the letters of each of the eight pairs of synonyms are in exactly the same position in each grid. Clues to each pair of synonyms are given in no particular order.

Example: The answers to the clue VAST are the words TOWERING in Grid One and GIGANTIC in Grid Two.

Find the remaining seven pairs of synonyms.

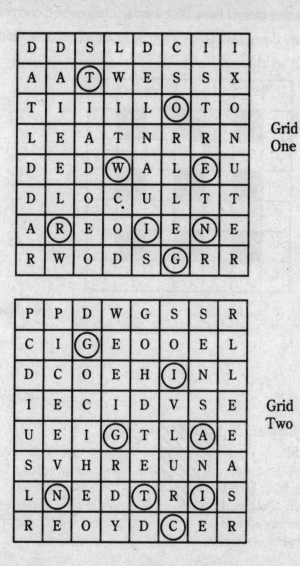

Grid One

D	D	S	L	D	C	I	I
A	A	T	W	E	S	S	X
T	I	I	I	L	O	T	O
L	E	A	T	N	R	R	N
D	E	D	W	A	L	E	U
D	L	O	C	U	L	T	T
A	R	E	O	I	E	N	E
R	W	O	D	S	G	R	R

Grid Two

P	P	D	W	G	S	S	R
C	I	G	E	O	O	E	L
D	C	O	E	H	I	N	L
I	E	C	I	D	V	S	E
U	E	I	G	T	L	A	E
S	V	H	R	E	U	N	A
L	N	E	D	T	R	I	S
R	E	O	Y	D	C	E	R

Clues: VAST, SLICK, CHIEF, LONE, TWISTER, DIARY, FORBID, BREADTH

(Solution 159)

121 Brain Strain

Insert the missing numbers so that the calculations are correct, both across and down. All numbers to be inserted are less than 10 (there is no zero).

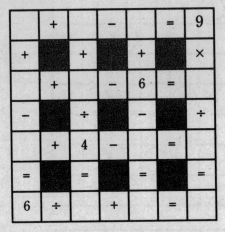

	+		−		=	9
+		+		+		×
	+		−	6	=	
−		÷		−		÷
	+	4	−		=	
=		=		=		=
6	÷		+		=	

(Solution 3)

122 Circle

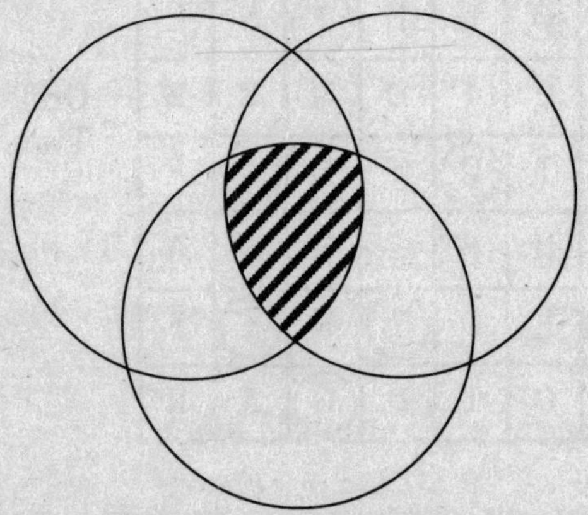

Approximately how much of one circle is shaded?

(Solution 7)

123 "E" Frame

All vowels are "E" and are not shown. All consonants are shown and all are used once only.

42 means 4 consonants and 2 vowels

DOWN

	1	2	3	4	5	6	7	8	
1	R	L	S	P	T	L	D	T	42
2	Y	P	L	S	D	T	L	P	52
3	B	B	B	P	D	H	W	L	42
4	K	J	R	N	S	N	N	T	42
5	L	D	N	P	L	S	N	S	52
6	N	R	L	K	R	T	N	B	42
7	W	R	C	R	F	B	D	M	32
8	N	T	H	T	M	R	F	M	32
	42	42	42	42	42	42	42	42	

ACROSS

Clues

Across

1 Arid land
2 Walked carefully
3 Duck like feet
4 Small house
5 Never ceasing
6 Dog's house
7 Put off
8 Go in

Down

1 Happening every seven days
2 Threefold
3 Man addicted to lewdness
4 Condiment
5 Nothing more
6 Baptist church
7 Yellow flowering plant
8 Symbolic representation

(Solution 12)

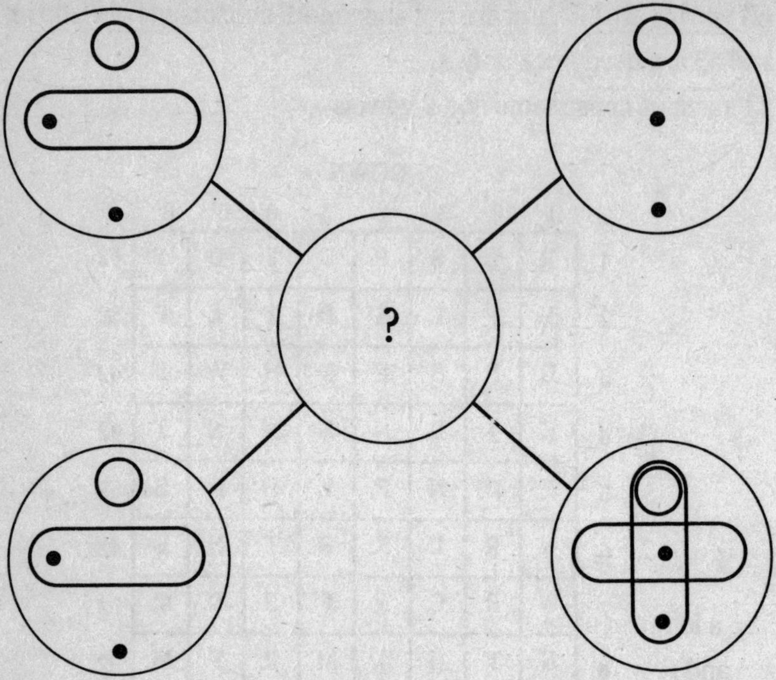

Each line and symbol which appears in the four outer circles, is transferred to the centre circle according to these rules.

If a line or symbol occurs in the outer circle:

once	it is	transferred
twice	it is	possibly transferred
3 times	it is	tranferred
4 times	it is	not transferred

Which of the circles A, B, C, D or E, shown opposite should appear at the centre of the diagram?

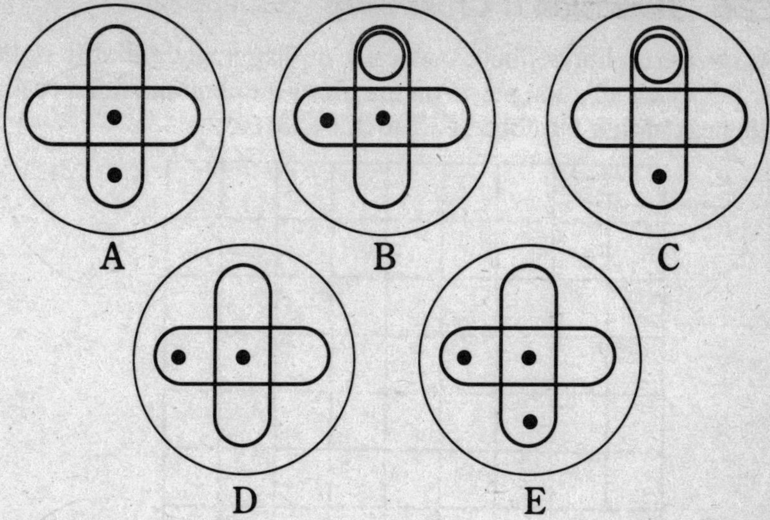

(Solution 15)

125 Add a Letter

Find a letter in place of ? When added to each of the five-letter sets and re-arranged will form six-letter words.
The six-letter words are names of plants and trees.

	C	H	E	W	S
	C	H	U	M	S
?	G	O	N	E	R
	C	H	O	R	E
	S	E	E	M	S

(Solution 19)

126 Directional Crossword

Answers run horizontally, vertically, or diagonally, either to right or left. Each solution starts on the lower number and finishes on the next higher number, i.e., 1 to 2, 2 to 3, etc.

1	5							4
10			13			12		7
	17						15	
	18						14	
				16				
11		8				9		6
3								2

1. Mislead
2. Anti-perspirant
3. Stormy
4. Wave passing around the earth
5. Learned
6. Talk over
7. Ship
8. Mechanical man
9. Controllable
10. Descriptive term
11. Leaves for smoking
12. Exposed
13. Girl's name
14. Gilbert and Sullivan's "____men" guardians
15. Hotchpotch
16. Musical instrument
17. Make a mistake

(Solution 24)

127 Quartering a Square

Divide the square into four quarters. Each quarter should be the same size and shape and contain the same four symbols.

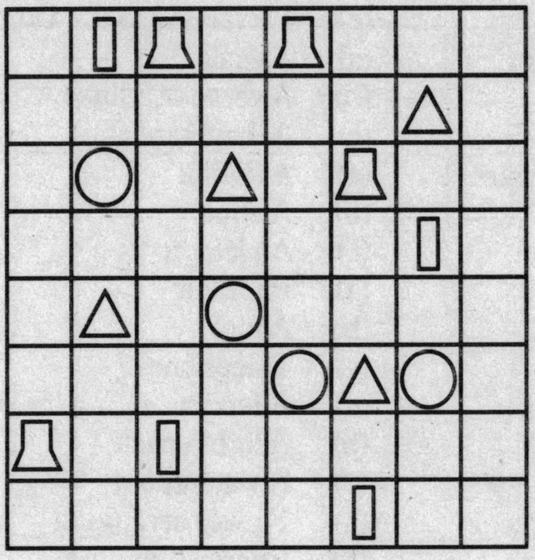

(Solution 28)

128 Concentration

A B C D E F G H

What letter is two to the right of the letter immediately to the right of the letter four to the left of the letter two to the right of the letter four to the right of the letter immediately to the left of the letter which comes midway between the letter two to the left of the letter 'C' and the letter three to the left of the letter 'F'?

(Solution 31)

129 Polling Day

At a recent bye-election a total of 23,968 votes were cast for the four candidates, the winner exceeding his opponents by 1026, 2822 and 6428 votes respectively.
How many votes were received by each candidate?

(Solution 35)

130 Alternatives

Select from the three alternatives the correct meaning.

1	Canicular	(a)	Oval-shaped
		(b)	Bearing flowers
		(c)	Pertaining to the Dog-Star
2	Dipsas	(a)	A snake
		(b)	A verse of 5 lines
		(c)	A drunkard
3	Escadrille	(a)	A flotilla
		(b)	A shoe
		(c)	A platoon
4	Fon	(a)	Phonetic
		(b)	A fool
		(c)	Telephone
5	Griffon	(a)	A terrier
		(b)	A light snack
		(c)	A waterspout
6	Ikebana	(a)	Flower arranging
		(b)	Exercise routine
		(c)	A waterfall
7	Lempira	(a)	Monetary unit of Honduras
		(b)	Circular motion
		(c)	A drug
8	Mazzard	(a)	Skull
		(b)	Drizzle
		(c)	Food

(Solution 39)

131 Ten-Digit Number

Write down a 10-digit number such that:
The 1st digit indicates the total number of 1's
The 2nd digit indicates the total number of 2's
The 3rd digit indicates the total number of 3's
etc, to the 10th digit which indicates the total number of zeroes.

(Solution 42)

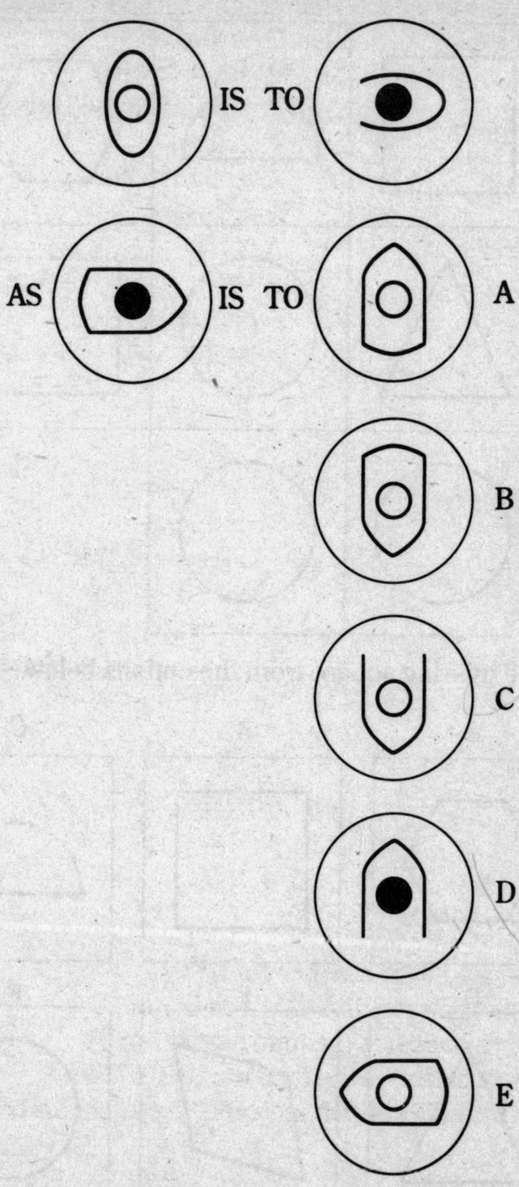

(Solution 45)

133 Work it Out

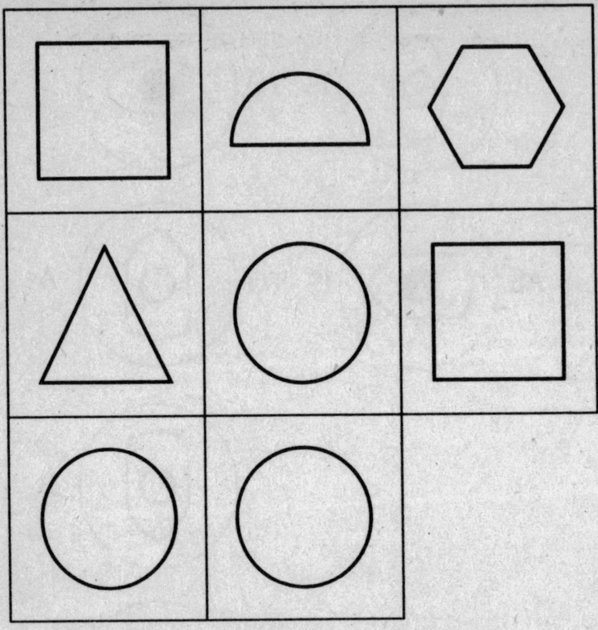

Choose the missing square from the options below.

A

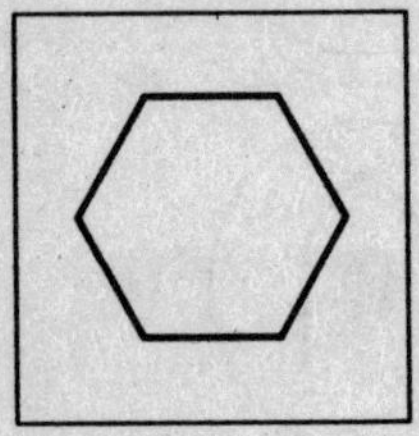

B

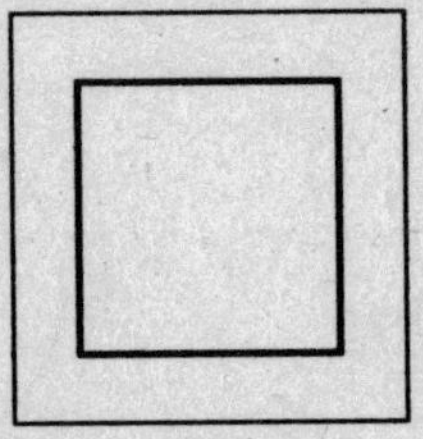

C

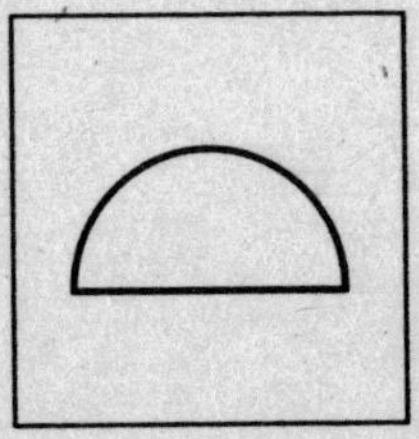

D

E

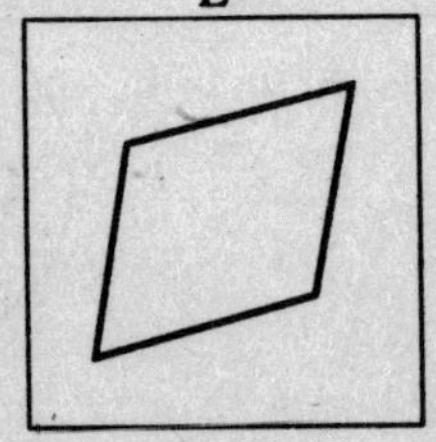

F

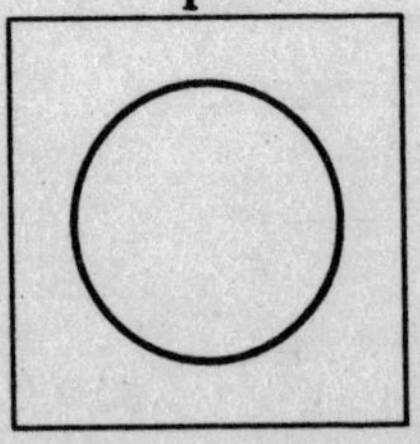

(Solution 49)

134 Found in the USA

All the following are anagrams of things which can be found in the USA.

1. MINUTE BATH STEEP GRID LIE
2. AND TRY NO CHANGE
3. SKATE ALERT GAL
4. NUN I'M STRAY COOK
5. HAIL GAME NICK
6. I HE SHE WE TO HUT

(Solution 53)

135 Odd One Out

Which is the odd one?

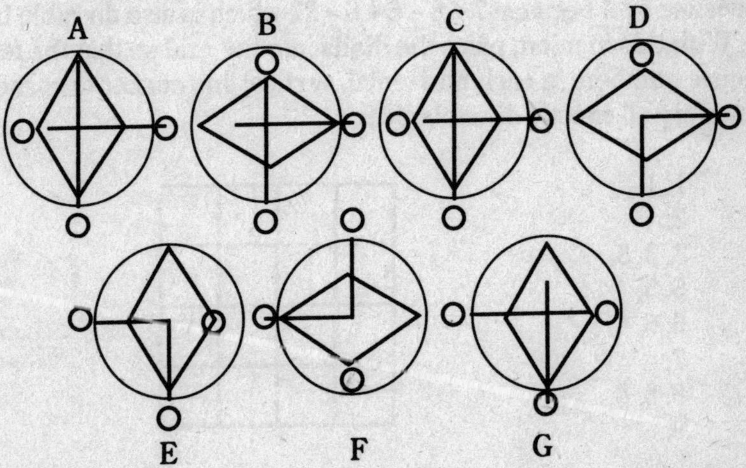

(Solution 56)

136 Anagram Theme

Arrange the 14 words in pairs so that each pair is an anagram of another word or name. The seven words produced will have a linking theme. For example, if the words TRY and CREASE were in the list, they could be paired to form an anagram of SECRETARY and the theme could be PROFESSIONS.

AGE	AURA	DIN	END	
FLAN	GAIN	GRAIN	HAY	SEW
IRE	NEAT	RAIL	RUNG	SIT

(Solution 62)

137 Nines

A number is divisible by 9 exactly when the sum of its digits are also divisible by 9 exactly. For example, the number 7866 is divisible by 9 because 7 + 8 + 6 + 6 = 27 which is also divisible by 9. With this in mind, place the digits into the grid so that the four-figure numbers in each horizontal, vertical and corner to corner lines are all exactly divisible by 9.

1, 1,
2,
3, 3, 3,
5, 5,
6, 6, 6,
7,
8, 8, 8,
9.

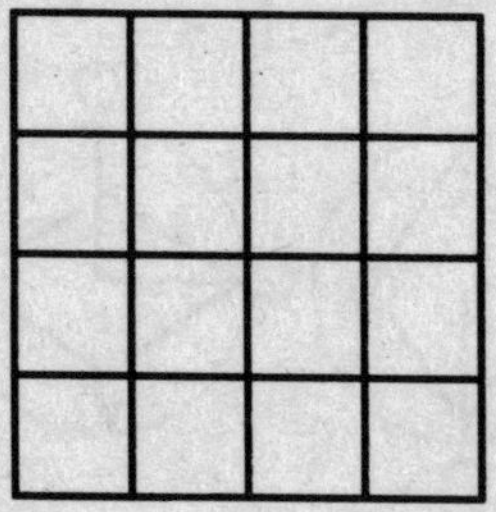

(Solution 65)

138 Missing Letters

Fill in the missing letters to make 10 occupations.

1 • N • T • M • S •
2 • T • N • M • N
3 • O • T • W • I •
4 • I • E • T • R
5 • A • A • N • R
6 • I • T • C • A •
7 • S • E • E • T •
8 • I • L • N • S •
9 • E • C • N • R •
10 • A • F • T • E •

(Solution 68)

139 Sequence

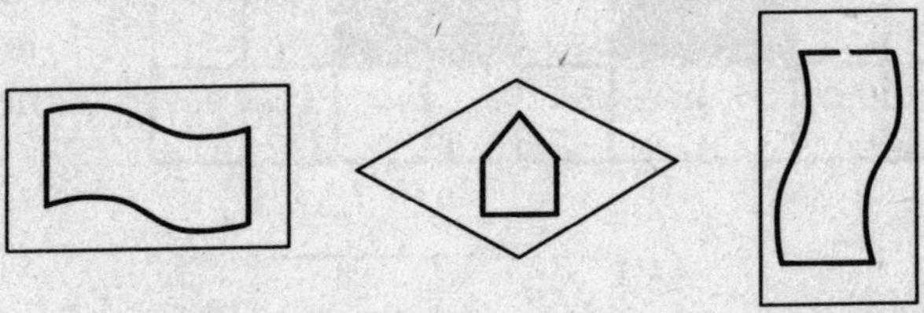

Which option below continues the above sequence?

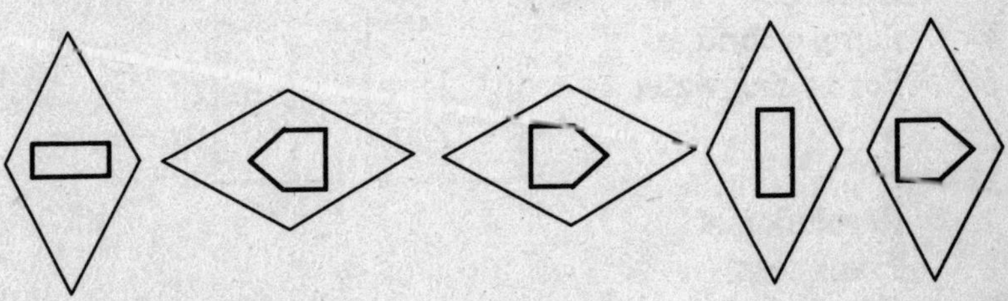

A B C D E

(Solution 73)

140 Niners

Solve the 8 clues.

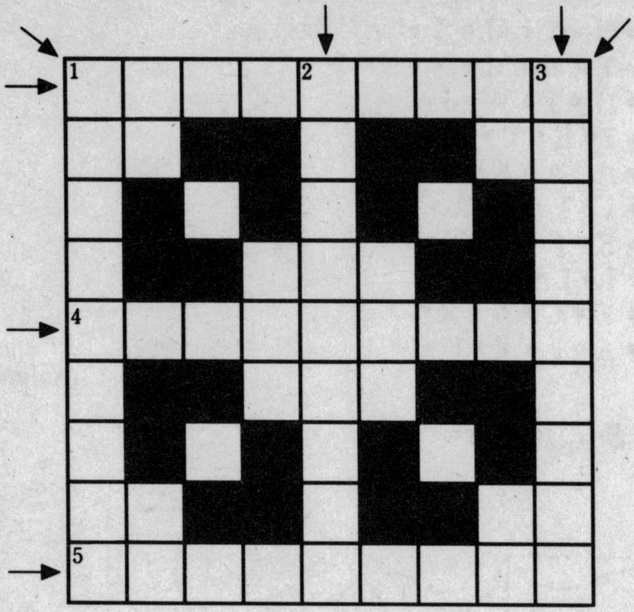

Clues

Across

1 Declarer
4 Ramp or bridge
5 For boiling water

Down

1 Revolutionist
2 Frankness
3 Of a definition

Diagonal

1 Chargeable
2 Coming into renewed life

(Solution 77)

141 Safe

The safe can only be opened by pressing the buttons in the correct order, following the directions on each button. The last button is marked (0)
You have to find the 1st button

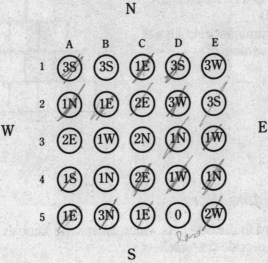

N

	A	B	C	D	E
1	3S	3S	1E	3S	3W
2	1N	1E	2E	3W	3S
3	2E	1W	2N	1N	1W
4	1S	1N	2E	1W	1N
5	1E	3N	1E	0	2W

W E

S

(Solution 82)

142 Song

This verse of an old song has had all of its vowels removed and is written in groups of 5. See if you can reconstitute it and make it into its words.

PNDDW NTHCT YRDNN
DTTHG LTHTS THWYT
HMNYG SPPGS THWSL

(Solution 86)

143 Pyramid Word

Solve the five clues, place the five words in the pyramid, then rearrange all fifteen letters to find a fifteen-letter word.

- abbreviation for pound sterling (1)
- the ratio of the circumference of a circle to its diameter (2)
- weapon (3)
- family of ruminant animals (4)
- convey in vehicle (5)

(Solution 90)

144 Middle Word

Place a word in the brackets which means the same as the words or phrases outside the brackets.

1 A Chinese idol (- - - -) Fate
2 Triangular sail (- - -) To balk
3 Branched chandelier (- - - - - - - - -) Rotating firework
4 Wolverine (- - - - - - -) One who eats to excess
5 To stuff (- - - - -) Buffoonery
6 Young deer (- - - -) To flatter
7 Polecat (- - - - - -) Search out
8 Polecat (- - - - -) Vetch
9 Darling (- - - - - -) Lathe-head
10 Broken piece (- - - - -) Beetle's wing case

(Solution 94)

145 Cross-Alphabet

Insert the letters of the alphabet once each only into the grid to form a crossword. Clues are given, but in no particular order.

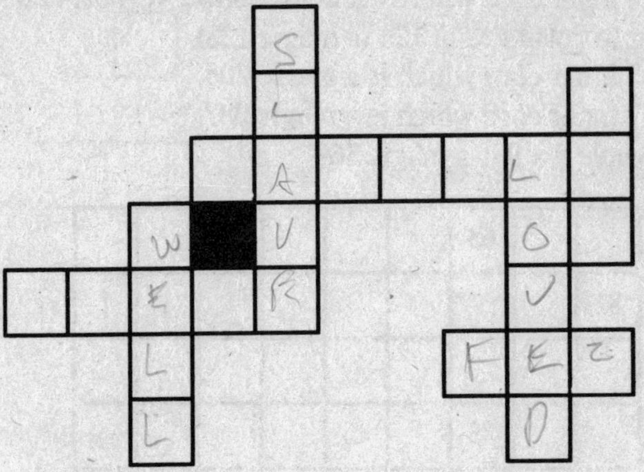

Clues:

- correctly
- side post of a door
- vessel in which consecrated host is preserved
- beast of burden
- adored
- speedy
- swagger
- Turkish cap

(Solution 97)

146 Number Sequence

What number comes next in this sequence?

1, 8, 70, 627, 5639 ?

(Solution 102)

147 Multiple Magic

Fill in the remaining numbers from 1 to 81 to form a multiple magic square to produce

1. A 3 × 3 inner core where each horizontal, vertical and corner to corner total 123 (a magic 123)
2. A 5 × 5 inner core which is a magic 205
3. A 7 × 7 inner core which is a magic 287
4. The whole 9 × 9 is a magic 369

		63						
81								1
		36		45				
	18							
	72							
						27	56	
					9			

(Solution 105)

148 Three Squares

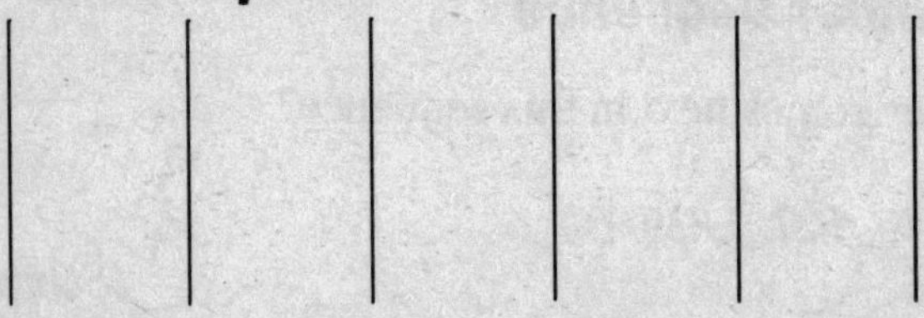

Using six matchsticks only create three squares of equal size. This one calls for a bit of lateral thinking.

(Solution 110)

149 Plan in Works

Change one letter from each word to make, in each case, a well-known phrase, for example:

PET RICE QUACK = GET RICH QUICK

1. GO PUT IN FIRE
2. PIN HARDS TOWN
3. BOOK HERS
4. PULL AT PITCH LATER
5. FASTS ON LINE
6. TALL IF FIRM
7. GO SICK SHE MUST
8. SET START
9. RUM TUM
10 FOE IN MY
11. NOW GO SAD
12. SO CRY BUT

(*Solution 115*)

150 Odd One Out

Which is the odd one?

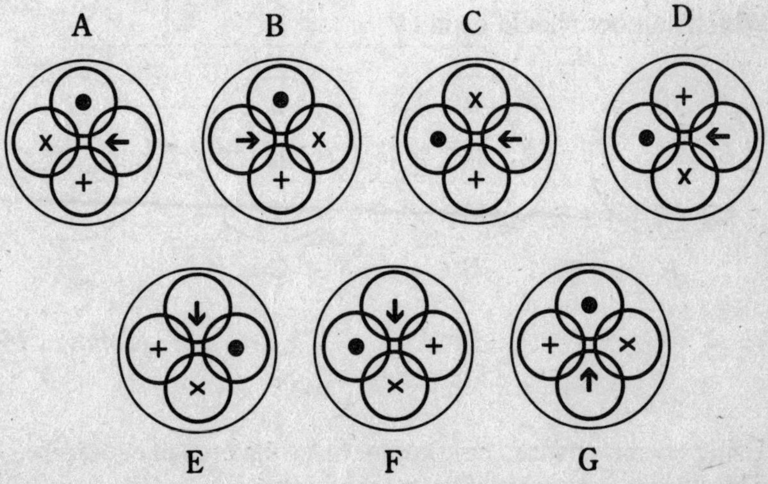

(*Solution 155*)

151 Trios

Complete the words to find, in each set, three words which are synonyms, for example:

IN • • N • = INVENT
• • I • I N • • • = ORIGINATE
• • • I • N = DESIGN

1. A • • • • T • • • T
• A • • A T • • •
A • T • • A T • • •

2. • • S S • • • O •
• O • • • • S • O •
• • S O • • • • • O •

3. • • V • • E
• E V E • E •
V E • E • • • • E

4. G • A • • • • • •
• • A • • • • G
• • • G A • •

5. • • • • I T • • •
I • I T • T I • •
• • • • T • • • • I T

6. • W • • E •
• • • E • • W • • E
W E • • E

(Solution 154)

152 Number

Which number should go in D?

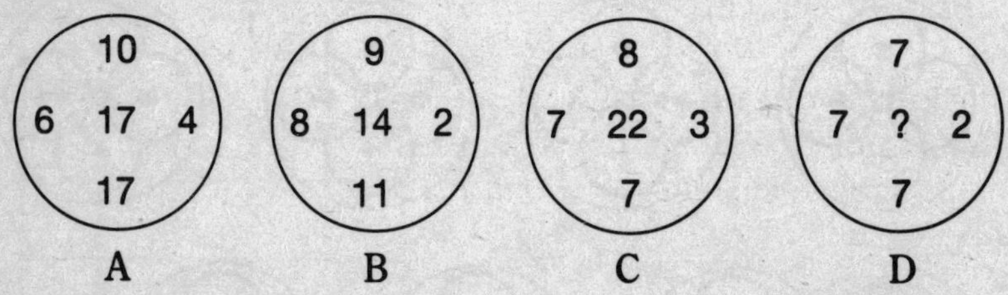

(Solution 150)

153 Brackets

Place a word in the brackets that when added on to the end of the first word forms a new word or phrase, and when placed in front of the second word also forms a new word or phrase.

1	RAIN	(- - - - -)	READER
2	LAMP	(- - - - -)	HOUSE
3	HORSE	(- - - -)	GROUND
4	HORSE	(- - - -)	HAND
5	FLINT	(- - - -)	SMITH
6	CROSS	(- - - -)	LAND
7	BRUSH	(- - - -)	WOOD
8	DRAGON	(- - -)	FISHING
9	DREAM	(- - - -)	LOCKED
10	BALL	(- - - - -)	LESS

(Solution 149)

154 Magic Square

The answers to the five clues are all five-letter words which when placed correctly in the grid form a magic word square where the same five words can be read both horizontally and vertically.

Clues (no particular order)

- In Roman times the ninth day before the Ides
- An appointed meeting
- Anguish
- Stiffness
- To bestow

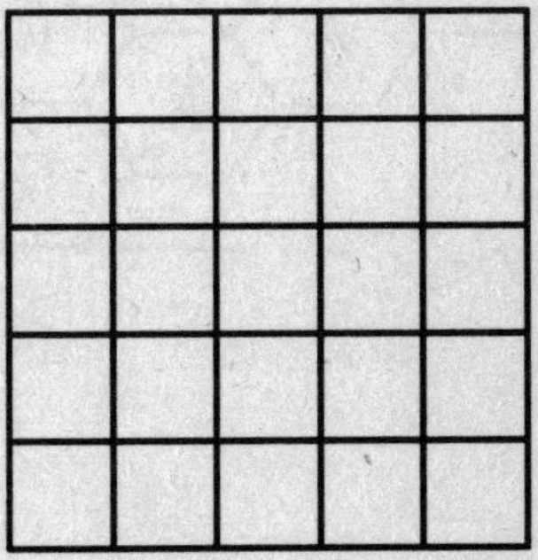

(Solution 145)

155 1 – 2 – 3

Fill in the last line to a regular rule.

1
11
21
1211
111221
312211
13112221
- - - - - - - - - - ?

(Solution 141)

156 Honeycomb

Reading in any direction, find 16 animals. Letters may be used more than once in the same word.

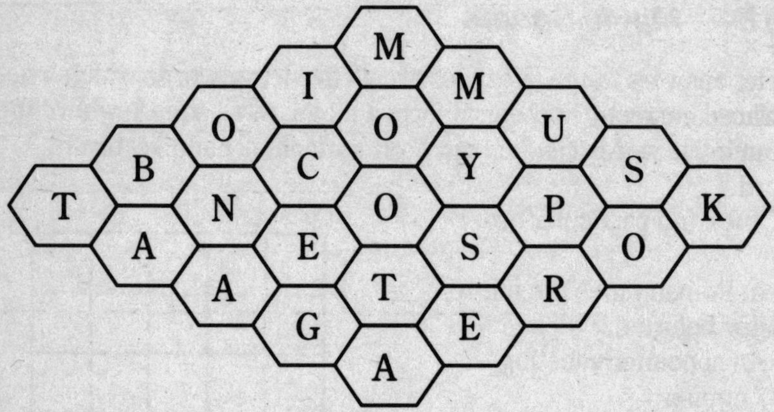

(Solution 137)

157 Missing Number

What is the missing number?

7	4	6	11
8	8	1	15
5	6	8	?

(Solution 132)

158 Pyramid Quotation

'Etiquette is the noise you don't make while having soup'

Using all 45 letters of the above quotation once each only, complete the pyramid with 1 × 1-letter, 1 × 2-letter, 1 × 3-letter words etc.
Clues are given, but in no particular order.

Clues:

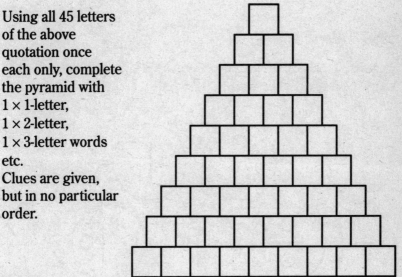

- Loud cry
- Crib
- Ornamental discs on dresses
- Large spotted dog
- An exclamation of surprise
- Steal
- Formal written application to persons in authority
- Very big
- The first person plural pronoun.

(Solution 128)

159 Circles

Which of these fit into the blank circle to carry on a logical sequence?

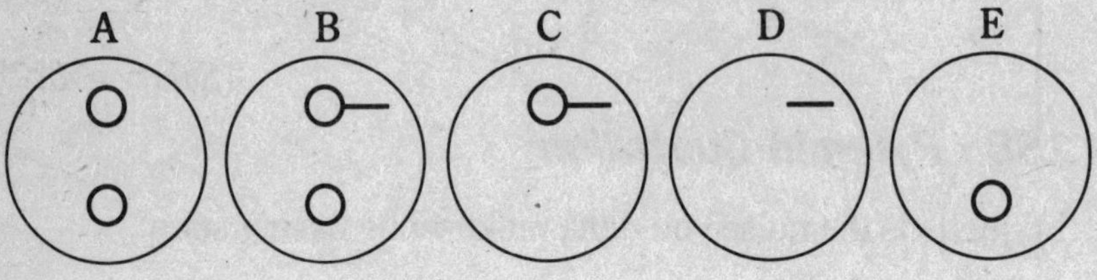

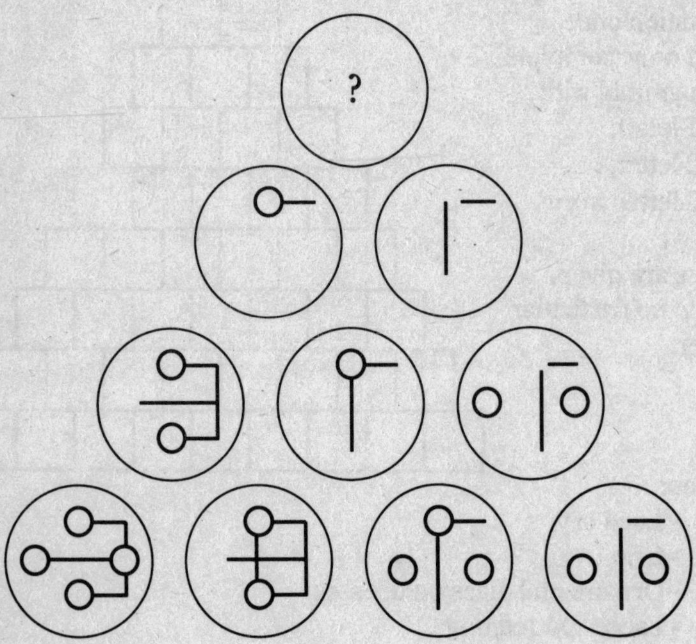

(Solution 125)

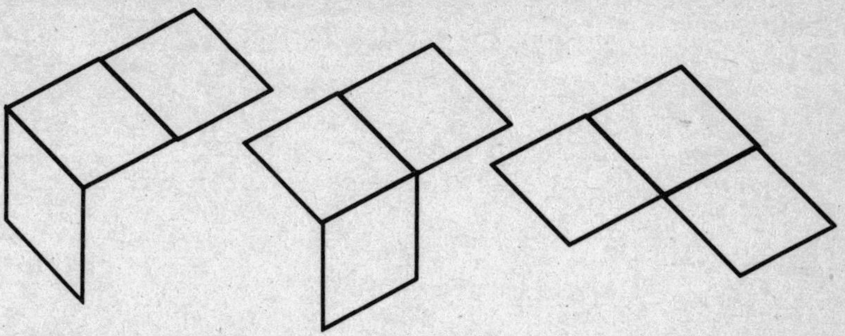

Which of the following options comes next in the above sequence?

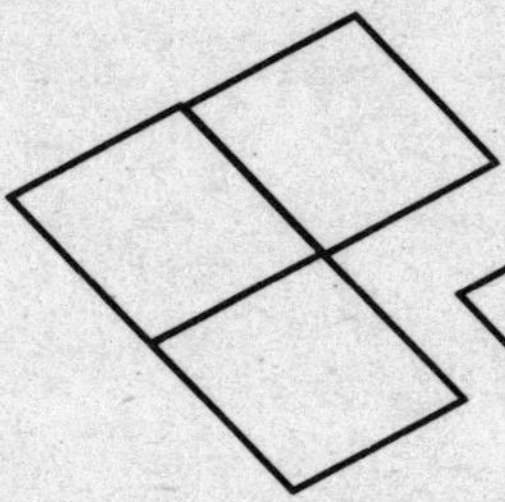

A

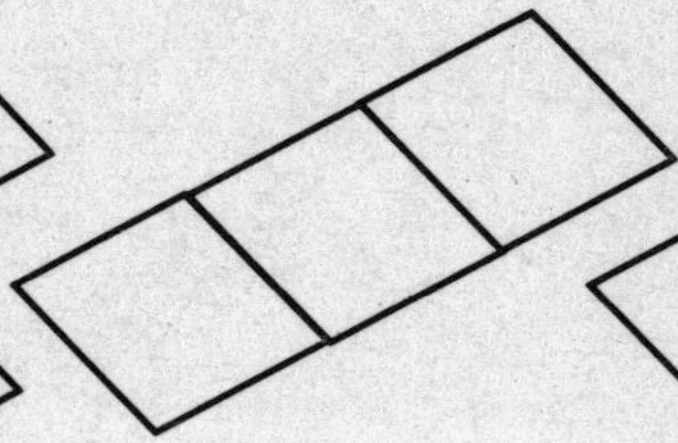

B

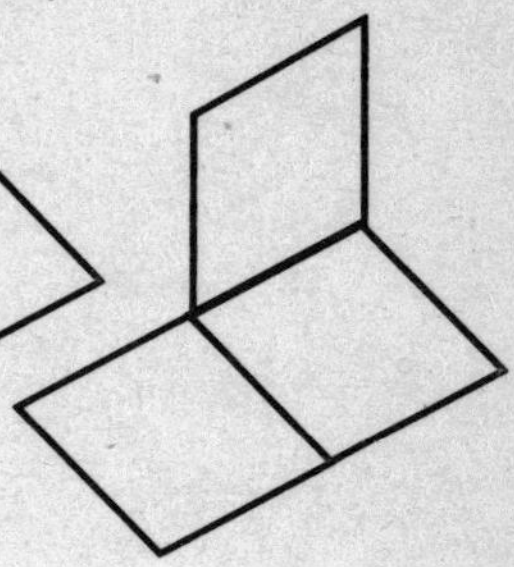

C

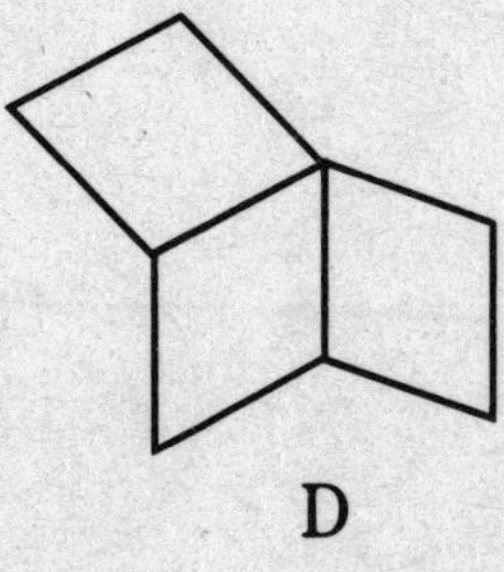

D

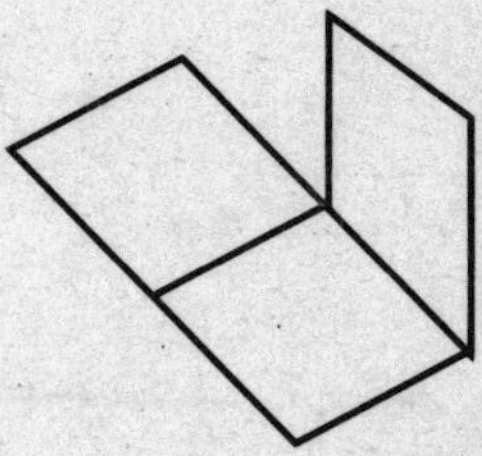

E

(Solution 119)

The Solutions

1 Find a Word

INVESTIGATION

(Puzzle 41)

2 Magic '34'

7	2	9	16
13	12	3	6
4	5	14	11
10	15	8	1

(Puzzle 80)

3 Brain Strain

7	+	5	–	3	=	9
+		+		+		×
7	+	3	–	6	=	4
–		÷		–		÷
8	+	4	–	6	=	6
=		=		=		=
6	÷	2	+	3	=	6

(Puzzle 121)

4 'X' Puzzle

Xiphoid, Xylene, Xylem, Xyloid, Dexter, Lynx, Rex, Lax, Ax, Axe, Hex, Exact, Text, Tax, Taxes, Exam, Sex, Ox, Pix, Nix, Pyx, Tux.

(Puzzle 1)

5 *Synonym Circles*

SIBLINGS
CHILDREN

(Puzzle 42)

6 *Square Numbers*

Across: 4489, 1681, 2916, 9604, 6241, 3025, 5776, 3136
Down: 4356, 1764, 9801, 2304, 5929, 1444, 3136, 2209

(Puzzle 81)

7 *Circle*

Less than 25%

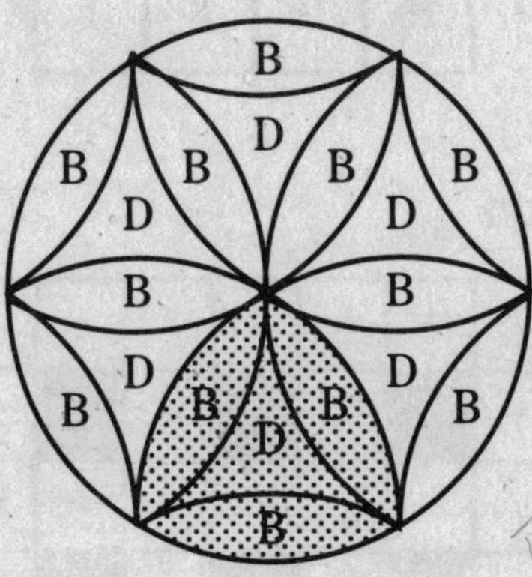

(Puzzle 122)

8 *Warehouse*

	C		
A	8×	B	4×
C	7×	D	6×

Starting at A each mile move towards B increases mileage per week by 8 but decreases 17 by 4 + 7 + 6 = 17.
From B to C we get + (8 + 4) – (7 + 6) – 1 so the number is still going down.
After C we get + (8 + 4 + 7) – 6 so it goes up. Therefore C is best.

(Puzzle 2)

9 Grid

2C

(Puzzle 43)

10 Middle Letters

FUSS-BUDGET
MISERLY
FUZZY-WUZZY
FRANGIPANI
FLUNKEYDOM
DUST-JACKET
FAR-FETCHED
EISTEDDFOD
DAISY-CHAIN
DAPPLE-GREY

(Puzzle 82)

11 Alphabet Crossword

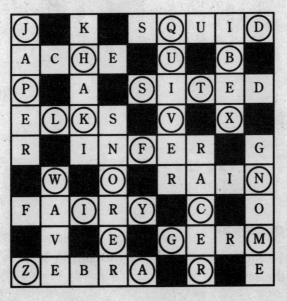

J		K		S	Q	U	I	D
A	C	H	E		U		B	
P		A		S	I	T	E	D
E	L	K	S		V		X	
R		I	N	F	E	R		G
	W		O		R	A	I	N
F	A	I	R	Y		C		O
	V		E		G	E	R	M
Z	E	B	R	A		R		E

(Puzzle 3)

12 'E' Frame

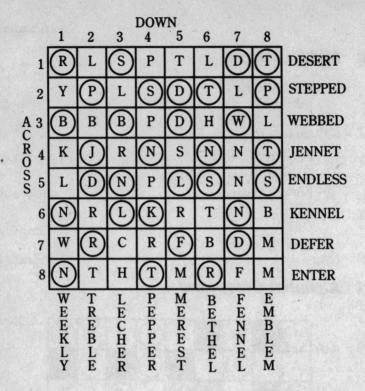

ACROSS \ DOWN	1	2	3	4	5	6	7	8	
1	**R**	L	**S**	P	T	L	**D**	**T**	DESERT
2	Y	**P**	L	**S**	**D**	**T**	L	**P**	STEPPED
3	**B**	B	**B**	P	**D**	H	**W**	L	WEBBED
4	K	**J**	R	**N**	S	**N**	N	**T**	JENNET
5	L	**D**	**N**	P	**L**	**S**	N	**S**	ENDLESS
6	**N**	R	**L**	**K**	R	T	**N**	B	KENNEL
7	W	**R**	C	R	**F**	B	**D**	M	DEFER
8	**N**	T	H	**T**	M	**R**	F	M	ENTER
	WEEKLY	TREBLE	LECHER	PEPPER	MEREST	BETHEL	FENNEL	EMBLEM	

(Puzzle 123)

13 Chairs

$$2 \times 7!$$
$$= 2 \times 7 \times 6 \times 5 \times 4 \times 3 \times 2 \times 1$$
$$= 10080$$

(Puzzle 44)

14 Sequence

B. The rectangle moves clockwise through 45 degrees each time, as does the square.

(Puzzle 83)

15 Symbols

D

(Puzzle 124)

16 Reverse Anagram

TAMBOURINE

(Puzzle 4)

17 Double Bigrams

HIPPOPOTAMUS, PHILOLOGY, SERENENESS, CONVIVIAL, BALALAIKA, ENTITIES, IMBIBING, STOWAWAY, PROTOTYPE, RHODODENDRON, UNINITIATED, TRAINING, SORDIDITY, CATATONIC.

(Puzzle 45)

18 Baby

7.2 lbs

12.96 ÷ 1.8 = 7.2

(Puzzle 84)

19 Add a Letter

A

CASHEW
SUMACH
ORANGE
ORACHE
SESAME

(Puzzle 125)

20 Number

The first two numbers in each line or column are divided by either 4 or 3, whichever is possible, and the quotients added together to produce the third number. i.e. (8 ÷ 4) + (12 ÷ 3) = 6 Thus the missing number is 4.

(Puzzle 46)

21 No Blanks

S	C	A	L	A	R		R	E	M	A	N	D
E		R	I	C	E	P	A	P	E	R		I
M	I	T	T	E	N		M	E	T	R	E	S
I		I		R	E	V	U	E		I		I
C	A	S	T		W	A	S		O	V	E	N
O		T	E	G		T		H	O	E		V
N			N	E	W		F	E	Z			E
D		C	O	T		M		N	E	T		S
U	P	O	N		L	A	C		S	O	F	T
C		V		D	O	N	O	R		I		M
T	R	E	P	A	N		M	E	A	L	I	E
O		R	E	M	E	D	I	A	T	E		N
R	O	T	T	E	R		C	R	E	D	I	T

(Puzzle 5)

22 Names

They all end countries:

AfghaniSTAN – PakiSTAN
ArgenTINA
DenMARK
JorDAN – SuDAN

(Puzzle 85)

23 Reserves

13.5 minutes $\frac{15 \times 36}{40}$

(Puzzle 6)

24 Directional Crossword

[1] M	[5] E	V	A	W	E	D	I	[4] T
[10] E	I	D	[13] N	E	P	[12] O	N	[7] S
P	L	S	U	E	C	E	T	S
I	[17] E	B	G	C	L	E	[15] O	U
T	R	O	A	U	A	L	E	C
H	[18] R	B	B	M	I	T	[14] Y	S
E	O	R	E	[16] O	A	D	E	I
[11] T	U	[8] R	O	B	O	[9] T	E	[6] D
[3] T	N	A	R	O	D	O	E	[2] D

1. Misguided
2. Deodorant
3. Turbulent
4. Tidewave
5. Educated
6. Discuss
7. Steamer
8. Robot
9. Tamable
10. Epithet
11. Tobacco
12. Open
13. Nelly
14. Yeo
15. Olio
16. Oboe
17. Err

(Puzzle 126)

25 Matrix

G. Looking both across and down, lines which are common in the first two squares are not carried forward to the third square.

(Puzzle 47)

26 Do-it-Yourself Crossword

I	L	L	U	S	T	R	A	T	E	D
N		A		O		O		O		U
T	U	T	O	R		B	A	T	O	N
E		H		T	H	E				E
R	U	E		S	I	S	T	E	R	S
		R			K			M		
D	E	S	I	R	E	D		B	A	R
O				A	R	E		A		I
L	I	K	E	N		B	U	R	N	T
T		E		E		U		G		E
S	U	G	G	E	S	T	I	O	N	S

(Puzzle 86)

27 Anagrammed Synonyms

1. TOO - BESIDES
2. WEAK - ENERVATED
3. HIND - POSTERIOR
4. KISS - OSCULATE
5. POST - PALISADE
6. EBB - RETREAT
7. WHET - STIMULATE
8. ACT - ORDINANCE
9. EAT - INGEST
10. VICE - WEAKNESS

(Puzzle 7)

28 Quartering a Square

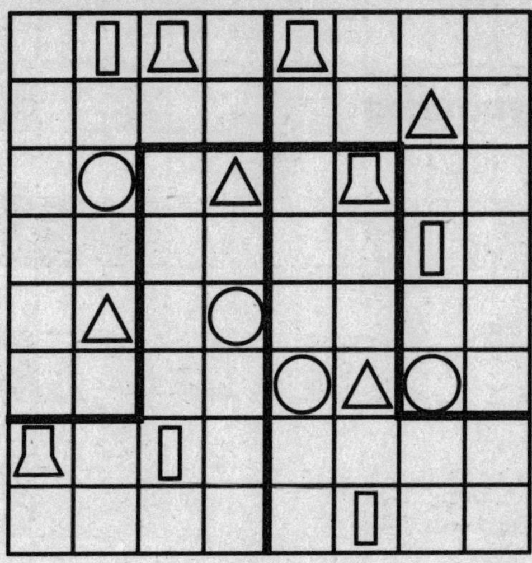

(Puzzle 127)

29 Anagrammed Magic Square

S	C	A	R	F
C	A	T	E	R
A	T	O	N	E
R	E	N	T	S
F	R	E	S	H

(Puzzle 48)

30 Comparison

C

(Puzzle 87)

31 Concentration

F

(Puzzle 128)

32 1984

```
          5
   780
   941
+  263
  1984
```

(Puzzle 8)

33 Stations

56
8×7

(Puzzle 49)

34 The Puzzling Puzzle

MYSTERY, CONUNDRUM, ENIGMA, PARADOX, PROBLEM, BEWILDERMENT.

(Puzzle 88)

35 Polling Day

Add 23,968 + 1026 + 2822 + 6428 = 34,244
Divide by four = 8561
8561 is the number of votes received by the successful candidate.
The second received 7535 (8561 – 1026),
the third 5739 (8561 – 2822) and fourth 2133 (8561 – 6428)

(Puzzle 129)

36 Round the Hexagons

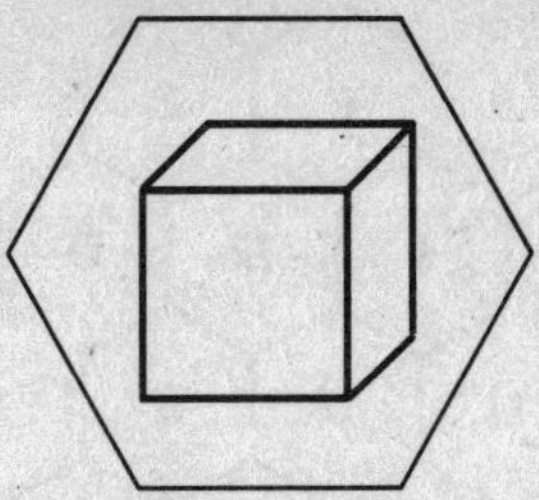

Working from top to bottom, every third hexagon contains the contents of the two previous hexagons.

(Puzzle 9)

37 Hexagram

SALMON, GRILSE, PLAICE, BLENNY, BURBOT, GROPER
Key = BARBEL

(Puzzle 50)

38 Bath

This is solved by reciprocals in the formula $(a^{-1} + b^{-1} - c^{-1})^{-1}$
$= (8^{-1} + 10^{-1} - 5^{-1})^{-1}$ i.e. $8^{-1} = \frac{1}{8}$
$= (0.125 + 0.1 - 0.2)^{-1} = 0.025^{-1}$
$= {}^{1}/_{0.025} = 40$ minutes

(Puzzle 89)

39 Alternatives

1	(c)	2	(a)
3	(a)	4	(b)
5	(a)	6	(a)
7	(a)	8	(a)

(Puzzle 130)

40 Hexagon

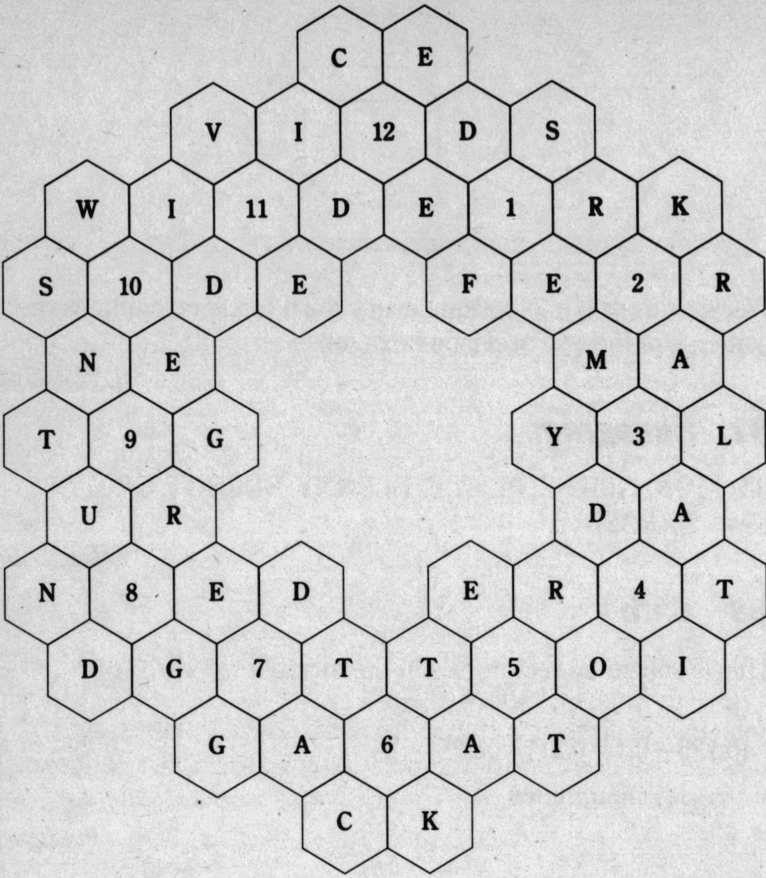

(Puzzle 10)

41 Homonym

YOU – EWE

(Puzzle 51)

42 Ten-Digit Number

2100010006

(Puzzle 131)

43 Circles

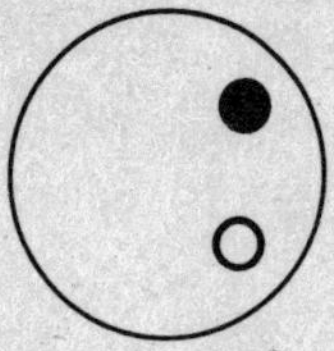

The contents of the middle circle are determined by the contents of the four circles surrounding it. Only when the same circle appears in the same position in three (and only three) of the surrounding circles is it carried forward to the middle circle.

(Puzzle 90)

44 Circles

C

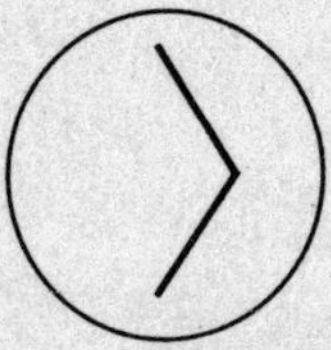

Each pair of circles produces the circle above by carrying forward the elements, only similar elements are carried forward.

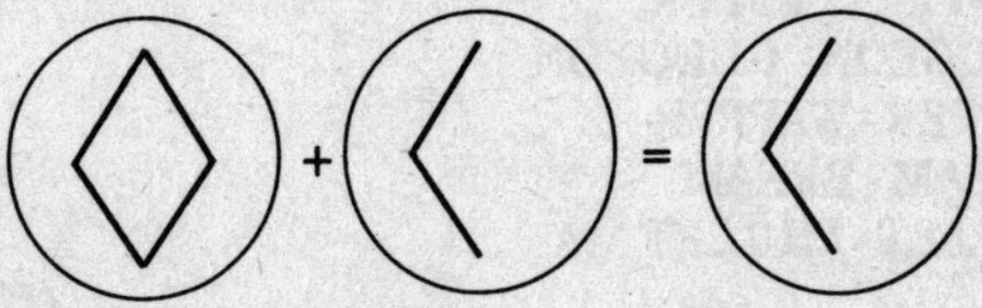

(Puzzle 11)

45 Comparison

C

(Puzzle 132)

46 Circles

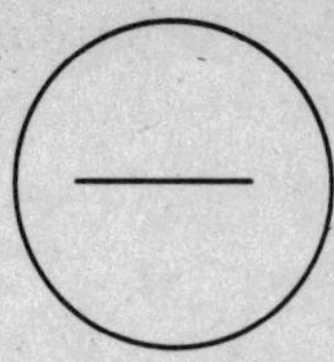

C

Each pair of circles produces the circle above by carrying forward the elements, only similar symbols are carried forward.

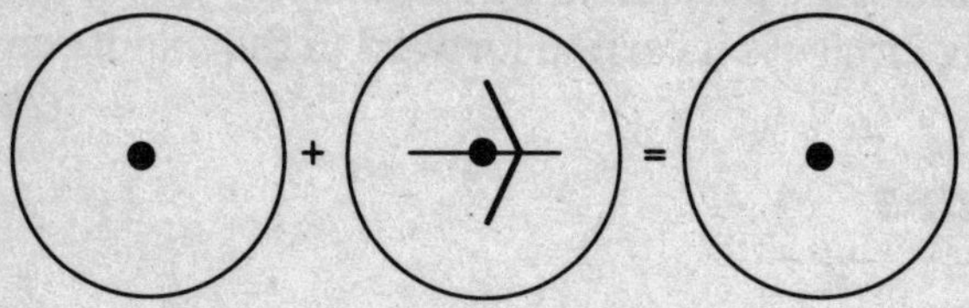

(Puzzle 52)

47 Fish

1 PROPER - GROPER
2 CATTLE - CUTTLE
3 GUNNER - GUNNEL
4 NIPPER - KIPPER
5 DUFFER - PUFFER
6 DUDGEON - GUDGEON
7 SAPPER - WAPPER
8 DREAM - BREAM
9 BULLET - MULLET

(Puzzle 91)

48 Pentagram

CIVET
CAMEL
PANDA Key COATI
STOAT
TAPIR

(Puzzle 53)

49 Work it Out

C. The final figure in each line is determined by the number of sides in each figure as follows:

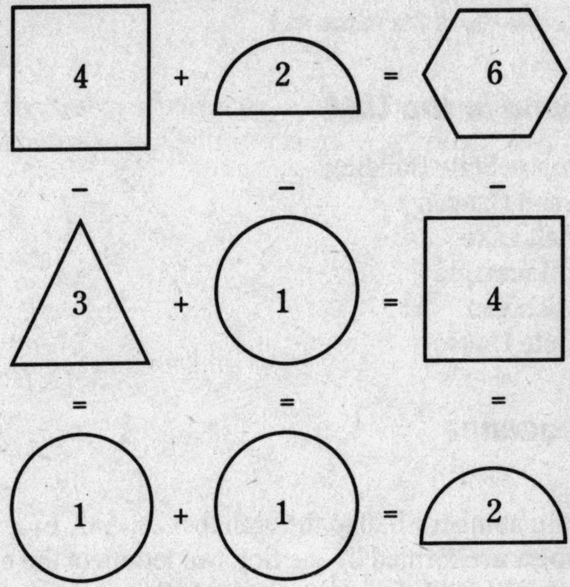

(Puzzle 133)

50 Target Crossword

- NOGGIN
- POSSUM
- SEXTON
- SEESAW
- EYELID
- PICNIC
- POSEUR
- SHANDY
- LINEAL
- SHAMAN
- ROUBLE
- PARODY
- SCONCE
- RIGHTS
- PIAZZA
- GINGKO

(Puzzle 12)

51 Something in Common

They are all names of ships or boats:
Packet, Punt, Barge, Liner, Smack, Tramp, Tender, Trader

(Puzzle 54)

52 Odd One Out

G
B is the same as E
A is the same as D
C is the same as F

(Puzzle 92)

53 Found in the USA

1. The Empire State Building
2. The Grand Canyon
3. Great Salt Lake
4. Rocky Mountains
5. Lake Michigan
6. The White House

(Puzzle 134)

54 Sequence

1021
Allocate the numbers 1-26 to the alphabet i.e. A=1, B=2, C=3 etc. The numbers are formed by the first two letters of the months of the year starting with January – J(10), A(1) = 101
The seventh month is, therefore July – J(10), U(21) = 1021.

(Puzzle 13)

55 Octagons

D. The shield twists round three sides of the octagon each time. The arrow moves from top to bottom of the shield in turn and points to the outside then the inside of the shield in turn.

(Puzzle 55)

56 Odd One Out

E
A is the same as C
B is the same as G
D is the same as F

(Puzzle 135)

57 Nursery Rhyme Crossword

M	A	J	E	S	T	Y
E		E		C		I
R	E	S	T	O	R	E
I		T		O		L
T	R	E	A	T	E	D
E		R		E		E
D	E	S	I	R	E	D

(Puzzle 93)

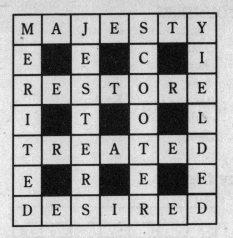

58 No Repeat Letters

SPECULATOR

(Puzzle 14)

59 Cards

$52p_4 = 52 \times 51 \times 50 \times 49$

$= 6{,}497{,}400$

(Puzzle 56)

60 Network

REPRESENTATIVE

(Puzzle 94)

61 Word Circle

STARCH, CHEESE, SENATE, TENURE, RESUME, METTLE, LEGACY, CYPHER, ERMINE, NEBULA, LAVISH, SHELVE, VENDOR, ORIGIN, INFEST.

(Puzzle 15)

62 Anagram Theme

The theme is COUNTRIES.

Nigeria	Gain	Ire
Finland	Flan	Din
Austria	Aura	Sit
Sweden	Sew	End
Argentina	Grain	Neat
Algeria	Rail	Age
Hungary	Rung	Hay

(Puzzle 136)

63 Number Logic

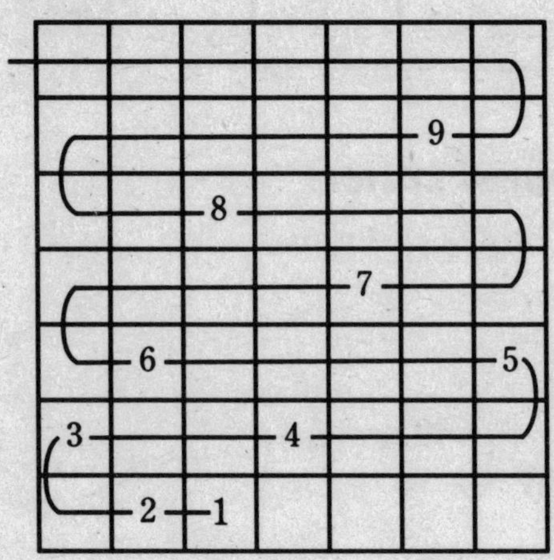

Start at the top left-hand corner and work in the direction indicated, counting the same number of squares as the next number each time.

(Puzzle 57)

64 Find Another Word

LONG. All words can be prefixed with FUR to form another word: Furbelow, Furore, Furrower, Furlong.

(Puzzle 95)

65 Nines

3	8	5	2
8	7	9	3
6	6	5	1
1	6	8	3

(Puzzle 137)

66 Missing Square

D. The number of sides in the figures in each horizontal, vertical and corner to corner line add up to 15.

(Puzzle 16)

67 Sequence

B.

The figure alternates:

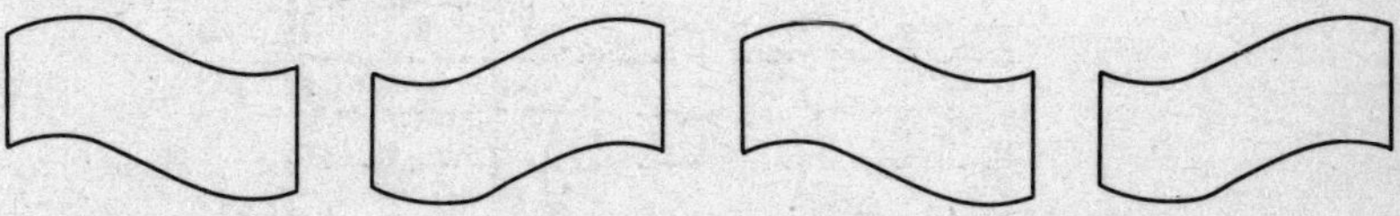

The lines are first introduced into the circles on the left, one at a time in rotation and then transfer to the circle on the right at the next stage.

(Puzzle 58)

68 Missing Letters

1 ANATOMIST
2 STUNTMAN
3 BOATSWAIN
4 RIVETTER
5 JAPANNER
6 DIETICIAN
7 USHERETTE
8 VIOLINIST
9 MERCENARY
10 GASFITTER

(Puzzle 138)

69 Connections

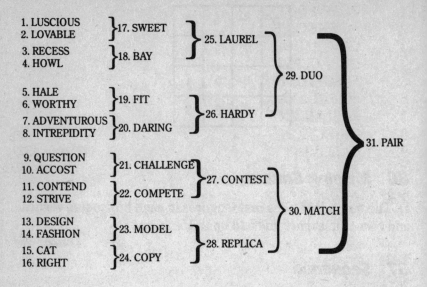

1. LUSCIOUS
2. LOVABLE } 17. SWEET

3. RECESS
4. HOWL } 18. BAY

17. SWEET, 18. BAY } 25. LAUREL

5. HALE
6. WORTHY } 19. FIT

7. ADVENTUROUS
8. INTREPIDITY } 20. DARING

19. FIT, 20. DARING } 26. HARDY

25. LAUREL, 26. HARDY } 29. DUO

9. QUESTION
10. ACCOST } 21. CHALLENGE

11. CONTEND
12. STRIVE } 22. COMPETE

21. CHALLENGE, 22. COMPETE } 27. CONTEST

13. DESIGN
14. FASHION } 23. MODEL

15. CAT
16. RIGHT } 24. COPY

23. MODEL, 24. COPY } 28. REPLICA

27. CONTEST, 28. REPLICA } 30. MATCH

29. DUO, 30. MATCH } 31. PAIR

(Puzzle 96)

70 Logic

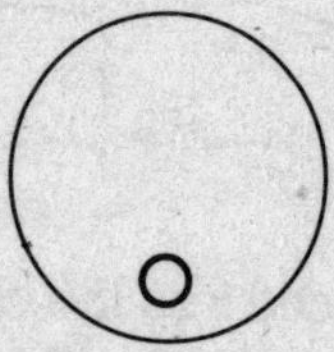

Row 1 A is added to B = C
Row 2 A is added to B = C
Row 3 A is added to B = C
Column A 1 is added to 2 = 3
Column B 1 is added to 2 = 3
Column C 1 is added to 2 = 3
But similar symbols only appear.

(Puzzle 17)

71 Word Power

1 PUSSYFOOT
2 MUSKETEER
3 CANTALOUP
4 DEBAUCHER
5 FLAGSTONE
6 MARIJUANA
7 RECUMBENT
8 OBJECTION
9 GALLIVANT

(Puzzle 59)

72 Ending

PER

HAMPER
PAMPER
HOPPER
WHIMPER
SUPPER
SLIPPER

(Puzzle 97)

73 Sequence

E. The rectangle and diamond form alternate sequences. First the rectangle turns through 90 degrees, then the diamond does the same.

(Puzzle 139)

74 Old Age

88

(Puzzle 19)

75 Logic

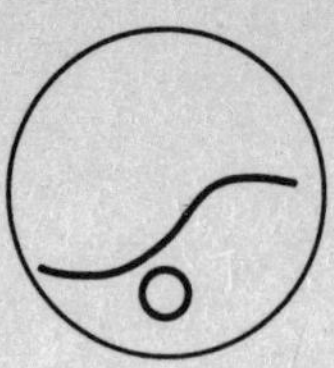

Row 1 A is added to B = C
Row 2 A is added to B = C
Row 3 A is added to B = C
Column A 1 is added to 2 = 3
Column B 1 is added to 2 = 3
Column C 1 is added to 2 = 3
But only similar symbols appear.

(Puzzle 60)

76 Arrows

F.
The arrow moves 45 degrees clockwise each time.
The arrow head alternates black/striped.
The arrow body alternates striped/black.
The ellipse rotates 45 degrees each time and moves from bottom to top etc. of arrow.
The circle moves from top to bottom etc. of arrow and black and white segments alternate.

(Puzzle 98)

77 Niners

Across	Down	Diagonal
1 Announcer	1 Anarchist	1 Accusable
4 Crossover	2 Unreserve	3 Renascent.
5 Teakettle	3 Recursive	

(Puzzle 140)

78 Pyramid

Unsportsmanlike

(Puzzle 61)

79 Sequence

D:

D	E F G H	I	(4)
I	J K L M N	O	(5)
O	P Q R S T U	V	(6)
V	W X Y Z A B C	D	(7)

(Puzzle 18)

80 Sequence

Trudy: The names can all be made from the days of the week starting SuNDAY (ANDY). Trudy can be produced from SaTURDaY.

(Puzzle 62)

81 Safe

Lynx

(Puzzle 99)

82 Safe

3W.

(Puzzle 141)

83 Word Search

DRINKS:
Chartreuse, Grenadine, Cappuccino, Cointreau, Muscadine, Orangeade, Martini, Arrack, Alcohol, Lager, Grog, Gimlet, Nog, Ale, Rosé, Cha, Hock, Tea, Fizz, Rye.

(Puzzle 20)

84 Clueless Crossword

P	L	U	M	B	E	R
L		P		U		E
A	P	P	A	R	E	L
T		E		S		I
E	R	R	A	T	I	C

(Puzzle 63)

85 Complete the Calculation

$$6^3 \div 36 = 6$$

(Puzzle 100)

86 Song

Up and down the city road,
In and out the eagle,
That's the way the money goes -
Pop goes the weasel!
Charles Twiggs (1853)

(Puzzle 142)

87 Letters Sequence

TH. They are the last two letters of each planet in reverse order from the Sun.

PluTO, NeptuNE, UranUS, SatuRN, JupitER, MaRS, EarTH.

(Puzzle 21)

88 Three Triangles

(Puzzle 64)

89 Grid

2A

(Puzzle 101)

90 Pyramid Word

L, PI, GUN, DEER, DRIVE.
15-letter word: UNDERPRIVILEGED

(Puzzle 143)

91 Bracket Word

ALTOGETHER

(Puzzle 22)

92 No Neighbours

TRANSMOGRIFICATION

(Puzzle 103)

93 Alternative Crossword

F	R	O	M	■	A	I	R	S
L	■	R	U	M	P	S	■	P
I	T	■	D	I	E	■	M	E
P	I	T	■	N	■	R	O	D
■	D	E	C	I	D	E	D	■
H	E	N	■	M	■	D	E	W
U	S	■	N	U	B	■	S	O
N	■	T	I	M	E	D	■	R
T	O	O	L	■	G	O	O	D

(Puzzle 65)

94 Middle Word

1 Joss
2 Jib
3 Girandole
4 Glutton
5 Farce
6 Fawn
7 Ferret
8 Fitch
9 Poppet
10 Shard

(Puzzle 144)

95 Odd One Out

B.
A is the same as D with Black and White reversed
C is the same as E with Black and White reversed

(Puzzle 23)

96 Circles

E

 moves 135° clockwise

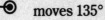

 moves 180°

 moves 90°

 moves 135°

(Puzzle 66)

97 Cross-Alphabet

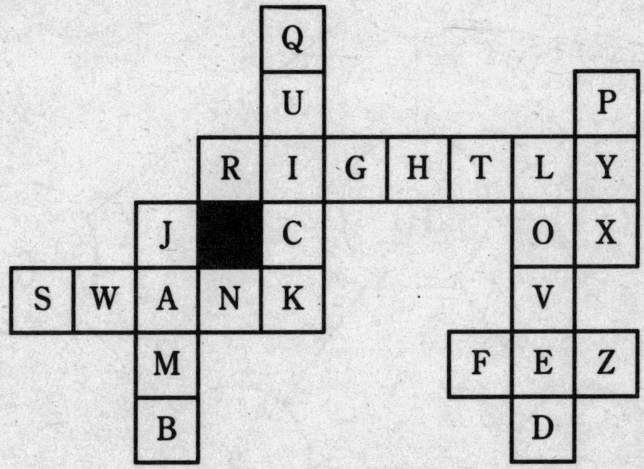

(Puzzle 145)

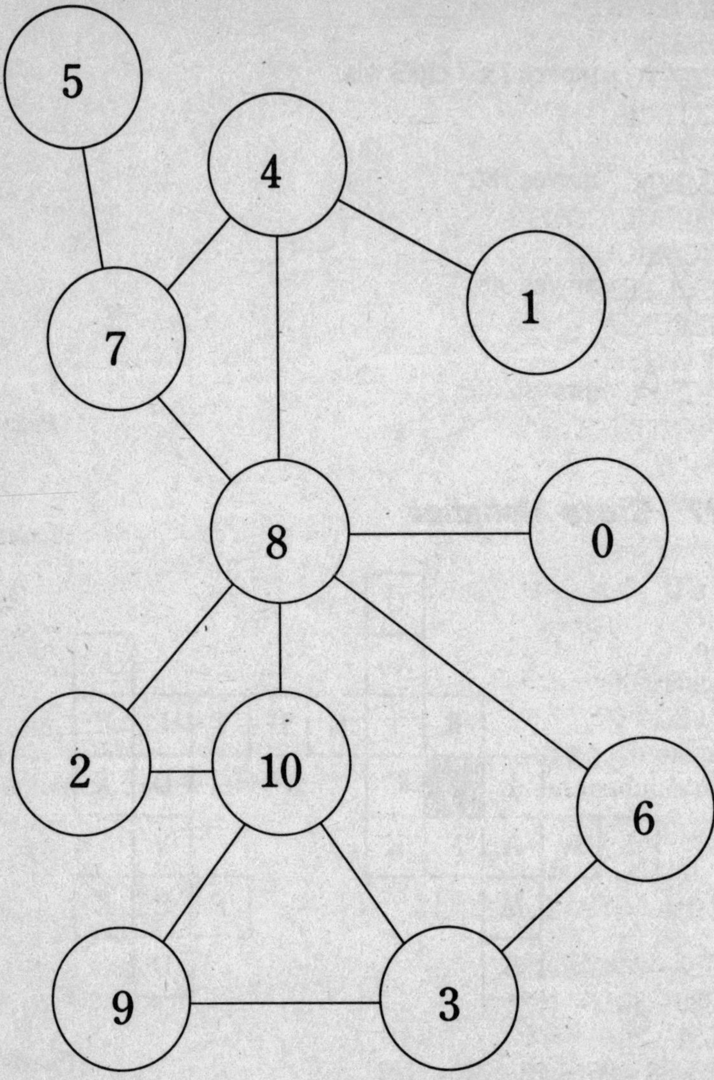

(Puzzle 102)

99 Word Power

ELDRICH
UKASE
REFECTION
EXTIRPATE
KOHL
AMAIN
IMPECUNIOUS
VICARIOUS
ESCULENT
GERUND
ODALISK
TERMAGANT
INANITION
TOLU
Eureka! I've got it. - ARCHIMEDES

(Puzzle 24)

100 Square Roots

No
Square these end digits and note last digit
0 1 2 3 4 5 6 7 8 9
Squared 0 1 4 9 6 5 6 9 4 1
No number ending in 2 - 3 - 7 - 8 can have a square root of integers only.

(Puzzle 67)

101 Missing Links

2798 – 2646 – 1196
4389 – 3827 – 1026
4051 – 2040 – 800
27 × 98 = 2646, 26 × 46 = 1196

(Puzzle 104)

102 Number Sequence

50746
1 x 9 – 1 = 8
8 x 9 – 2 = 70
70 x 9 – 3 = 627
627 x 9 – 4 = 5639
5639 x 9 – 5 = 50746

(Puzzle 146)

103 Greek Cross to Square Puzzle

The lines AB and CD are drawn from the centre of their respective sides of the Greek cross.

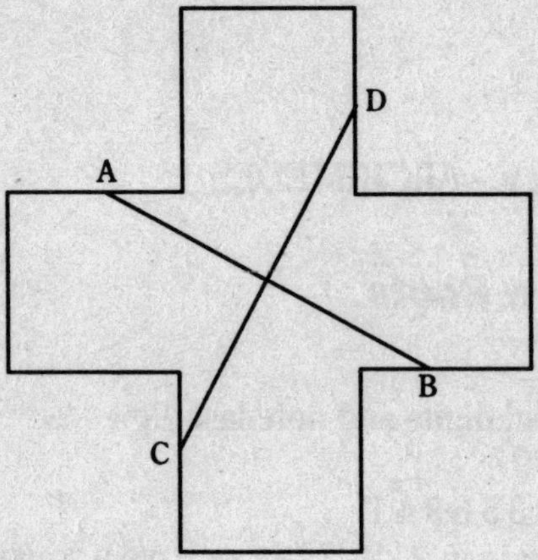

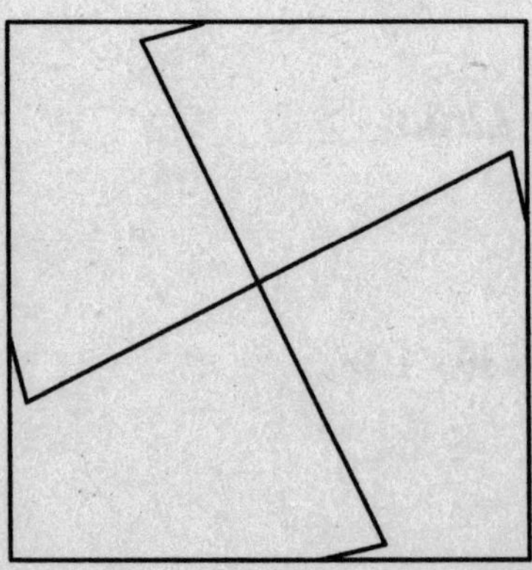

(Puzzle 25)

104 Wine

	hours	reciprocal	decimal
Man	2.5	$^1/_{2.5}$	.400
Wife	1.5	$^1/_{1.5}$	.667
		Add	1.067

Take reciprocal

$^1/_{1.067}$ = .9375 hrs.

= .9375 × 60

= 56.25 minutes.

(Puzzle 68)

105 Multiple Magic

13	12	63	3	61	73	59	80	5
81	26	71	28	57	30	55	20	1
78	68	35	60	29	50	31	14	4
6	24	36	40	45	38	46	58	76
75	17	49	39	41	43	33	65	7
8	18	34	44	37	42	48	64	74
15	72	51	22	53	32	47	10	67
16	62	11	54	25	52	27	56	66
77	70	19	79	21	9	23	2	69

(Puzzle 147)

106 Occupations

Ploughman
Professor
Major-domo
Puppeteer
Harpooner
Geologist
Osteopath
Zookeeper
Ropemaker
Gondolier
Herbalist
Hypnotist

(Puzzle 105)

107 Appropriate Anagrams

Dead Respire Again
Is Lit For Seamen
Causes Sin
Is No Meal
Sit Not At Ale Bars
A Stew Sir
Apt Is The Cure
No Hat, A Smile
Noted Miscalculations
Faces One At The End

(Puzzle 26)

108 Alternative Crossword

S	W	A	G	E
H	A	R	E	M
O	V	O	L	O
R	E	M	I	T
T	R	A	D	E

(Puzzle 69)

109 Sea Level

8.7 miles

The formula is

$$\text{Height} = \frac{2n^2}{3} \text{ feet}$$

(where n = distance in miles)

$$\therefore 50 = \frac{2n^2}{3}$$

$$150 = 2n^2$$

$$75 = n^2$$

$$n = \sqrt{75}$$

$$n = 8.7 \text{ miles}$$

(Puzzle 106)

110 Three squares

Sorry if this was a bit sneaky, but we didn't say that you couldn't break the matches.

(Puzzle 148)

111 Jumble

VACCINATION
VENTILATION
VENTURESOME
VICEROYSHIP
VERSATILITY
VERMICULATE
VICARIOUSLY
VEXATIOUSLY

(Puzzle 27)

112 Anagrammed Phrases

1. Let sleeping dogs lie
2. To give up the ghost
3. To beg the question
4. A fly on the wall
5. Play fast and loose

(Puzzle 70)

113 Logic

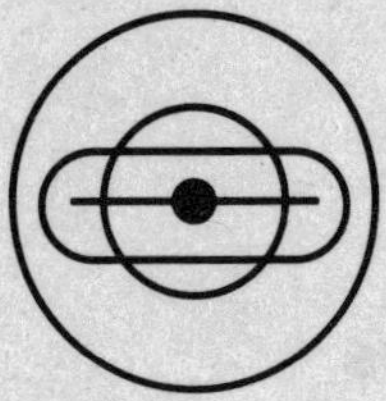

Row 1 A is added to B = C
Row 2 A is added to B = C
Row 3 A is added to B = C
Column A 1 is added to 2 = 3
Column B 1 is added to 2 = 3
Column C 1 is added to 2 = 3
But similar symbols disappear.

(Puzzle 107)

114 Four Integers

A = 9
B = 6
C = 3
D = 1
CABA = 3969
DCBA = 1369
DACB = 1936

(Puzzle 28)

115 Plan in Works

1. To cut it fine
2. Win hands down
3. Look here
4. Dull as ditch water
5. Facts of life
6. Ball of fire
7. To lick the dust
8. See stars
9. Yum yum
10. Woe is me
11. Not to say
12. To try out

(Puzzle 149)

116 Symbols

A

(Puzzle 29)

117 Work it Out

63 : $\frac{15 \times 3 \times 7}{5}$

Likewise : $\frac{4 \times 3 \times 8}{6} = 16$

$\frac{9 \times 12 \times 2}{9} = 24$

(Puzzle 71)

118 Cheeses

63 moves $(2^6 - 1)$

(Puzzle 30)

119 Logical Movement

B. There are three components:

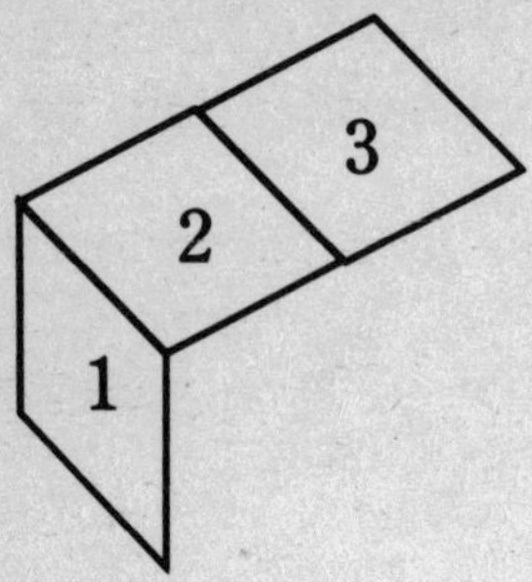

All pieces are laid flat.
Pieces 2 and 3 never move.
Piece 1 moves by rotating anti-clockwise and clamping itself onto the next available side.

Thus option 2:-

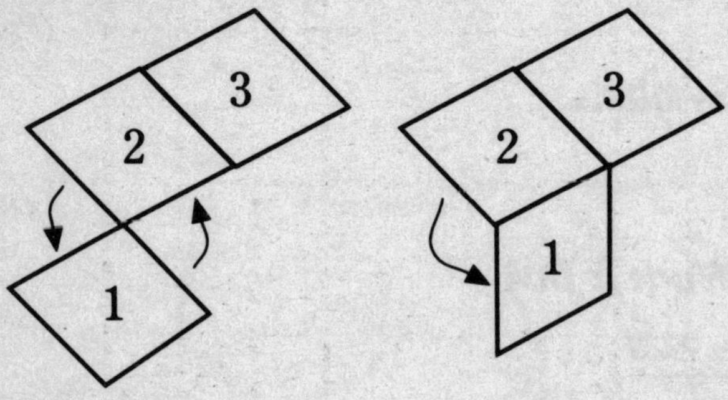

(Puzzle 160)

120 Quotation

Anyone who thinks that there is a safety in numbers has not looked at the stock market pages - Irene Peter.

(Puzzle 108)

121 Comparison

A

(Puzzle 34)

122 Cryptogram

Write we know is written right, when we see it written write;
But when we see it written wright, we know 'tis not then written right;
For write to have it written right, must not be written right nor wright;
Nor yet should it be written rite, but write – for so 'tis written right.

(Puzzle 72)

123 Dominoes

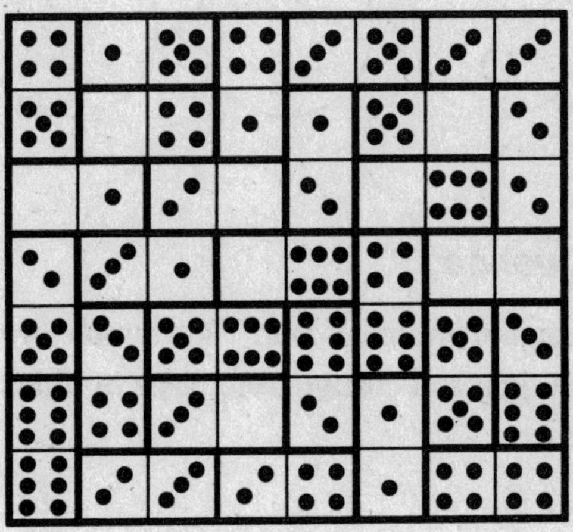

(Puzzle 109)

124 The Gallopers

ANNOYING (Exasperating), LAG (Delay)
LING (Heather), OBLONG (Rectangular)
PRIG (Puritan), EVERLASTING (Imperishable)
ROUSING (Stimulating), SPRING (Fountainhead)

(Puzzle 31)

125 Circles

D

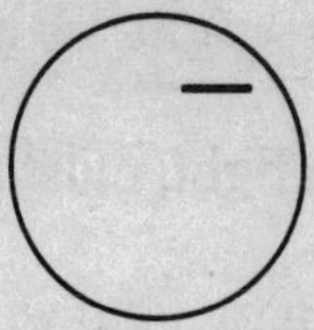

Each pair of circles produces the circle above by carrying forward the elements, only similar symbols are carried forward.

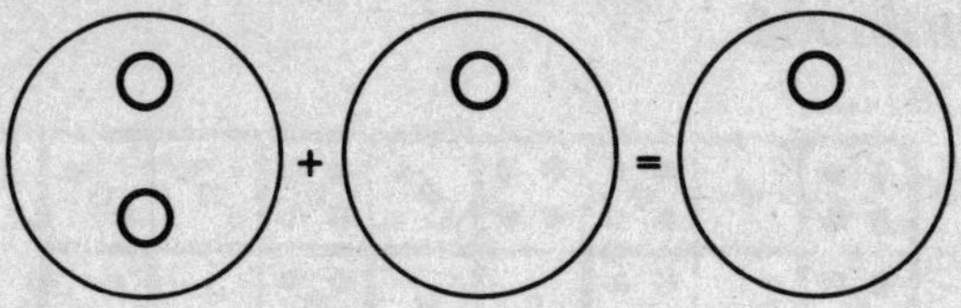

(Puzzle 159)

126 Sequence

C. Break them into groups of four. They tumble over one at a time from the right and change from black to white one at a time from the left.

(Puzzle 73)

127 Letter Sequence

R. They are all alternate letters in

ThE uNiTeD sTaTeS oF aMeRica

(Puzzle 110)

128 Pyramid Quotation

O, we, key, huge, shout, thieve, sequins, petition, dalmation

(Puzzle 158)

129 Analogy

C. The figure is inverted and the inverted figure placed on top on the original figure touching the top and bottom of it.
The external parts in the figure created are shaded.

(Puzzle 32)

130 Sequence

REEF:
RAY (ON E) PAULE (T WO) R (TH REE) F

(Puzzle 74)

131 Odd One Out

Open.
All other words are made up from the initials of the numbers 1-10 : OTTFFSSENT.

(Puzzle 111)

132 Missing Number

1. The link is in each horizontal line

$$7 = \frac{4 + 6 + 11}{3}$$

$$8 = \frac{8 + 1 + 15}{3}$$

$$5 = \frac{6 + 8 + 1}{3}$$

(Puzzle 157)

133 Birds

Crested	Grebe
Carrier	Pigeon
Stormy	Petrel
Snow	Goose
Muscovy	Duck
Tawny	Owl
Night	Hawk
Water	Ousel
Turtle	Dove
House	Martin
Willow	Warbler
Black	Cockatoo

Odd word – PEACOCK

(Puzzle 33)

134 Missing Number

4.

The number inside the octagon is produced by doing the opposite calculation to that indicated immediately above.

i.e. $7 + 3$ ∴ actual calculation $7 - 3 = 4$
3×3 ∴ actual calculation $3 \div 3 = 1$
$3 - 2$ ∴ actual calculation $3 + 2 = 5$
$2 - 7$ ∴ actual calculation $2 + 7 = 9$

(Puzzle 112)

135 Knight

We find it hard to believe that other people's thoughts are as silly as our own, but they probably are.

(Puzzle 35)

136 Threes

They are all names of groups.

Pack	Hyenas, Wolves, Cigarettes
Rookery	Penguins, Rooks, Seals
Drove	Pigs, Swine, Oxen
Nest	Machine Guns, Wasps, Mice
Pod	Peas, Whales, Hippopotamuses
Troop	Scouts, Baboons, Actors

(Puzzle 75)

137 Honeycomb

ANIMALS

Moose	Coyote	Coypu
Pup	Puppy	Sore
Mice	Possum	Teg
Musk	Cob	Bat
Nag	Tat	Moco
Stag		

(Puzzle 156)

138 Series

The step each time is to multiply by 3

e.g. $6 \times 3 = 9$

We require the 10th term, i.e., 6×3^9

$= 6 \times 19683$

$= 118098$

(Puzzle 36)

139 Common

They all begin with things associated with water but, with letters reversed.

1. Bib
2. Carp
3. Dab
4. Crab
5. Gar
6. Tide
7. Newt
8. Orca

(Puzzle 76)

140 Middle Words

1. By
2. King
3. Fish
4. Wood
5. Me
6. Ring
7. Ate
8. Lock
9. He
10. Cap

(Puzzle 113)

141 1-2-3

1113213211:

Each line describes the number above it.

For example, 1221 would be:

One 1, Two 2, One 1, etc.

(Puzzle 155)

142 Division

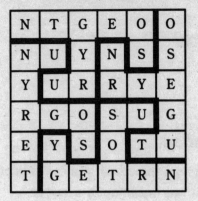

YOUNGSTER

N	T	G	E	O	O
N	U	Y	N	S	S
Y	U	R	R	Y	E
R	G	O	S	U	G
E	Y	S	O	T	U
T	G	E	T	R	N

(Puzzle 37)

143 Scales

13.5 grams

$9 \times 6 = 4 \times 13.5$

(Puzzle 77)

144 Track Word

INSTANTANEOUSLY

(Puzzle 114)

145 Magic Square

G	R	A	N	T
R	I	G	O	R
A	G	O	N	Y
N	O	N	E	S
T	R	Y	S	T

(Puzzle 154)

146 Three Animals

Panther, Antelope, Llama

(Puzzle 38)

147 Symbols

A

(Puzzle 78)

148 Quotation

The minute you read something you can't understand, you can almost be sure it was drawn up by a lawyer.

- Will Rogers

(Puzzle 115)

149 Brackets

1. Proof
2. Light
3. Play
4. Whip
5. Lock
6. Over
7. Fire
8. Fly
9. Land
10. Point

(Puzzle 153)

150 Number

14

$(7 \times 2) + 7 - 7 = 14$

(Puzzle 152)

151 Equilateral Triangle

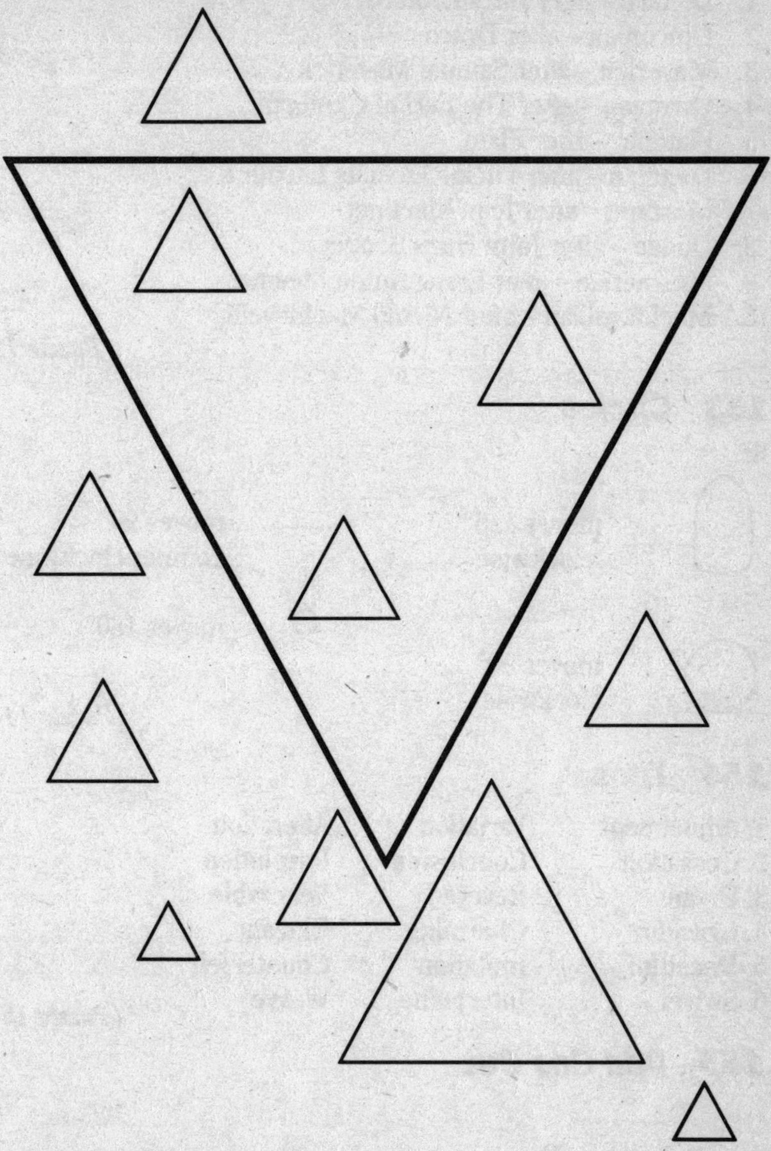

(Puzzle 39)

152 Eponyms

1. Leotard – after Jules Léotard
2. Draconian – after Draco
3. Maverick – after Samual Maverick
4. Cardigan – after The Earl of Cardigan
5. Platonic – after Plato
6. Lucullan – after Lucius Licinius Lucullus
7. Martinet – after Jean Martinet
8. Dunce – after John Duns Scotus
9. Mesmerize – after Franz Anton Mesmer
10. Machiavellian – after Nicolò Machiavelli

(Puzzle 79)

153 Circles

B:

moves 135° clockwise

moves 90° counter-clockwise

moves 180°

moves 90° clockwise

(Puzzle 116)

154 Trios

1. Adjustment	Variation	Alteration
2. Cessation	Conclusion	Resolution
3. Divine	Revered	Venerable
4. Graceful	Charming	Elegant
5. Deceitful	Imitation	Counterfeit
6. Swivel	Intertwine	Weave

(Puzzle 151)

155 Odd One Out

D:
A is the same as F
B is the same as E
C is the same as G

(Puzzle 150)

156 Quotation

"I have made it a rule never to smoke more than one cigar at a time." – *Mark Twain*

(Puzzle 117)

157 Directional Numbers

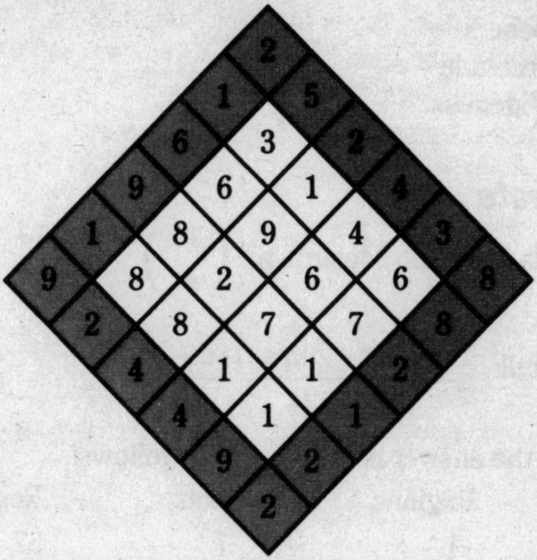

(Puzzle 40)

158 The Hexagonal Pyramid

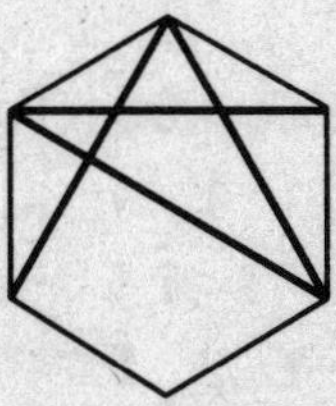

The content of each hexagon is made up by merging the contents of the two hexagons directly below, with the exception that where two identical lines appear they are not carried forward.

(Puzzle 119)

159 Synchronized Synonyms

Towering, Gigantic
Dextrous, Polished
Director, Governor
Isolated, Solitary
Swindler, Deceiver
Calendar, Schedule
Disallow, Preclude
Latitude, Wideness

(Puzzle 120)

160 Spots

The formula is by Leo Moser: $n + \binom{n}{4} \binom{n-1}{2}$

Written in full: $$\frac{n^4 - 6n^3 + 23n^2 - 18n + 24}{24}$$

Amazingly the answer is not 32. It is as follows:

Spots	Regions	Spots	Regions
1	1	7	57
2	2	8	99
3	4	9	163
4	8	10	256
5	16	11	386
6	31		

Answers can be obtained by a cut from Pascal's triangle.

```
            1
           1 1
          1 2 1
         1 3 3 1
        1 4 6 4 1 /
      1 5 10 10 5 /1
    1 6 15 20 15/6 1
  1 7 21 35 35/21 7 1
```

(Puzzle 118)

IQ
Hotshot

1 *Alternative Crossword*

Select the correct letters to complete the crossword.

1	5	5	3	2	2	6	7
5	■	■	1	5	7	■	2
7	5	■	2	1	7	■	6
7	3	6	■	4	5	6	2
2	4	1	5	■	6	2	5
7	■	8	5	8	■	8	2
2	■	2	8	1	■	■	4
2	3	4	1	7	5	6	9

KEY

1	A	B	C
2	D	E	F
3	G	H	I
4	J	K	L
5	M	N	O
6	P	Q	R
7	S	T	U
8	V	W	X
9	Y	Z	–

	■	■				■	
		■				■	
			■				
				■			
	■				■		
	■				■	■	

(Solution 4)

2 Batteries

A day's production of batteries has 10% spoilage.
If three batteries are selected at random, what are the chances that all three will be defective?

(Solution 8)

3 Link Word

Find a 5-letter word that when placed in front of these words produces new words.

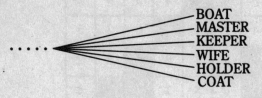

. . . . . — BOAT
MASTER
KEEPER
WIFE
HOLDER
COAT

(Solution 10)

4 Common Clues

What does each pair of words have in common?

Vex
Summit

Implement
A fine silk net

Necessity
Pound

Strip
Forbidden

Reconsider
A light entertainment

Meter
A pledge

Encroach
Railed

(Solution 16)

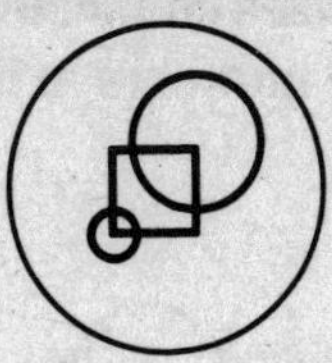 IS TO 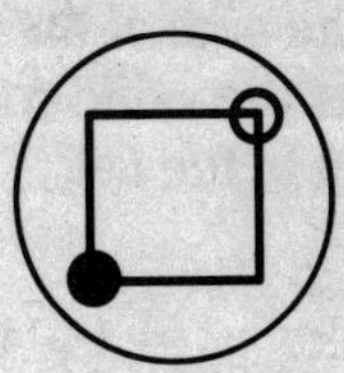

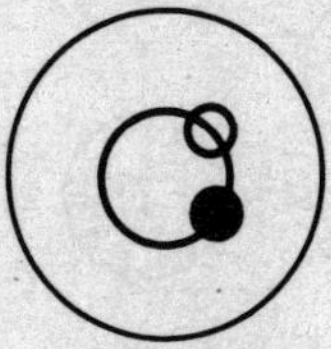 IS TO ?

A 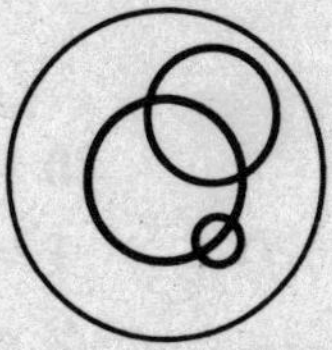

B 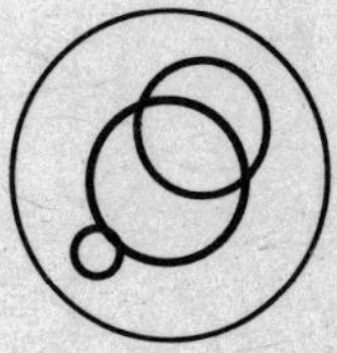

C 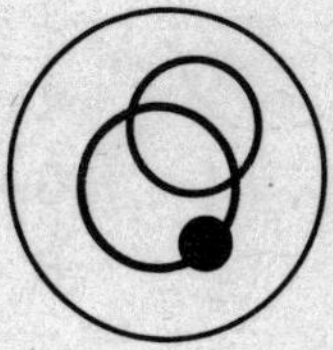

D 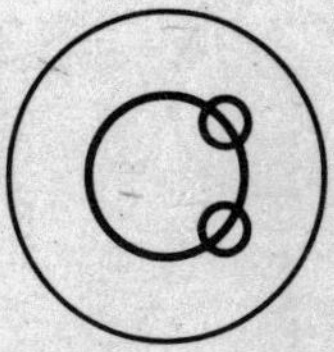

E 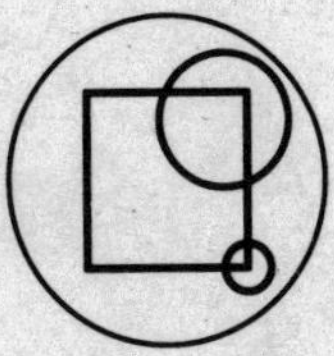

(Solution 20)

6 Connections

Insert the numbers 0–10 in the circles so that for any particular circle the sum of the numbers in the circles connected directly to it equals the value corresponding to the numbers in that circle, as given in the list.

Example: 1 = 14 (4 + 7 + 3)
4 = 8 (7 + 1)
7 = 5 (4 + 1)
3 = 1

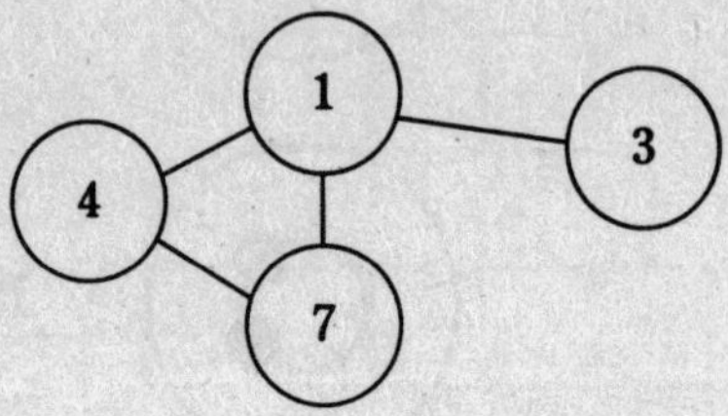

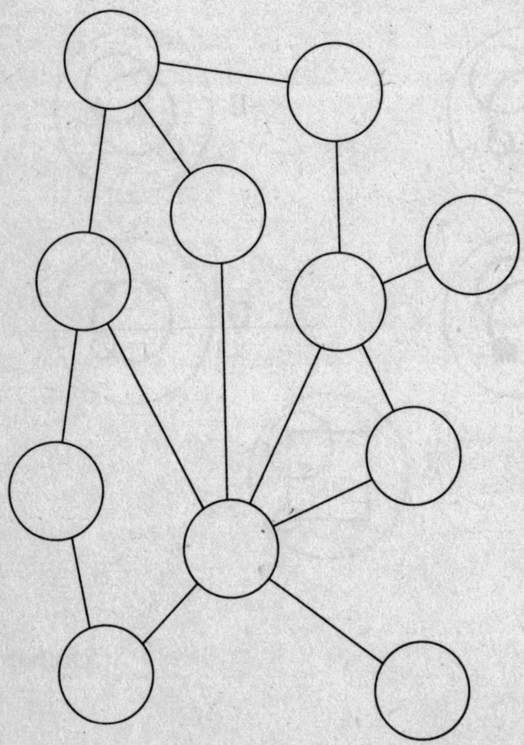

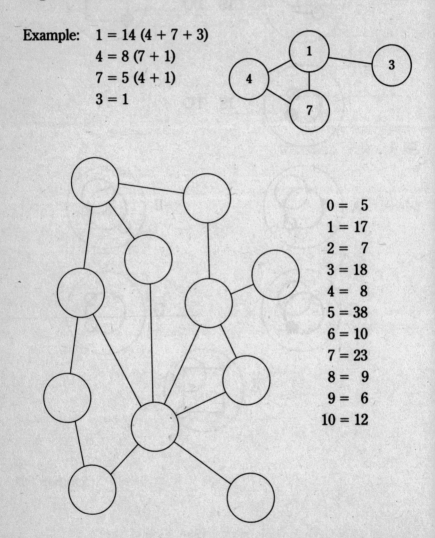

0 = 5
1 = 17
2 = 7
3 = 18
4 = 8
5 = 38
6 = 10
7 = 23
8 = 9
9 = 6
10 = 12

(Solution 24)

7 Pyramid Word

Solve the five clues, enter the correct words in the pyramid, and then rearrange all the letters to find a 15-letter word.

1. The first known quantity in an algebraic expression
2. Denoting direction to or towards
3. To droop
4. To plunge
5. Noise

(Solution 28)

8 Twelve Letters

Find the four 12-letter words. The first half is inside the star. The second half is outside the star and is joined to the first half by a hyphen

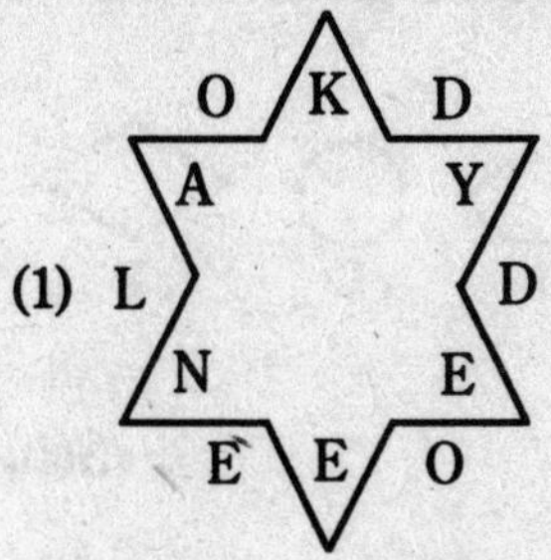

Clue: Bit of a dandy!

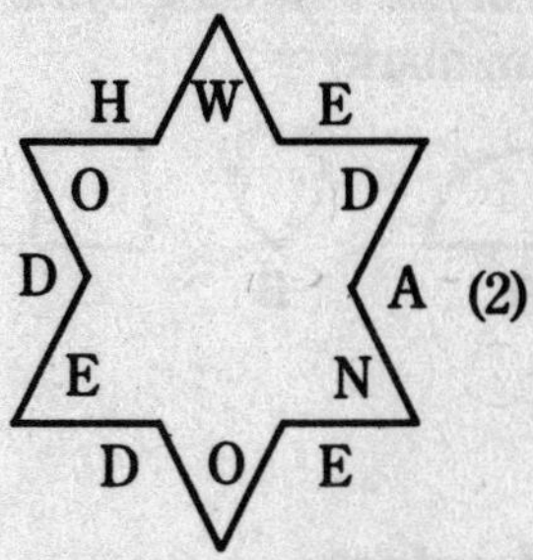

Clue: Don't scratch it!

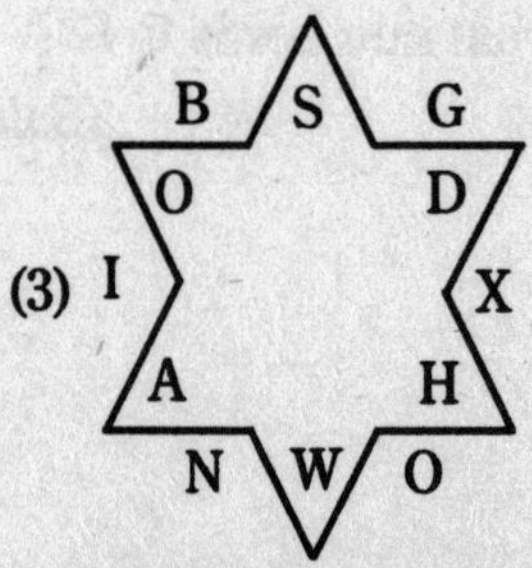

Clue: Win on points?

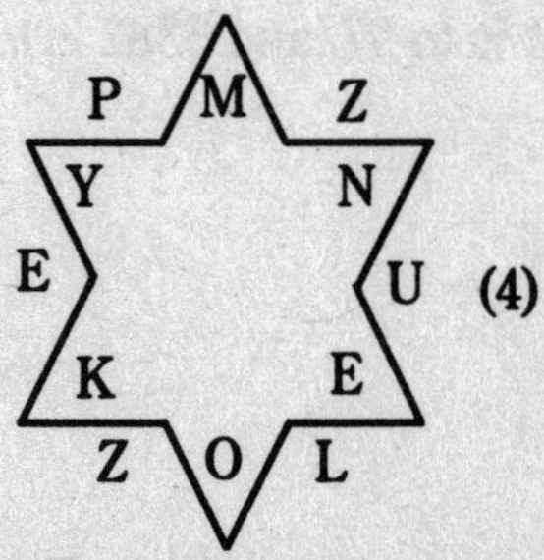

Clue: Kind of tree?

(Solution 29)

9 Pyramidal Logic

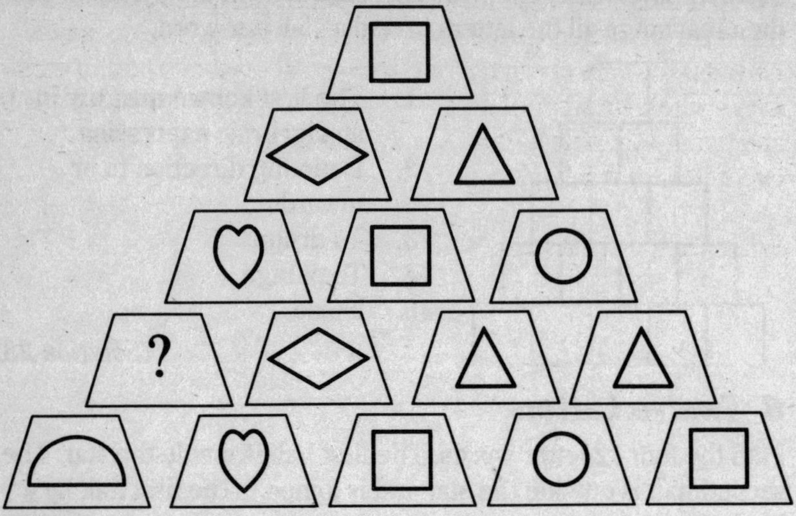

Which of the following symbols should logically replace the question mark?

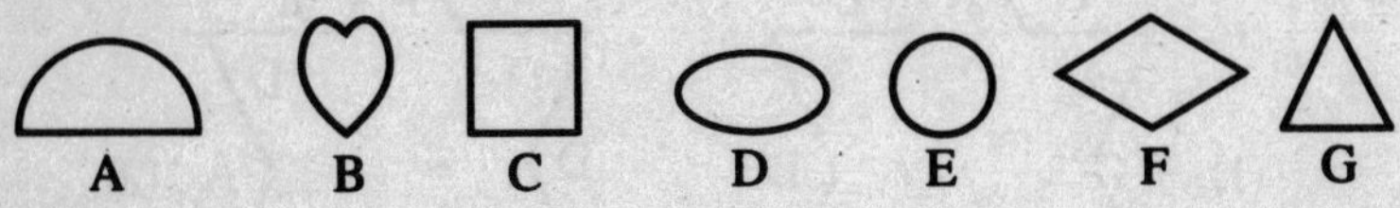

(Solution 36)

10 Analogy

If 3694 is to 97, and 5382 is to 54, what number is to 83?

(Solution 40)

11 Racetrack

There is a circular racetrack twenty-seven miles long. On the track are six racing cars that have broken down. The distances between the cars are such that between at least one pair of cars every whole number of miles can be measured between one mile and twenty-six miles. Thus A may be a mile from B, D may be two miles from E, and so on.

What are the six distances between the cars?

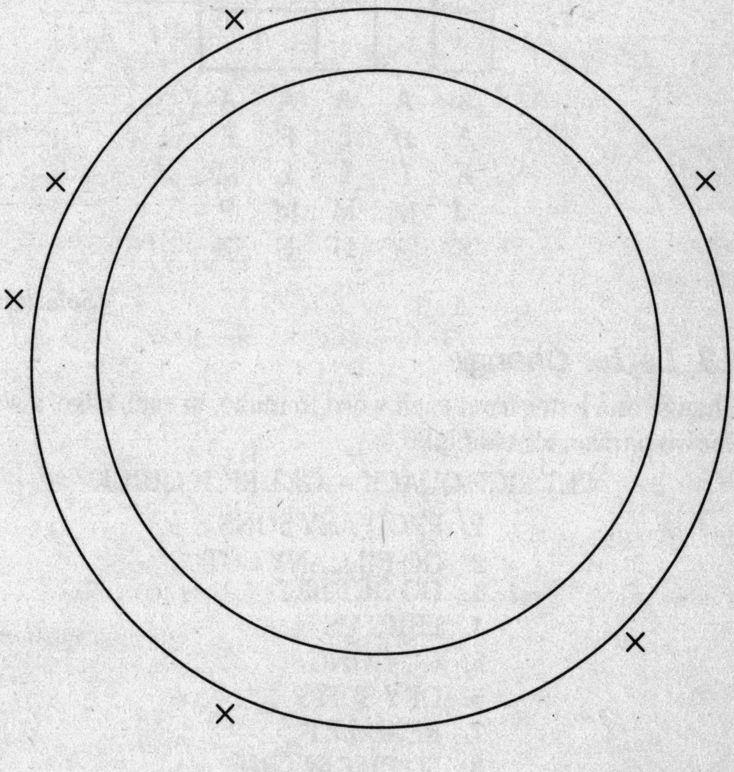

(Solution 44)

12 Magic Word Square

Place the letters in the grid. Words are the same across and down. (One of the words is a proper noun.)

				S
			M	
		D		
	M			
S				

A	A	A	A	A
A	~~D~~	E	E	E
E	L	L	L	M
M	M	~~M~~	~~M~~	P
~~S~~	~~S~~	U	U	Z

(Solution 48)

13 Letter Change

Change one letter from each word to make, in each case, a well-known phrase, for example:

PET RICE QUACK = GET RICH QUICK

1. PROD ANY SONS
2. GO FILL ANY COT
3. DO BET FRY
4. I BEG US
5. GO GONG
6. DRY SUITS
7. READ LET
8. SO PUT IN LINE
9. TALL GUN
10. SO NIP US

(Solution 52)

14 Grid

Each of the nine squares marked 1A to 3C should incorporate all the lines and symbols that are shown in the squares A, B, or C and 1, 2, or 3. Thus 2B should incorporate all the lines and symbols in 2 and B.

One of the squares, 1A to 3C, is incorrect. Which one is it?

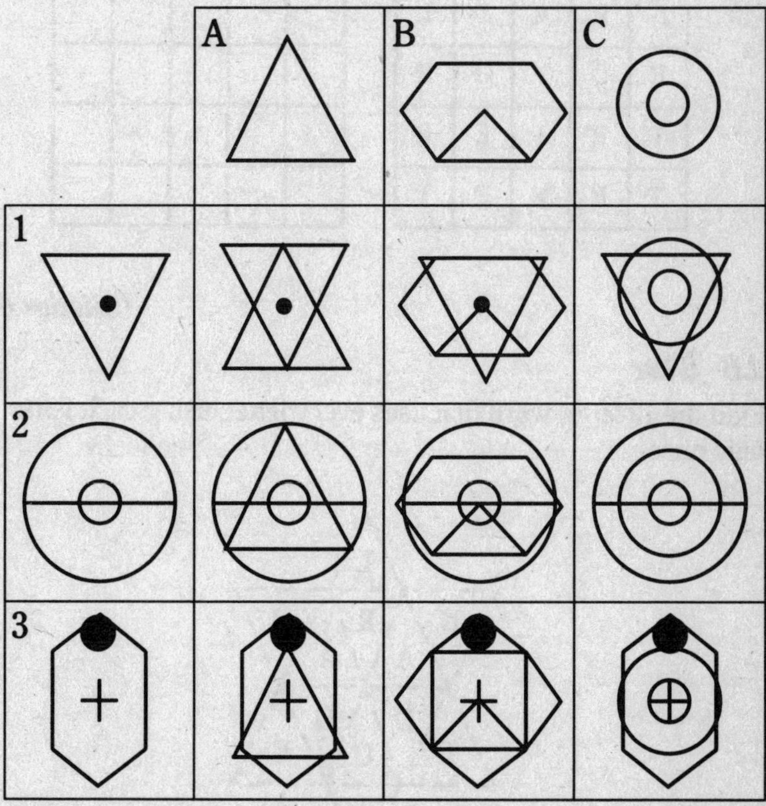

(Solution 56)

15 Magic Square

Rearrange the twenty-five letters to form five new words so that when placed in the correct order in the blank grid a magic word square will be formed, where the same five words can be read both across and down.

E	A	G	L	E
G	R	A	I	L
R	O	T	O	R
T	R	I	E	R
T	E	M	P	T

(Solution 61)

16 Star

Find the 12-letter word that uses every letter, using each letter only once.

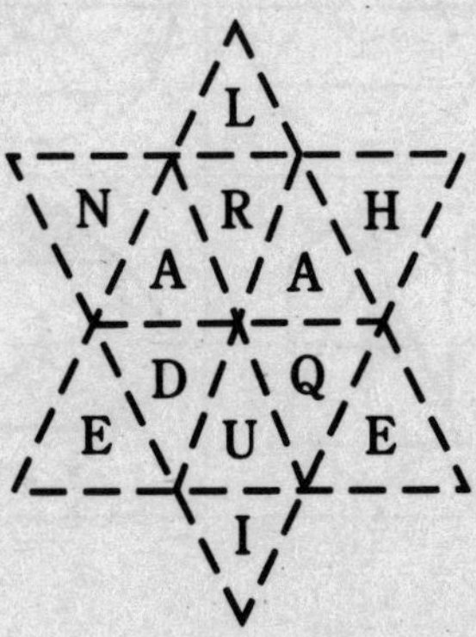

(Solution 64)

17 Analogy

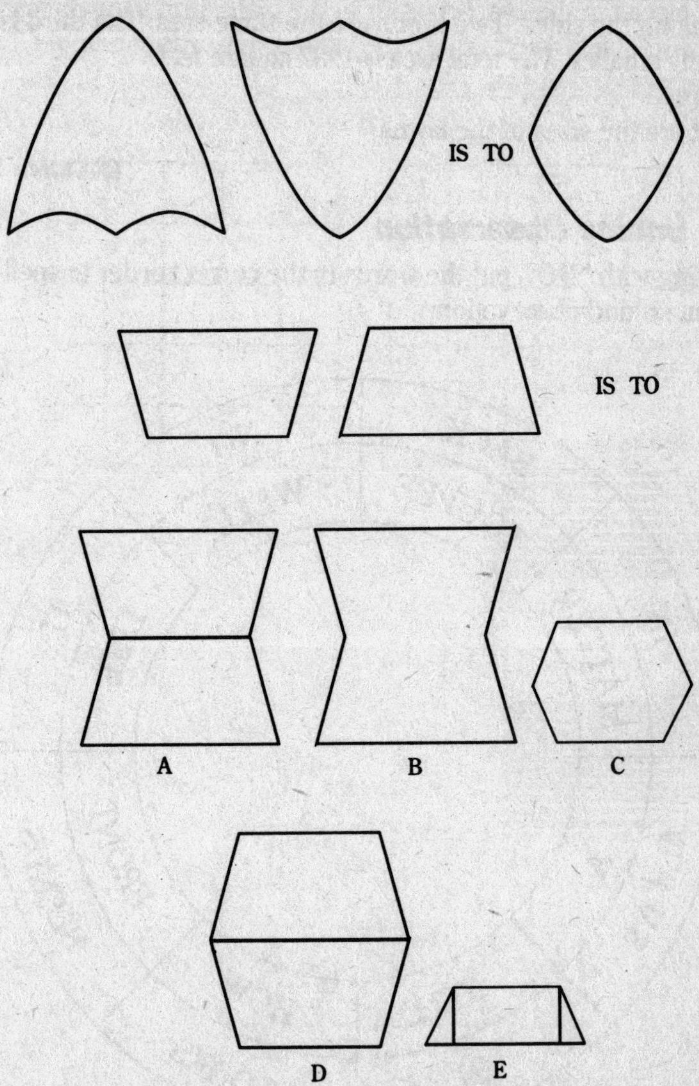

(Solution 68)

18 Lawns

My garden has three square lawns. Each has a whole number of feet along the sides. Two lawns are the same area. The third is slightly smaller. The total area is 1987 square feet.

What are the sizes of the lawns?

(Solution 72)

19 Unkind Observation

Starting with "NO", put the words in the correct order to spell out an unkind observation.

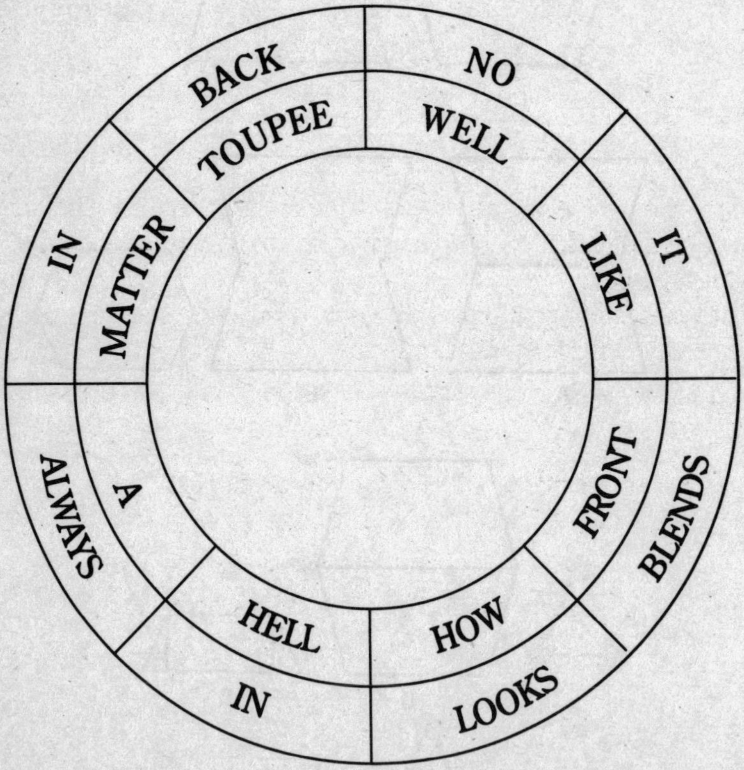

(Solution 76)

20 Links Jigsaw Puzzle

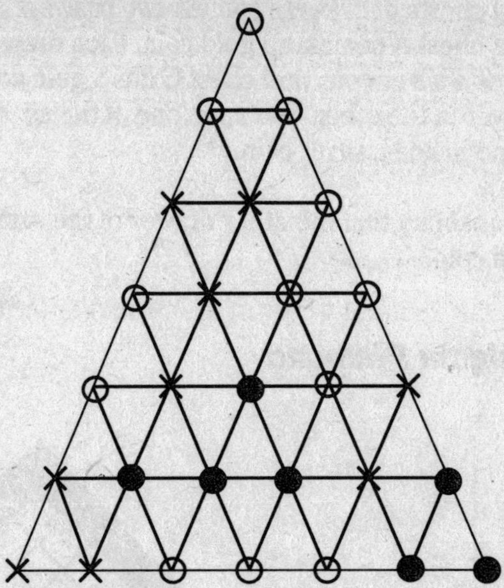

Place the twelve segments, below, over the triangular grid, above, in such a way that each link symbol is covered by exactly the same symbol.
The connecting segments must not be rotated. Note that not all the connecting lines will be covered.

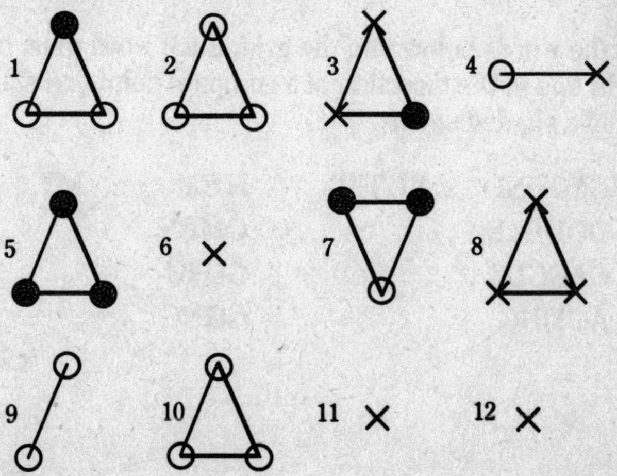

(Solution 80)

21 Bertrand's Paradox

Three identical chests of drawers contain two drawers each. Each drawer of chest A contains a gold coin, each drawer of chest B contains a silver coin, and chest C has a gold coin in one drawer and silver in the other. You open one of the six drawers at random and find inside a silver coin.

What is the probability that the other drawer of the same chest contains a gold coin?

(Solution 84)

22 The Enigma Diamond

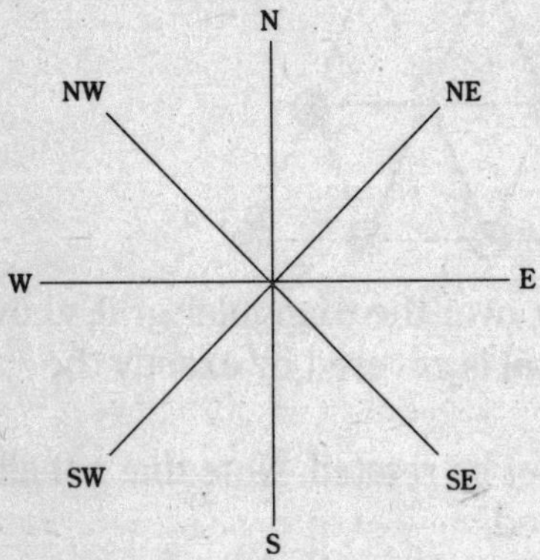

Fit all the words below into the grid. Each word must travel in a straight line in the direction of a compass point and start and finish in a shaded square.

GROUND	NOTED	ITEM	MY
DOUBLE		OMEN	
GAGGLE		GURU	
ACTING		GONG	

(Solution 89)

23 Find Another Word

Consider the following words:
MARE, CAP, LIGHT

Now choose one of the following words that has something in common with all the words above.
IN, OUT, CLIMB, FALL

(Solution 92)

24 Circles Matrix

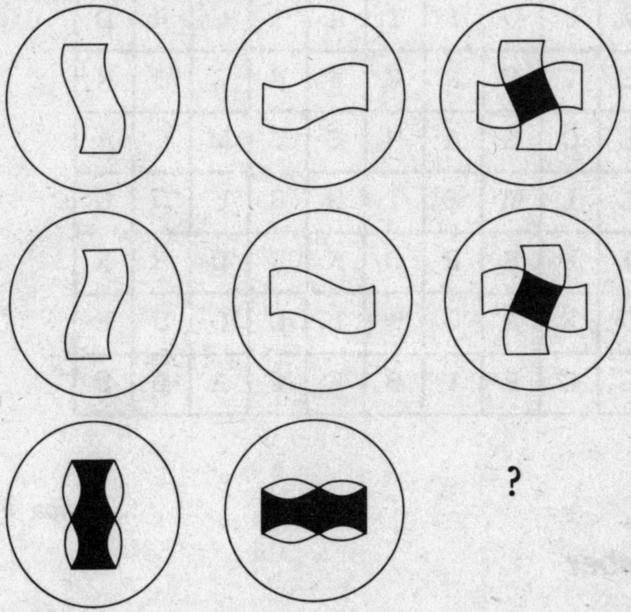

Which circle is missing from the arrangement above?

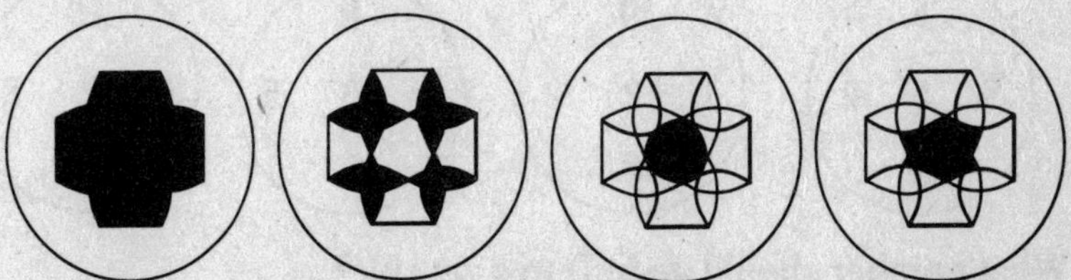

A B C D

(Solution 96)

25 Word Search

Find the names of twenty-two birds in this puzzle. Words can be found in any direction but only in a straight line.

R	E	D	S	H	A	N	K	U	H
T	A	M	E	W	T	E	O	C	R
O	R	G	A	O	S	B	N	U	E
M	E	D	I	T	A	I	C	R	D
E	V	R	R	R	F	R	E	O	N
L	O	E	A	N	E	T	M	C	A
L	L	M	E	T	S	G	U	O	G
I	P	E	R	O	K	R	D	B	R
U	R	A	O	W	L	U	O	U	E
G	D	R	I	B	K	C	A	L	B

(Solution 101)

26 Number

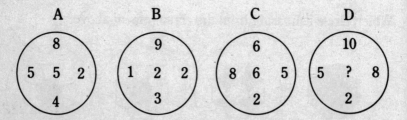

A	B	C	D
8	9	6	10
5 5 2	1 2 2	8 6 5	5 ? 8
4	3	2	2

What number should go in D to a set rule?

(Solution 104)

27 Diamond

Find the names of twelve fish moving in any direction, not necessarily in a straight line. Letters may be used more than once in each word. Corners count as connected.

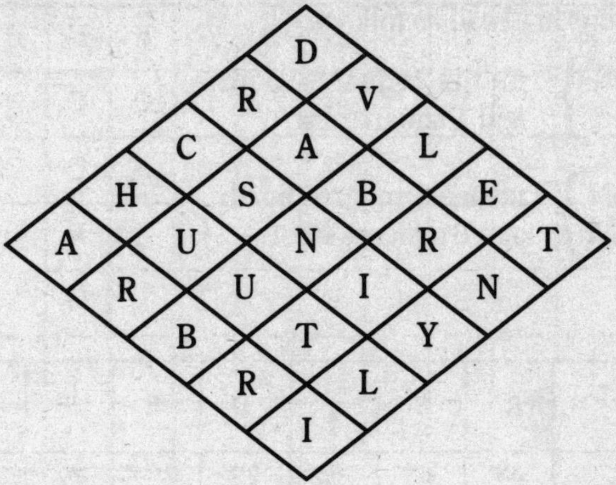

(Solution 108)

28 Circles

What number should replace the question mark?

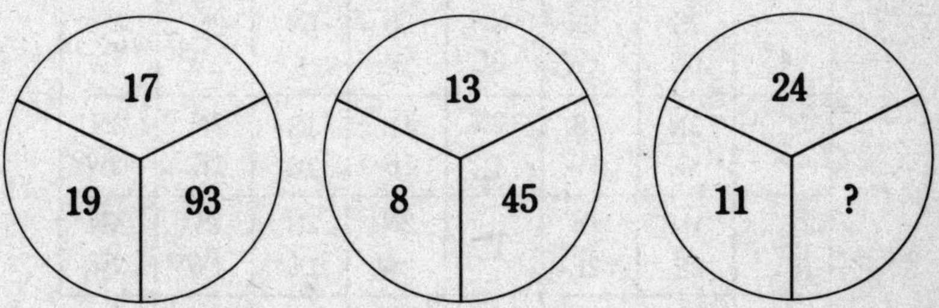

(Solution 112)

29 Treasure

The treasure is on square C6. You have to find the starting square that will lead to the treasure.

Instructions are read as follows:

2S } means 2 squares south
1E } and 1 square east

6N } means 6 squares north
6W } and 6 squares west

N

	A	B	C	D	E	F	G
1	3S 3E	6S 4E	6S 1W	2S 2W	3S 2E	4S 4W	2S 3W
2	2S 4E	5S 1E	1N 1E	4S 1E	1N 2W	1N 1E	4S 3W
3	2S 3E	1N 1W	3S 2W	2N 2W	2N 1E	2S 1W	1S 5W
4	2S 6E	1N 1W	2N 3E	3S 3E	1N 1E	2N 3W	2S 1W
5	3N 1E	2S 1W	3N 1E	4N 1E	1S 2W	2N 1E	2N 2W
6	1N 2E	1S 2E	T	2N 3W	2N 1E	1S 1W	4N 2W
7	1N 1E	4N 1E	2N 4E	2N 2E	5N 2E	2N 5W	3N 4W

W — E

S

(Solution 114)

30 The Enigmasig Wheel

This puzzle is named after "Enigmasig" the special interest group (SIG) within MENSA devoted to the setting and solving of puzzles that is run jointly by the two authors.

Complete the words in each column, all of which end in E. The scrambled letters in the section to the right of each column are an anagram of a word that will give you a clue to the word you are trying to find, to put in the column.

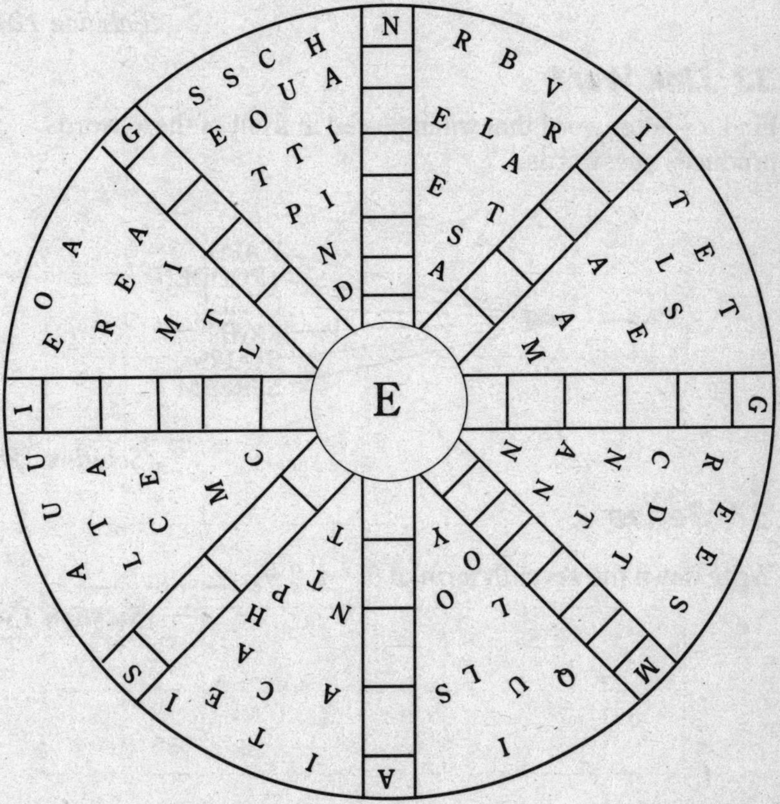

(Solution 120)

31 Categories

Arrange the twelve words below into four groups of three.

Copper	Knot
Fawn	Lemon
Foot	Palm
Gold	Perch
Gum	Plane
Hazel	Stone

(Solution 124)

32 Link Word

Find a 4-letter word that when placed in front of these words produces new words.

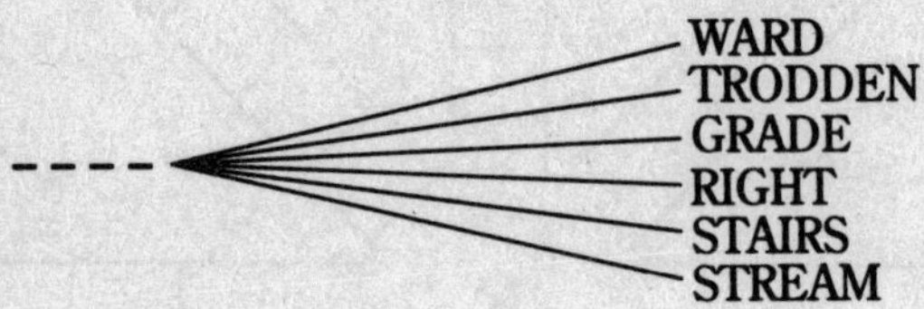

(Solution 128)

33 Series

Write down the seventh term of 6, -4, $2\,{}^{2}/_{3}$, _____.

(Solution 134)

34 The Triangle and Hexagon

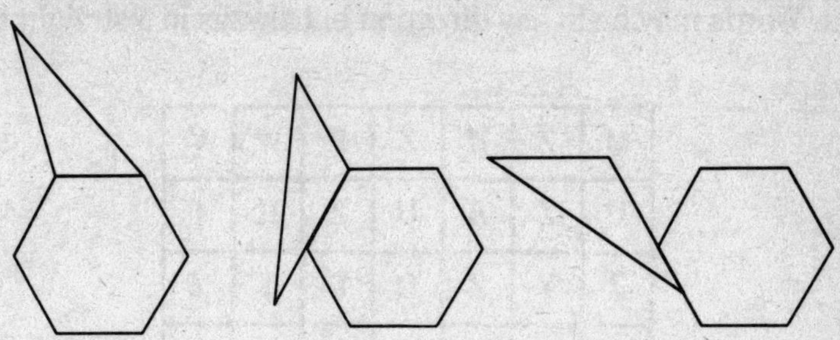

Which option below continues the above sequence?

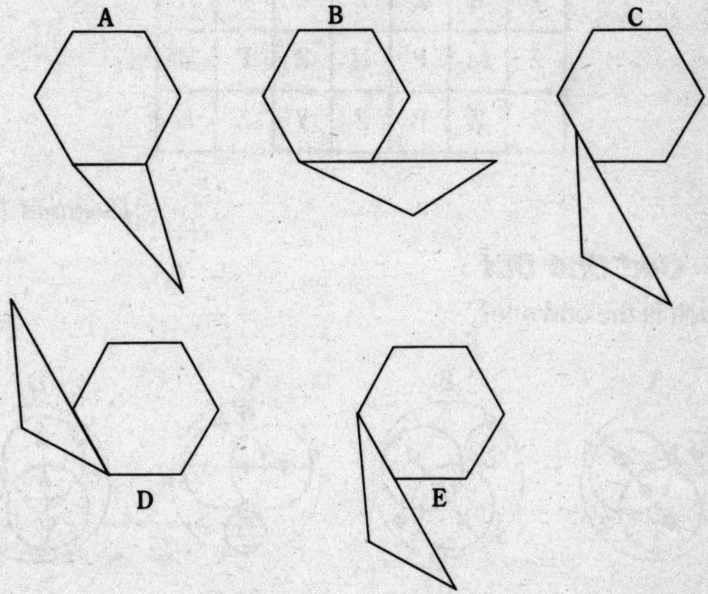

(Solution 136)

35 "Z" Puzzle

Find fourteen words in the grid. Each must have at least one "Z" in it. Words may be in any direction but always in a straight line.

M	Z	H	Z	F	W	V
U	Z	A	U	Z	H	I
Z	Y	Z	O	D	I	Z
Z	Z	Y	U	I	Z	F
Y	A	Z	L	Z	I	A
Z	M	P	U	Z	P	Z
Z	Z	B	Z	Y	Z	E

(Solution 140)

36 Odd One Out

Which is the odd one?

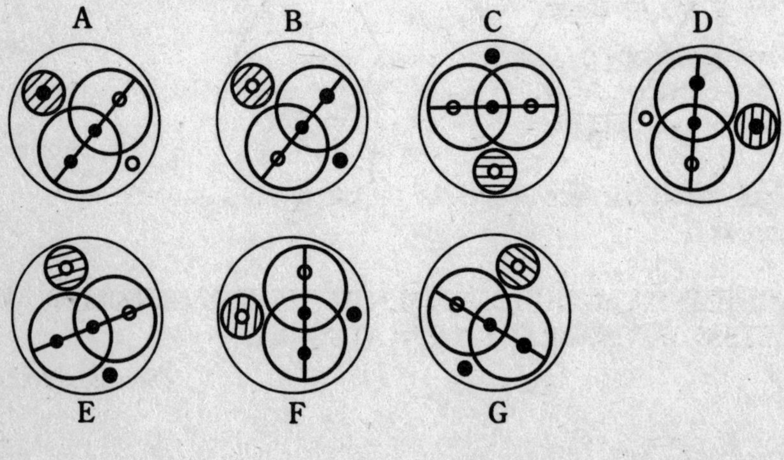

(Solution 144)

37 *Anagrammed Synonyms*

In each of the following, study the list of three words. Your task is to discover which two of the three words can be paired to form an anagram of a word that is a synonym of the word remaining. For example:

LEG – MEEK – NET

The words LEG and NET are an anagram of GENTLE, which is a synonym of the word remaining, MEEK.

1. SHIM – SHAM – HASH
2. SNIP – THEM – LOAD
3. FEN – OLD – PET
4. GALE – MET – STEP
5. TIN – SEQUENCES – PITH
6. MUSE – SPUR – PIT
7. RED – VERSE – COY
8. RULE – BLUE – CANE
9. TROUP – DUN – MINE
10. VANE – TITLE – AIR

(Solution 148)

38 *Two in One*

Two quotations by Charles Caleb Colton (1780 – 1832) have been fused together. All letters remain in the correct order. Can you find the two quotations?

Cross out the letters to one and the other will automatically appear.

WIHEMNIYTAOTIUHONAIVSENTOTHEHISNIGNTCEOSR
AEYSSTAFYORNMOTOHFIFNLATTEGRY.

(Solution 152)

39 Brain Strain

Insert the missing numbers so that the calculations are correct, both across and down. All numbers to be inserted are less than 10 (there is no zero).

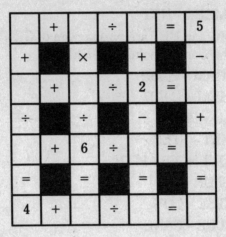

	+		÷		=	5
+		×		+		−
	+		÷	2	=	
÷		÷		−		+
	+	6	÷		=	
=		=		=		=
4	+		÷		=	

(Solution 157)

40 Hexagons

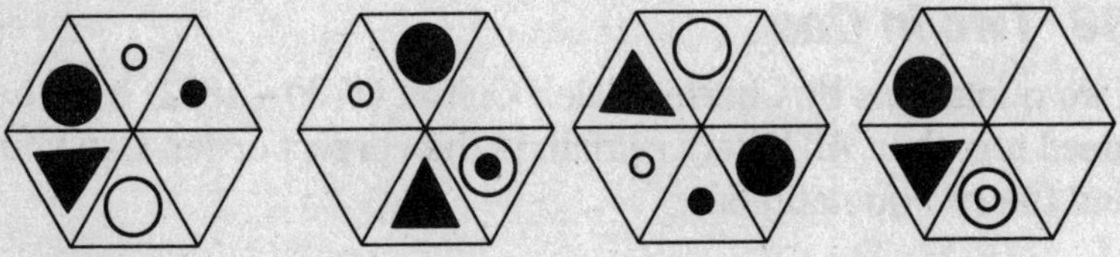

Which hexagon below continues the sequence above?

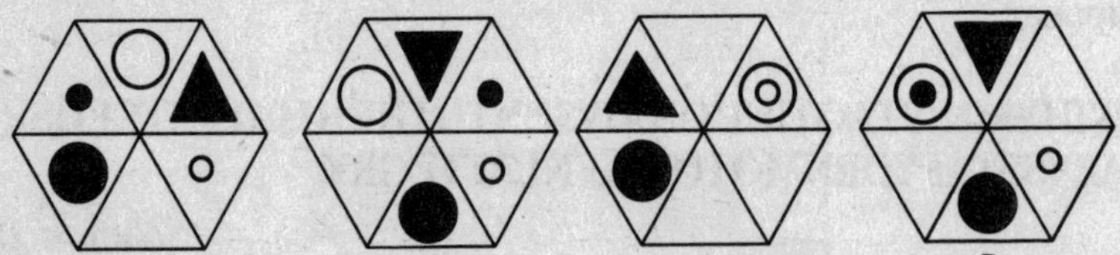

A B C D

(Solution 2)

41 *WOT! No Vowels*

Find sixteen words of three or more letters contained in the grid. Words run in any direction, backward and forward, horizontal, vertical and diagonal, but only in a straight line.

C	W	H	Y	R	D
R	F	R	P	Y	X
Y	L	R	L	H	Y
P	Y	Y	Y	T	R
T	R	M	C	P	P
W	N	Y	Y	H	S

(Solution 6)

42 *Three Too Many*

Delete three of the letters in each 4-letter square in order to complete the crossword.

ST LR	E	DR TN	U	CR DP	E	DL BC
E		E		A		E
VR TD	I	SL MN	I	RL VT	O	RS DL
I		I		E		I
SL TV	U	TG PN	A	RG NL	E	DM PR
E		N		E		E
DT SR	E	SL BC	I	RG TL	E	DF NL

(Solution 11)

43 Committee

A committee of six is to be formed from a group of seven men and four women. How many different committees can be formed if at least two women are always included in each committee?

(Solution 14)

44 Odd One Out

Which is the odd one?

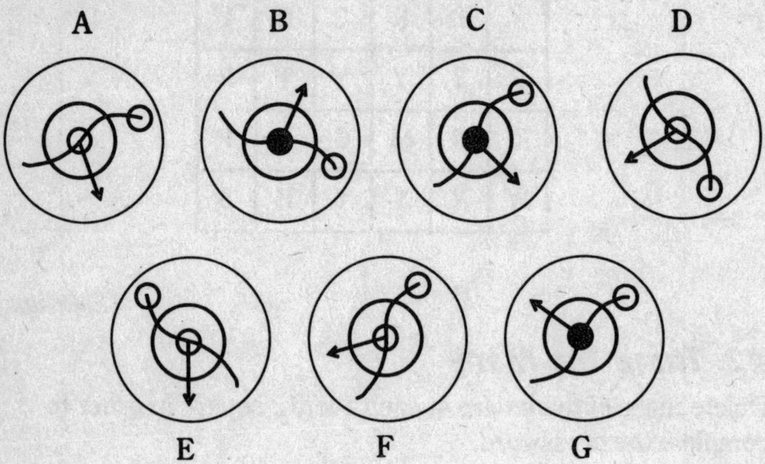

(Solution 18)

45 Subtraction

100, 90, 84, 74, 63, 53, 43, 33, ?

What number comes next?

(Solution 22)

46 Sequence

ACE, LANDING, SNIPE, REFLATE, TEMPO, ?

Which word below continues the sequence that is occurring above?

PRIDE, CHART, TRAMP, NEVER, REGAL

(Solution 26)

47 Segments

What is the smallest number of segments of equal area that the rectangle can be divided up into so that each segment contains the same number of triangles, bells, and circles?

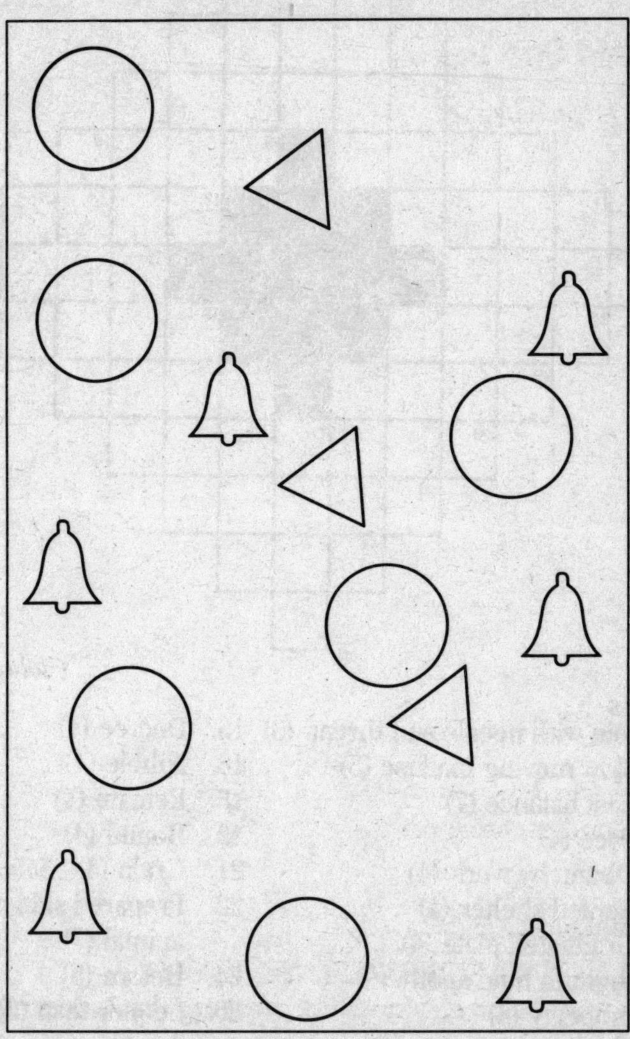

(Solution 30)

48 Word-Cross Puzzle

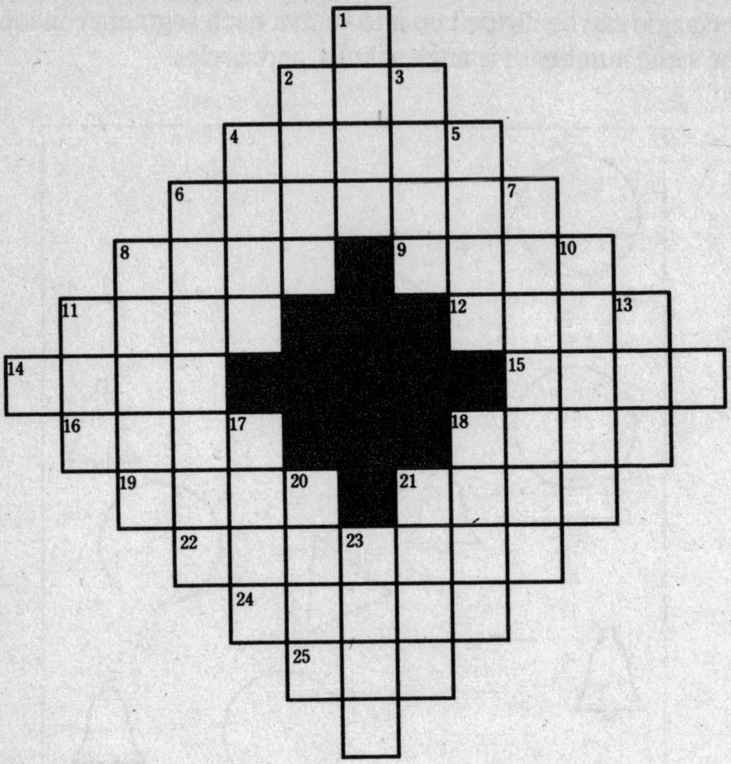

Across

2. Join with needle and thread (3)
4. Slow moving mollusc (5)
6. Lost balance (7)
8. Pace (4)
9. Obtain by work (4)
11. Roofed shelter (4)
12. Graduated plate (4)
14. Right to hold another's property (4)
15. Decree (4)
16. Nibble (4)
18. Remain (4)
19 Bound (4)
21. Grain (4)
22. Prepared skin of animal (7)
24. Before (5)
25. Sooner than (3)

Down

1. Jump (4)
2. Cut (4)
3. Rub so as to clean (4)
4. Toboggan (4)
5. Guide (4)
6. Thin sheet pierced with pattern (7)
7. Aimless person (7)
8. Broad piece of material (5)
10. Water nymph (5)
11. Drink in small portions (3)
13. Minstrel's song (3)
17. Retain (4)
18. Prophet (4)
20. Venture (4)
21. Covering for foot (4)
23. Exhaust (4)

(Solution 33)

49 Square

How many 3-letter words can you find in any direction if you arrange the following letters as the example? (Maximum possible = 12.)

AABDGOOOT

Example:

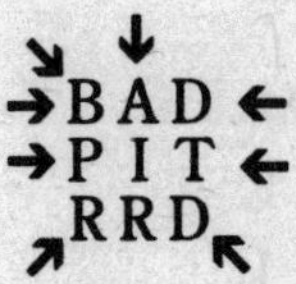

RID	TIP
BID	DIB
AIR	BAD
PIT	DAB

(Solution 38)

50 Missing Number

Find the missing number.

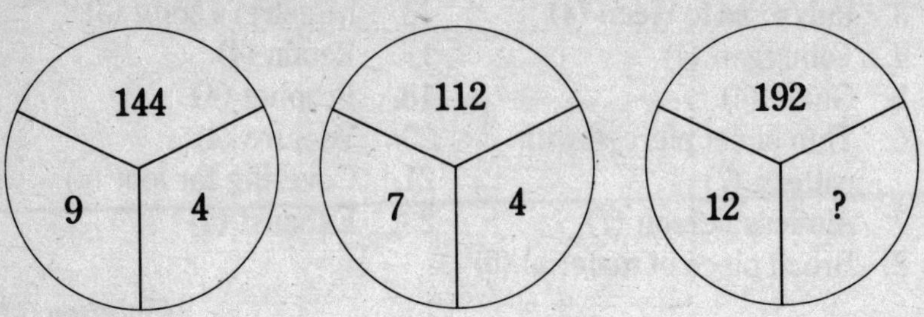

(Solution 42)

51 Bracket Word

Place two letters in each bracket so that these finish the word on the left and start the word on the right. The letters in the brackets, read downwards in pairs, will spell out a 12-letter word.

SA	(_ _)	AR
CL	(_ _)	LE
E	(_ _)	TE
GRA	(_ _)	IAL
T	(_ _)	E
RE	(_ _)	L

(Solution 46)

52 Nursery Rhyme Crossword

The clues are hidden in the narrative, in parentheses.

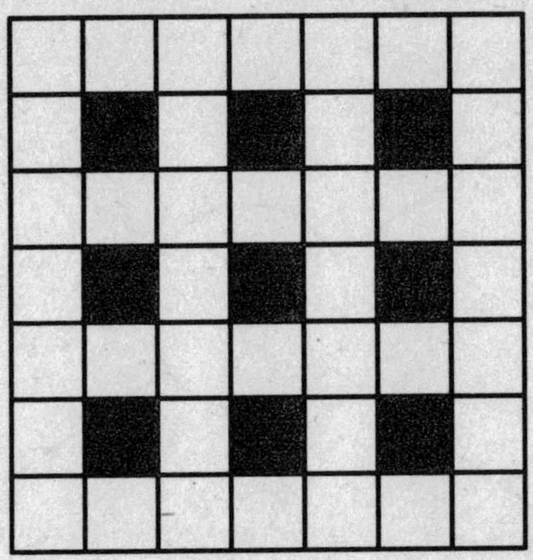

Solve the clues and determine where to place the answers in the grid.

Clues

1. Little boy blue who was one of the (Spanish ladies) brothers,
2. And (was one of those who cut fleece).
3. And whose (kidney was troubled) come blow your horn.
4. (The llamas) are in the meadow
5. (The deer) are in the corn.
   Where is the boy that looks after the sheep?
6. The lady (observes) that he has been
7. Knocked down like a (bottle-shaped pin)
8. And the (notion) is that he is asleep.

(Solution 50)

53 Symbols

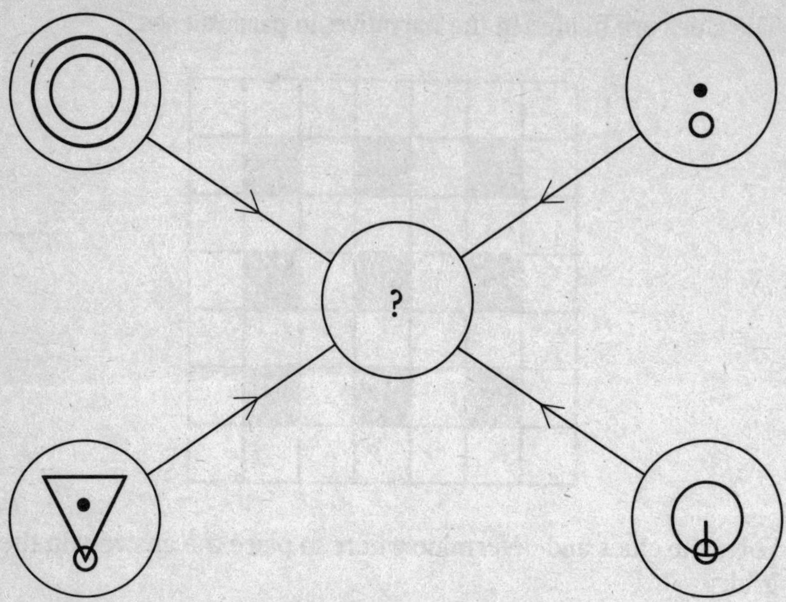

Each line and symbol that appears in the four outer circles is transferred to the middle circle according to these rules:

If a line or symbol occurs in the outer circle:

once	it is transferred
twice	it is possibly transferred
3 times	it is transferred
4 times	it is not transferred

Which of the circles A, B, C, D, or E, shown on the next page should appear in the middle of the diagram?

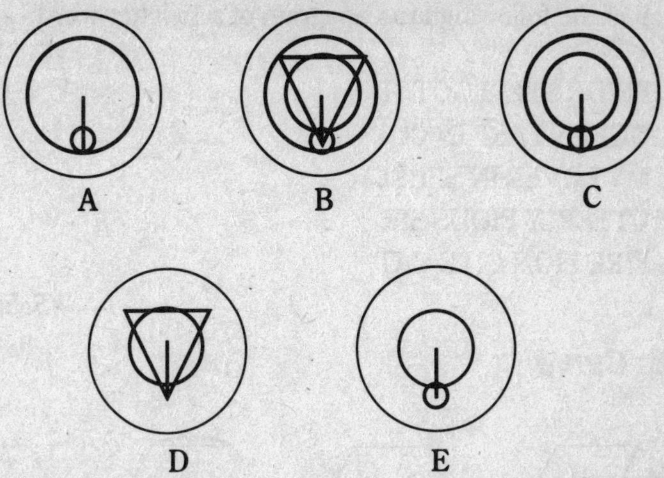

(Solution 54)

54 Round Table

Five people are seated at a round table. In how many different ways can the people be seated, where two arrangements in which everyone has the same neighbours are considered the same? For example, consider these arrangements of just four people:

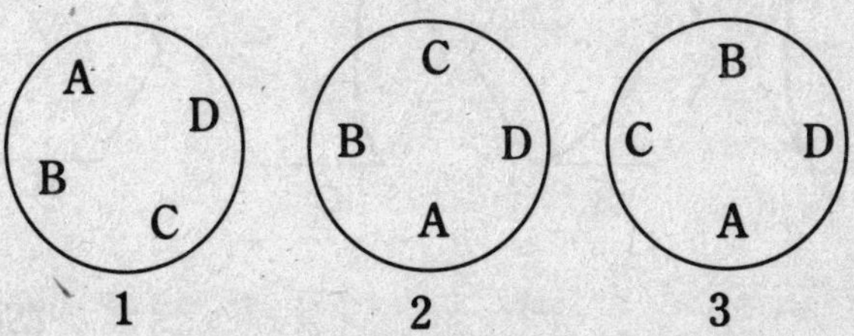

Figures 1 and 2 would be considered the same because everyone has the same neighbours, but 1 and 3 and 2 and 3 are different.

(Solution 58)

55 15-Letter Words

Each of the following is an anagram of a 15-letter word:

1. PRIDE STAIR GOT IT
2. QUEEN LAST IN COIN
3. MY LOVER IN SPEECH
4. UTTERLY PIOUS SIR
5. FIRE LION CITE CAT

(Solution 62)

56 Curve

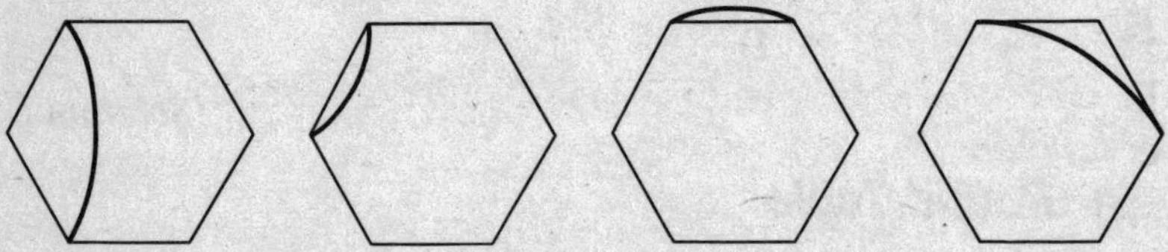

Which option below continues the above sequence?

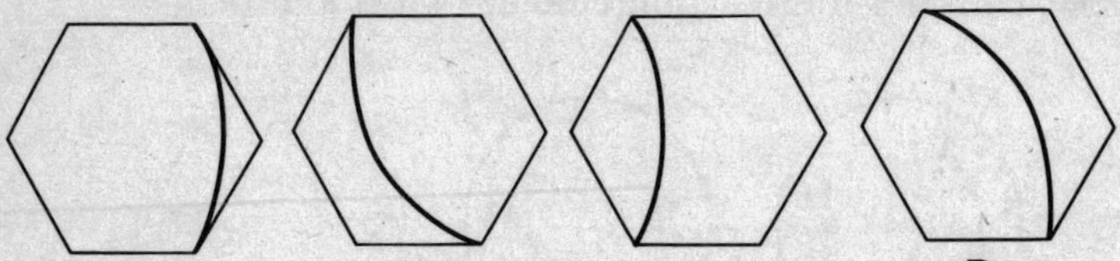

A B C D

(Solution 66)

57 Common

What do all of these words have in common?

1. HUNGER
2. GANNET
3. MARKER
4. GETTING
5. GODLY
6. TACTIC
7. FLOWER
8. TABBED
9. REPAIR
10. UPSALA

(Solution 70)

58 Alphabet Clueless-Cross

Insert the twenty-six letters of the alphabet to complete the crossword.

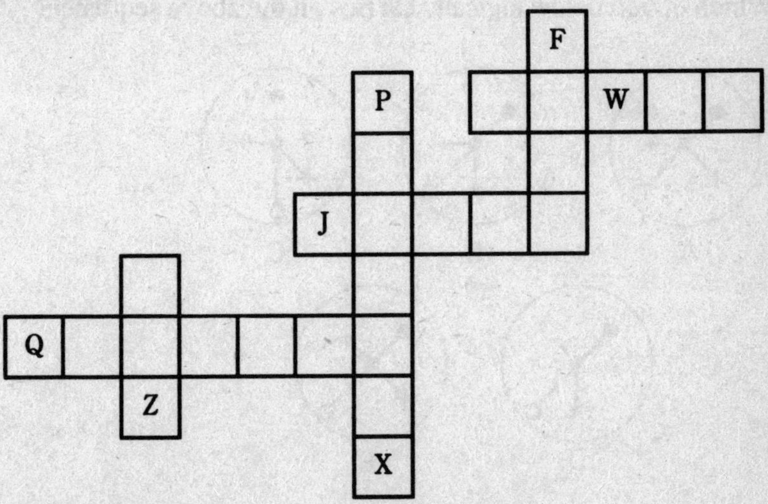

Seven of the letters have already been inserted.

A B C D E ~~F~~ G H I ~~J~~ K L M

N O ~~P~~ ~~Q~~ R S T U V ~~W~~ ~~X~~ Y ~~Z~~

(Solution 74)

59 Alphametics

Replace the letters with numbers:

```
  LABEL
    ALL
+  SEAL
-------
  BALES
```

(Solution 78)

60 Sequence

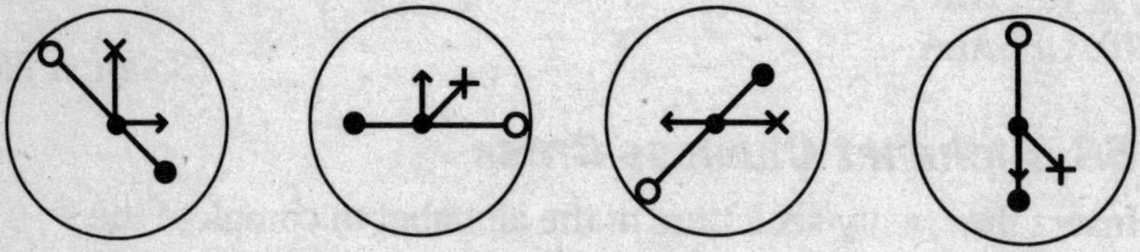

Which option below logically carries on the above sequence?

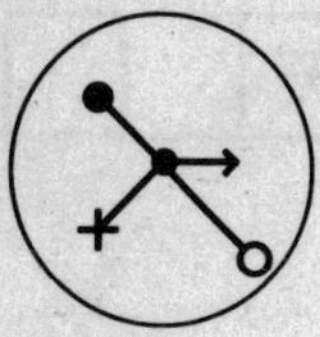

A

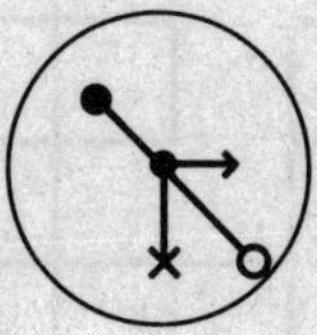

B

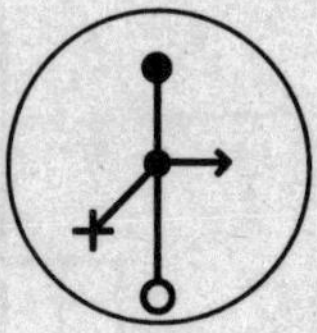

C

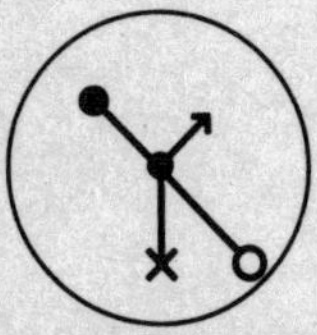

D

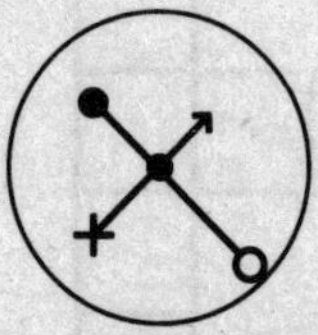

E

(Solution 82)

61 Network

Find the starting point and travel along the connecting lines in a continuous path to adjacent circles to spell out a 14-letter word. Every circle must be visited once only.

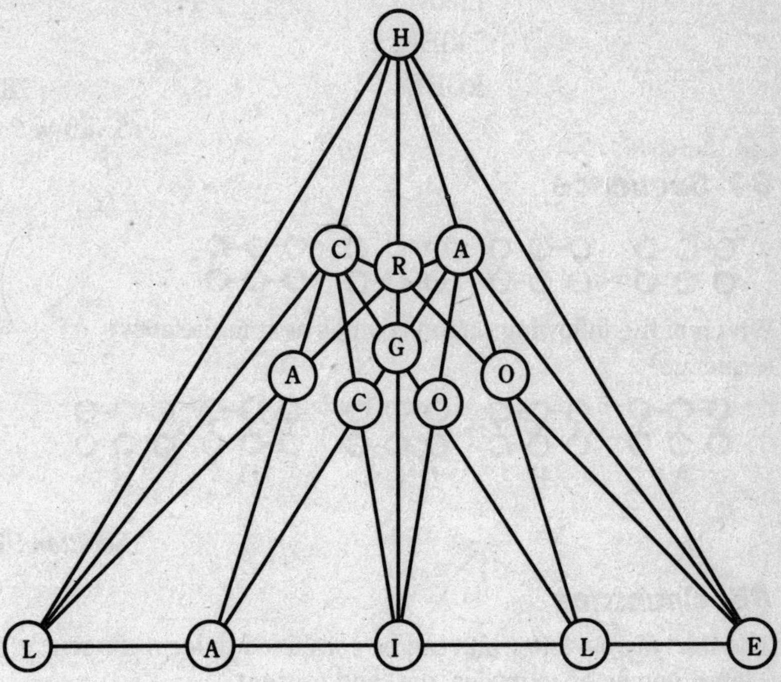

(Solution 86)

62 Array

Study the array of numbers below. What numbers should replace the question mark?

8	15	17
18	80	82
27	36	45
42	56	?

(Solution 90)

63 A Common Thread

What do these words have in common?

HOUNDS
PLEAT
LINE
TRIBE
ROBE

(Solution 94)

64 Sequence

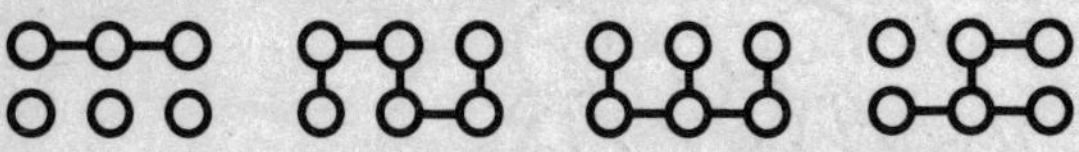

Which of the following options comes next in the above sequence?

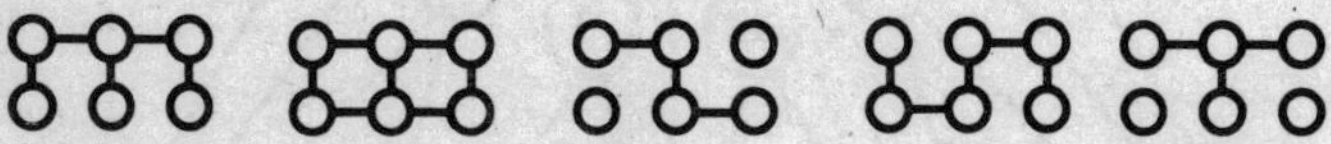

A B C D E

(Solution 97)

65 Countries

The thirty-two 4-letter bits can be combined to form sixteen 8-letter names of countries, past and present.

INIA	IDAD	CAMB	ZANZ
PAKI	OLIA	MALA	TANZ
RHOD	IBAR	STAN	BULG
ARIA	ZIMB	ADOS	HOND
PARA	URAS	MONG	TRIN
LAND	BARB	UGAL	ABWE
PORT	GUAY	SCOT	YSIA
ANIA	ESIA	ODIA	SARD

(Solution 102)

66 Soccer Ball

A soccer ball is to be made up of leather squares and triangles that are to be sewn together. The squares are all of the same size and triangles are also identical. How many squares and triangles are needed?

(Solution 106)

67 Niners

Solve the eight clues.

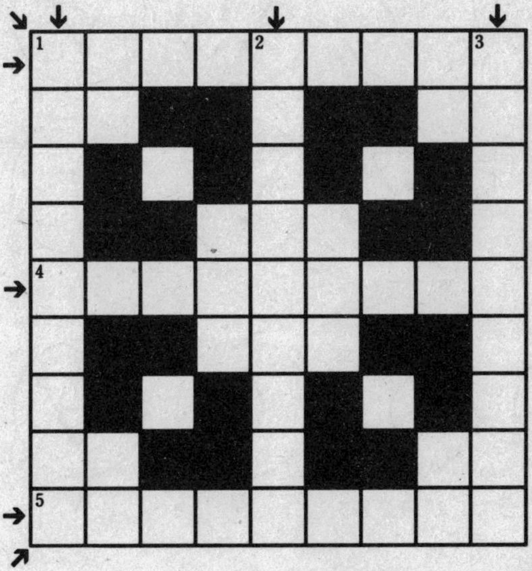

Across

1. Act of going away
4. Imparting secrets
5. To bargain

Down

1. A careful likeness
2. Unvarying person
3. Coming out

Diagonal

1. Interchange of embraces
5. Blackness

(Solution 110)

68 Logic

Logically, which arrangement should be placed in the final circle?

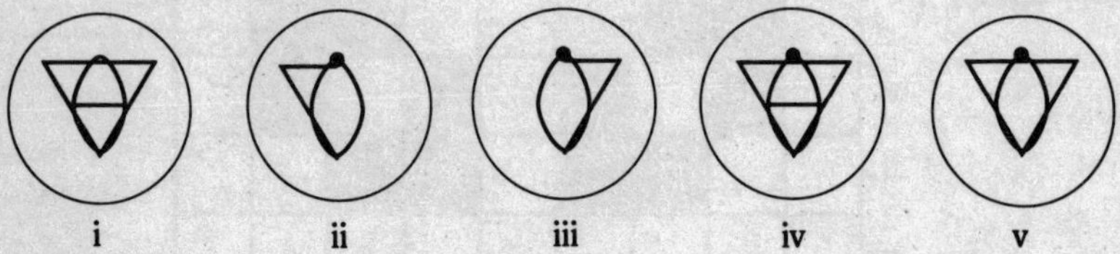

(Solution 115)

69 Percussion

Use all the letters of the sentence below once each to spell out three percussion instruments.

STAB MAN, I ACT, ARREST A MOB

(Solution 117)

70 Double Digits

In the following multiplication sum each letter stands for a different digit; in other words, each of the digits 0–9 occurs twice.

Can you complete the sum?

```
  GHA
  FFB
  ---
  HGD
 PJC
PJC
-----
BKKAD
```

(Solution 122)

71 Diamonds

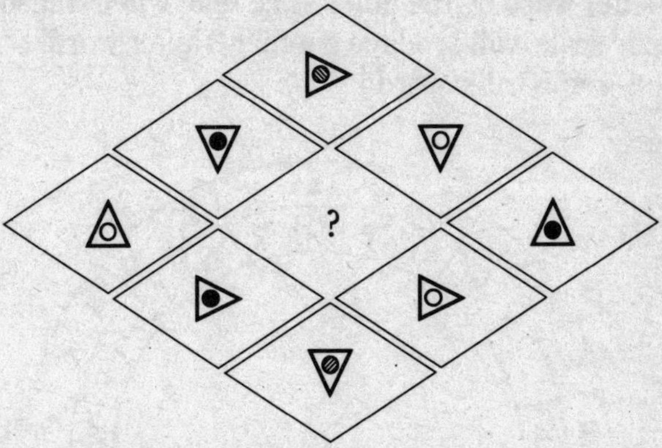

Which diamond below belongs in the middle of the above pattern?

A B C D

(Solution 126)

72 Anagram Theme

Arrange the fourteen words in pairs so that each pair is an anagram of a name. The seven names produced will have a linking theme. For example, if the words DIAL and THAN were in the list, they could be paired to form an anagram of THAILAND and the theme would be countries.

ANY	CAR	CLIP
HALT	HELL	JUT
LIE	LIT	ME
NOT	TOO	SEA
SEER	SOUR	

(Solution 131)

73 Zoetrope

Find a 3-letter word on the inner scale that, when transposed on to the outer scale, will produce another 3-letter word.
Then try 4- and 5-letter words.

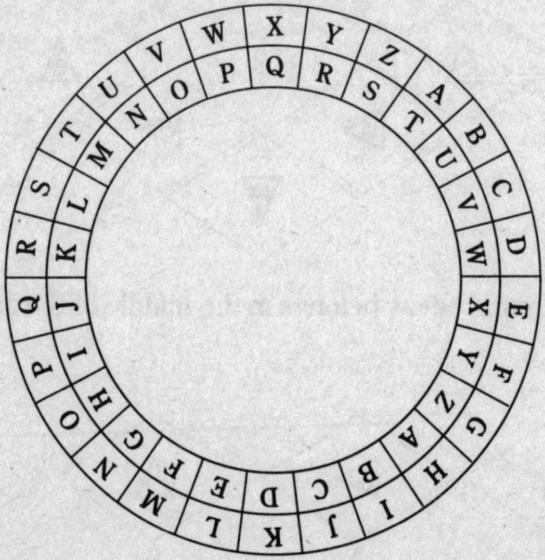

(Solution 133)

74 Darts

At the fairground one had to score 100 exactly with just six darts to win a prize. Three players scored 120, 110, 100. If every dart was a scoring dart, how did each player score?

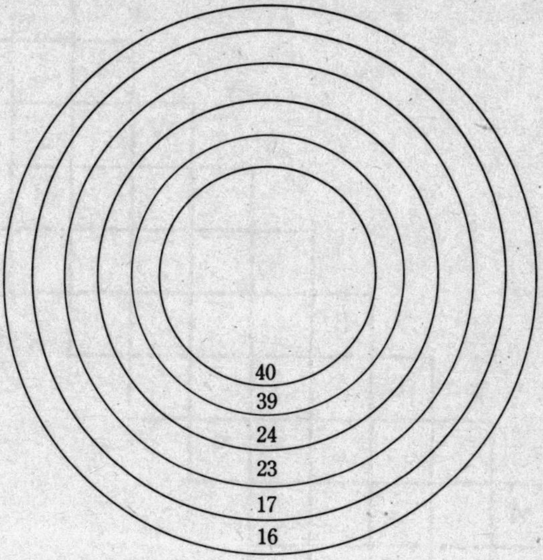

(Solution 138)

75 Dice

With a standard 6-sided die, how many throws on average are required before each of the six numbers has landed face upwards?

(Solution 142)

76 No Blanks

Place the twenty words in the crossword (some vertically, some horizontally) so that each horizontal and vertical line forms a word.

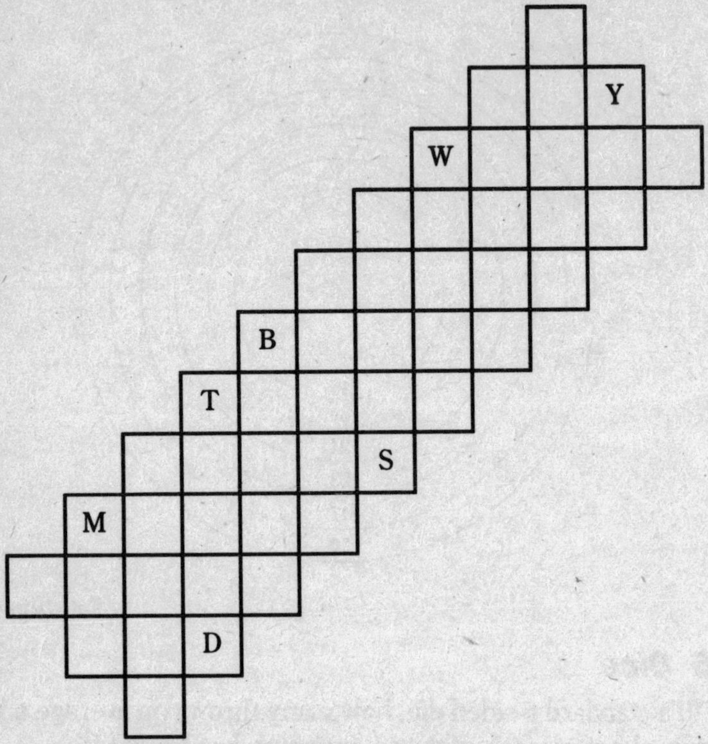

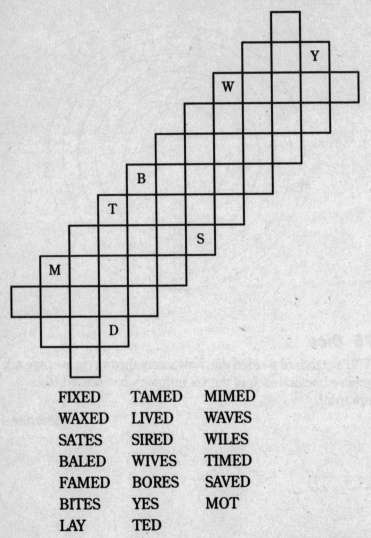

FIXED	TAMED	MIMED
WAXED	LIVED	WAVES
SATES	SIRED	WILES
BALED	WIVES	TIMED
FAMED	BORES	SAVED
BITES	YES	MOT
LAY	TED	

(Solution 147)

77 Logic

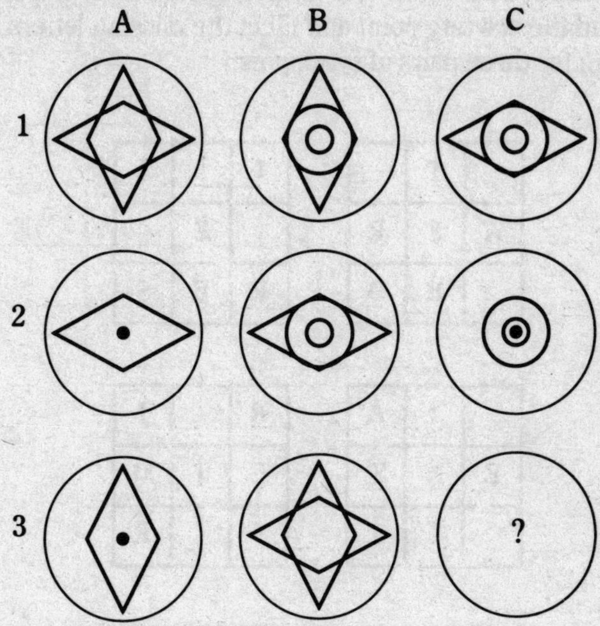

Logically, which circle fits the pattern?

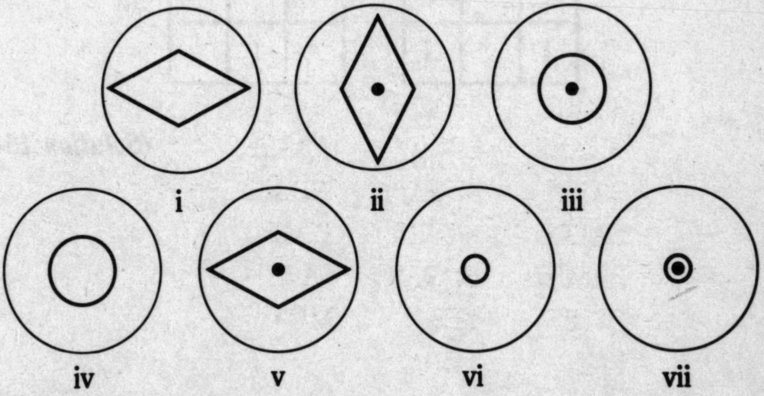

(Solution 151)

78 Square Words

In each of the following, start at a corner square and spiral clockwise around the perimeter to spell out a 9-letter word. You have to find the starting point and fill in the missing letters. You are looking for three pairs of synonyms.

	T	
A	E	R
	E	D

I		A
	E	
R	E	S

	I	A
E	N	T
		I

R		I
E	T	M
		E

E	N	
D		O
I		N

I	T	
L		O
A	I	

(Solution 154)

79 Clueless Crossword

In each square there are four letters. Your task is to cross out three of each four, leaving one letter in each square so that the crossword is made up in the usual way with interlocking words.

P J A D	C Y R D	A N E I	V P A E	T A M E	E I T L	E R C D
I O R N		I E U X		O E X R		E I R A
I G M O	R E A N	U V R G	O B M E	B N I A	G N E L	G E D B
I D E N		E D H S		N A E P		H A E L
S T E R	T H R I	E N T R	E K R A	L T E Y	I E R L	T E D R

(Solution 160)

80 Saying

This saying has had all of its vowels removed. The consonants are in the correct order but have been broken up into groups of four. Replace the vowels and reconstitute the saying.

THMN WHKN WSHW WLLL WYSH
VJBT HMNW HKNW SWHY WLLL
WYSB HSBS S.

(Solution 1)

81 Squares

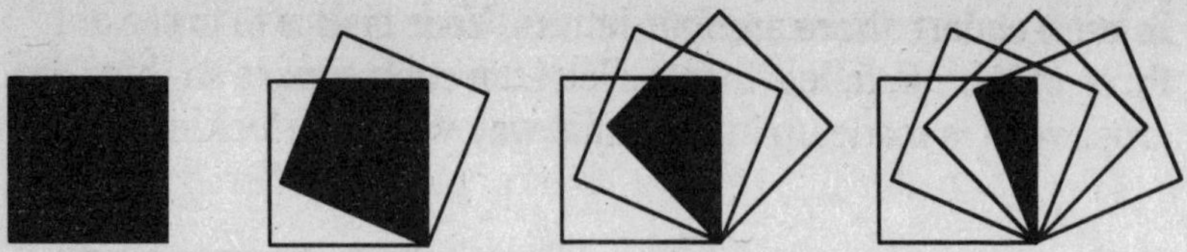

Which option below continues the above sequence?

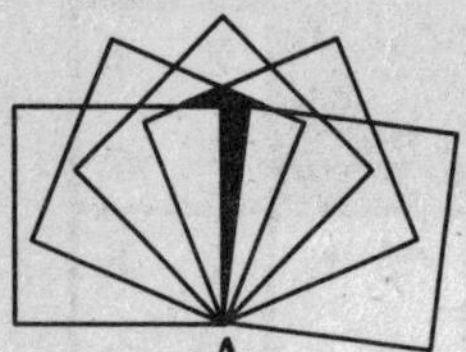

A

B

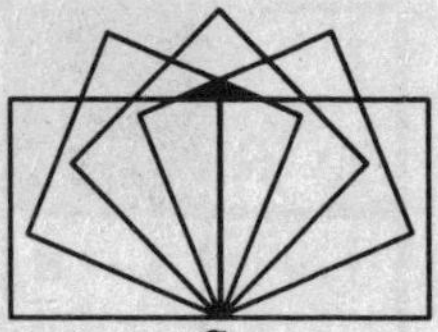

C

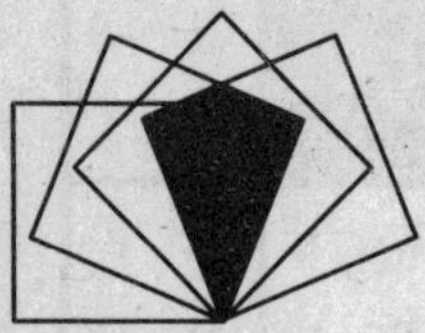

D

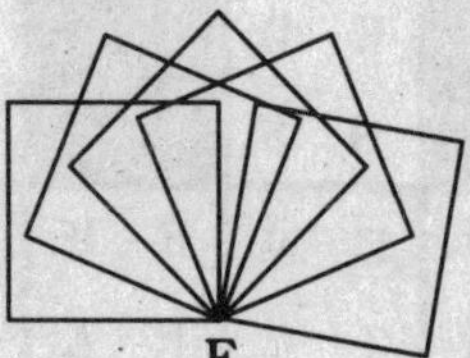

E

(Solution 5)

82 Horse Race

In a 7-horse race, a bookmaker has laid the following odds on six of the horses.

No. 1	4 to 1 against
No. 2	4 to 1 against
No. 3	4 to 1 against
No. 4	5 to 1 against
No. 5	6 to 1 against
No. 6	7 to 1 against
No. 7	?

What odds should he give on the seventh horse in order to give himself approximately 20% margin of profit?

(Solution 9)

83 Triple Choice

Select the correct meaning from the three choices.

1. FRANGIPANI: (a) Red-flowered tree
   (b) Mincemeat
   (c) Bird of partridge family

2. GLOTTIS: (a) A veil
   (b) Musical Instrument
   (c) Entrance to the windpipe

3. PERSIMMON: (a) Date-plum
   (b) Flippancy
   (c) Cambric

4. HYPERBOLE: (a) Exaggerated speech
   (b) Part of a tree
   (c) Living in the north

5. KINKAJOU: (a) Relative of raccoon
   (b) Type of kingfisher
   (c) Type of squid

6. VALGUS: (a) Bow-legged
   (b) Brave and foolish
   (c) Smaller intestine

7. BRASSARD: (a) Arm band
   (b) Vegetable
   (c) Braggart

8. CASSATA: (a) Root yielding starch
   (b) Kind of cinnamon
   (c) Italian ice cream

(Solution 13)

84 Circles

Which of these fit into the blank circle to create a logical sequence?

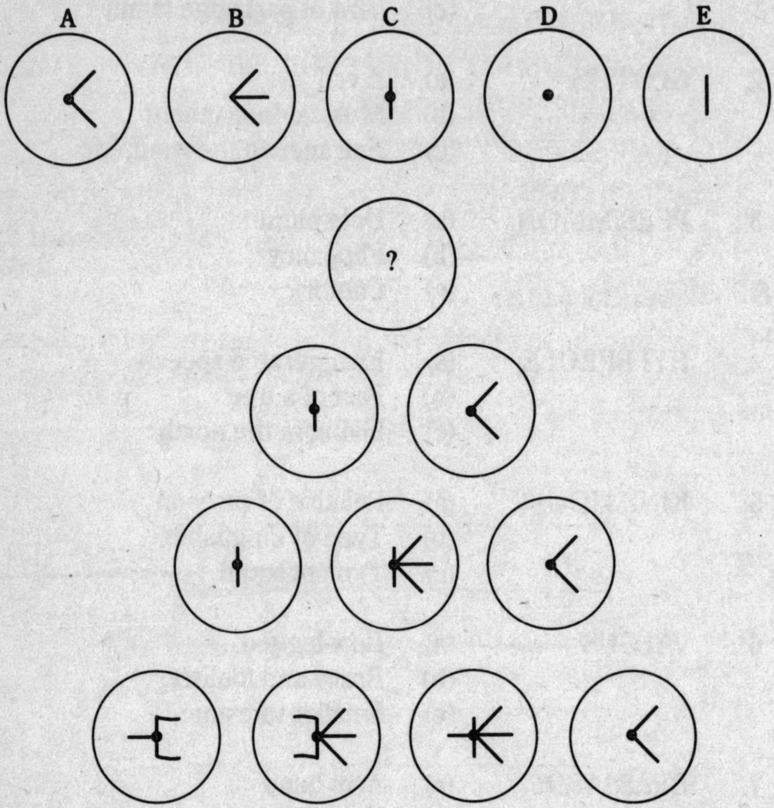

(Solution 17)

85 Two Letters

Can you think of two common English 2-letter words that double their length when pluralized and end in different suffixes?

(Solution 21)

86 Anagram Phrases

Each of the following is an anagram of a well-known phrase or saying. For example: SO NOTE HOLE = ON THE LOOSE.

1. TRAINED STONES HOW TO WHIP
2. KESTREL SHOT DOWN I BOIL TIT NOW
3. FLAT LIE WOKE POOPER
4. RAW SEVENTY TO COME LOOSE
5. TAG I OWN SHOCK

(Solution 25)

87 Missing Links

Fill in the missing numbers. The link between each of the three numbers is the same in each row, and just enough information has been provided to enable you to carry out your task.

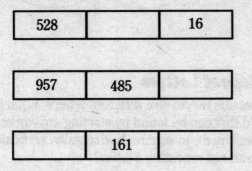

528		16

957	485	

	161	

(Solution 31)

88 Decadice

With a pair of 10-sided dice, what are the odds of scoring at least eleven in one throw of the pair?

(Solution 34)

89 Elliptical Illusion

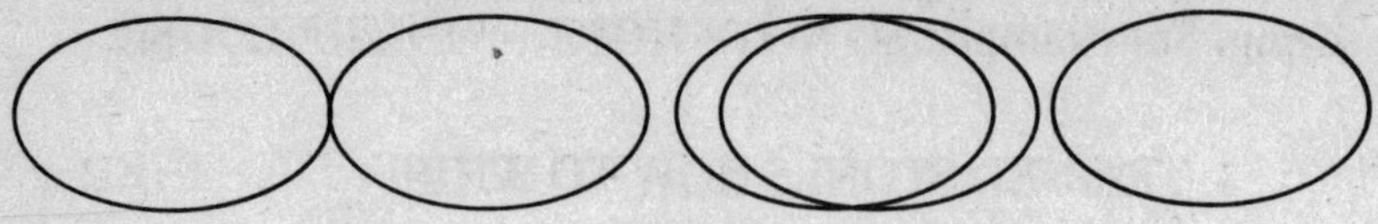

Which option below continues the above sequence?

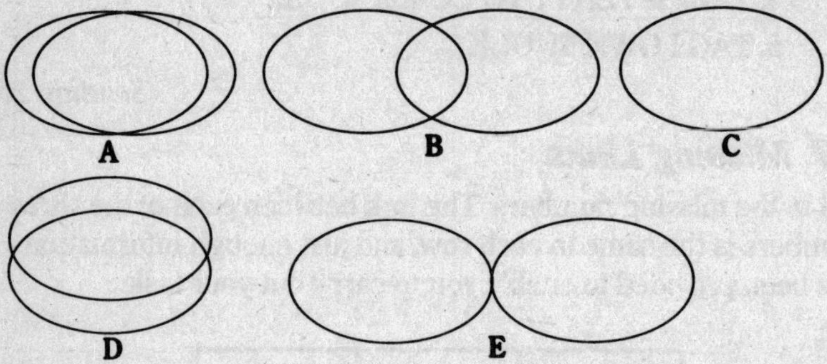

(Solution 37)

90 No Repeat Letters

The grid contains twenty-five different letters. What is the longest word that can be found by starting anywhere and working from square to square, horizontally, vertically, or diagonally, and not repeating a letter?

B	G	W	L	R
P	X	J	O	Y
K	A	T	U	F
C	V	D	Q	E
N	I	S	H	M

(Solution 41)

91 Rebuses

A rebus is an arrangement of letters or symbols to represent a familiar word or phrase. For example:

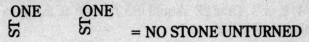

ONE ONE
ST ST = NO STONE UNTURNED

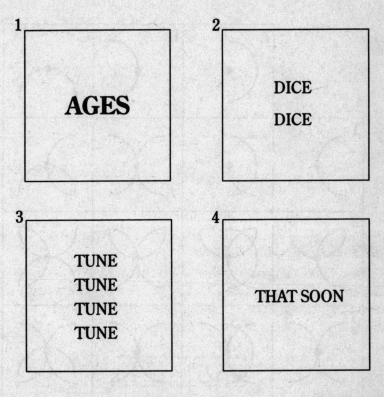

Now try these.

1

AGES

2

DICE

DICE

3

TUNE

TUNE

TUNE

TUNE

4

THAT SOON

(Solution 45)

92 Grid

Each of the nine squares marked 1A to 3C should incorporate all the lines and symbols that are shown in the squares A, B, or C and 1, 2, or 3. Thus 2B should incorporate all the lines and symbols in 2 and B.

One of the squares, 1A to 3C, is incorrect. Which one is it?

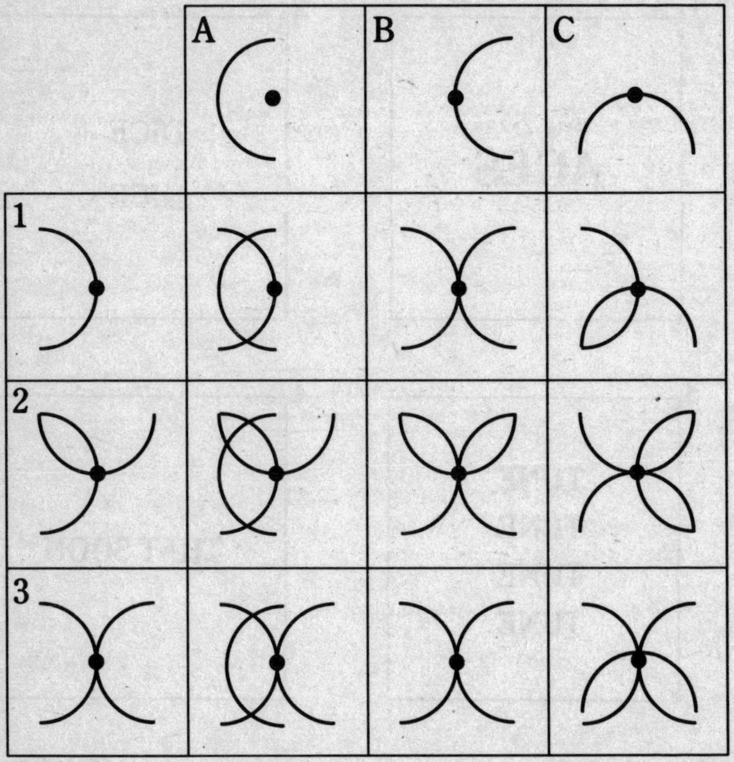

(Solution 49)

93 Cryptogram

The following is a straightforward substitution cryptogram in which each letter of the alphabet has been substituted for another.

QU M AQFFAL HSCPALBVL QY BMSVLICKY,
PJLIL QY FJL DMS PJC JMY YC
DXRJ MY FC GL CXF CU BMSVLI?

F. J. JXZALO

(Solution 53)

94 Magic Square

Insert the remaining numbers from 1 to 25 to form a magic square where each horizontal, vertical, and corner-to-corner line adds up to 65.

5				25
				10
20				
		15		

(Solution 57)

95 Pyramid Quotation

"All I know is that I am not a Marxist." – *Karl Marx*

Using all 28 letters of the above quotation only once, complete the pyramid with one 1-letter, one 2-letter, one 3-letter word, and so on.

Clues are given, but in no particular order.

Clues

- Gland in throat
- Which thing
- The Roman numeral for 1000
- Request
- Pertaining to a line around which a body revolves
- Type of cocktail
- In the direction of

(Solution 60)

96 Words

What have the following words all got in common?

TRY	VIABLE
ABLE	VISION
DURING	GRAVE
SHRINE	SIGN

(Solution 65)

97 The Hexagonal Pyramid

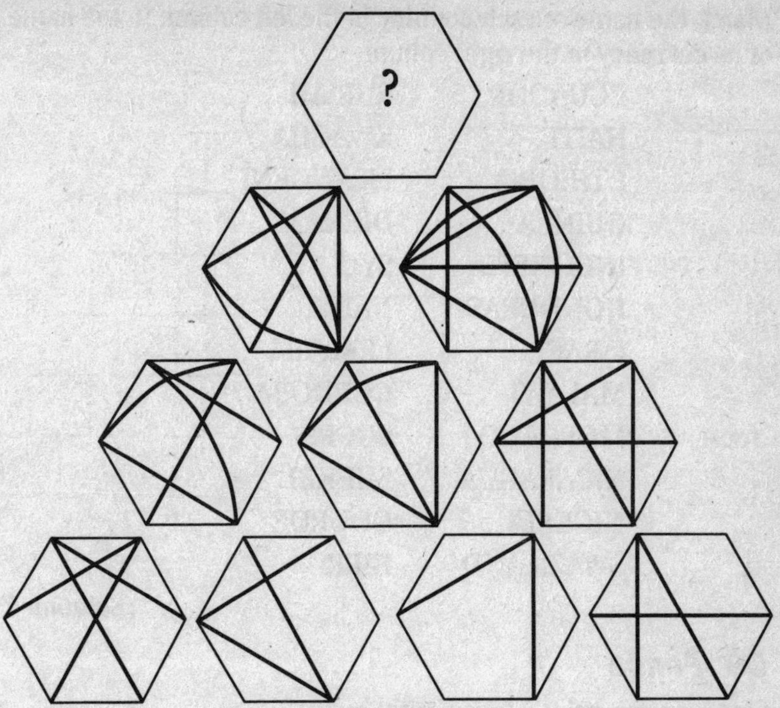

Which of the options below belongs at the top of the pyramid?

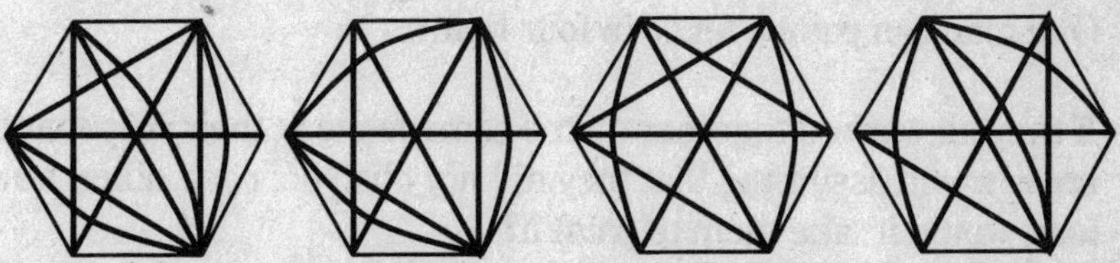

A B C D

(Solution 69)

98 Mixed Currency

Match the name of each country in the left column to the name of its currency in the right column.

ECUADOR	RUPIAH
HAITI	KWACHA
ETHIOPIA	LILANGENI
GUINEA	DIRHAM
INDONESIA	SYLI
HONDURAS	NAIRA
ISRAEL	LEMPIRA
MALAWI	CORDOBA
MOROCCO	SUCRE
NICARAGUA	SHEKEL
NIGERIA	GOURDE
SWAZILAND	BIRR

(Solution 73)

99 Fence

One man can paint a fence in six hours.
One man can paint a fence in three hours.
One man can paint a fence in two hours.
One man can paint a fence in four hours.

If they all worked together on the same fence at their respective speeds, and assuming that they did not obstruct each other, how long would it take them to paint it?

(Solution 77)

100 Nine Letters

Find the eight 9-letter words. The first three letters of each word have been given. The other two sets of three letters can be found somewhere in the letter groupings below.

1.	TAU		
2.	PIT		
3.	NIT		
4.	LAI		
5.	HAR		
6.	DIA		
7.	CHA		
8.	BLO		

KER	TOL
SIS	ANG
ILY	PIC
HIP	NTE
OGY	TCH
UER	CHF
ORK	RDS
USE	GNO

(Solution 81)

101 Grid

Each of the nine squares marked 1A to 3C should incorporate all the lines and sybols that are shown in the squares A, B, or C and 1, 2, or 3. Thus 2B should incorporate all the lines and symbols in 2 and B.

One of the squares, 1A to 3C, is incorrect. Which one is it?

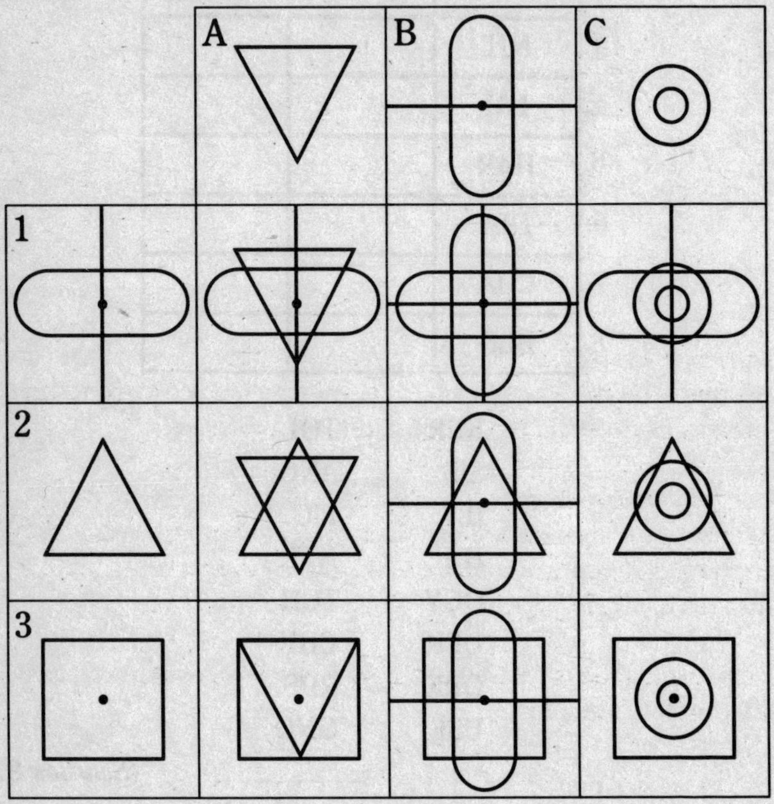

(Solution 85)

102 Stacking Cubes

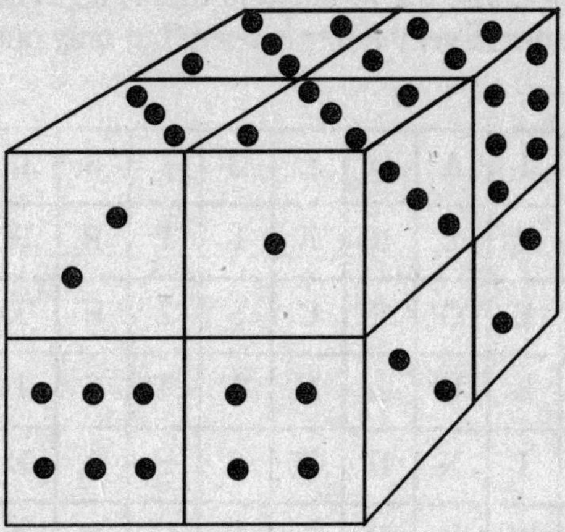

Eight dice are stacked together to form a cube. One example of how this is possible is shown above. In how many different ways is it possible to stack the cubes together in this way?

Note that simply changing two dice and retaining the same position of the spots is not considered a different assembly since the spots that appear on the outside of the cube will be identical and thus it will, in appearance, be the same cube.

If, however, a die is rotated in any way, this is considered different for example:

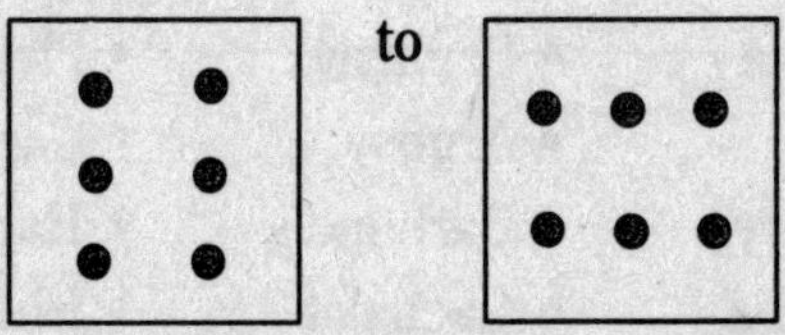

(Solution 88)

103 Lads and Lasses

Each horizontal line contains the jumbled letters of a boy's name and each vertical line the jumbled letters of a girl's name. Find the twenty names. Every letter is used, but only once each.

A	I	A	O	L	B	I	S	L	E
A	Y	L	R	A	L	P	R	H	I
T	E	O	S	C	S	Z	H	T	A
R	E	U	L	N	W	T	S	I	C
H	I	N	D	T	S	E	A	E	K
Y	W	H	R	I	R	M	N	A	E
L	E	A	D	K	A	E	S	C	R
A	D	S	V	A	L	G	N	I	L
U	S	A	I	T	J	I	N	I	O
A	N	S	R	I	Y	N	A	A	B

(Solution 93)

104 Group Puzzle

Arrange the following words into groups of three.

- Porbeagle
- Hyacinth
- Corncrake
- Tumbrel
- Cassowary
- Barkentine
- Pinnace
- Snapper
- Popinjay
- Argosy
- Carbuncle
- Cachalot
- Grayling
- Tonneau
- Pichiciago
- Capybara
- Hackney
- Iridium

(Solution 98)

105 Arcs Matrix

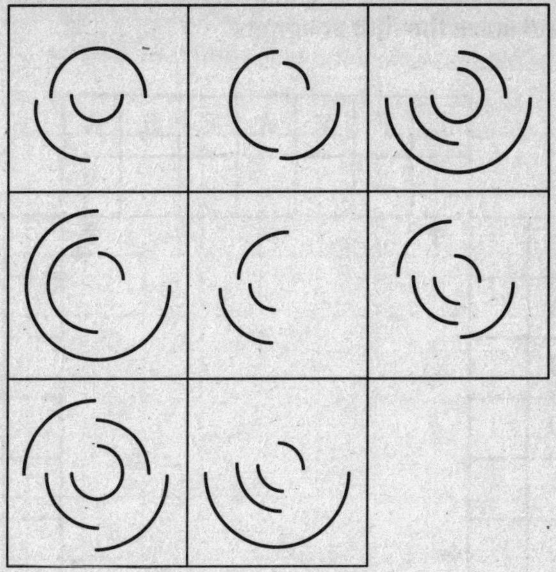

Choose the missing tile from the options below.

A

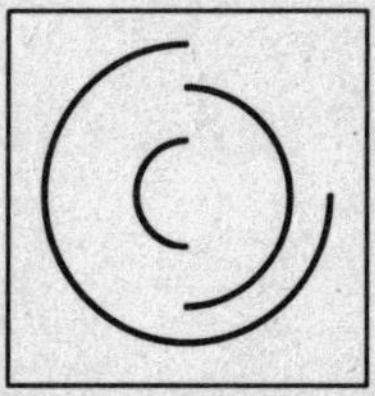

B

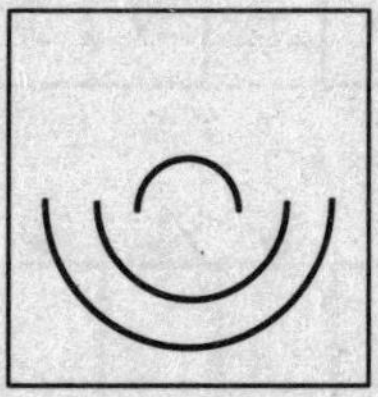

C

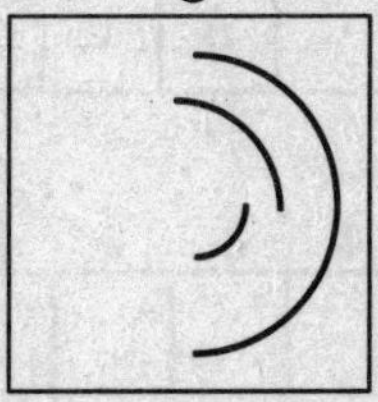

D

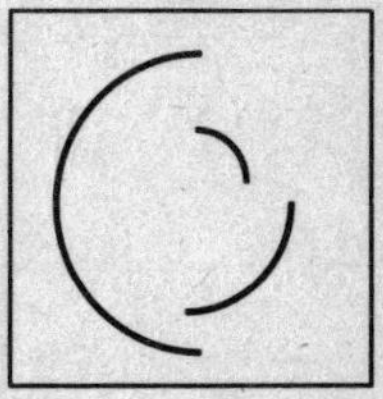

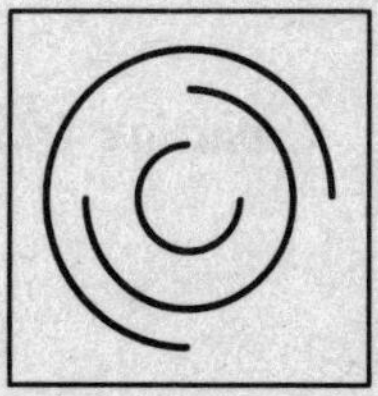

E

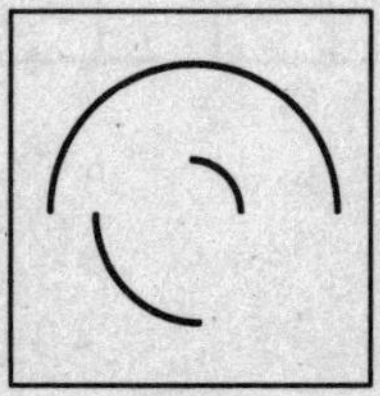

F

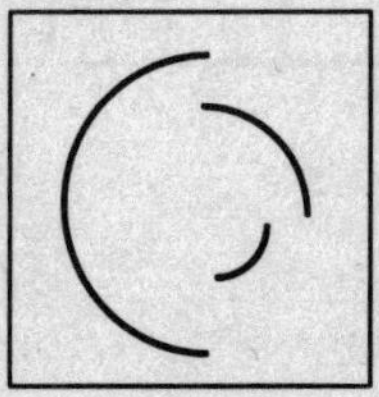

G

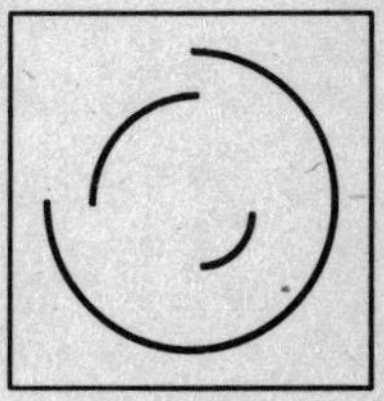

H

(Solution 100)

106 Enigmagram

Solve the four anagrams of types of boats. Transfer the arrowed letters and solve the fifth anagram.

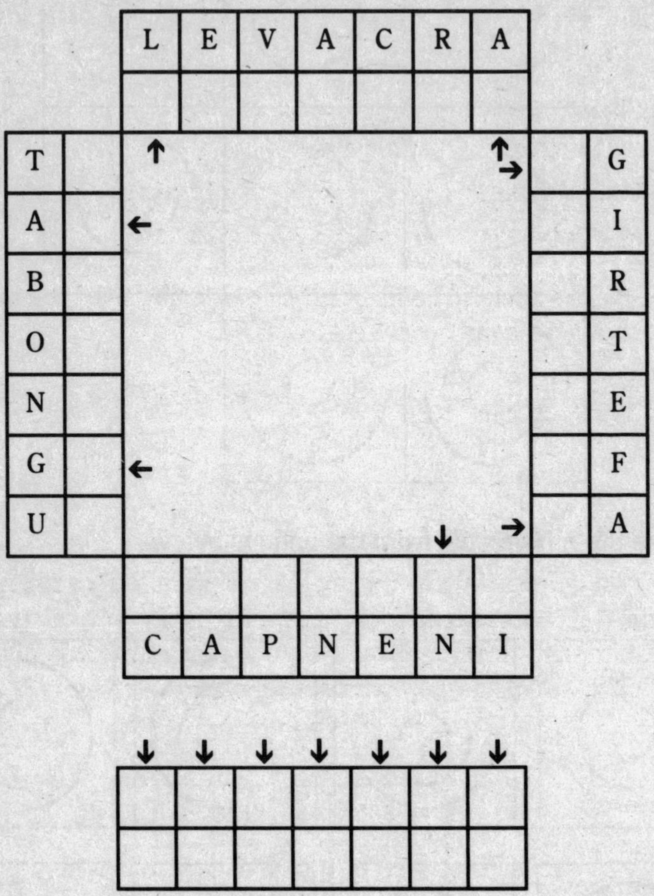

(Solution 105)

107 Tennis

At the local tennis club the following members entered the championships for singles and doubles.

	Men	Women
Men's Singles	41	
Women's Singles		29
Men's Doubles	20 pairs	
Women's Doubles		14 pairs
Mixed Doubles	26 pairs	26 pairs

They were knockout competitions so by using byes the numbers first had to be reduced to 32 – 16 – 8 – 4 – 2 –

How many matches had been played by the end of Championship Day?

(Solution 109)

108 No Repeat Letters

The grid below contains twenty-five different letters of the alphabet. What is the longest word that can be found by starting anywhere and working from square to square horizontally, vertically, and diagonally, and not repeating a letter?

B	V	R	U	Q
M	Y	I	E	J
L	N	P	W	F
G	T	O	K	S
H	X	D	C	A

(Solution 113)

109 Links Jigsaw Puzzle

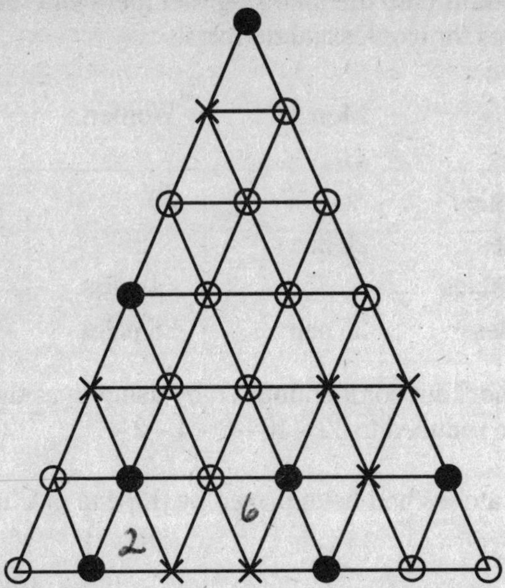

Place the twelve segment links, below, over the triangular grid above, in such a way that each link symbol is covered by exactly the same symbol.
The connecting segments must not be rotated. Note that not all the connecting lines will be covered.

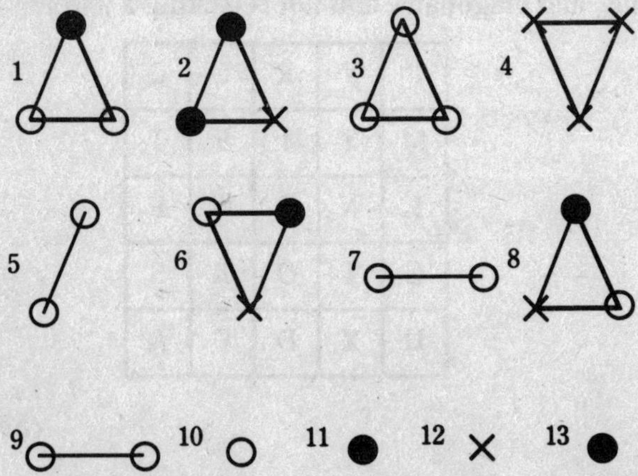

(Solution 118)

110 Cubes

Each horizontal and vertical line contains the digits of a 5-figure cube number. The digits are always in the correct order, but not necessarily adjacent. Each digit is used once only, and they are all used. Find the twenty 5-figure cube numbers.

6	4	1	6	6	8	5	6	1	5
8	3	3	5	7	9	1	7	3	7
9	1	3	2	1	5	2	9	7	5
1	9	2	1	4	1	6	7	5	4
9	2	4	1	3	8	8	5	9	8
9	3	8	7	0	3	9	3	6	7
2	3	2	9	8	2	6	7	6	8
5	0	4	5	9	3	1	0	7	9
1	4	5	6	8	4	8	2	5	2
1	1	0	2	6	4	3	7	6	8

(Solution 121)

111 Sequence

What number comes next in this sequence?

149, 162, 536, 496, 481, ?

(Solution 125)

112 Sequence

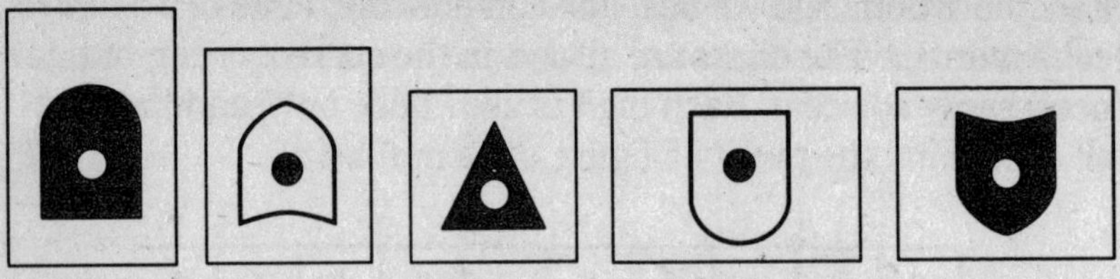

Which option below continues the above sequence?

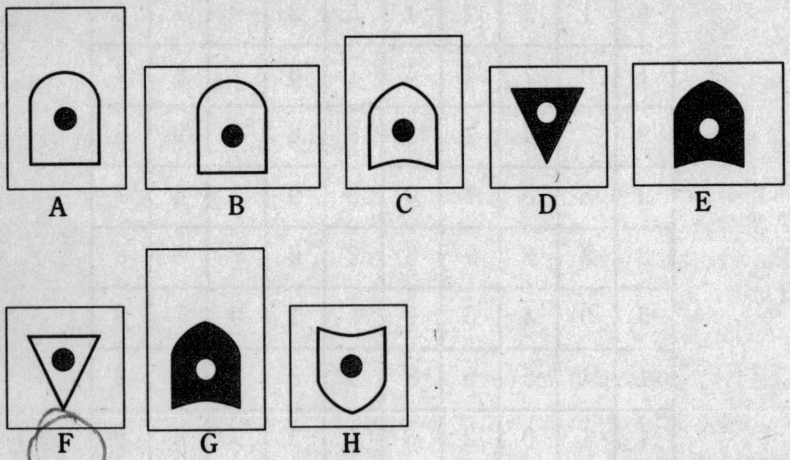

(Solution 129)

113 Cliff

The height of a cliff can be measured by dropping a stone from the top and timing its descent. How is this calculated?

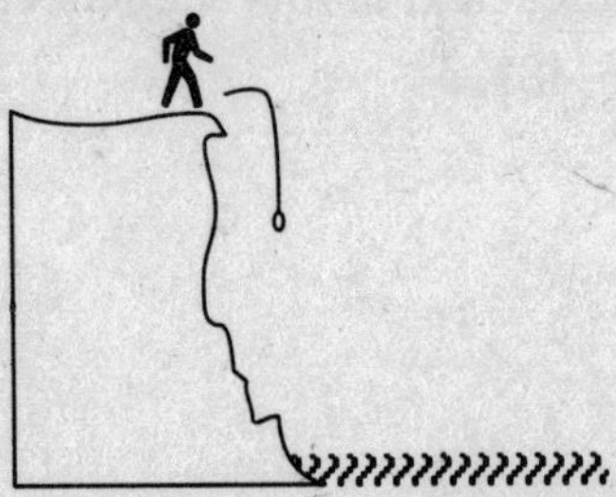

(Solution 130)

114 Tampa

Place the letters in the grid to spell five 5-letter words. Five letters have been placed. Clues are not necessarily in the correct order.

1.	T					K K A A E
2.		A				G G H K L
3.			M			L M M M M
4.				P		N O P P T
5.					A	T U U V Y

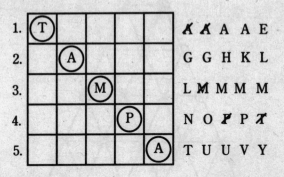

Fleshy body in throat
A pasty or doughy mass
A dance
Pure water
Tidy

(Solution 137)

115 Hidden Lands

Can you find the words that include the names of these countries?

• W A • • L E S
• • • • • T U N I S •
• • T • • • O G • • • O •
C • • U • B A • • • •
• • C H A • D
N A T • • • A L • • •
• • I T • A L • Y
• • • O M • • • • A • • • N
• • P E R • • • U •
C O N G • • • • • • • • • • O • •

(Solution 141)

116 Links Jigsaw Puzzle

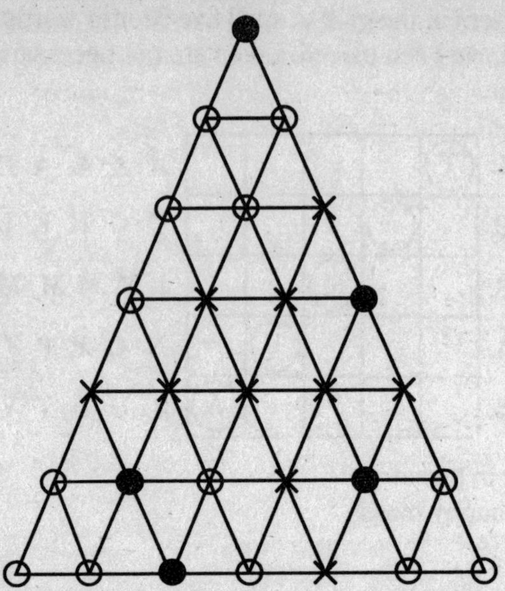

Place the twelve segment links, below, over the triangular grid above, in such a way that each link symbol is covered by exactly the same symbol.
The connecting segments must not be rotated. Note that not all the connecting lines will be covered.

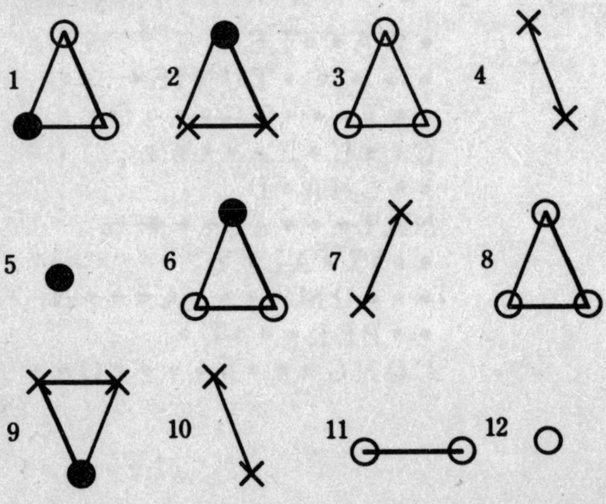

(Solution 145)

117 Margana

If we presented you with the words MAR, AM, and FAR and asked you to find the shortest English word that contained all the letters from which these words could be produced, we would expect you to come up with the word FARM.

Here is another list of words:

STAIN, YES, COUNT, CLEAN

What is the shortest English word from which all these words can be produced?

(Solution 149)

118 Unscramble a Sequence

Start at the starred square and work from square to square horizontally, vertically, and diagonally to unscramble a meaningful sequence. Every square must be visited once only. Finish at the top left-hand square.

← 3	0	1	6	2	8
5	1	5	3	1	3
1	6	1	2	6	5
3	2	*	4	5	5
1	1	0	1	7	6
5	0	1	8	9	6

(Solution 153)

119 Track Word

Work around the track to find a 14-letter word. You have to provide the missing letters and find the starting point. The word might appear reading clockwise or counter-clockwise, and the overlapping letter appears twice.

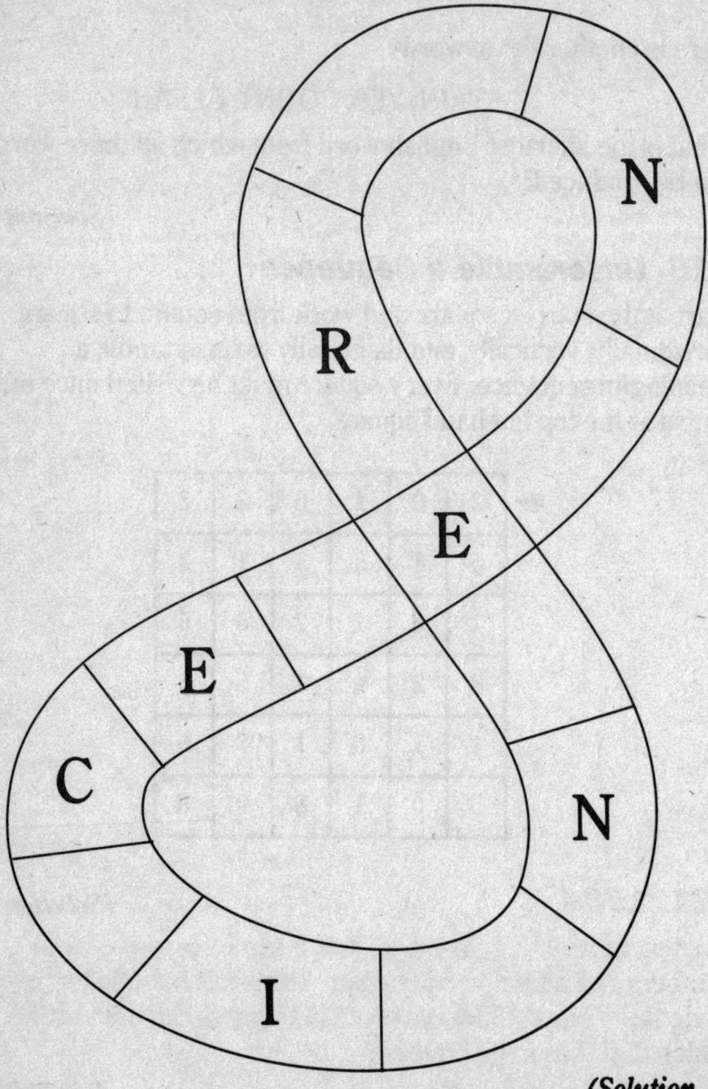

(Solution 159)

120 Octagons

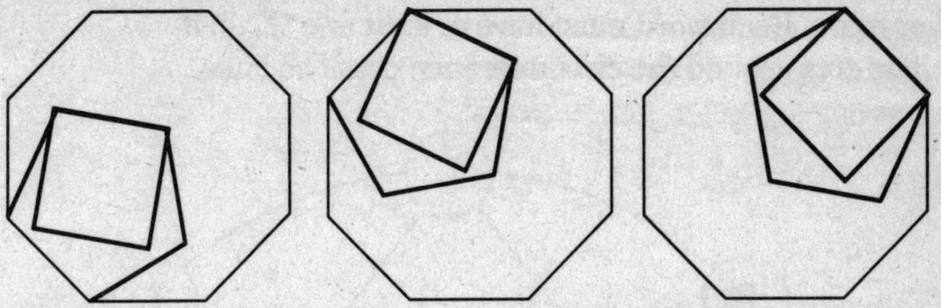

Which octagon below continues the above sequence?

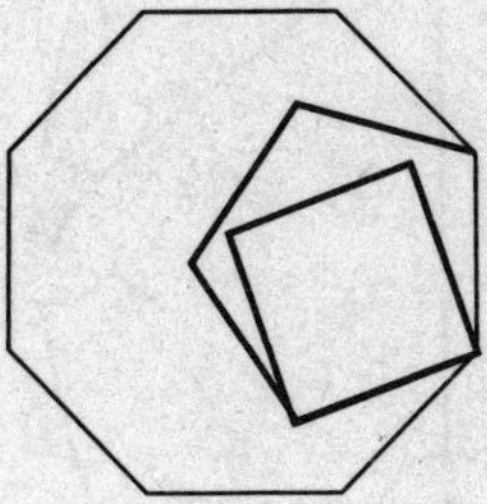

A

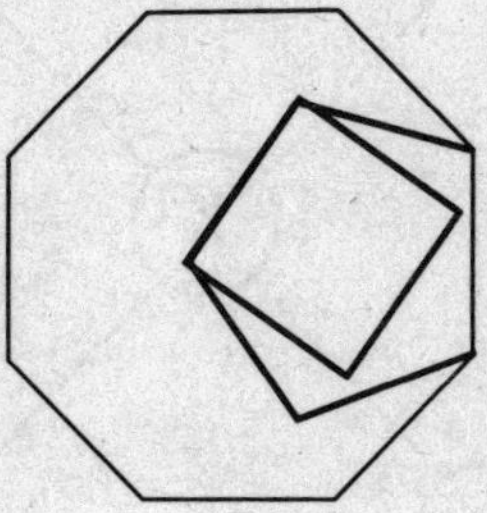

B

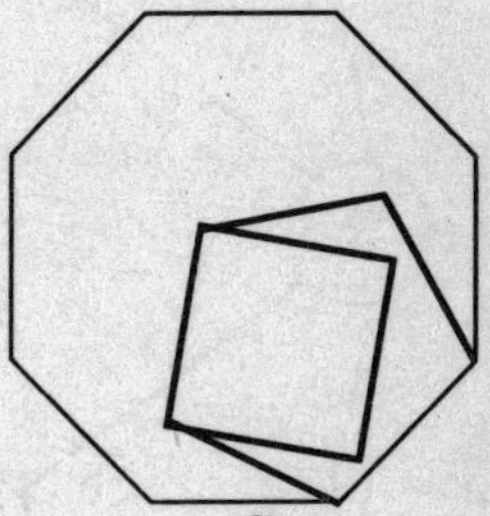

C

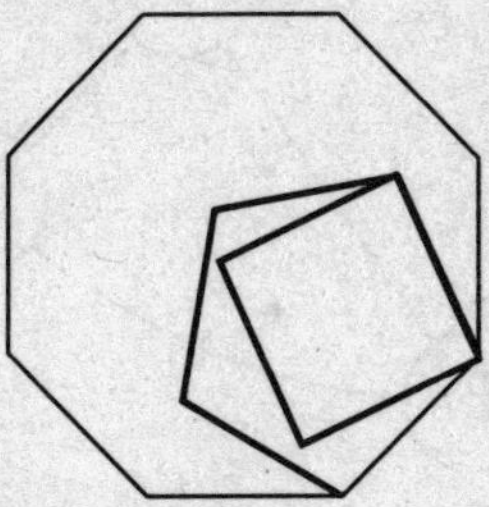

D

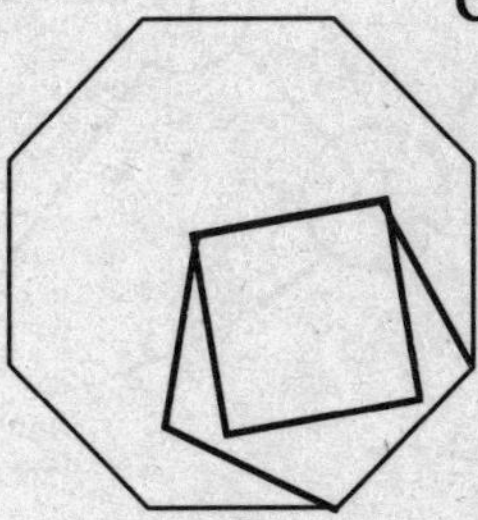

E

(Solution 3)

121 1984

The ten digits 0, 1, 2, 3, 4, 5, 6, 7, 8, 9 can be arranged into numbers and added to equal many totals but nobody has ever made them equal 1984. However, nine digits can equal 1984. Which digit has to be omitted?

(Solution 7)

122 "X" Puzzle

Move from letter to letter along the lines to spell out thirty words or more. Each word must have at least one "X" in it.
The arcs around the circumference count as lines.

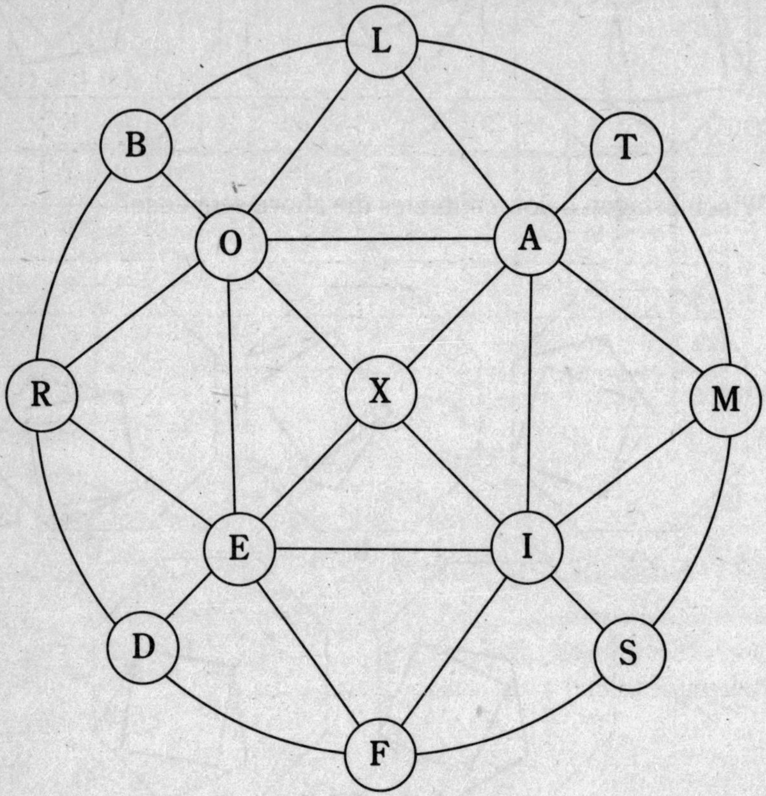

(Solution 12)

123 Playing Cards

Here is a pack of fifty-two playing cards. Each card has been designated a letter. Select no more than twelve cards and arrange into a word to make the highest score that you can. The maximum score possible is 160.

											(11)	(12)	(13)	(15)
POINTS		2	3	4	5	6	7	8	9	10	J	Q	K	A
SUITS	♡	L	R	S	Z	H	X	Q	J	C	U	P	I	T
	◇	B	M	A	Z	Y	G	V	E	Q	J	A	N	I
	♤	S	D	N	F	Y	X	K	W	D	K	T	R	E
	♧	G	W	L	O	C	P	H	B	M	F	U	O	V
POINTS		2	3	4	5	6	7	8	9	10	J	Q	K	A
											(11)	(12)	(13)	(15)

(Solution 15)

124 Biblical Characters

Complete the names of the biblical characters below. Only alternate letters are shown. Then rearrange the first letters of each name to find a tenth biblical character.

• I • A •
• P • R • I •
• A • N • B • S
• A • O •
• I • O • H •
• E • J • M • N
• H • D • A • H
• B • A • A •
• E • O •

(Solution 19)

125 Treasure

The treasure is on square D7. You have to find the starting square that will lead to the treasure.

Instructions are read as follows:

2S } means 2 squares South
1E } and 1 square East

6N } means 6 squares North
6W } and 6 squares West

N

	A	B	C	D	E	F	G
1	2S 2E	2S 4E	3S 4E	3S 1W	6S 3W	5S 1W	6S 6W
2	1N 1E	2S 1W	4S 4E	1N 1E	5S 2W	4S 4W	1N 1W
3	1N 3E	3S 1W	3S 3E	2N 3W	2S 2W	2N 2W	1S 2W
4	2N 2E	3N 1E	1N 1W	3S 3E	1S 1W	1N 2W	2N 6W
5	3N 4E	2S 2E	1N 1E	1S 1W	2S 1E	2N 1E	2N 6W
6	1N 4E	3N 3E	2N 1W	1S 1E	1N 3W	1N 1E	1N 1W
7	5N 5E	2N 1W	1N 1E	(T)	2N 1E	5N 1E	5N 5W

W — E

S

(Solution 23)

126 The Palindromic Biennium

A palindrome is a word, phrase or number that reads the same both backwards and forwards. For example,

MADAM I'M ADAM, CIVIC, or 1881.

When is the next time that two consecutive palindromic years will occur?

(Solution 27)

127 Word Compasses

Place the letters in the correct sectors in each quadrant to obtain two 8-letter words, one reading clockwise and the other counter-clockwise. The two words are antonyms.

NE : EIFA
SE : NLUG
NW : LANC
SW : RUGY

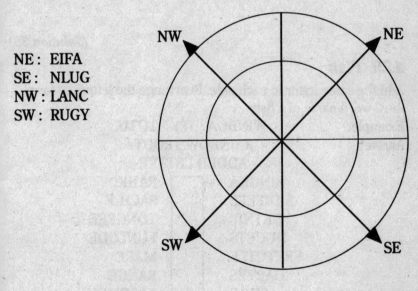

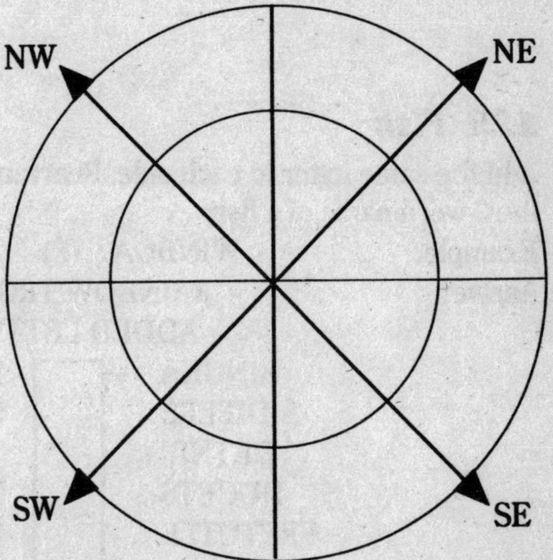

(Solution 32)

128 Triangles

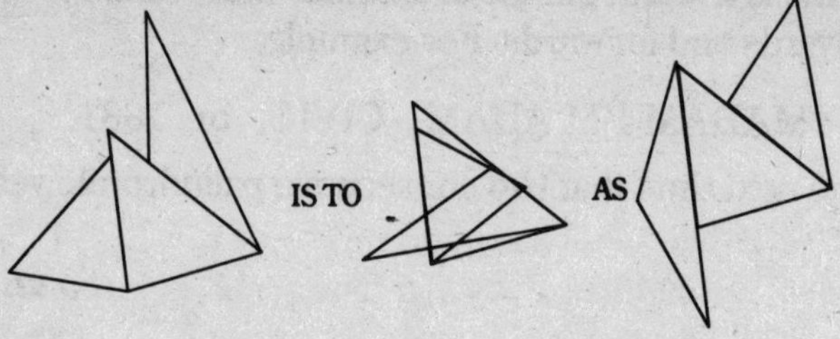

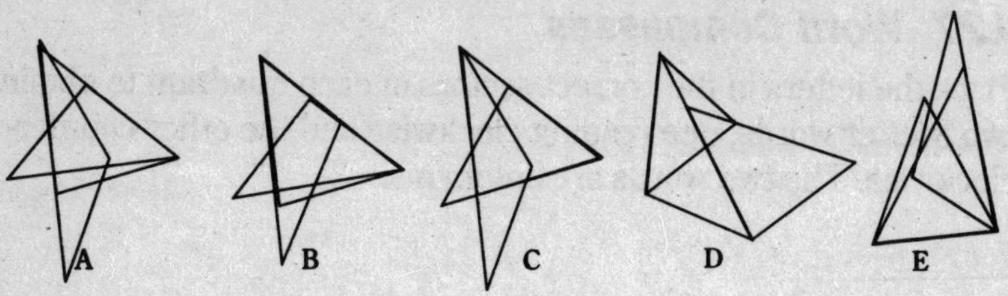

(Solution 35)

129 Fish

Add the same letter to each side. Rearrange the letters to form the 2-word name of a fish.

Example: WINBOA (R) TOTU

Answer: RAINBOW TROUT

	ADDED LETTER	
BINGKA		RAHK
DIPERS		SACHIF
DETNIP		TONGRED
DUCETS		FUNLODE
FRYTUTLE		MARE
CARTES		RANGE
SHOE		LACEMEK
DRABE		FAGHIS
NOBW		PEGOR
NIPY		HOSEARE

(Solution 39)

130 Aliens

100 aliens attended the intergalactic meeting on earth.

73 had two heads
28 had three eyes
21 had four arms
12 had two heads and three eyes
9 had three eyes and four arms
8 had two heads and four arms
3 had all three unusual features

How many had none of these unusual features?

(Solution 43)

131 Saying

Letters have been omitted from the saying. See if you can fill them in the grid.

A		W	A		S	
O	R		I		E	
O	U	R			E	
I	E		N	O		H
I	N		A	N	N	
	S		H	E		S
O	M		C			

E	M	T
F	M	U
G	N	V
G	O	Y
H	S	Y
L	T	Y

(Solution 47)

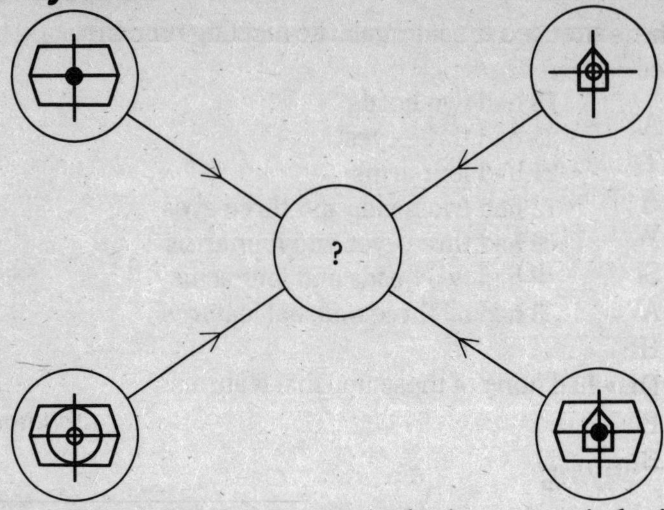

Each line and symbol that appears in the four outer circles is transferred to the middle circle according to these rules:

If a line or symbol occurs in the outer circle:

once	it is transferred
twice	it is possibly tranferred
3 times	it is transferred
4 times	it is not transferred

Which of the circles A, B, C, D, or E, shown below should appear in the middle of the diagram?

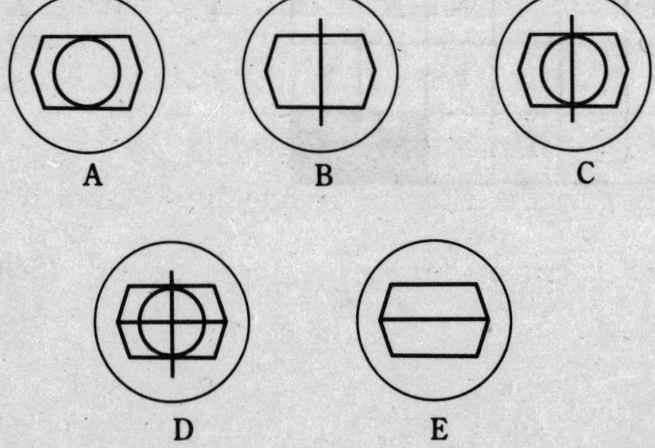

(Solution 51)

133 Found in America

All the following are anagrams of things that can be found in the United States of America.

1. ACHED NOT A BAY
2. TALES AND TINS
3. A FEISTY HOTEL BUTTER
4. WASTE SHEER ROT
5. SLUM ABOUT NINE
6. AVERSE A DRAIN
7. HELL YET VADA
8. DID GET COY
9. POUR LAD A COOL TEA
10. BARE ON GOUT

(Solution 55)

134 Work it Out

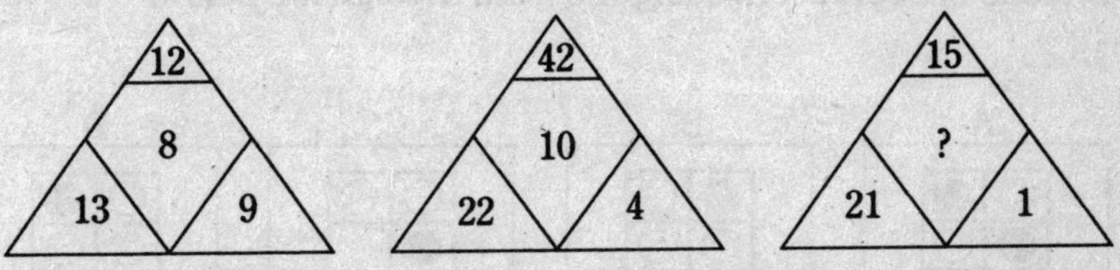

Work out the number that should replace the question mark in the third triangle.

(Solution 59)

135 Three Birds and a Fish

Rearrange all of the letters below into three birds and a fish.

HARD BEHIND SIT SAFER

(Solution 63)

136 Dots Matrix

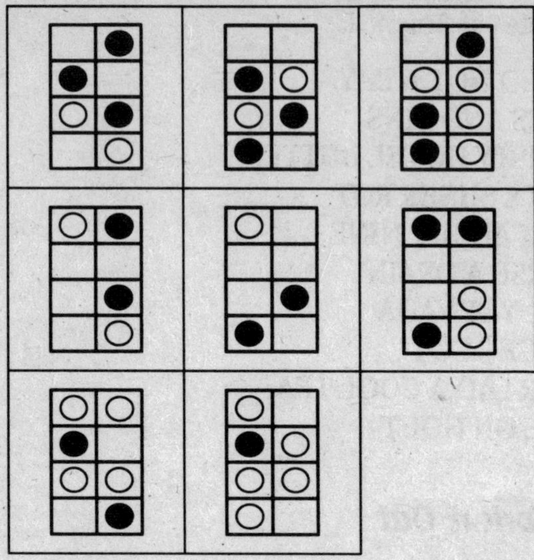

Choose the correct missing tile from the options below.

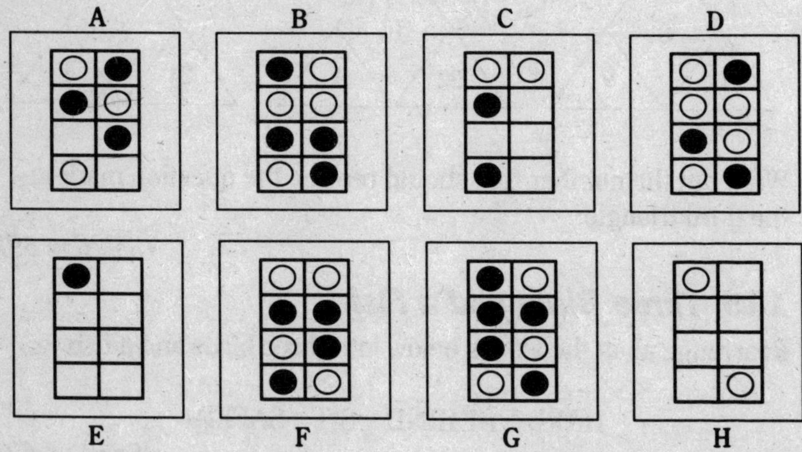

(Solution 67)

137 Bull's Eye

Find the answer to the sixteen questions.

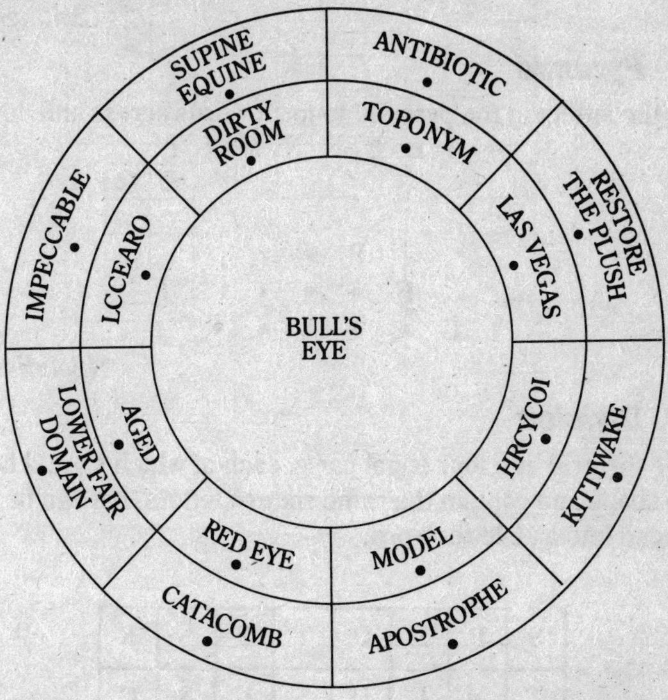

1. Vegetable (anag.)
2. One familiar word (anag.)
3. Person named after a place
4. Salvages (anag.)
5. West to East overnight
6. Dormitory (anag.)
7. A direct address to a dead person
8. Opposite of peccable
9. Sleeping donkey
10. Kidnapped (4 consecutive letters of the alphabet missing)
11. Tomb
12. Boat (anag.)
13. The upholsterers (anag.)
14. Species of gull
15. Cheesecake
16. Opposite to biotic (relating to life)

(Solution 71)

138 Cycle

How many revolutions are made by a 28” bicycle wheel over one mile?

(Solution 75)

139 Pyramid

Place the letters in the pyramid to form words across and down.

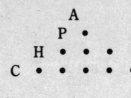

A A B E E N R R T

A
P •
H • • •
C • • • • •

(Solution 79)

140 Division

Divide the grid into four equal parts, each of which should be the same shape and contain the same sixteen letters that can be arranged into a 16-letter word.

S	P	P	O	T	S	S	R
T	M	E	U	S	U	S	O
U	E	U	U	P	U	R	T
S	P	S	E	P	U	O	U
S	O	R	S	E	E	N	P
R	M	S	N	M	N	S	U
N	S	E	U	M	S	E	E
T	S	P	U	S	P	S	U

(Solution 83)

141 Symbols

Which of the circles A, B, C, D, or E should appear in the middle circle?

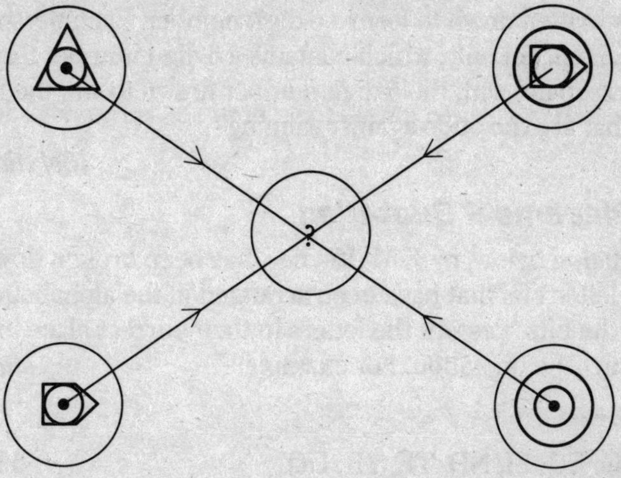

Each line and symbol that appears in the four outer circles is transferred to the middle circle according to these rules:

If a line or symbol occurs in the outer circle:

once	it is transferred
twice	it is possibly transferred
3 times	it is transferred
4 times	it is not transferred

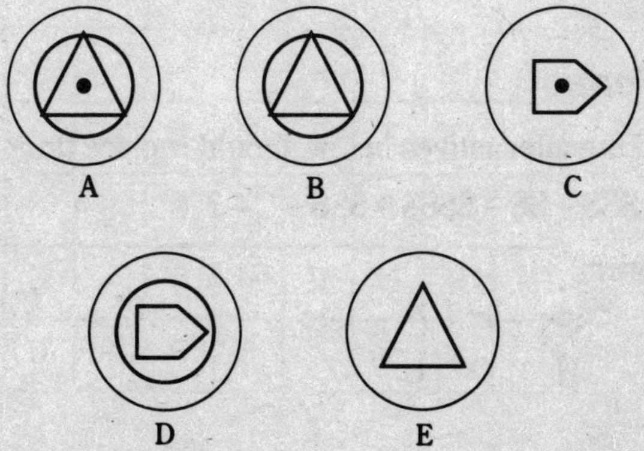

(Solution 87)

142 Sweepstakes

A bag contains nine balls numbered 1–9. To decide the winner of a sweepstake, six balls are drawn out successively and their numbers written down to form a 6-digit number. Each person is allowed one ticket only, which contains a 6-digit number that must correspond with the 6-digit number drawn to win the first prize. What are the odds against winning?

(Solution 91)

143 Piecemeal Quotation

The quotation below, by J. M. Keynes, has been broken down into two-letter bits that have been arranged in the alphabetical order of the bits. Restore the letters to their correct place to reconstruct the quotation. For example:

- - - - / - - - / - - - - -

Bits: EQ, FI, ND, TE, TH, UO
Answer: Find the Quote.

- - - - - - - - - - / - - - / - - - - - / - - - - - /
- - - - - - - - - - - - / - - - / - - - / - / - - - - /
- - - / - - / - - - - - / - - - / - / - - - .

AD, AM, AN, AV, AY, EF, EN, ER, ES, EV, FW, GS, HI, IN, IV, KF, LL, OR, OR, OU, TO, UP, US, UT, WH, YO, YO .

(Solution 95)

144 Series

Which of the alternatives below should replace the ?

S – SC – SSS – SS – SSSS – SSS – C – ?

Choose from:

SC	SS	SSS	C	C	SSS
P	T	H	O	U	Z

(Solution 99)

145 Circles

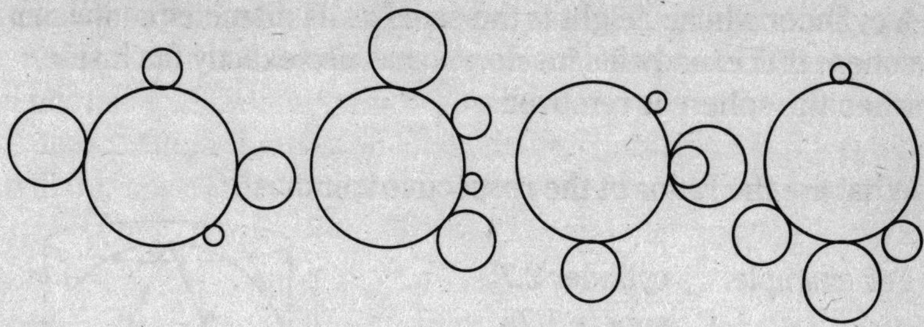

Which option below continues the above sequence?

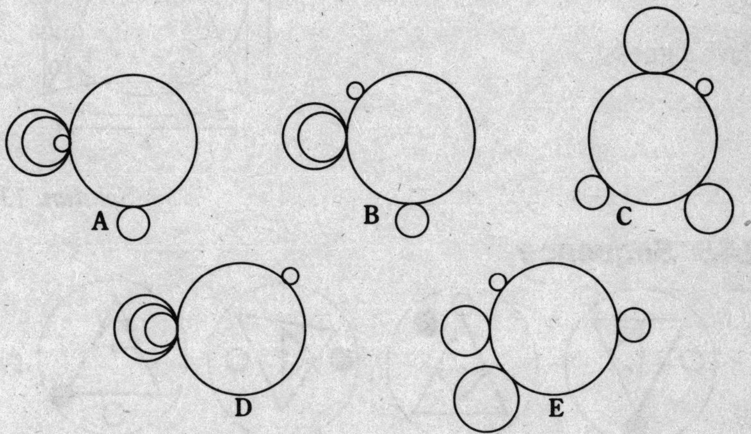

(Solution 103)

146 Ten Letters

Strike out ten letters to leave a word that can be found in the dictionary.

COTNEGNRLAETTULTATEIORNSS

(Solution 107)

147 Cylinder

A cylinder whose height is the same as its diameter contains a sphere that exactly fits inside. A cone also exactly fits inside when the sphere is removed.

What are the ratios of the respective volumes?

For example: cylinder 2.75
sphere 1.75
cone 1

Have a guess!

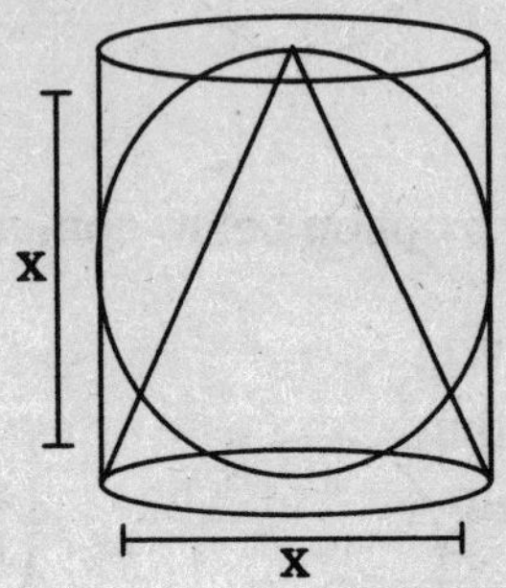

(Solution 111)

148 Sequence

Which option continues the above sequence?

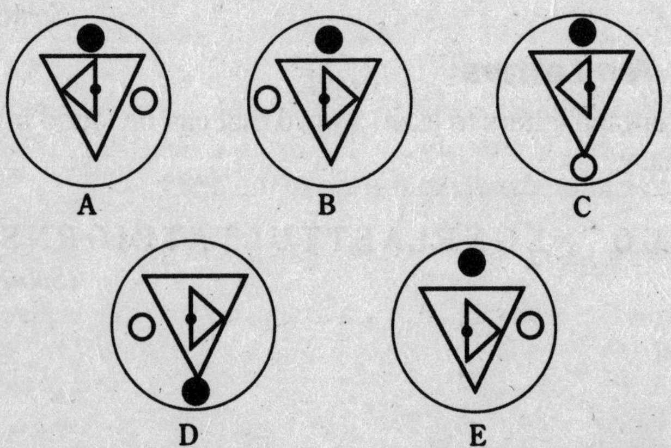

(Solution 116)

149 Letter Search

K	D	G	A	N
R	O	U	L	E
P	J	C	T	Q
Y	S	F	B	I
H	V	M	X	W

1. What letter is two above the letter immediately to the right of the letter three below the letter two to the right of the letter immediately above the letter "J"?

2. What letter is immediately to the left of the letter immediately below the letter two to the left of the letter two below the letter three to the right of the letter three letters above the letter "S"?

3. What letter is two to the right of the letter immediately above the letter two to the left of the letter two letters above the letter immediately to the right of the letter immediately below the letter which is midway between the letters "T" and "V"?

4. What letter is two to the left of the letter immediately above the letter two to the left of the letter immediately to the right of the letter immediately below the letter that is midway between the letter two to the right of the letter "D" and the letter immediately to the left of the letter "W"?

(Solution 119)

150 Plurals

Can you find a word that is a plural of a word that is also a plural?

(Solution 123)

151 Nines

When the sum of the digits of a number will divide exactly by nine, then the number itself will also divide by nine. For example, 2673; 2 + 6 + 7 + 3 = 18. With this in mind, place the digits into the grid so that each horizontal and vertical line, when read both forwards and backwards, will divide exactly by nine.

1 1 1
2 2 2
3 3
4 4
5 5 5
6 6 6 6
7 7 7
8 8
9 9 9

(Solution 127)

152 Analogy

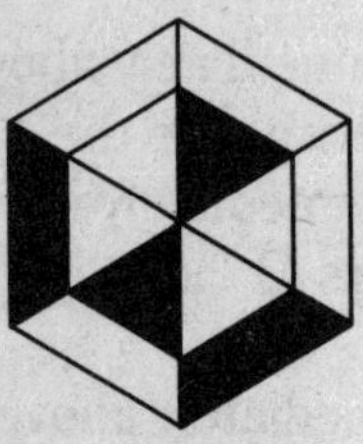

IS TO

AS

IS TO

A

B

C

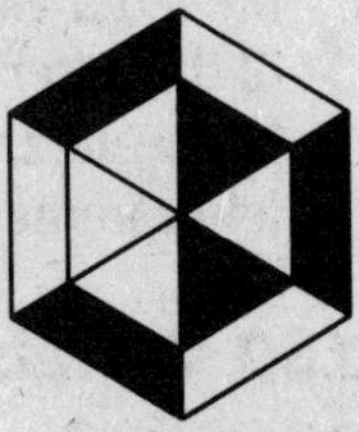

D

(Solution 132)

153 Nine Letters

The twenty-five words can be grouped into twelve pairs of words that belong together, which will leave one odd word. Find the odd word.

GUINEVERE	CATAMOUNT
FOMALHAUT	FARANDOLE
SHILLALAH	HIPPODROME
SHELDRAKE	FRICASSEE
AUBERGINE	NICOTIANA
MERCENARY	DROMEDARY
BODYGUARD	ALDEBARAN
ARGONAUTS	WHITEBEAM
MARSUPIAL	MONOTREME
JACARANDA	MANGETOUT
PYRACANTHA	MERGANSER
SUCCOTASH	DERRINGER
POUSSETTE	

(Solution 135)

154 12 Letters

Thirty 4-letter bits can be formed into ten 12-letter words. (Four of the answers are hyphenated.)

OGRA	HIGH	RDEN
OARD	MENT	NDED
GENE	PHIC	FLEB
AWED	MARK	SHUF
ERNJ	WISH	PHON
SHRE	ICAL	ENCE
NESS	PING	STEP
SING	ELOC	LEHA
NIST	LANT	COMM
UTIO	ETGA	ALOG

(Solution 139)

155 Boat

A boat is to be rowed straight across a river, which has a constant current that flows downstream at six metres a minute. The rower makes a constant effort, which through still water is at the rate of ten metres a minute.

In which direction must the rower head and how far will he travel across the river in one minute?

(Solution 143)

156 Circles

Which of these fits into the blank circle to carry on a logical sequence?

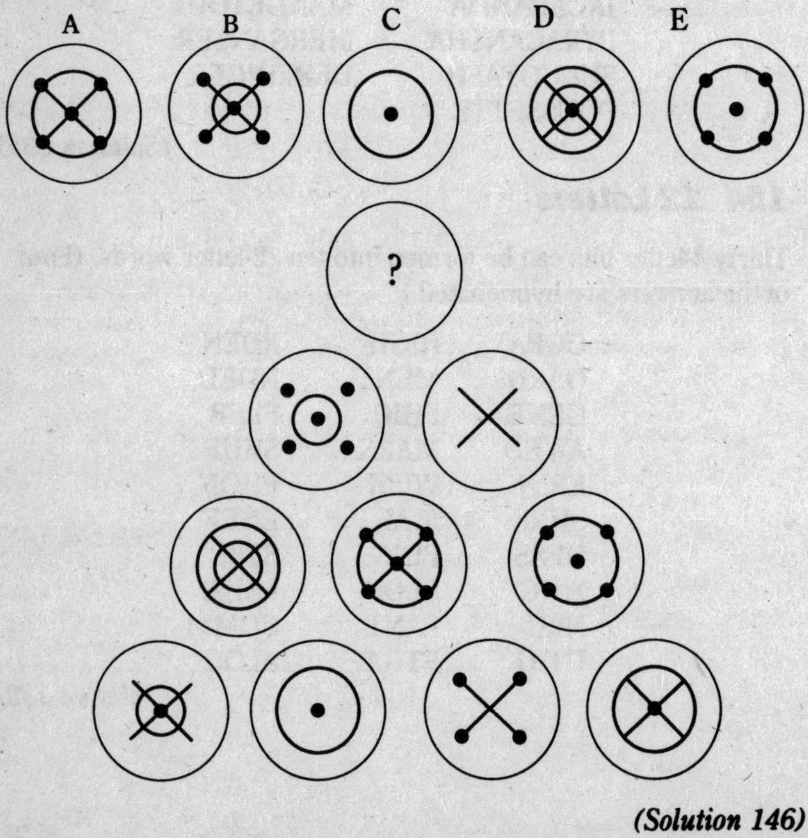

(Solution 146)

157 Synonyms

In each of the following a number of synonyms of the keyword are shown. Take one letter from each of the synonyms to find a further synonym of the keyword. The letters appear in the correct order.

1. Keyword : FAST
   Synonyms : HASTY, MERCURIAL, RAPID, BRISK, SWIFT, FLEET, WINGED

2. Keyword : EVIDENT
   Synonyms : PATENT, MANIFEST, BLATANT, CONSPICUOUS, PLAIN, OBVIOUS, VISIBLE, CLEAR

3. Keyword : ECCENTRIC
   Synonyms : ERRATIC, BIZARRE, PECULIAR, ABERRANT, FREAKISH, IDIOSYNCRATIC, IRREGULAR, ODD, ANOMALOUS, OUTLANDISH

4. Keyword : HAZY
   Synonyms : OVERCAST, NEBULOUS, DIM, BLURRY, OBSCURE, DULL

5. Keyword : SCURRILOUS
   Synonyms : OBSCENE, SCANDALOUS, RIBALD, INFAMOUS, INDECENT, VITUPERATIVE, COARSE, INSULTING, OFFENSIVE

(Solution 150)

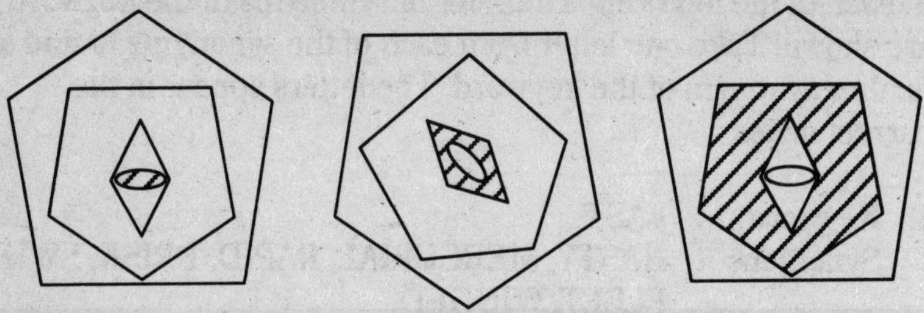

Which option below continues the above sequence?

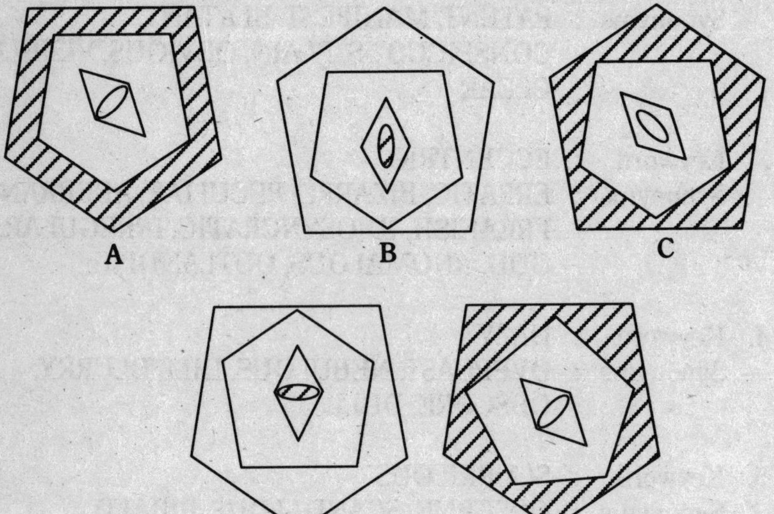

(Solution 158)

159 Synonym Circles

Work clockwise to find a pair of synonyms. You must provide the missing letters.

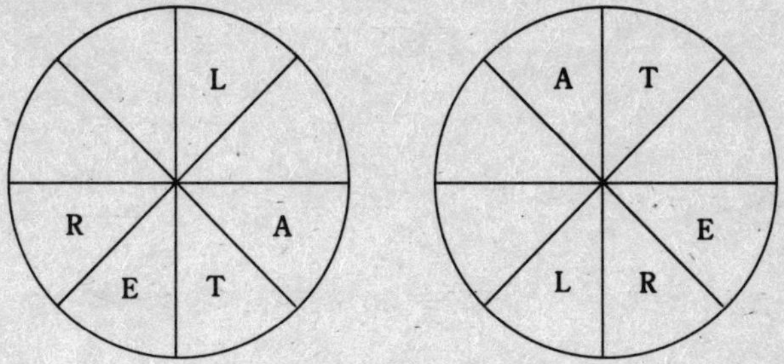

(Solution 155)

160 Sensible

Start at the middle square and move from square to square horizontally, vertically, or diagonally to spell out seven synonyms of SENSIBLE. Visit every square once, and once only. Finish at the top right-hand square.

U	D	P	O	I	A	E	→
E	R	L	N	T	N	S	
N	C	A	A	T	I	C	
T	Y	A	*	R	S	L	
S	R	N	N	I	I	A	
H	W	E	D	C	U	E	
D	J	U	I	O	R	S	

(Solution 156)

The Solutions

(Solutions are presented out of numerical sequence so that reading the answer to one puzzle will not inadvertently reveal the answer to the next.)

1 *Saying*

"The man who knows how will always have a job. The man who knows why will always be his boss." *(Anon.)*

(Puzzle 80)

2 *Hexagons*

D. Each symbol moves in its own sequence.

● moves one clockwise, then two clockwise, then three clockwise, etc.

◯ moves one counter-clockwise, then two counter-clockwise, then three counter-clockwise, etc.

▲ moves one counter-clockwise, then two clockwise, then one counter-clockwise, etc.

○ moves one counter-clockwise each time.

• moves one clockwise each time (in the fourth hexagon this symbol is hidden by the triangle).

(Puzzle 40)

3 *Octagons*

D. The pentagon moves two sides of the octagon clockwise each time. The square moves one side of the pentagon counter-clockwise each time.

(Puzzle 120)

4 Alternative Crossword

C	O	N	I	F	E	R	S
O	■	■	C	O	S	■	E
S	O	■	E	A	T	■	R
S	I	R	■	L	O	P	E
E	L	A	N	■	P	E	N
T	■	V	O	W	■	W	E
E	■	E	V	A	■	■	L
D	I	L	A	T	O	R	Y

(Puzzle 1)

5 Squares

E. Another square is added at each stage and this rotates by half the length of the side of a square clockwise at each stage, and all squares are attached to the same pivot. Only the section common to all squares at a particular stage is shaded.

(Puzzle 81)

6 WOT! No Vowels

Wry	Wryly	Hymn
Thy	Fly	Pry
Fry	Shy	Spy
Pyx	Crypt	Why
Cry	Dry	
Spry	Myrrh	

(Puzzle 41)

7 1984

5:

$$\begin{array}{r} 869 \\ 702 \\ 413 \\ \hline 1984 \end{array}$$

(Puzzle 121)

8 Batteries

$$\frac{1}{10} \times \frac{1}{10} \times \frac{1}{10} = \frac{1}{1000}$$

1 in one thousand chance.

(Puzzle 2)

9 Horse Race

No.	Odds	Stake to win 100, including stake returned
1	4 – 1	20
2	4 – 1	20
3	4 – 1	20
4	5 – 1	16.67
5	6 – 1	14.28
6	7 – 1	12.5
7	5 – 1	16.67
		120.12 total stake
		100.00 less payout
		20.12 profit

$$\frac{20}{100} = 20\%$$

(Puzzle 82)

10 Link Word

House

(Puzzle 3)

11 Three Too Many

R	E	D	U	C	E	D
E	■	E	■	A	■	E
V	I	S	I	T	O	R
I	■	I	■	E	■	I
S	U	G	A	R	E	D
E	■	N	■	E	■	E
D	E	S	I	R	E	D

(Puzzle 42)

12 "X" Puzzle

Tax	Taxi	Axis	Taxis
Taxed	Axe	Axed	Six
Fix	Fixed	Fixer	Rex
Exam	Maxim	Maxims	Maxi
Maxis	Ax	Ox	Box
Boxed	Boxer	Lax	Lox
Laxed	Exalt	Exams	Mix
Mixed	Mixer	Laxer	Taxied

(Puzzle 122)

13 Triple Choice

1. (a) Red-flowered tree
2. (c) Entrance to the windpipe
3. (A) Date-plum
4. (a) Exaggerated speech
5. (a) Relative of raccoon
6. (a) Bow-legged
7. (a) Arm band
8. (c) Italian ice cream

(Puzzle 83)

14 Committee

Assume two women and four men

Then $$\frac{4 \times 3}{2 \times 1} \times \frac{7 \times 6 \times 5 \times 4}{4 \times 3 \times 2 \times 1} = 6 \times 35 = 210$$

Assume three women and three men

Then $$\frac{4 \times 3 \times 2}{3 \times 2 \times 1} \times \frac{7 \times 6 \times 5}{3 \times 2 \times 1} = 4 \times 35 = 140$$

Assume four women and two men

Then $$\frac{4 \times 3 \times 2 \times 1}{4 \times 3 \times 2 \times 1} \times \frac{7 \times 6}{2 \times 1} = 1 \times 21 = 21$$

$$\overline{371}$$

Can be written as

$$\frac{4! - 2!}{2!} \times \frac{7! - 3!}{4!}$$

$$+ \quad \frac{4! - 1!}{3!} \times \frac{7! - 4!}{3!}$$

$$+ \quad \frac{4!}{4!} \times \frac{7! - 5!}{2!}$$

(Puzzle 43)

15 Playing Cards

Score	VITUPERATION
AC	15 - V
AD	15 - I
AH	15 - T
QC	12 - U
QH	12 - P
AS	15 - E
KS	13 - R
QD	12 - A
QS	12 - T
KH	13 - I
KC	13 - O
KD	13 - N
	160

(Puzzle 123)

16 Common Clues

They are pairs of homonyms: Pique, Peak; Tool, Tulle; Need, Knead; Band, Banned; Review, Revue; Gauge, Gage; Invade, Inveighed.

(Puzzle 4)

17 Circles

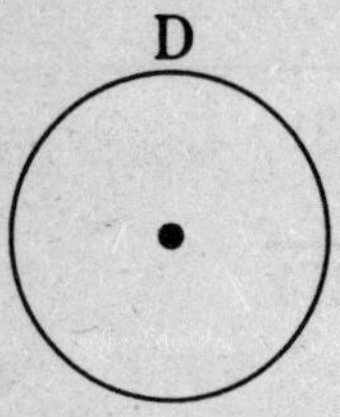

Starting at the base, each pair of circles determines the one above. Similar symbols only are carried forward.

(Puzzle 84)

18 Odd One Out

C:
A is the same as D
B is the same as G
E is the same as F

(Puzzle 44)

19 Biblical Characters

Hiram, Ephraim, Barnabas, Aaron, Timothy, Benjamin, Shadrach, Abraham, Herod.
Anagram: Bathsheba

(Puzzle 124)

20 Comparison

A.

(Puzzle 5)

21 Two Letters

OX – OXEN
NO – NOES
(As in, for example, "the ayes to the right, the noes to the left.")

(Puzzle 85)

22 Subtraction

22:
Subtract the number of letters in the previous number each time. For example, one hundred (10 letters), therefore 100 − 10 = 90. Ninety (6 letters), therefore 90 − 6 = 84.

(Puzzle 45)

23 Treasure

G1.

(Puzzle 125)

24 Connections

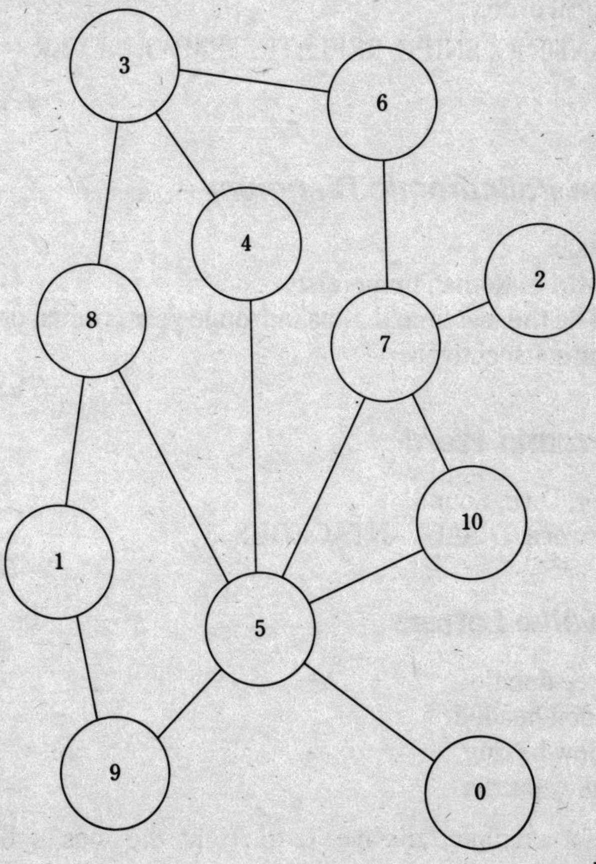

Puzzle 6)

25 Anagram Phrases

1. Hoist with one's own petard
2. To kill two birds with one stone
3. To keep a low profile
4. To overstay one's welcome
5. What's cooking

(Puzzle 86)

26 Sequence

Never:
The middle letter of each word is a roman numeral in alphabetical order.

ACE, LANDING, SNIPE, REFLATE, TEMPO, NEVER

(Puzzle 46)

27 The Palindromic Biennium

1999 – 2000:
MIM – MM in Roman numerals!
This will be the last time that palindromic years roman or arabic will occur consecutively.

(Puzzle 126)

28 Pyramid Word

A, At, Sag, Dive, Sound
15-letter word: DISADVANTAGEOUS

(Puzzle 7)

29 Twelve Letters

(1) Yankee-doodle
(2) Wooden-headed
(3) Shadow-boxing
(4) Monkey-puzzle

(Puzzle 8)

30 Segments

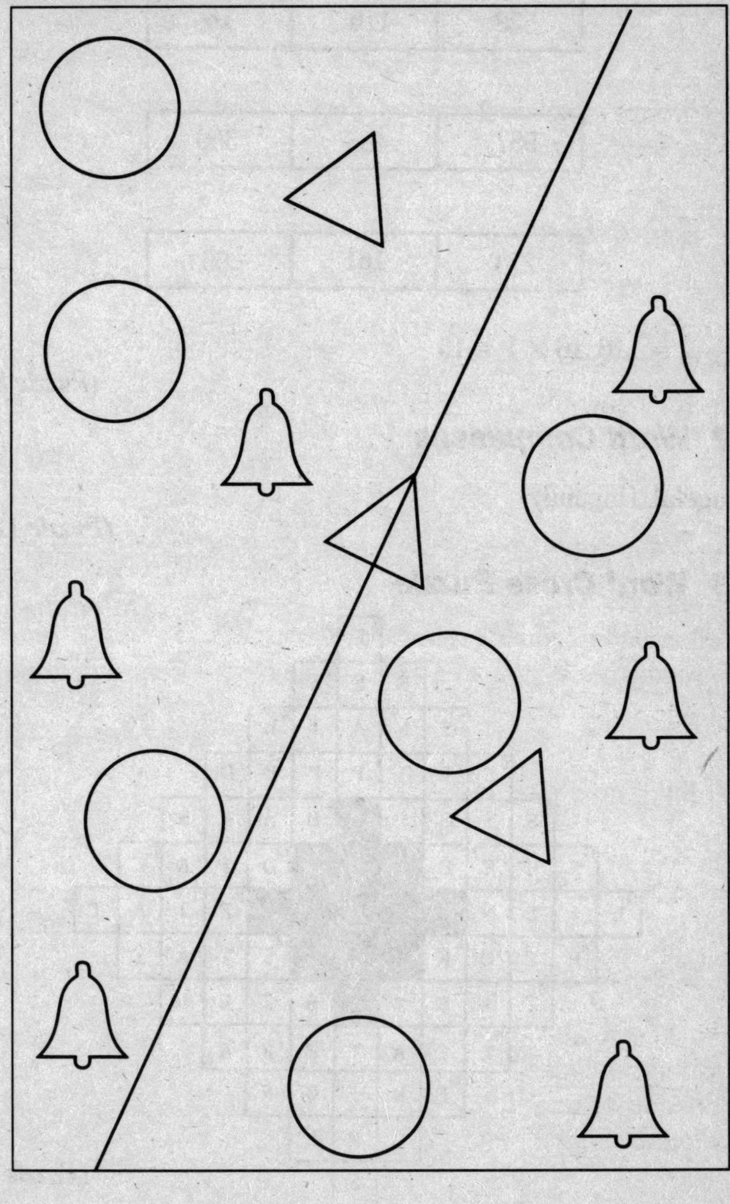

(Puzzle 47)

31 Missing Links

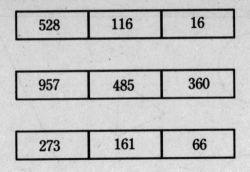

528	116	16

957	485	360

273	161	66

$58 \times 2 = 116$, $16 \times 1 = 16$

(Puzzle 87)

32 Word Compasses

Graceful, Ungainly

(Puzzle 127)

33 Word Cross Puzzle

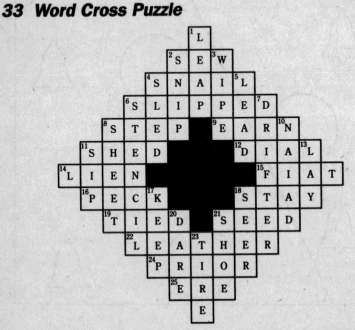

						1 L						
					2 S	E	3 W					
				4 S	N	A	I	5 L				
			6 S	L	I	P	P	E	7 D			
		8 S	T	E	P	■	9 E	A	R	10 N		
	11 S	H	E	D	■	■	■	12 D	I	A	13 L	
14 L	I	E	N	■	■	■	■	■	15 F	I	A	T
	16 P	E	C	17 K	■	■	■	18 S	T	A	Y	
		19 T	I	E	20 D	■	21 S	E	E	D		
			22 L	E	A	23 T	H	E	R			
				24 P	R	I	O	R				
					25 E	R	E					
						E						

(Puzzle 48)

34 Decadice

Lose

1-1	2-1	3-1	4-1	5-1	6-1	7-1	8-1	9-1	10-1
1-2	2-2	3-2	4-2	5-2	6-2	7-2	8-2	9-2	10-2
1-3	2-3	3-3	4-3	5-3	6-3	7-3	8-3	9-3	10-3
1-4	2-4	3-4	4-4	5-4	6-4	7-4	8-4	9-4	10-4
1-5	2-5	3-5	4-5	5-5	6-5	7-5	8-5	9-5	10-5
1-6	2-6	3-4	4-6	5-6	6-6	7-6	8-6	9-6	10-6
1-7	2-7	3-7	4-7	5-7	6-7	7-7	8-7	9-7	10-7
1-8	2-8	3-8	4-8	5-8	6-8	7-8	8-8	9-8	10-8
1-9	2-9	3-9	4-9	5-9	6-9	7-9	8-9	9-9	10-9
1-10	2-10	3-10	4-10	5-10	6-10	7-10	8-10	9-10	10-10

Win

Lose	Win
9	1
8	2
7	3
6	4
5	5
4	6
3	7
2	8
1	9
–	10
45	55

Win 55–45 Lose
or 55–45 Odds on

(Puzzle 88)

35 Triangles

A. There are three triangles. The middle triangle remains stationary and the two outer triangles are folded inwards along their adjoining edges of the middle triangle.

(Puzzle 128)

36 Pyramidal Logic

D

By logical process of elimination this is the only possible answer. Each symbol is linked to the two symbols below it. The same symbol never appears above the two symbols below it.
The symbols are produced as follows:

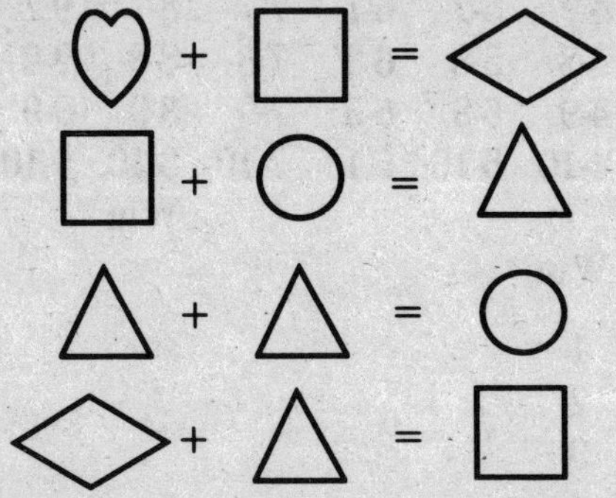

So that  +  must equal something completely different to anything above. Of the other options shown this can only be 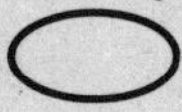.

(Puzzle 9)

37 Elliptical Illusion

A. The right-hand ellipse is moving across the left-hand ellipse. In the second stage it has moved across so that it touches the left-hand ellipse halfway across top and bottom. In the third stage it completely covers the left-hand ellipse.

In the answer, option A, it has reappeared having moved the same distance again and, in fact, now becomes the left-hand ellipse.

(Puzzle 89)

38 Square

D	O	G
A	O	O
B	A	T

Dog
Bat
God
Tab
Got
Tog
Dab
Bad
Gob
Bog
Dot
Tod

(Puzzle 49)

39 Fish

		Added letter
Basking	Shark	S
Striped	Catfish	T
Painted	Dragonet	A
Crusted	Flounder	R
Butterfly	Bream	B
Scarlet	Angler	L
Horse	Mackerel	R
Barred	Garfish	R
Brown	Groper	R
Spiny	Seahorse	S

(Puzzle 129)

40 Analogy

6512:

3694 : $\frac{63}{7}\ \frac{49}{7} = 97$

5382 : $\frac{35}{7}\ \frac{28}{7} = 54$

6512 : $\frac{56}{7}\ \frac{21}{7} = 83$

(Puzzle 10)

41 No Repeat Letters

Judicatory

(Puzzle 90)

42 Missing Number

$144 \div 9 = 16, \sqrt{16} = 4$

$112 \div 7 = 16, \sqrt{16} = 4$

$192 \div 12 = 16, \sqrt{16} = \textcircled{4}$

(Puzzle 50)

43 Aliens

To solve this problem use a Venn diagram.

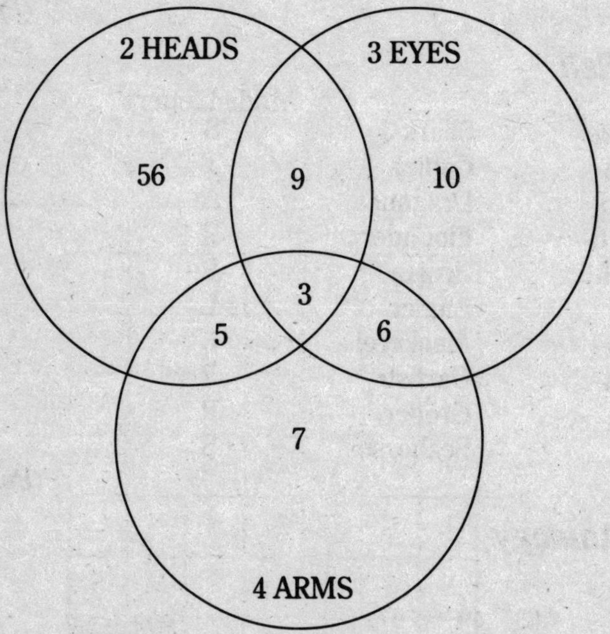

$$\begin{array}{lr} & 100 \\ 10 + 56 + 9 + 3 + 5 + 6 + 7 = & 96 \\ \hline \text{Answer} & 4 \end{array}$$

(Puzzle 130)

44 Racetrack

1 – 1 – 4 – 4 – 3 – 14
Other answers are possible.

(Puzzle 11)

45 Rebuses

1. Dark Ages
2. Paradise
3. Fortunes
4. Soon after that

(Puzzle 91)

46 Bracket Word

GEOGRAPHICAL

(Puzzle 51)

47 Saying

"Always forgive your enemies, nothing annoys them so much."
– *Oscar Wilde*

A	L	W	A	Y	S	F
O	R	G	I	V	E	Y
O	U	R	E	N	E	M
I	E	S	N	O	T	H
I	N	G	A	N	N	O
Y	S	T	H	E	M	S
O	M	U	C	H		

(Puzzle 131)

48 Magic Word Square

P	U	M	A	S
U	L	E	M	A
M	E	D	A	L
A	M	A	Z	E
S	A	L	E	M

(Puzzle 12)

49 Grid

2C.

(Puzzle 92)

50 Nursery Rhyme Crossword

V	E	N	I	S	O	N
I	■	I	■	H	■	O
C	O	N	C	E	P	T
U	■	E	■	A	■	I
N	E	P	H	R	I	C
A	■	I	■	E	■	E
S	E	N	O	R	A	S

(Puzzle 52)

51 Symbols

A.

(Puzzle 132)

52 *Letter Change*

1. Pros and cons
2. To bill and coo
3. To let fly
4. A leg up
5. So long
6. Cry quits
7. Dead set
8. To cut it fine
9. Fall guy
10. To zip up

(Puzzle 13)

53 *Cryptogram*

"If a little knowledge is dangerous, where is the man who has so much as to be out of danger?" – *T. H. Huxley*

(Puzzle 93)

54 *Symbols*

B.

(Puzzle 53)

55 *Found in America*

1. Daytona Beach
2. Staten Island
3. The Statue of Liberty
4. The Sears Tower
5. Blue Mountains
6. Sierra Nevada
7. Death Valley
8. Dodge City
9. Colorado Plateau
10. Baton Rouge

(Puzzle 133)

56 *Grid*

1C.

(Puzzle 14)

57 Magic Square

5	2	11	22	25
16	18	9	12	10
23	7	13	19	3
20	14	17	8	6
1	24	15	4	21

(Puzzle 94)

58 Round Table

Twelve different ways:
Calling the people 1, 2, 3, 4, 5, it is irrelevant where 1 is seated. The remaining four people can be seated in 4! or $4 \times 3 \times 2 \times 1 = 24$ ways. However, as left and right are considered the same, the answer is $24 \div 2 = 12$ different ways.

(Puzzle 54)

59 Work it Out

7:
$15 + 21 = 36 \qquad \sqrt{36} + \sqrt{1} = 7$

Similarly in the first two triangles:
$12 + 13 = 25 \qquad \sqrt{25} + \sqrt{9} = 8$
$42 + 22 = 64 \qquad \sqrt{64} + \sqrt{4} = 10$

(Puzzle 134)

60 Pyramid Quotation

M, To, Ask, What, Axial, Tonsil, Martini

(Puzzle 95)

61 Magic Square

L	A	R	G	O
A	L	E	R	T
R	E	M	I	T
G	R	I	P	E
O	T	T	E	R

(Puzzle 15)

62 15-Letter Words

1. Prestidigitator
2. Inconsequential
3. Comprehensively
4. Surreptitiously
5. Electrification

(Puzzle 55)

63 Three Birds and a Fish

Three birds and a fish

(Puzzle 135)

64 Star

Harlequinade

(Puzzle 16)

65 Words

All words can be prefixed with EN-:
Entry, Enable, Enduring, Enshrine, Enviable, Envision, Engrave, Ensign.

(Puzzle 96)

66 Curve

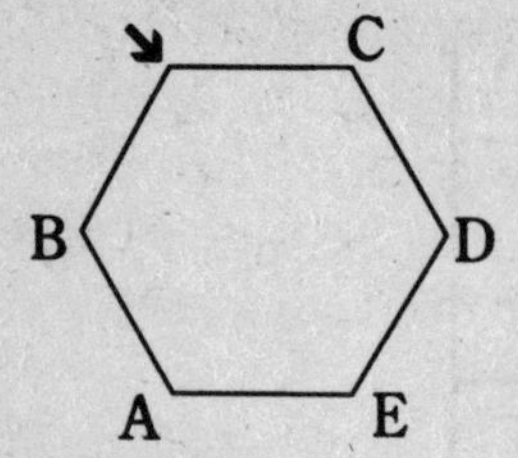

D. The curve has its pivot on the corner of the hexagon indicated below at all times. The curve moves clockwise around this pivot and adjusts its length to join corners A, B, C, D, and E in turn.

(Puzzle 56)

67 Dots Matrix

B. The end square in each horizontal and vertical line is determined by the contents of the previous two squares. The two previous squares are combined to form the third square. However, where two black spots appear in the same position in the previous two squares they appear as a white spot in the third square, and where two white spots coincide they appear as a black spot in the third square.

(Puzzle 136)

68 Analogy

C. One figure is superimposed on the other but only the internal lines are produced (i.e., only lines common to both figures appear).

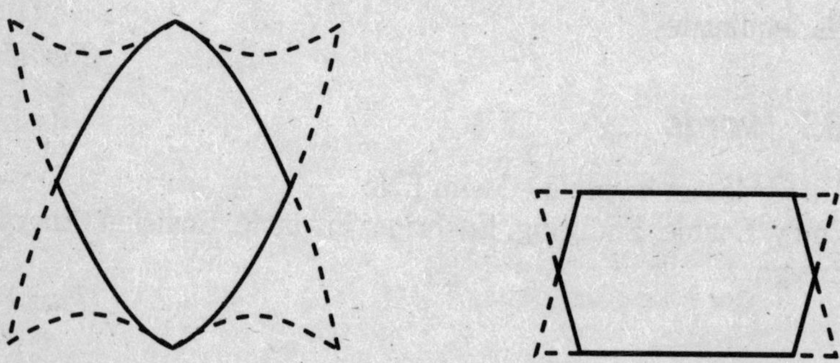

(Puzzle 17)

69 The Hexagonal Pyramid

B. The contents of each pyramid from the second row up are determined by the contents of the two pyramids below it. All lines are carried forward with the complication that if two straight lines coincide in the same position they become a curved line in the pyramid above, and if two curved lines coincide they become straight.

(Puzzle 97)

70 Common

They all contain the names of creatures spelled backward.

1. Gnu	6. Cat
2. Nag	7. Wolf
3. Ram	8. Bat
4. Nit	9. Ape
5. Dog	10. Asp

(Puzzle 57)

71 Bull's Eye

1. Chicory (anag. HRCYCOI)
2. Lower fair domain
3. Toponym
4. Las Vegas (anag.)
5. Red eye
6. Dirty room
7. Apostrophe
8. Impeccable
9. Supine equine
10. Aced (hijacked)
11. Catacomb
12. Coracle (anag. LCCEARO)
13. Restore the plush (anag.)
14. Kittiwake
15. Model
16. Antibiotic

(Puzzle 137)

72 Lawns

$1987 = 27^2 + 27^2 + 23^2$
$1987 = 33^2 + 27^2 + 13^2$
$1987 = 39^2 + 21^2 + 5^2$
$1987 = 41^2 + 15^2 + 9^2$

Only $27^2 + 27^2 + 23^2$ fits the question.

(Puzzle 18)

73 Mixed Currency

Ecuador	–	Sucre
Haiti	–	Gourde
Ethiopia	–	Birr
Guinea	–	Syli
Indonesia	–	Rupiah
Honduras	–	Lempira
Israel	–	Shekel
Malawi	–	Kwacha
Morocco	–	Dirham
Nicaragua	–	Cordoba
Nigeria	–	Naira
Swaziland	–	Lilangeni

(Puzzle 98)

74 Alphabet Clueless-Cross

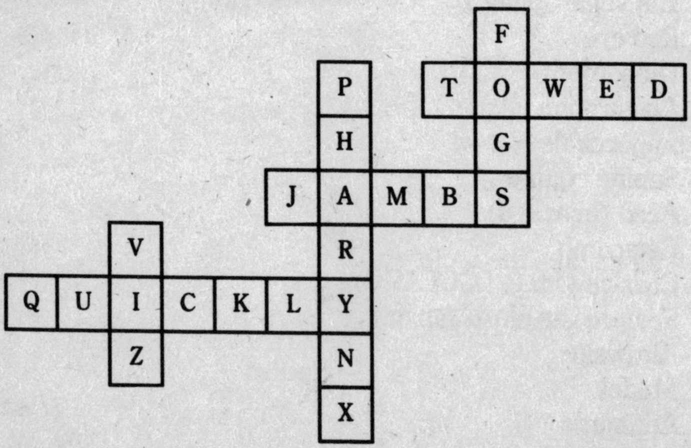

(Puzzle 58)

75 Cycle

(Take π as $\frac{22}{7}$)

Then $C = \frac{22}{7} \times 28 = 88$ inches

Number of revolutions

$$= \frac{1760 \times 3 \times 12}{88}$$

$$= 720$$

(Puzzle 138)

76 Unkind Observation

"No matter how well a toupee blends in back, it always looks like hell in front." – *Sam Levenson*

(Puzzle 19)

77 Fence

	Takes	Reciprocal	Decimal
1 man	6	$\frac{1}{6}$	.166
1 man	3	$\frac{1}{3}$	.333
1 man	2	$\frac{1}{2}$	.500
1 man	4	$\frac{1}{3}$	.250
	Add		1.250

Now again take the reciprocal

$$\therefore \quad \frac{1}{1.250} = .8 \text{ hrs}$$

$$\therefore \quad .8 \times 60 = 48 \text{ minutes}$$

(Puzzle 99)

78 Alphametics

$$
\begin{array}{r}
37413 \\
733 \\
9173 \\
\hline
47319
\end{array}
$$

(Puzzle 59)

79 Pyramid

A
P A
H E R B
C A N T E R

(Puzzle 139)

80 Links Jigsaw Puzzle

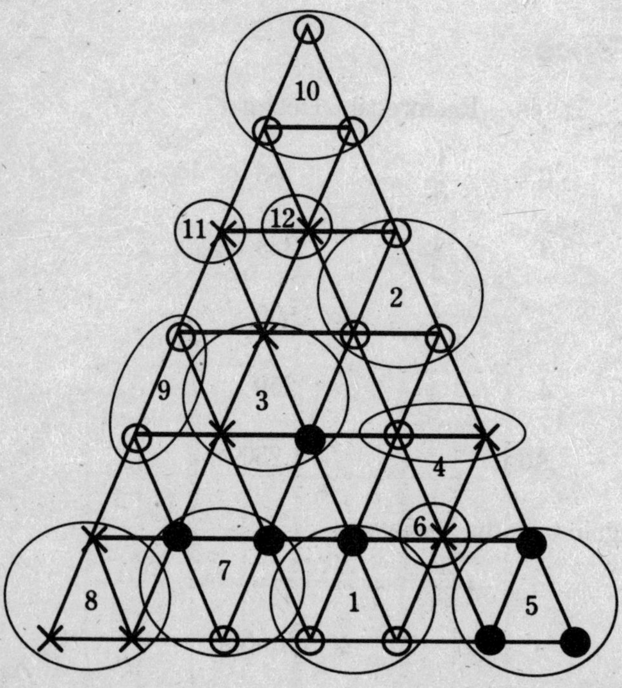

(Puzzle 20)

81 Nine Letters

1. Tautology
2. Pitchfork
3. Nitpicker
4. Lairdship
5. Haranguer
6. Diagnosis
7. Chanteuse
8. Blotchily

(Puzzle 100)

82 Sequence

B:
In each successive circle

•⟶	moves 45° counter-clockwise
•—○	moves 135° clockwise
•—×	moves 45° clockwise
•—•	moves 135° clockwise

(Puzzle 60)

83 Division

S	P	P	O	T	S	S	R
T	M	E	U	S	U	S	O
U	E	U	U	P	U	R	T
S	P	S	E	P	U	O	U
S	O	R	S	E	E	N	P
R	M	S	N	M	N	S	U
N	S	E	U	M	S	E	E
T	S	P	U	S	P	S	U

Presumptuousness

(Puzzle 140)

84 Bertrand's Paradox

Knowing that a drawer of either chest B or C has been opened would lead most people to believe that the probability is 1/2. However we are dealing here with drawers and not chests. The answer is actually 1/3.

The three drawers containing silver coins represent equally likely cases, and only one of these is favourable. That is the drawer with the silver coin in chest C. The probability that chest C has been opened is initially 1/3 and remains 1/3 when a drawer has been opened and found to have a silver coin, because gold and silver are distributed identically over drawers and chests. Someone having gambled on chest C would not regard his chances as better or worse after a silver coin has been found in the first drawer to be opened.

(Puzzle 21)

85 Grid

1C.

(Puzzle 101)

86 Network

ARCHAEOLOGICAL

(Puzzle 61)

87 Symbols

A.

(Puzzle 141)

88 Stacking Cubes

Taking just one die any one of six faces can be chosen as a base. These six faces can each be rotated 90° so that any one of four faces is at the front. This gives $6 \times 4 = 24$ different ways of positioning one cube. The same applies for each of the eight dice that are stacked to form the cube. The number of different ways in which they can be stacked, therefore, is 24^8, or 110,075,314,176.

(Puzzle 102)

89 The Enigma Diamond

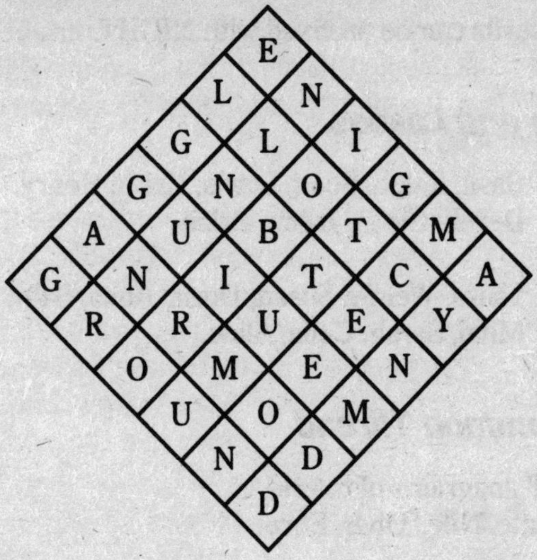

Or rotations of the same grid.

(Puzzle 22)

90 Array

70:
Reading across they are groups of Pythagorean numbers.

$17^2 = 15^2 + 8^2$

$82^2 = 18^2 + 80^2$

$45^2 = 27^2 + 36^2$

$70^2 = 42^2 + 56^2$

(Puzzle 62)

91 Sweepstake

60479 to 1:
The number of ways in which the drawing of the six balls is possible is $9 \times 8 \times 7 \times 6 \times 5 \times 4 = 60480$.

or $\dfrac{9!}{3!} = \dfrac{9 \times 8 \times 7 \times 6 \times 5 \times 4 \times 3 \times 2 \times 1}{3 \times 2 \times 1}$

(Puzzle 142)

92 Find Another Word

FALL. All words can be prefixed with NIGHT.

(Puzzle 23)

93 Lads and Lasses

Across: Basil, Ralph, Scott, Lewis, Keith, Henry, Derek, Gavin, Jason, Brian

Down: Laura, Wendy, Susan, Doris, Anita, Sally, Mitzi, Sarah, Celia, Alice.

(Puzzle 103)

94 A Common Thread

They are all anagrams of rivers:
Hudson, Plate, Nile, Tiber, Ebro.

(Puzzle 63)

95 Piecemeal Quotation

"Whenever you save five shillings you put a man out of work for a day."

(Puzzle 143)

96 Circles Matrix

C. Looking both across and down, the figures in the first two circles are merged to produce the figure in the final circle, and the sections common to all components are shaded.

(Puzzle 24)

97 Sequence

D. It is the numbers 1, 2, 3, 4, 5 laid on their side. If in doubt look at the page sideways.

(Puzzle 64)

98 Group Puzzle

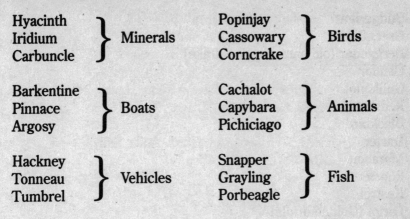

Hyacinth, Iridium, Carbuncle	Minerals	Popinjay, Cassowary, Corncrake	Birds
Barkentine, Pinnace, Argosy	Boats	Cachalot, Capybara, Pichiciago	Animals
Hackney, Tonneau, Tumbrel	Vehicles	Snapper, Grayling, Porbeagle	Fish

(Puzzle 104)

99 Series

The series describes the shape of letters of the alphabet.
i.e., A = Straight, Straight, Straight = SSS

The series is the run of letters
I – J – K – L – M – N – O – ?

Answer is P = SC (Straight line/Curved line).

(Puzzle 144)

100 Arcs Matrix

G. Looking both across and down, the final square is arrived at by combining the contents of the previous two squares, with the exception that lines that are common to the first two squares are not carried forward.

(Puzzle 105)

101 Word Search

Budgerigar
Greenfinch
Bergander (old name for Sheldrake)
Gander
Guillemot
Redshank
Blackbird
Darter
Marabou
Rooster
Kestrel
Loriot (Golden oriole)
Auk
Cob
Emu
Owl
Ruc (old form of Roc)
Roc
Plover
Daw
Mew
Finch

(Puzzle 25)

102 Countries

Paraguay	Mongolia
Tanzania	Sardinia
Cambodia	Honduras
Pakistan	Portugal
Zanzibar	Zimbabwe
Malaysia	Barbados
Rhodesia	Bulgaria
Scotland	Trinidad

(Puzzle 65)

103 Circles

B. There are five circles, in order of size A, B, C, D, E. The largest circle A remains stationary. The remaining circles move around the circumference of A as follows:

Circle B moves clockwise 90°
Circle C moves clockwise 45°
Circle D moves clockwise 45°
Circle E moves counter-clockwise 45°

(Puzzle 145)

104 Number

2:
(10 ÷ 2) + 5 − 8 = 2

(Puzzle 26)

105 Enigmagram

Caravel
Frigate
Gunboat
Pinnace

Key: FELUCCA

(Puzzle 106)

106 Soccer Ball

18 squares
8 triangles

(Puzzle 66)

107 Ten Letters

C O ~~T~~ N ~~E~~ G ~~N~~ R ~~L~~ A ~~E~~ T ~~T~~ U L ~~T~~ A T ~~E~~ I O ~~R~~ N S ~~S~~

(Puzzle 146)

108 Diamond

Anabas	Bass
Bret (Turbot)	Blenny
Brill	Bib (Whiting Pout)
Brit	Dab
Eel	Tuna
Char	Chub

(Puzzle 27)

109 Tennis

If there were 41 men in the singles there must have been 1 winner and 40 losers. So there must have been 40 matches. Therefore:

	Matches
Men's singles	40
Women's singles	28
Men's doubles	19
Women's doubles	13
Mixed doubles	25
	125

(Puzzle 107)

110 Niners

Across
1. Departure
4. Confiding
5. Negotiate

Diagonal
1. Dalliance
5. Nigritude

Down
1. Depiction
2. Routinist
3. Emergence

(Puzzle 67)

111 Cylinder

Volume:

Cylinder: $\frac{\pi d^2 h}{4} = \frac{\pi d^3}{4}$ (since d = h)

Sphere: $\frac{4}{3}\pi r^3 = \frac{\pi d^3}{6}$

Cone: $\frac{1}{3}\frac{\pi d^2 h}{4} = \frac{\pi d^3}{12}$

Ratio is therefore

3 : 2 : 1

Cylinder : sphere : cone

(Puzzle 147)

112 Circles

68:

93 − 17 (÷ 4) = 19

45 − 13 (÷ 4) = 8

68 − 24 (÷ 4) = 11

(Puzzle 28)

113 No Repeat Letters

Toweringly

(Puzzle 108)

114 Treasure

1A.

(Puzzle 29)

115 Logic

iv 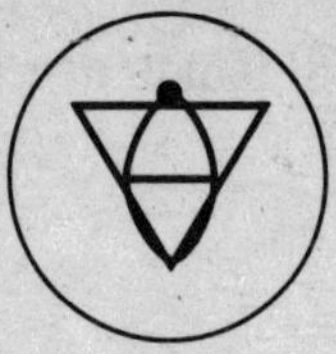

Row 1	A is added to B = C
Row 2	A is added to B = C
Row 3	A is added to B = C
Column A	1 is added to 2 = 3
Column B	1 is added to 2 = 3
Column C	1 is added to 2 = 3

But similar symbols disappear.

(Puzzle 68)

116 Sequence

B:
In each circle

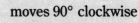

▷ moves 90° clockwise

△ moves 180° clockwise

○ moves 90° clockwise

● moves 225° clockwise

(Puzzle 148)

117 Percussion

Marimba, Castanets, Tabor

(Puzzle 69)

118 Links Jigsaw Puzzle

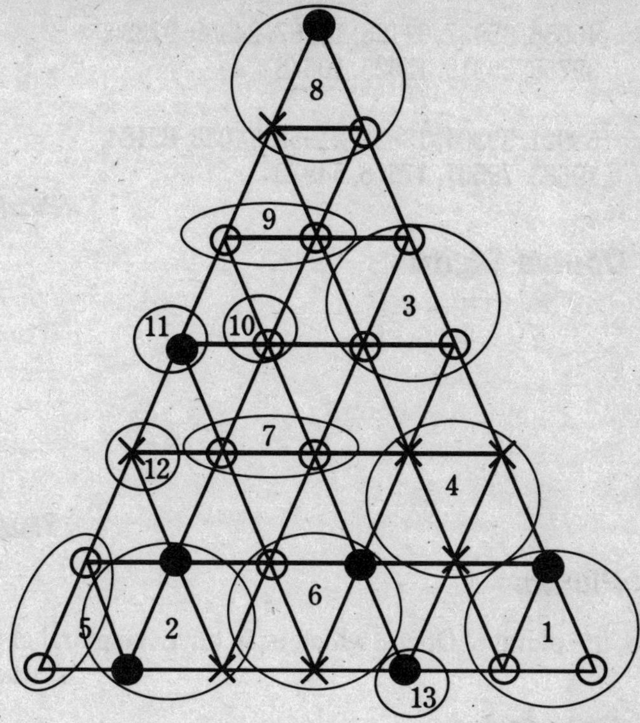

(Puzzle 109)

119 Letter Search

1. Q 2. S 3. L 4. P

(Puzzle 149)

120 The Enigmasig Wheel

NAVIGABLE (Traversable)
IMPASSE (Stalemate)
GODLIKE (Transcendent)
MONOLOGUE (Soliloquy)
AVERSE (Antipathetic)
STORE (Accumulate)
IMPROVE (Ameliorate)
GAUCHE (Unsophisticated)

(Puzzle 30)

121 Cubes

Across: 46656, 35937, 91125, 12167, 24389, 97336, 32768, 59319, 15625, 10648

Down: 68921, 39304, 13824, 21952, 74088, 85184, 19683, 79507, 17576, 54872

(Puzzle 110)

122 Double Digits

```
  179
  224
  ---
  716
 358
358
-----
40096
```

(Puzzle 70)

123 Plurals

Operas, the plural of Opera, which is, in turn, the plural of Opus.

(Puzzle 150)

124 Categories

Lemon, Hazel, Plane	– all trees
Palm, Gum, Foot	– parts of the body
Gold, Fawn, Copper	– all colours
Knot, Perch, Stone	– all measurements

(Puzzle 31)

125 Sequence

100. They are consecutive square numbers, starting with 1 and divided into groups of three numbers.
149, 162, 536, 496, 481, 100
1, 4, 9, 16, 25, 36, 49, 64, 81, 100

(Puzzle 111)

126 Diamonds

A. So that in each line of three, pointing SW/NE and NW/SE there is a black/white/striped circle and a triangle pointing North, South, and East.

(Puzzle 71)

127 Nines

4	8	7	6	2
2	7	3	1	5
7	1	6	9	4
5	8	6	2	6
9	3	5	9	1

(Puzzle 151)

128 Link Word

Down

(Puzzle 32)

129 Sequence

F. Each of the rectangles, after the first three stages, is repeated but rotates 90°. Each of the three internal figures, after the first three stages, is repeated but rotates 180°. The circle appears white/black alternately and the internal figures appear black/white alternately.

(Puzzle 112)

130 Cliff

Say 7 seconds.
Then distance = $16x^2$ feet
$\therefore 16 \times 7 \times 7 = 784$ feet

(Puzzle 113)

131 Anagram Theme

They are all Shakespearean characters whose names have appeared in titles of Shakespeare plays:

OTHELLO (Hell too)
JULIET (Jut lie)
ANTONY (Any not)
CAESAR (Sea car)
TROILUS (Sour lit)
PERICLES (Clip seer)
HAMLET (Halt me)

(Puzzle 72)

132 Analogy

C. This is **almost** a mirror-image puzzle. The shaded sections in the hexagon are **a mirror image** of the shaded sections in the circle and vice-versa, with the added complication that shaded and white sections are reversed in the image.

For example, in a simple version the following would occur:

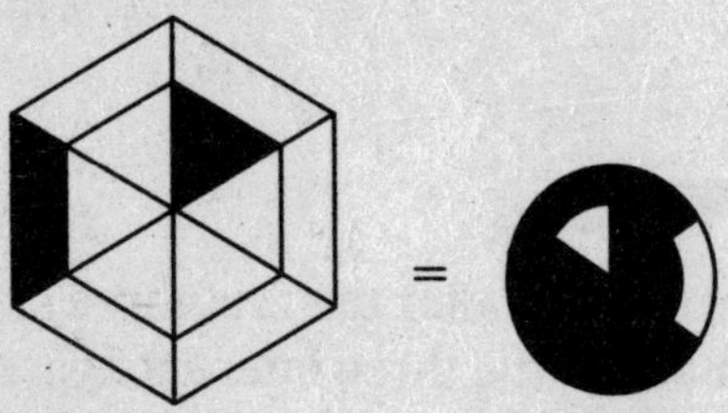

In effect the hexagon has flipped over, turned into a circle, and black has turned to white, white to black.

(Puzzle 152)

133 Zoetrope

Tee – All	Ate – Hal
Ling – Spun	Ibex – Pile
Later – Shaly	Cheer – Jolly

(Puzzle 73)

134 Series

The step each time is to multiply by $-\,^{2}/_{3}$

e.g. $6 \times (-\,^{2}/_{3}) = -4$

We require the 7th term, i.e. $6 \times (-\,^{2}/_{3})^{6}$

$= 6 \times .0878$

$= .5268$

(Puzzle 33)

135 Nine Letters

HIPPODROME

Marsupial Monotreme	Orders of mammals	Sheldrake Merganser	Birds
Whitebeam Jacaranda	Trees	Catamount Dromedary	Animals
Aubergine Mangetout	Vegetables	Fricassee Succotash	Food
Guinevere Argonauts	Mythology	Farandole Poussette	Dances
Nicotiana Pyracantha	Plants	Shillalah Derringer	Weapons
Fomalhaut Aldebaran	Stars	Mercenary Bodyguard	Professionals

(Puzzle 153)

136 The Triangle and Hexagon

C. The hexagon remains stationary and the triangle flips round the sides using as its pivot its southernmost touching point on the hexagon each time and clamping itself on the next available side in a counter-clockwise direction.

(Puzzle 34)

137 Tampa

1. Tango
2. Magma
3. Lymph
4. Kempt
5. Uvula

(Puzzle 114)

138 Darts

Player	A	B	C
	40	23	17
	16	23	17
	16	16	17
	16	16	17
	16	16	16
	16	16	16
	120	110	100

(Puzzle 74)

139 12 Letters

High-stepping
Commencement
Elocutionist
Genealogical
Lantern-jawed
Market-garden
Phonographic
Shrewishness
Shuffleboard
Single-handed

(Puzzle 154)

140 "Z" Puzzle

Buzz	Whiz
Zulu	Fizz
Zip	Dizzy
Fuzzy	Hazy
Muzzy	Dozy
Mazy	Zap
Faze	Viz

(Puzzle 35)

141 Hidden Lands

Swaddles
Opportunist
Interrogation
Conurbation
Pochard
Nationality
Initially
Recommendation
Impervious
Congratulations

(Puzzle 115)

142 Dice

14.7 throws:
Say 2 appears face upwards on the first throw. Then continue until another number appears. The probability of this occuring on the next throw is 5/6, the average number of throws needed to obtain a different number being 6/5. Say the number 6 is next to appear, then it is necessary to continue until a number differing from 2 or 6 appears. The probability of this occuring on the next throw (irrespective of how many throws have occurred up to now) is 4/6. The calculation for all six numbers is therefore:

$$1 + \frac{6}{5} + \frac{6}{4} + \frac{6}{3} + \frac{6}{2} + \frac{6}{1} = 14.7$$

(Puzzle 75)

143 Boat

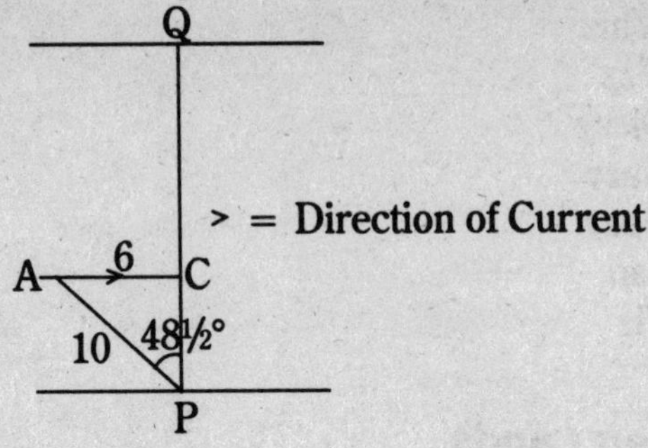

To get from P to Q the rower must head in the direction
$48\frac{1}{2}° = x$
His speed across will be CP
PA = 10
AC = 6

$\therefore \quad (AP)^2 = (AC)^2 + (CP)^2$

$\therefore \quad 10^2 = 6^2 + (CP)^2$

$\therefore \quad (CP)^2 = 10^2 - 6^2$

$\therefore \quad (CP)^2 = 64$

$\therefore \quad CP = \sqrt{64}$

$\therefore \quad CP = 8$ metres per minute

(Puzzle 155)

144 Odd One Out

C:
A is the same as D
E is the same as F
B is the same as G

(Puzzle 36)

145 Links Jigsaw Puzzle

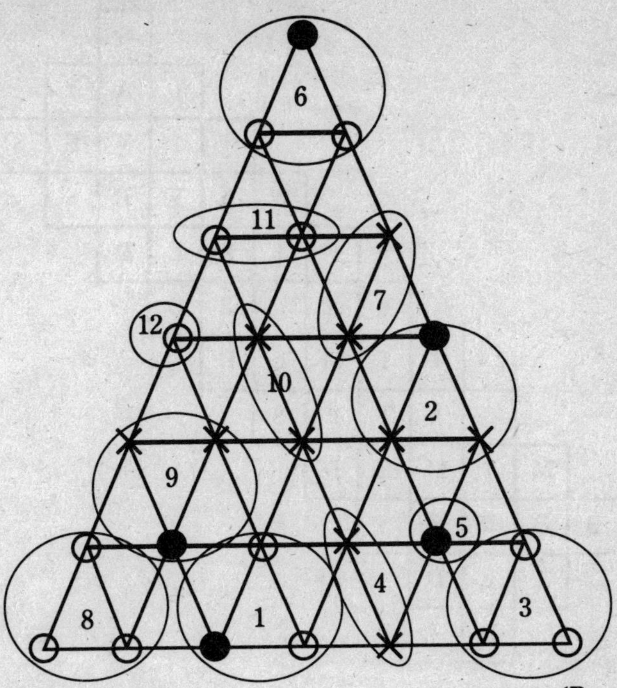

(Puzzle 116)

146 No Blanks

Each pair of circles produces the circle above by carrying forward the elements, but similar elements are cancelled out; e.g.:

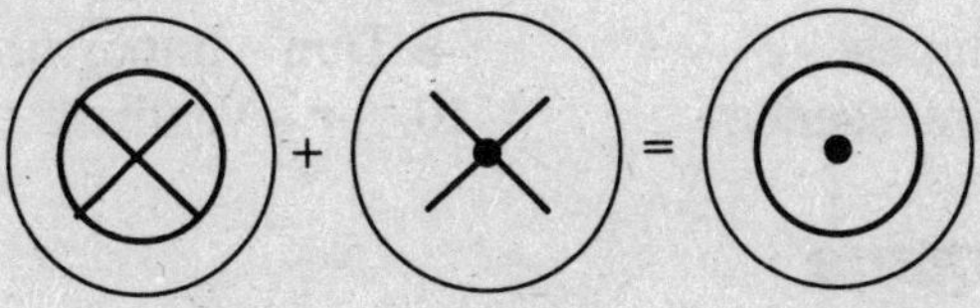

ANSWER

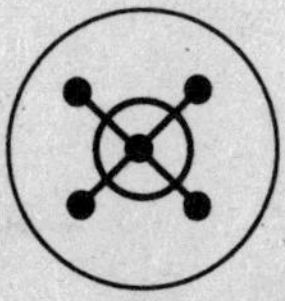

B

(Puzzle 156)

147 No Blanks

									S		
								L	A	Y	
							W	I	V	E	S
						W	A	V	E	S	
					F	I	X	E	D		
				B	A	L	E	D			
			T	I	M	E	D				
		S	A	T	E	S					
	M	I	M	E	D						
B	O	R	E	S							
	T	E	D								
		D									

(Puzzle 76)

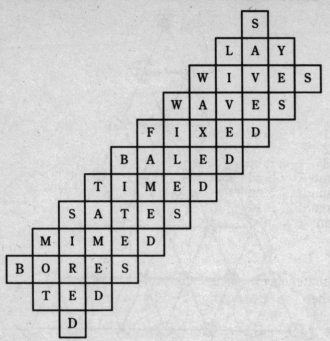

148 Anagrammed Synonyms

1. Hash – Mishmash
2. Load – Shipment
3. Pet – Fondle
4. Gale – Tempest
5. Pith – Quintessence
6. Spur – Impetus
7. Coy – Reserved
8. Blue – Cerulean
9. Dun – Importune
10. Air – Ventilate

(Puzzle 37)

149 Margana

Tenaciously

(Puzzle 117)

150 Synonyms

1. Hurried
2. Palpable
3. Capricious
4. Veiled
5. Salacious

(Puzzle 157)

151 Logic

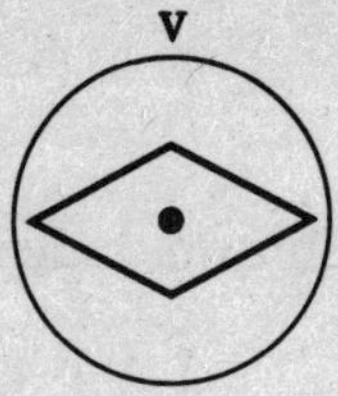

Row 1 A is added to B = C
Row 2 A is added to B = C
Row 3 A is added to B = C
Column A 1 is added to 2 = 3
Column B 1 is added to 2 = 3
Column C 1 is added to 2 = 3
But similar symbols disappear.

(Puzzle 77)

152 Two in One

1. "Imitation is the sincerest form of flattery."
2. "When you have nothing to say, say nothing."

(Puzzle 38)

153 Unscramble a Sequence

Proceed via triangular numbers: 1, 3, 6, 10, 15, 21, 28, 36, 45, 55, 66, 78, 91, 105, 120, 136, 153. Triangular numbers are numbers arranged in triangular form in one layer.

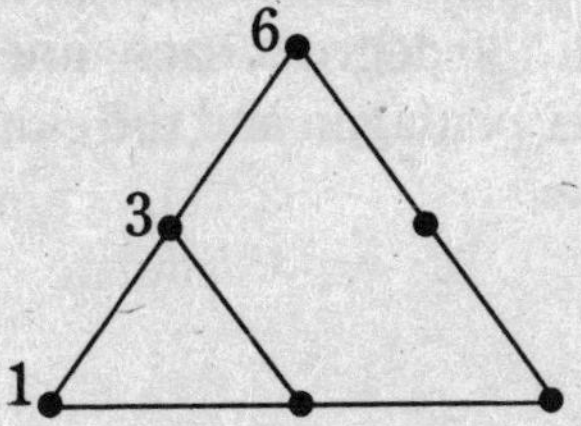

(Puzzle 118)

154 Square Words

Departure, Assertive, Deviation, Merriment, Confident, Joviality.

The three pairs of synonyms are: Departure – Deviation, Assertive – Confident, Merriment – Joviality.

(Puzzle 78)

155 Synonym Circles

Paternal, Fatherly

(Puzzle 159)

156 Sensible

Rational, Prudent, Canny, Shrewd, Judicious, Realistic, Sane

(Puzzle 160)

157 Brain Strain

7	+	8	÷	3	=	5
+	■	×	■	+	■	−
5	+	3	÷	2	=	4
÷	■	÷	■	−	■	+
3	+	6	÷	3	=	3
=	■	=	■	=	■	=
4	+	4	÷	2	=	4

(Puzzle 39)

158 Twist and Turn

E. The shaded segment moves outwards to each portion in turn. The pentagon moves through 180 degrees each time. The diamond moves with the inner pentagon and the ellipse turns 90 degrees within the diamond.

(Puzzle 158)

159 Track Word

Electioneering

(Puzzle 119)

D	Y	N	A	M	I	C
I	■	U	■	E	■	R
G	A	R	B	A	G	E
I	■	S	■	N	■	E
T	R	E	A	T	E	D

(Puzzle 79)

IQ
Countdown

1 Knight's Saying

Using the knight's move as in chess, spell out the message. You have to find the starting point. The two left-over words are the name of the author.

↙FINISH

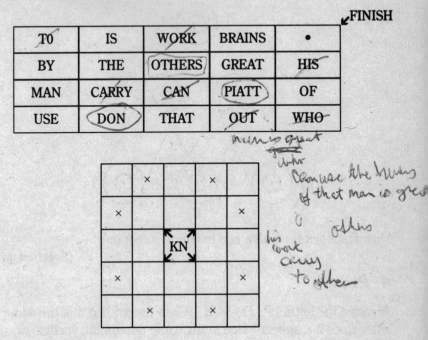

TO	IS	WORK	BRAINS	•
BY	THE	OTHERS	GREAT	HIS
MAN	CARRY	CAN	PIATT	OF
USE	DON	THAT	OUT	WHO

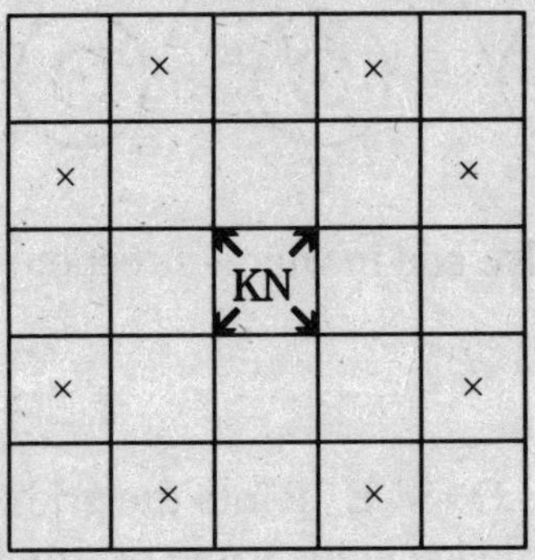

(Solution 3)

2 Centre Word

Find a 3-letter word that completes all three words on the left-hand side and prefixes all three words on the right-hand side.

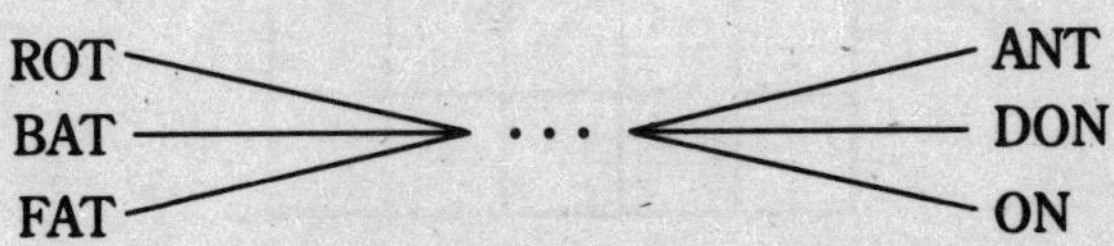

(Solution 7)

3 Pulleys

The inner wheel is 50 per cent of the outer wheel's diameter. A revolves at a speed of 10.

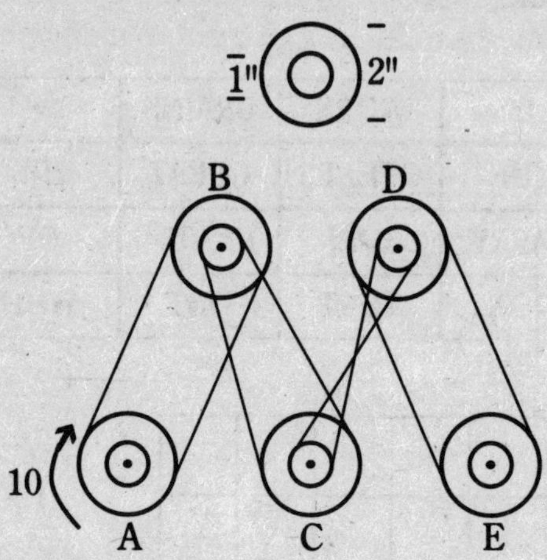

How fast does E revolve and in which direction?

(Solution 11)

4 Poser

Arrange the letters P - O - S - E - R into the grid so that the same letter does not appear twice in the same horizontal, vertical or diagonal line.

P	O	S	E	R

(Solution 15)

5 Grid

Each of the nine squares 1A to 3C should incorporate all the lines and symbols shown in the outer squares A, B or C and 1, 2 or 3. Thus 2B should incorporate all the lines and symbols in 2 and B. One of the squares, 1A to 3C, is incorrect. Which one is it?

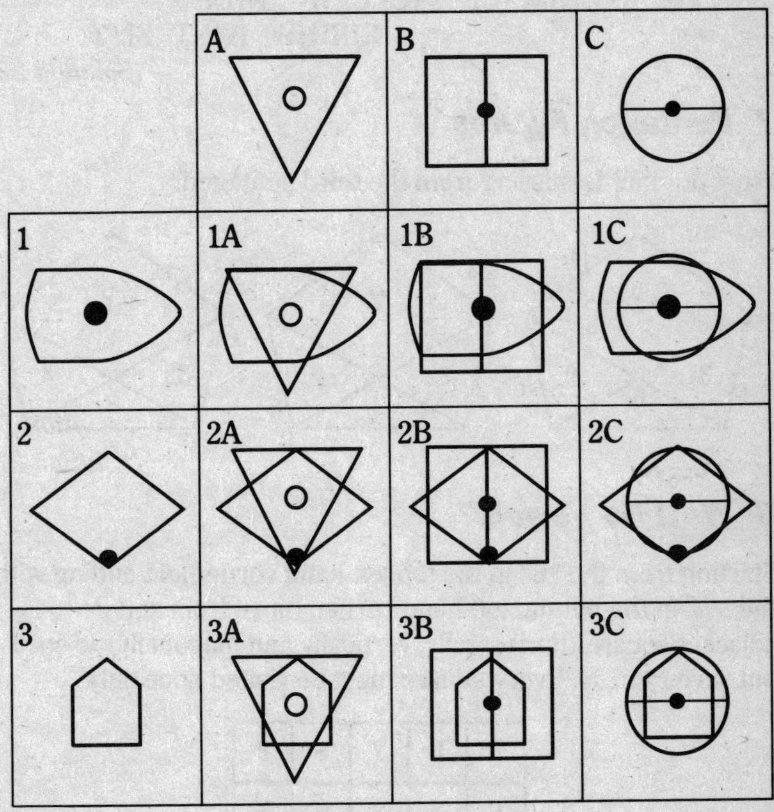

(Solution 19)

6 Cryptogram I

This is a straightforward cryptogram in which each letter of the quotation has been replaced by another.

XW XKHM. JL RKV 'UW ZKJTZ CK ONSW
NT WUUKU, ONSW N MKKER, NTM MKT'C
XW NLUNJM CK PJC CPW XNHH
– XJHHJW IWNT SJTZ

(Solution 22)

7 Pentagon Figures

What number is missing from the third pentagon?

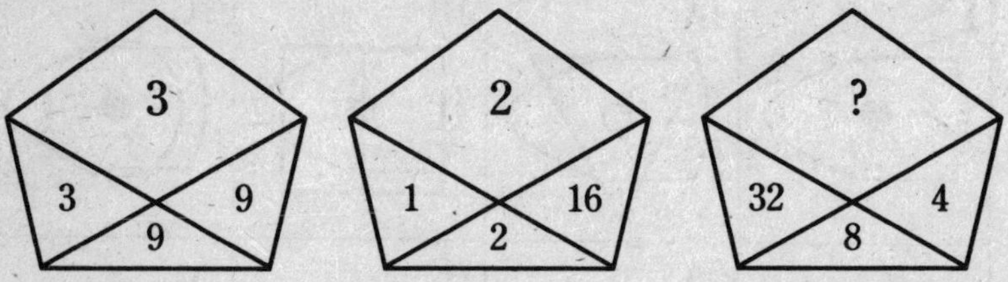

(Solution 27)

8 Wot! No Vowels?

Starting from the "B" in the top left-hand corner and ending with the "Y" in the bottom left-hand corner, move from square to adjacent square (horizontally, vertically and diagonally) to spell out seven words. Every square must be visited once only.

B	L	Y	S	P
P	Y	Y	H	Y
Y	Y	S	M	N
L	L	W	T	R
Y	R	T	S	Y

(Solution 31)

9 Sequence

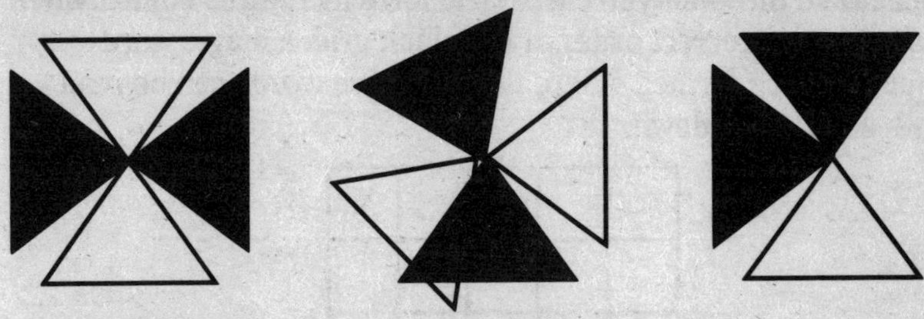

Which option below continues the above sequence?

A

B

C

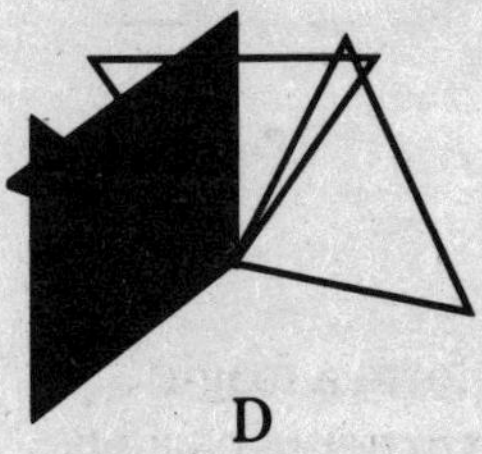

D

E

F

(Solution 35)

10 Children

In a class of thirty children, fifteen can play table tennis and nineteen can play soccer.
Six cannot play either table tennis or soccer.
How many children can play both table tennis and soccer?

(Solution 40)

11 Magic Word Square

Rearrange the twenty-five letters to form five words so that when placed in the correct order in the blank grid, a magic word square will be formed where the same five words can be read both across and down.

				T
			M	
		C		
	M			
T				

A	A	A	A	A
A	~~C~~	D	E	E
G	I	I	L	L
~~M~~	~~M~~	O	O	R
S	~~T~~	~~T~~	V	V

(Solution 43)

12 Magic '65'

Insert the remaining numbers from 1 to 25 to form a magic square whereby each horizontal, vertical and corner-to-corner line totals 65.

20				
				5
				10
		25		
15				

(Solution 47)

13 12 Letters

Find the four 12-letter words (each word consists of two 6-letter parts). The first half is inside the star, the second half is outside the star.

(1) 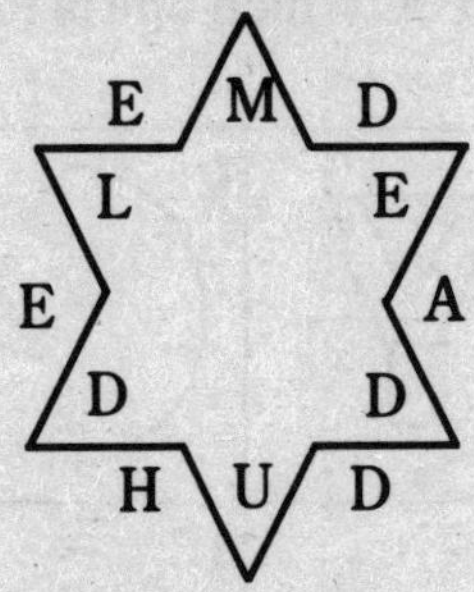

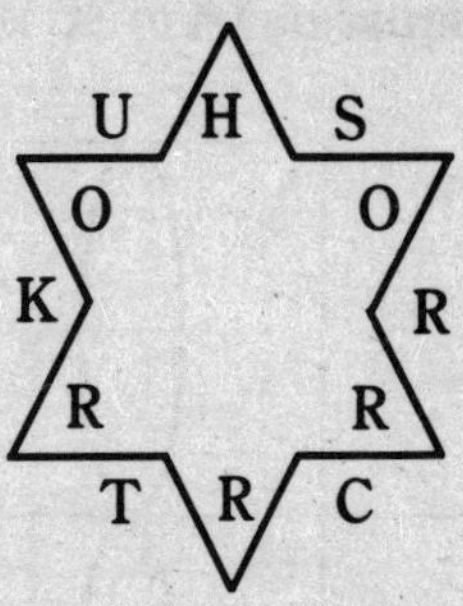 (2)

Clue: Mixed Up!

Clue: Hit by a Ghost!

(3) 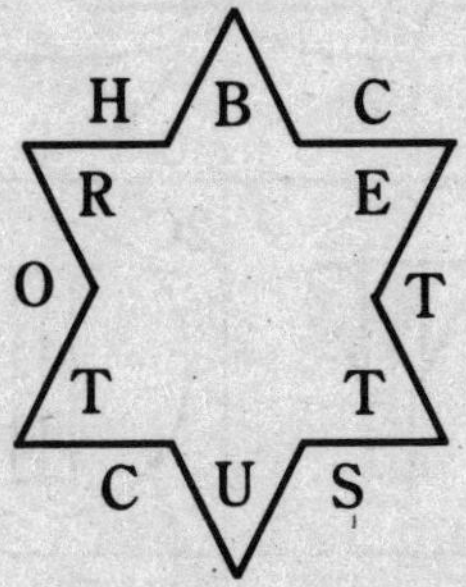

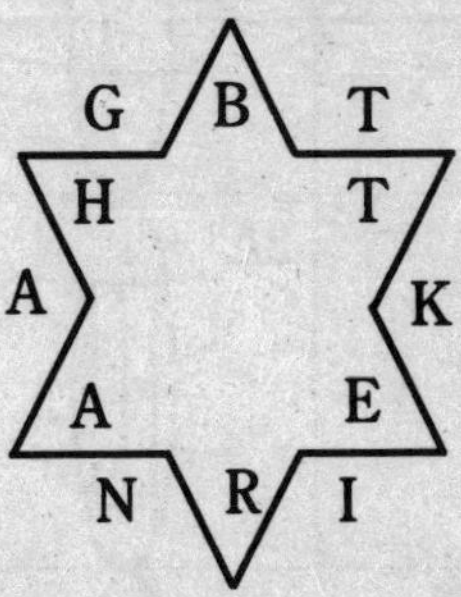 (4)

Clue: Whisky from a Cow?

Clue: Blowing up a Balloon!

(Solution 51)

14 Odd One Out

Who is the odd one out?

Ethel	Noble
Cyril	Lord
Stella	Strong
Clive	Cliff
Lloyd	Grey

(Solution 55)

15 Grid

Each of the nine squares 1A to 3C should incorporate all the lines and symbols shown in the outer squares A, B or C and 1, 2 or 3. Thus 2B should incorporate all the lines and symbols in 2 and B. One of the squares, 1A to 3C is incorrect. Which one is it?

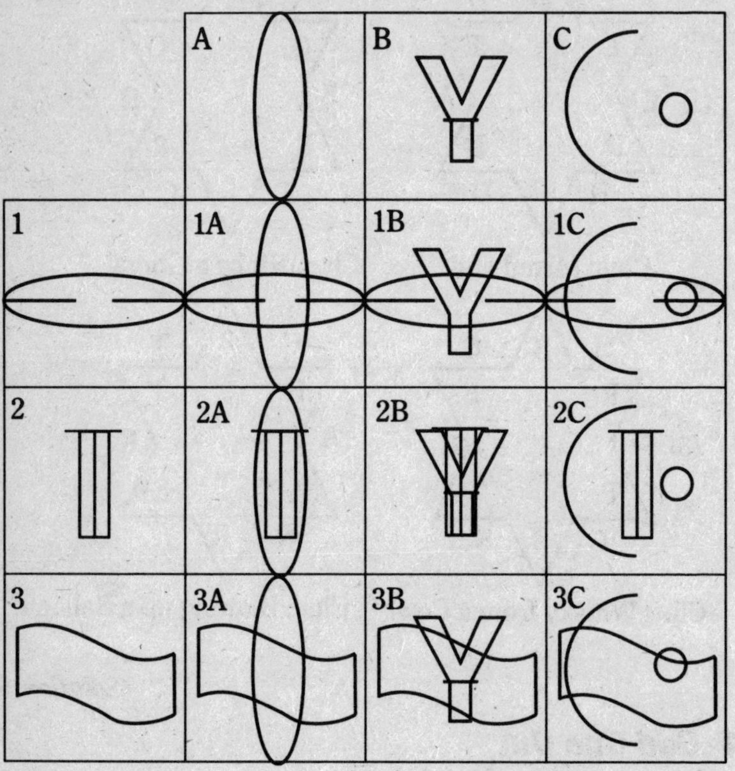

(Solution 59)

16 Do-It-Yourself Diamond Crossword

Insert into the grid all the words listed so that each word travels in a straight line in the direction of one of the compass points indicated.

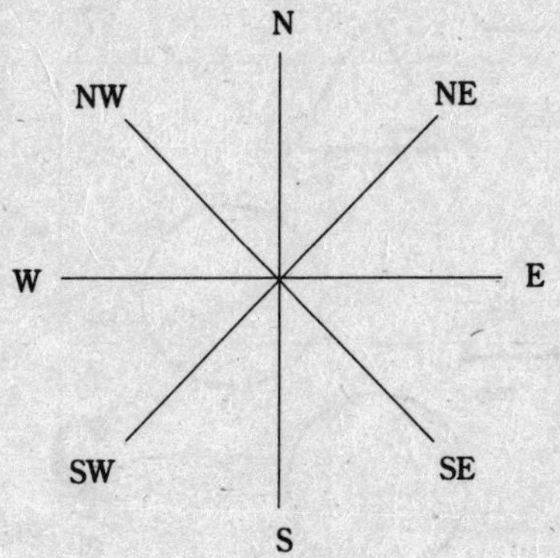

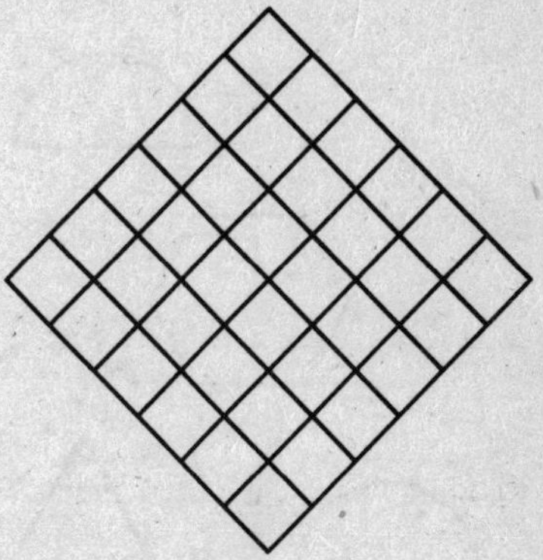

TROPHY	EXPECT
YELLOW	NOBODY
SINEWY	TITLES
WHISKY	INSERT

(Solution 63)

17 Survey

A survey was carried out on one hundred people concerning their eating habits:

20	had breakfast
23	had lunch
40	had dinner
6	had breakfast and lunch
7	had breakfast and dinner
5	had lunch and dinner
2	had breakfast, lunch and dinner

How many had only one meal?

(Solution 68)

18 Pyramid

What symbol should replace the question mark?

(Solution 71)

19 Honeycomb

Find eighteen names of food. A word may move in any direction as long as letters are adjacent. But a letter can only be visited once in each word.

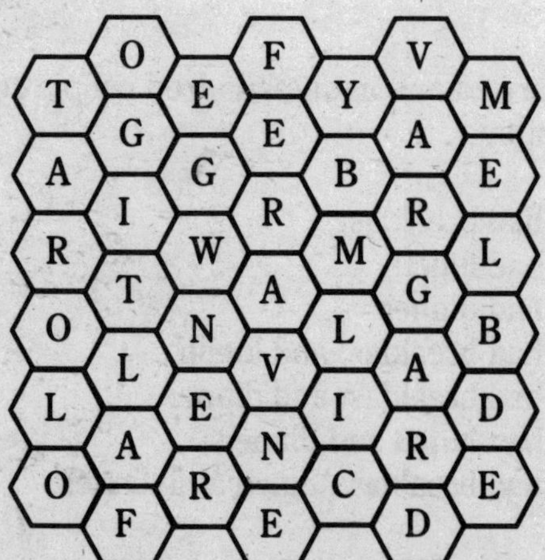

(Solution 74)

20 Find a Word

Trace out a 13-letter word by travelling along the lines. You need to find the starting letter and it cannot be crossed twice.

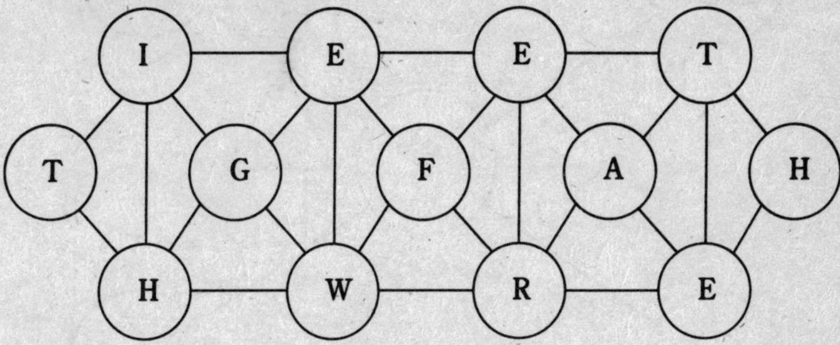

(Solution 79)

21 No Repeat Letters

The grid contains twenty-five different letters of the alphabet. What is the longest word that can be found by starting anywhere and working from square to square horizontally, vertically, or diagonally, without repeating a letter?

P	L	A	H	W
D	Q	N	T	V
X	E	U	G	O
J	S	I	R	F
Y	M	K	C	B

(Solution 83)

22 Symbols

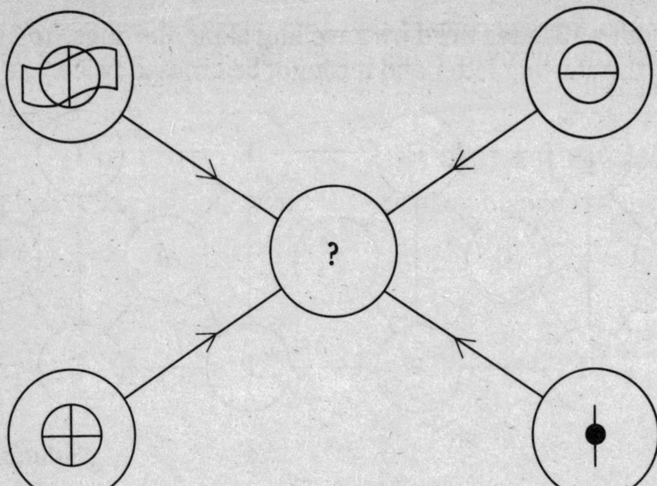

Each line and symbol that appears in the four outer circles is transferred to the centre circle according to these rules:
If a line or symbol occurs in the outer circles:

once	it is	transferred
twice	it is	possibly transferred
three times	it is	transferred
four times	it is	not transferred

Which of the circles A, B, C, D or E shown below, should appear at the centre of the diagram?

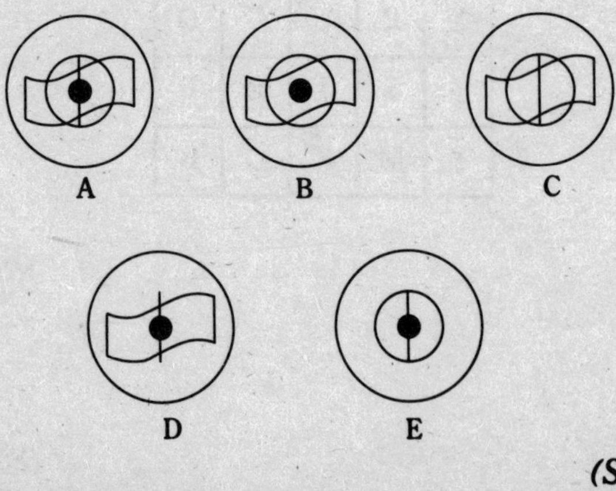

(Solution 87)

23 The Five Pennies

Someone tosses five coins in the air at the same time and you are betting on the outcome. What are the chances that at least four of the coins will finish up either all heads or all tails?

(Solution 91)

24 Hexagon Logic

What symbols should go inside the hexagons marked A and B?

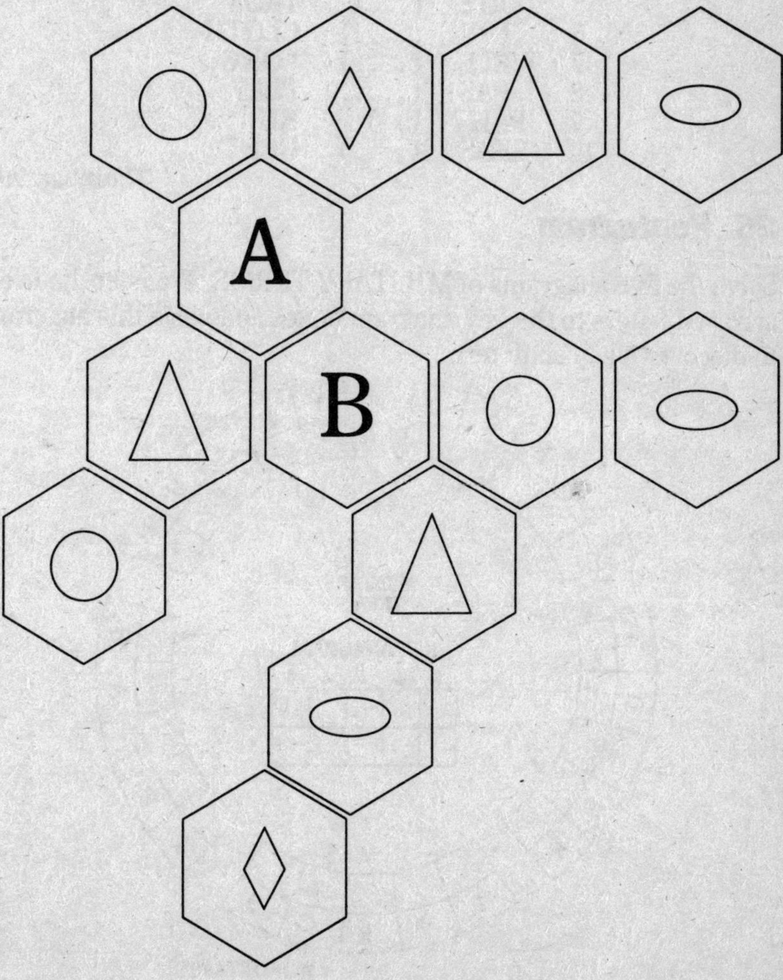

(Solution 96)

25 Links

Find the words that when placed in the brackets will complete the first word and start the second. One word is hyphenated. The number of dots equals the number of letters in the missing word.

1.	MAR	(. . . .)	BOAT
2.	ROUND	(. .)	PITY
3.	RIB	(. . .)	IRON
4.	BACK	(. . . . .)	ROOM
5.	OUT	(. . .)	TROT
6.	TRY	(. . . .)	CLOTH
7.	WELL	(. . . .)	LONG
8.	PAS	(. . . . .)	PLAY
9.	PALL	(. .)	BIT
10.	SEAS	(. . . .)	BENT

(Solution 99)

26 Pentagram

Solve the five anagrams of MILITARY TERMS. Transfer the five arrowed letters to the key anagram boxes and solve this anagram to discover a key sixth term.

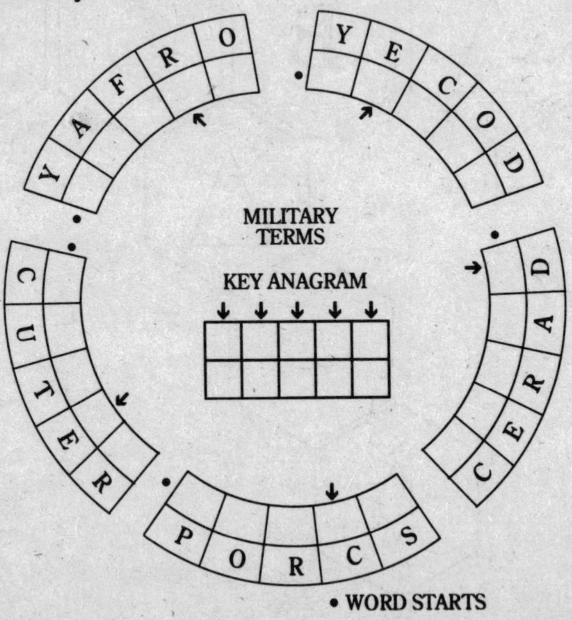

(Solution 103)

27 Three to Choose

Select the correct meaning from the three alternatives.

1. Tarn	(a)	Sick cow
	(b)	Hobgoblin
	(c)	Highland lake
2. Furlough	(a)	Legal possession
	(b)	Leave of absence
	(c)	Free transport
3. Gharry	(a)	Horse-drawn carriage
	(b)	Ale house
	(c)	Pension
4. Izzard	(a)	The letter "Z"
	(b)	Bird's throat
	(c)	Mythical sea
5. Mountebank	(a)	Jasmine
	(b)	Rogue
	(c)	Marshy area
6. Machete	(a)	Sharp cutting knife
	(b)	Farm machinery
	(c)	Platform for tiger shooting
7. Marchpane	(a)	Wild flower
	(b)	Marzipan
	(c)	Heat haze
8.Nuncio	(a)	Papal envoy
	(b)	Idiot
	(c)	Novice nun
9. Ounce	(a)	Lynx
	(b)	Trivial object
	(c)	Bone in the ear
10. Rutabaga	(a)	Turnip
	(b)	Hungarian dance
	(c)	Mêlée

(Solution 107)

28 Cricket Ground

One man can mow a cricket ground in two hours.
One man can mow a cricket ground in three hours.
One man can mow a cricket ground in four hours.
One man can mow a cricket ground in five hours.
One man can mow a cricket ground in six hours.

If they all worked together over the same area at their respective speeds, and assuming that they did not obstruct each other, how long would they take collectively to finish the job.

(Solution 110)

29 Word Circles

Reading clockwise, provide the missing letters to spell an 8-letter word in each circle. You are looking for a pair of synonyms and a pair of antonyms.

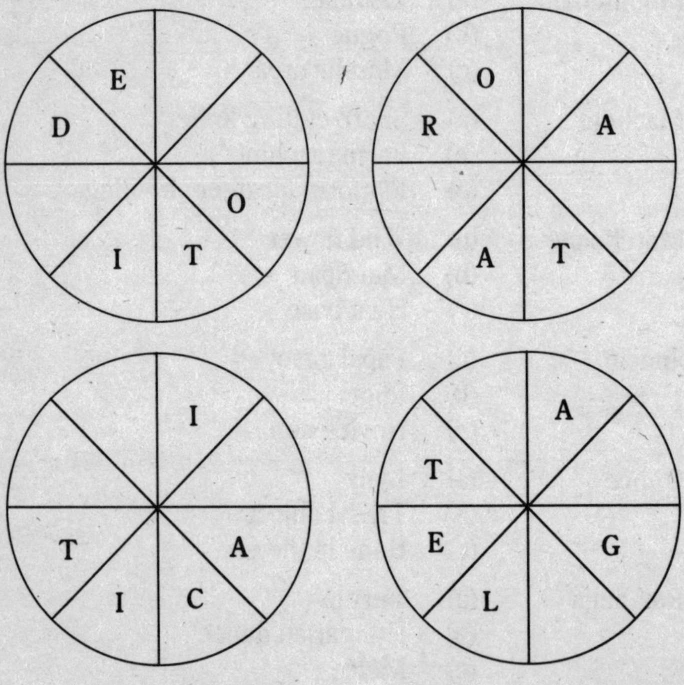

(Solution 115)

30 Circles

Which of these fit into the blank circle to carry out the pattern?

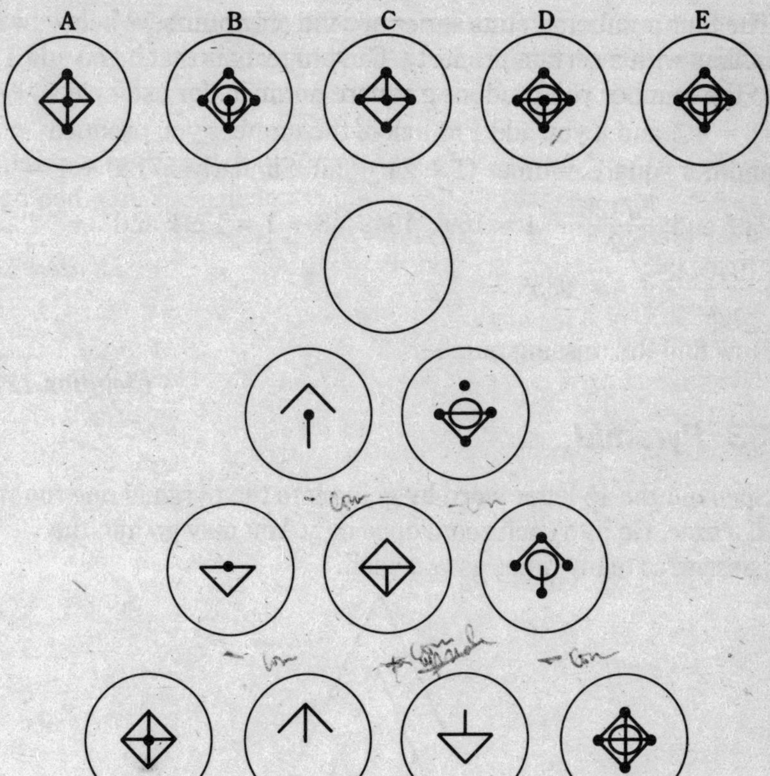

(Solution 119)

31 Eggs

In a crate of eggs, six out of one hundred are bad. What are the chances of drawing out two and finding them both bad?

(Solution 123)

32 Number Crunching Series

48, ? , 57210, 1940448

The four numbers in this series are the only numbers below two million with a certain property. The property is that if you add 1 to the number you produce a square number (for example, 1 + 48 = 49) and if you add 1 to half of the number you produce another square number (1 + 24 = 25). Similarly, 57120 + 1 =

239^2 and $\frac{57120}{2} + 1 = 169^2$. $1940448 + 1 = 1393^2$ and

$\frac{1940448}{2} + 1 = 985^2$.

Now find the missing number.

(Solution 127)

33 Pyramid

Spell out the 15-letter word by going into the pyramid one room at a time. Go into each room once only. You may go into the passage as many times as you wish.

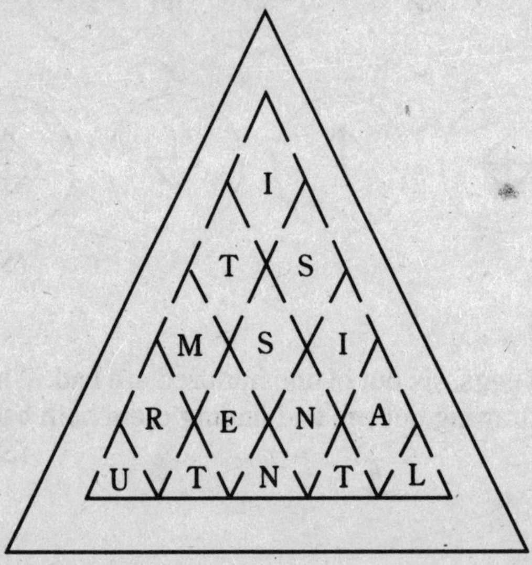

(Solution 131)

34 Track Word

Work around the track and provide the missing letters to find a 15-letter word. The word might appear clockwise or counter-clockwise, and the overlapping letter appears twice.

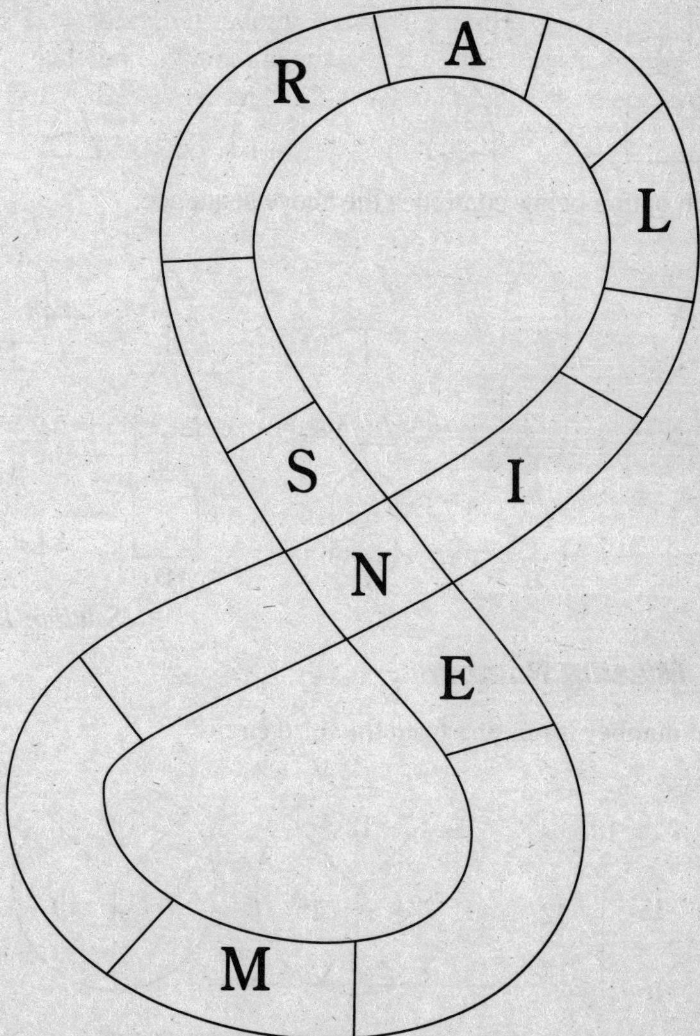

(Solution 135)

35 Sequence

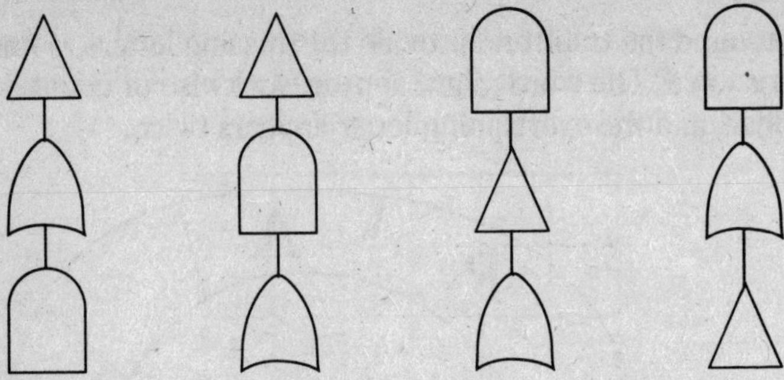

Which option below continues the above sequence?

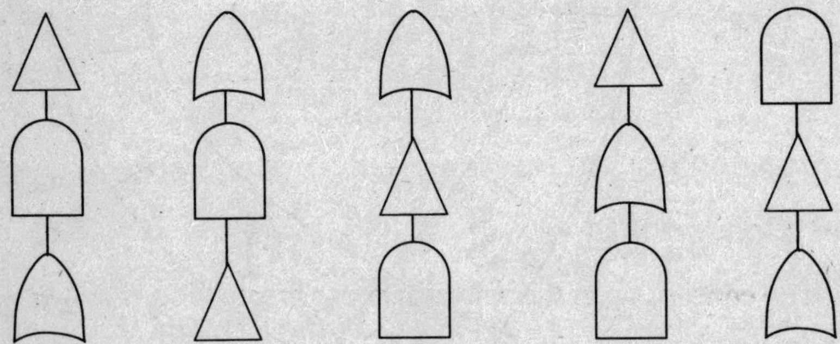

A B C D E

(Solution 139)

36 Missing Number

What number is missing from the third circle?

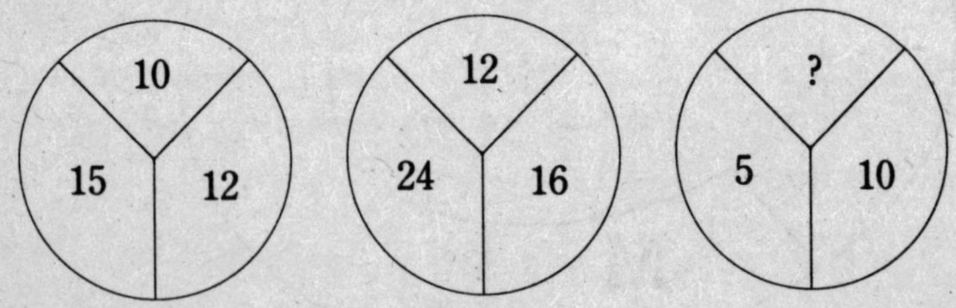

(Solution 143)

37 Wot! No Vowels?

Find sixteen words of three or more letters contained in the grid. Words run in any direction (backward and forward, horizontally, vertically, and diagonally), but only in a straight line.

C	D	S	Y	L	P
N	R	L	L	R	Y
Y	Y	Y	Y	R	F
S	C	L	P	Y	Y
H	F	Y	R	T	R
Y	X	W	Y	N	D

(Solution 147)

38 Consonants

Restore consonants to the words below to create groups of four synonyms.

1. • A • • • • I • •
   • E • • • • A • •
   • • A • • A • •
   • • I • E • I O •

2. • E • A • • I • • A • •
   O • • • I • A • E
   • A • • A • •
   I • • • A • • A • • E

3. E • • • A • •
   • E • I • • •
   • E • I • • •
   • E • • E • I • E

4. • O • U • I O •
   A • • I • U • A • I O •
   I • • O • A • I O •
   A • • E • •

5. A • • E • O • •
   • A • A • • E
   A • O • O • U E
   • A • • E

6. • U I • E • U •
   • U • • I • •
   U • • E • • A • •
   • E • E I • • U •

(Solution 151)

39 Grid

Each of the nine squares 1A to 3C should incorporate all the lines and symbols shown in the outer squares A, B, or C and 1, 2, or 3. Thus 2B should incorporate all the lines and symbols in 2 and B. One of the squares, 1A to 3C, is incorrect. Which one is it?

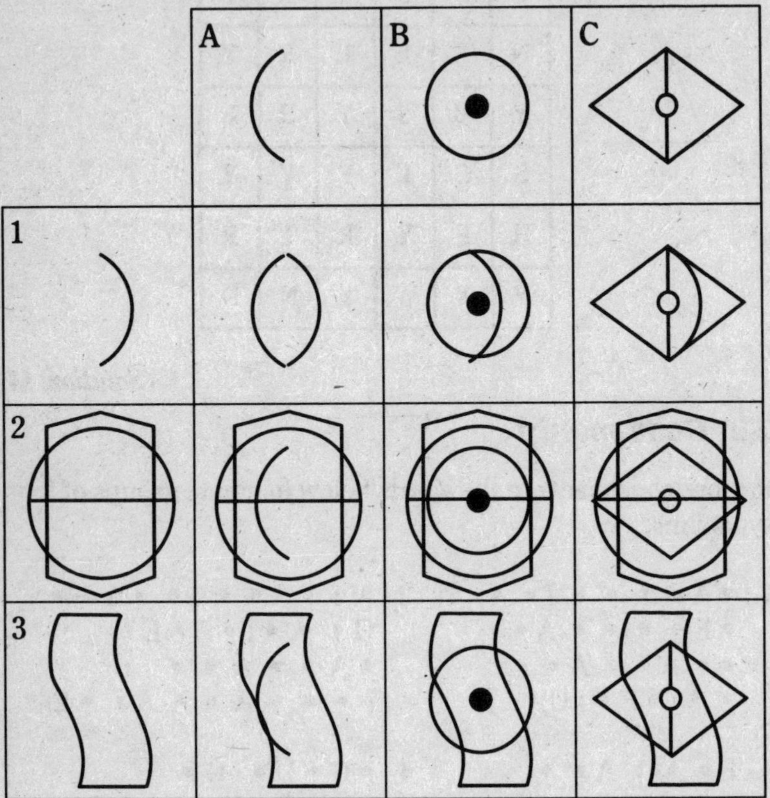

(Solution 155)

40 Analogy

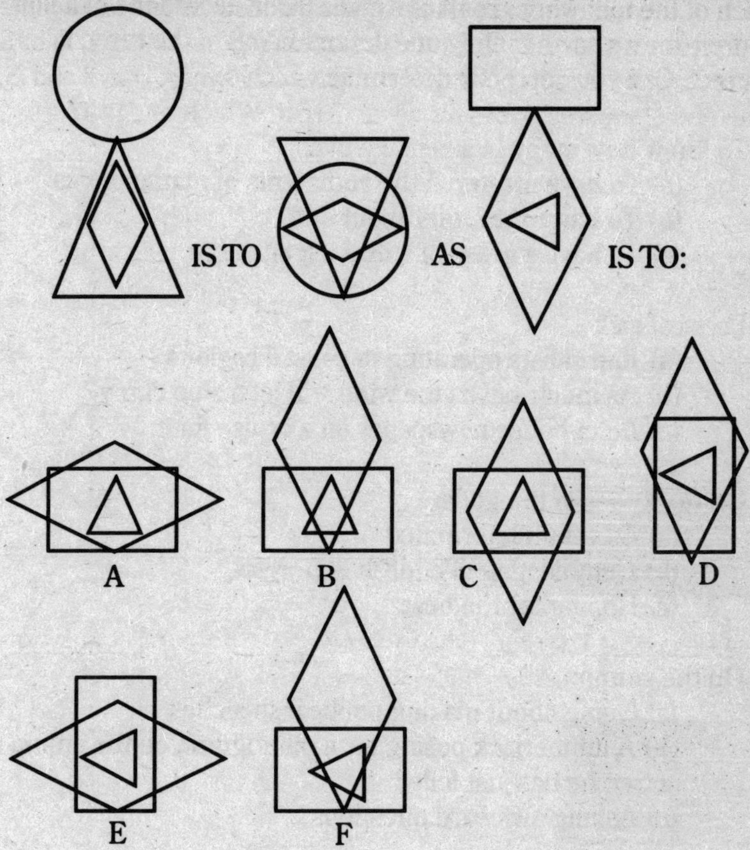

(Solution 159)

41 Triple Choice

Each of the following groupings gives three definitions of a not-so-well-known saying. Only one definition out of the three is correct. Can you correctly determine which one?

1. To know how many beans make five:
   (a) To have mastered the rudiments of mathematics
   (b) To have one's wits about one
   (c) To have a grasp of a difficult situation

2. Press of sail:
   (a) Journalists operating in coastal regions
   (b) As much sail as the wind will let a ship carry
   (c) An in-house newspaper on a cruise liner

3. On the knees of the gods:
   (a) As yet undetermined
   (b) Genuflecting at church in prayer
   (c) Hoping for the best

4. On the stump:
   (a) Going about making political speeches
   (b) A lumberjack posing for a photograph on the stump of a tree he has just felled
   (c) Asking awkward questions

5. To kick against the pricks:
   (a) To disobey the rules of authority in the armed forces
   (b) To campaign against someone in high authority
   (c) To hurt oneself in an unavailing struggle against something

6. Lop and top:
   (a) Trimmings of trees
   (b) A quick haircut
   (c) Execution by guillotine

7. To take to the heather:
   (a) To take a walking tour
   (b) To adopt a nomadic lifestyle
   (c) To become an outlaw

8. In the pouts:
   (a) Sullen
   (b) Sexy
   (c) Carefree

9. To row down:
   (a) To collide with another boat
   (b) To win a heated argument
   (c) To overtake by rowing

10. To heap coals of fire:
   (a) To return good for evil
   (b) To fuel an argument
   (c) To earn great riches

(Solution 4)

42 Link Words

Find a 3-letter word that, when placed on the end of these words, will produce new words.

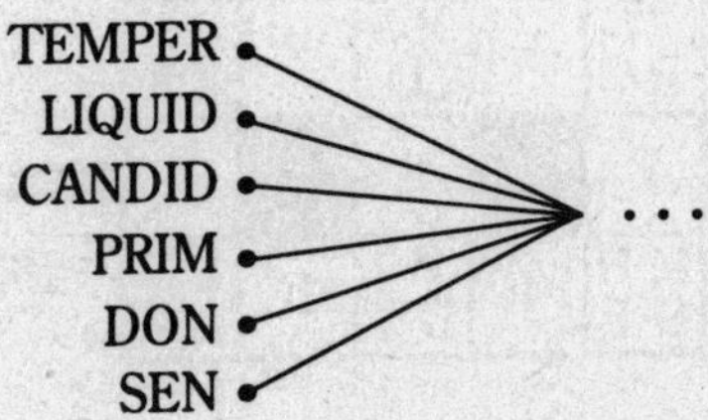

(Solution 8)

43 Horse Race

In a 5-horse race, a bookmaker laid the following odds on four of the horses:

No.	Odds
1	2 to 1 against
2	3 to 1 against
3	4 to 1 against
4	5 to 1 against
5	?

What odds should he give on horse no. 5 in order to give himself a 15 per cent margin of profit?

(Solution 12)

44 Three Too Many

Delete three of the letters in each 4-letter box to solve the crossword.

LS TR	E	TD SV	I	PR NL	E	LD MN
E		A		E		E
DC BR	I	DL GM	I	TP SR	A	TN LP
U		E		I		U
LD NC	A	TN PC	E	RS DL	E	DN TR
E		E		E		E
SD RL	E	MN SP	I	RS DT	E	LN DG

(Solution 16)

45 Symbols

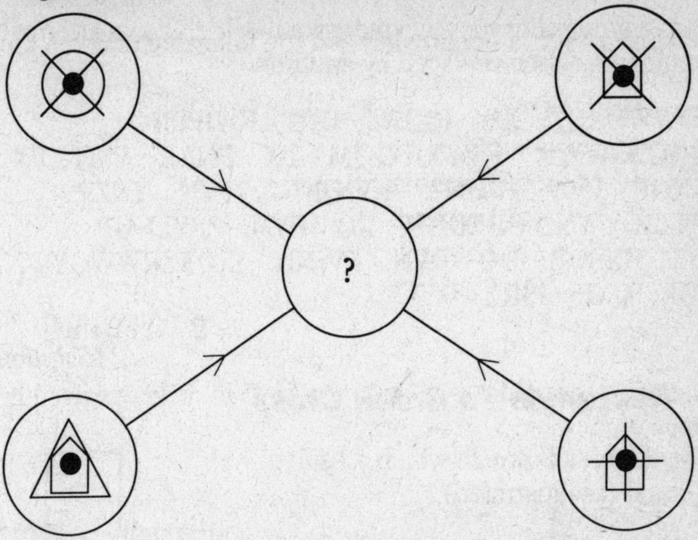

Each line and symbol that appears in the four outer circles is transferred to the centre circle according to these rules:
If a line or symbol occurs in the outer circles

once	it is	transferred
twice	it is	possibly transferred
three times	it is	transferred
four times	it is	not transferred

Which of the circles A, B, C, D, or E shown below should appear in the centre of the diagram?

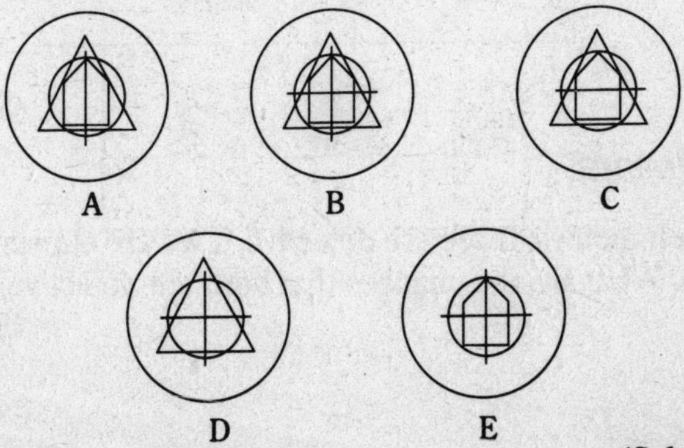

(Solution 20)

46 Cryptogram II

This is a straightforward cryptogram in which each letter of the quotation has been replaced by another.

IDWWDXQZ XH KXJBZ GJN KJDPPNQ GQQSGWWR, FSJFXJPDQM PX PNAA VXK PX YNGP PVN JGUNZ, KVNJNGZ PVN YNZP FXZZDYWN GBEDUN XQ PVN ZSYLNUP DZ HXSQB DQ PVN PVJNN IXQXZRWWGYWNZ: "BX QXP PJR".

– BGQ FGJANJ

(Solution 23)

47 Rectangle To Greek Cross

A Greek cross is one in which all sides are equal (as illustrated).

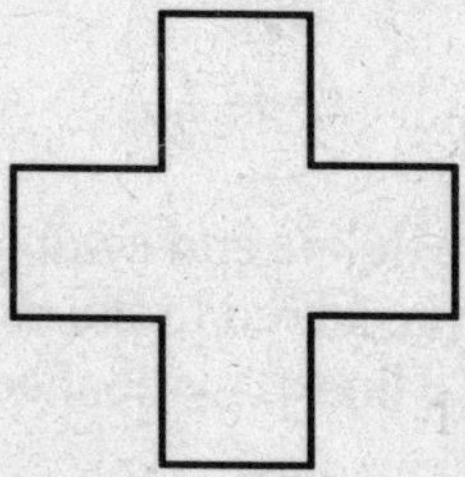

Divide a rectangle measuring 6″ × 3″ into three pieces that can be assembled into the shape of a Greek cross.

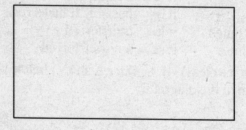

(Solution 28)

48 Motors

Out of ten motors, three are defective. Two are chosen at random. What are the chances that both are defective?

(Solution 32)

49 Word Circles

Place the letters in the correct boxes in each quadrant to obtain two 8-letter words, one reading clockwise and the other counter-clockwise. The two words are antonyms.

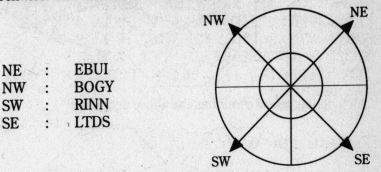

NE	:	EBUI
NW	:	BOGY
SW	:	RINN
SE	:	LTDS

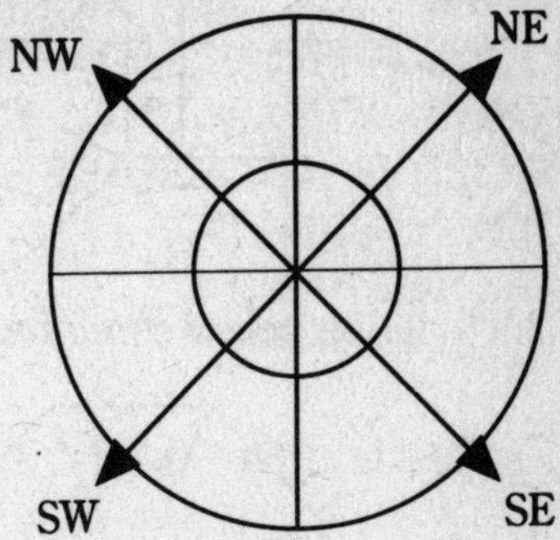

Now use the same method to find two synonyms.

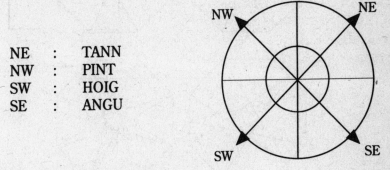

NE	:	TANN
NW	:	PINT
SW	:	HOIG
SE	:	ANGU

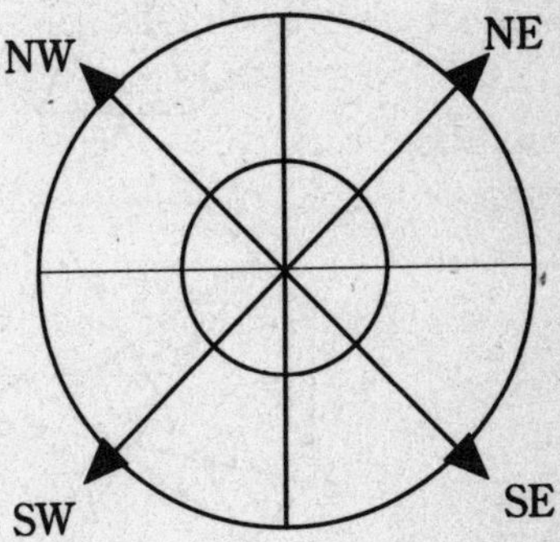

(Solution 36)

50 Number Crunching Squares

The number 65 can be expressed as the sum of two squares in two different ways:

$$8^2 + 1^2\ (64 + 1) \text{ and } 7^2 + 4^2\ (49 + 16).$$

What is the smallest number that can be expressed as the sum of two squares in twelve different ways?

(Solution 41)

51 Sequence

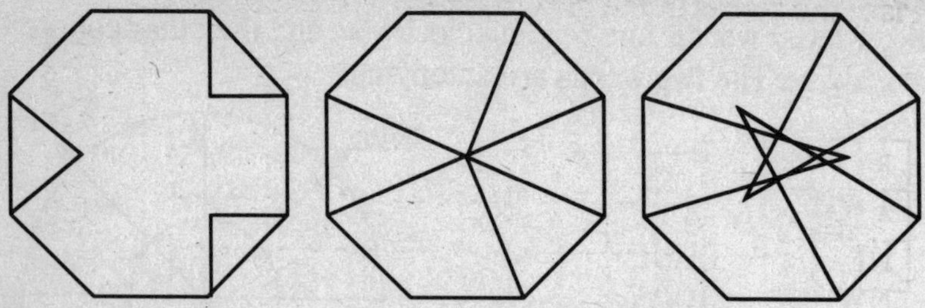

Which option below continues the above sequence?

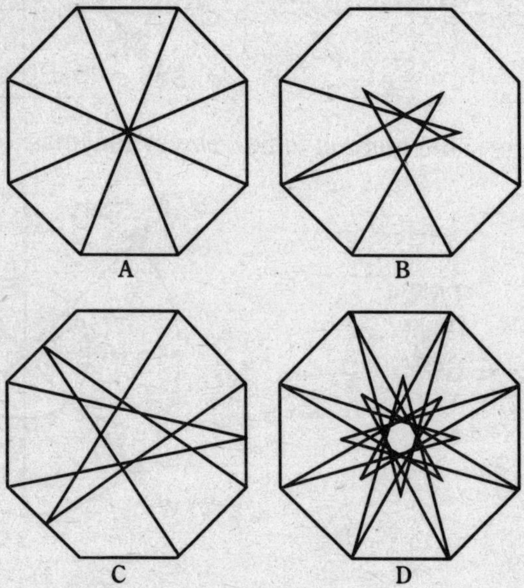

(Solution 45)

Do-It-Yourself Crossword

Place the pieces in the grid to complete the crossword.

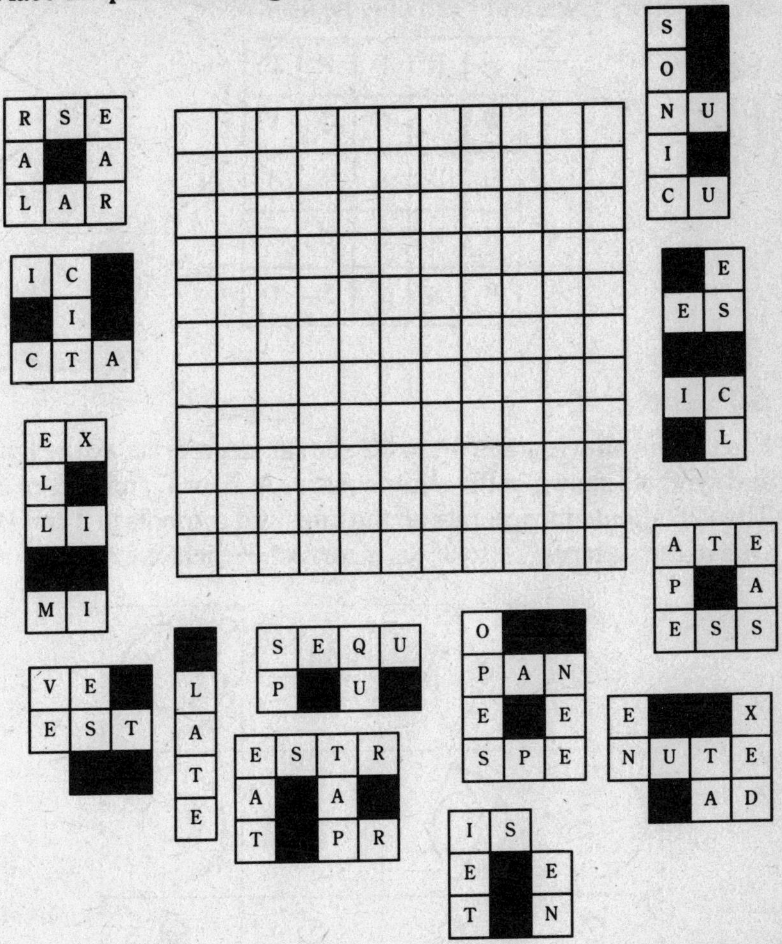

(Solution 48)

53 Longest Word

Find the longest word by moving from letter to adjacent letter in any direction. Each letter can only be used once.

R	E	F	P	C
W	T	G	O	V
H	D	A	I	J
K	N	L	U	Y
B	S	M	X	Q

(Solution 52)

54 Grid

Each of the nine squares 1A to 3C should incorporate all the lines and symbols shown in the outer squares A, B, or C and 1, 2, or 3. Thus 2B should incorporate all the lines and symbols in 2 and B. One of the squares, 1A to 3C, is incorrect. Which one is it?

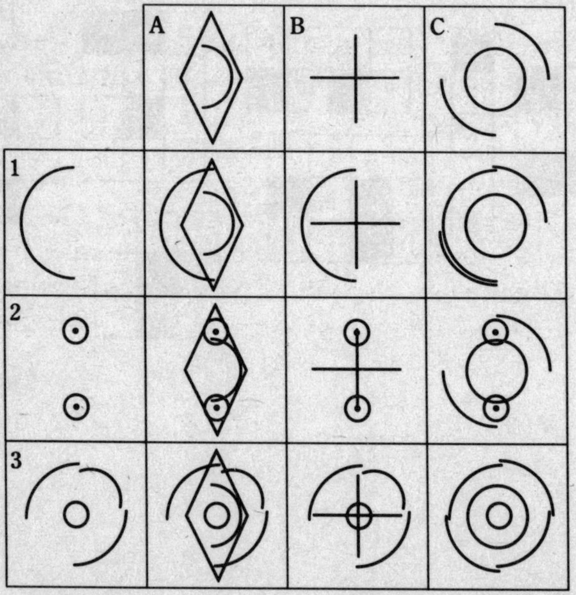

(Solution 56)

55 The Paradox of the Unexpected Gift

This is our presentation of a famous paradox which is more of an exercise in logic than a puzzle. Like all good paradoxes, it is designed to provide food for thought and philosophical discussion.

For the sake of argument I am retiring next week and am to be presented with a gift. However, the day of presentation is meant to be a surprise; in other words, although I know I am to receive the gift, I do not know whether it is to be presented on the Monday, Tuesday, Wednesday, Thursday, or Friday.

The question to consider is, can such a surprise gift be given? I know that it cannot be given on Friday, the last day, for if it was left until then, the only day left, it would not be a surprise. So it must be on Thursday. But then Thursday has in effect become the last day left, so it wouldn't be a surprise on that day either. The logic continues right back to Monday. Thus an unexpected gift is impossible.

Are there any other ways of solving the paradox? We make several suggestions in the answers section, some of which you may think better than others.

At first, when you read the paradox with a clear mind, you may think the argument propounded ridiculous. But, like all good paradoxes, it is designed to confuse, and the more you think about it the more unclear your mind is likely to become about it.

(Solution 60)

56 Cross-Alphabet

Insert all twenty-six letters of the alphabet into the grid once each to form a crossword. Clues are given, but in no particular order.

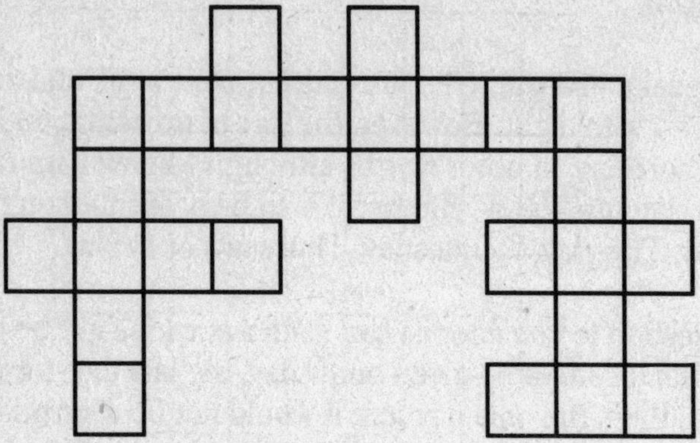

Clues:

- An opening in a house roof
- A valuable collection
- To spring into the air
- A Japanese sect of Buddhism
- Close at hand
- Bovine animal
- To make firm
- Small group of military personnel

(Solution 64)

57 Odd One Out

Which is the odd one out?

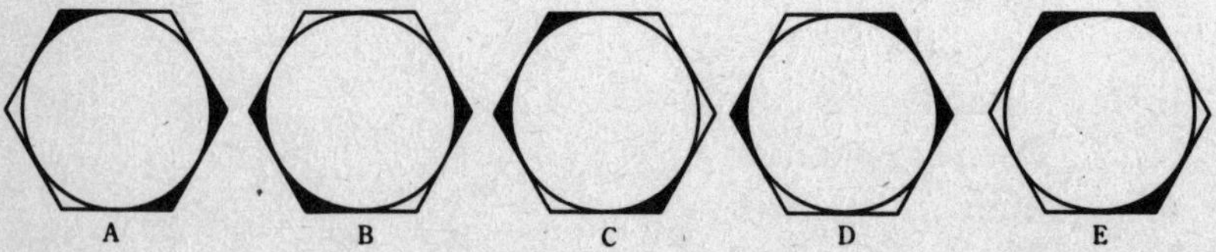

(Solution 67)

58 Directional Crossword

Answers run horizontally, vertically, or diagonally, either to the right or left. Each solution starts on the lower number and finishes on the next higher number, i.e. 1 to 2, 2 to 3, etc.

1	5							4
10			13			12		7
	17						15	
							14	
				16				
11		8				9		6
3								2

Clues:

1. Make worse
2. Illegal behaviour
3. Pain along a nerve
4. Wing or lifting surface
5. Embrocation
6. A rich confection
7. Small part
8. Thesis
9. Comes out
10. Specious argument
11. Wed
12. Canines
13. Grain storage containers
14. Result of addition
15. Shift
16. Ages
17. Steep in liquid

(Solution 72)

59 Lawns

My garden has two square lawns. Each has a whole number of feet along the sides. The total area is 8845 square feet.

What are the sizes of the lawns if one lawn has a side that is one foot longer than the other lawn?

(Solution 76)

60 Same Word

Place a word in the parentheses that means the same as the two words or phrases outside the brackets.

1. Blockhead	(------)	Pasta
2. Pot	(-----)	Decrepit person
3. Vessel	(-------)	Baseball thrower
4. Line of people	(-----)	Braid of hair
5. Set of three	(----)	Aquatic bird
6. Cask	(--------)	Post supporting roof
7. Goblin	(----)	Ice hockey disc
8. One who staggers	(-------)	Crossed greyhound and collie
9. Grease over	(-----)	Tack in sewing
10. Small hound	(------)	Spy or informer

(Solution 80)

61 The Train in the Tunnel

A train travelling at a speed of 75 m.p.h. enters a tunnel that is $2\frac{1}{2}$ miles long. The length of the train is $\frac{1}{4}$ mile. How long does it take for all of the train to pass through the tunnel, from the moment the front enters to the moment the rear emerges?

(Solution 84)

62 Links Jigsaw Puzzle

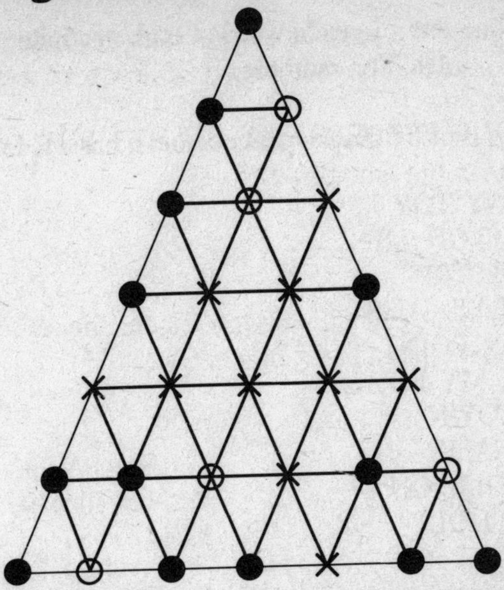

Place the twelve segment links below over the triangular grid above, in such a way that each link symbol is covered by exactly the same symbol. The connecting segments must not be rotated. Note that not all the connecting lines will be covered.

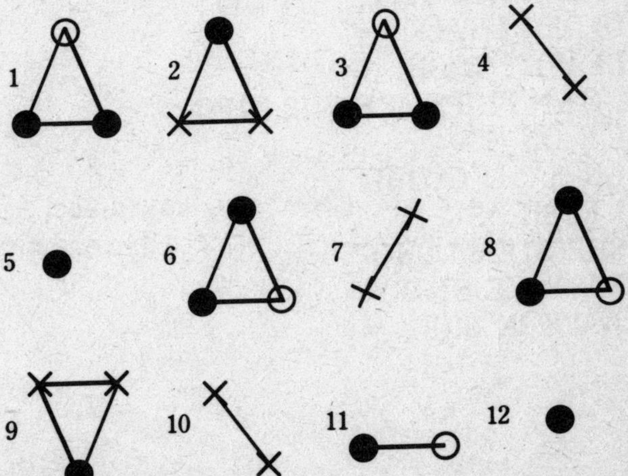

(Solution 88)

63 Plan in Works

A. Change one letter in each word of each grouping to make a well-known phrase. For example,

GO PAT OUR FEEDERS will become TO PUT OUT FEELERS.

1. TAN ANY TOY
2. O PUCK ON LIPS
3. IF PULL TRY
4. SO TREAT GUSS
5. PUT ON POINT
6. CHEER MY FOWL
7. PINE TOWN
8. PLAN SALE
9. LAD COLD ON
10. JIVING DOLT

B. The following are more difficult because the order of the words has also been changed. For example,

OUR FEEDERS PAT GO will become TO PUT OUT FEELERS.

1. ANDS ADDS ANY
2. OLDER I TALK
3. BEAST PAY SHE GO
4. GOWN SHIPS ACE SHE THEN
5. LIE ON SO
6. ON SAND GLOBE
7. I RUSH AS
8. SHE STEAM SHOP
9. MY FAKE STORY
10. WAVE IN SHE

(Solution 93)

64 Piecemeal Quotation

A quotation has been divided into letter groups and arranged in alphabetical order. For example, FIND THE QUOTE would be presented as EQ, FI, ND, TE, TH, UO (4, 3, 5). Rearrange the following letters to find a quotation by Goethe (2, 5, 4, 7, 6, 2, 2, 4, 3, 2, 7, 2, 8, 3, 7).

AN, BE, DK, EA, ER, ER, IF, IO, KI, LE, MB, ND,
NO, NO, NO, NX, OA, ON, RE, RE, SE, TH, TO,
TS, TT, UL, US, WE, WE, WE, WO, WM.

__/_____/____/_______/______/
__/__/____/___/__/_______/__/
________/___/_______

(Solution 95)

65 Birds

Solve the clues, then change one letter, to find the name of ten birds. The asterisk represents the letter to be changed.

	Answer	Birds
1. Stray away	* • • • • •	• • • • • •
2. Rolled up	• • • • • *	• • • • • •
3. Four-leafed is lucky	* • • • • •	• • • • • •
4. Best toasted with butter	* • • • • •	• • • • • •
5. Type of flag	* • • • • •	• • • • • •
6. What a dropped catch is	• • • • • *	• • • • • •
7. Animal found in rivers	* • • • • •	• • • • • •
8. Muffle	* • • • • •	• • • • • •
9. Type of fish	• • • • • *	• • • • • •
10. A lie	• • • • • *	• • • • • •

(Solution 100)

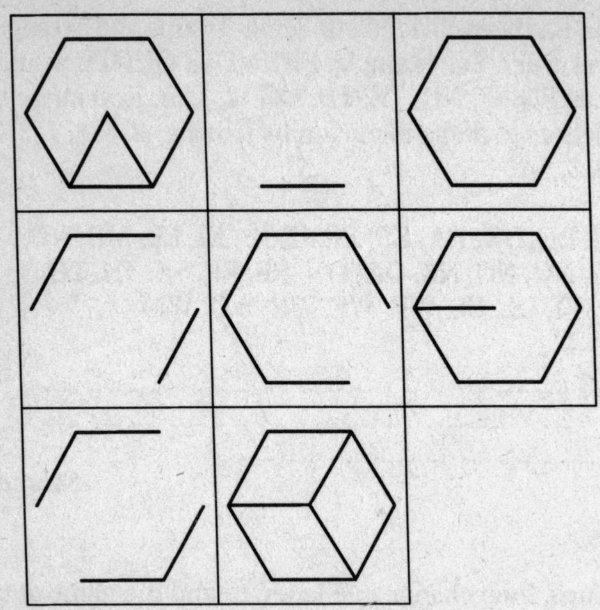

Find the missing tile from the choice below:

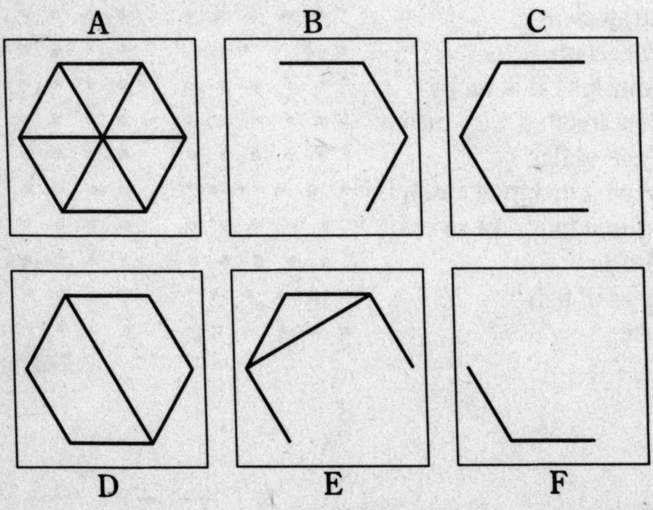

(Solution 104)

67 Links Jigsaw Puzzle

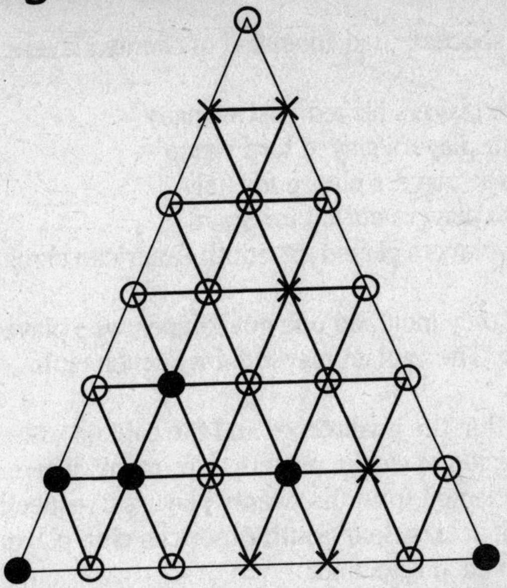

Place the twelve segment links below over the triangular grid above, in such a way that each link symbol is covered by exactly the same symbol.
The connecting segments must not be rotated. Note that not all the connecting lines will be covered.

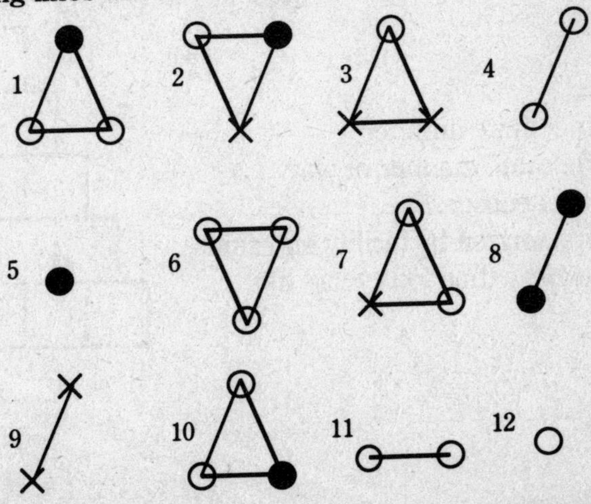

(Solution 108)

68 World Cup 1994

A national soccer squad consisted of twenty players:

Five players played for Germany
Four players played for France
Three players played for Italy
Two players played for Spain
Six players played for South American clubs

The squad only included one goalkeeper, who played for an Italian club. The captain played for a French club.

Assuming that the goalkeeper and the captain were included in every selection of eleven players, how many different teams could be selected from the twenty players irrespective of positions, if at least four South American club players were included in each selection?

(Solution 113)

69 Pyramid Word

Solve the five clues, enter the correct words in the pyramid, and then rearrange all the answer letters to find one 15-letter word.

Clues:
1. An indefinite number
2. In the same manner or way
3. Holds a possession
4. Characterized by facility and skill
5. An ox less than four years old

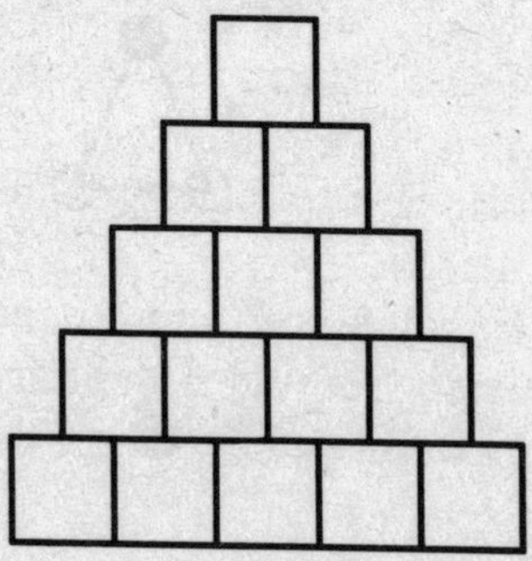

(Solution 116)

70 Two Quick Teasers

1. By what fractional part does four-fourths exceed three-fourths?
2. Write down quickly in figures the sum of 13 thousand and 13 hundred and 13.

(Solution 120)

71 Clueless Crossword

Delete three letters in each 4-letter box to solve the crossword.

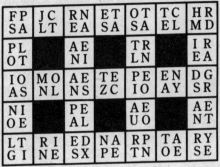

FP SA	JC LT	RN EA	ET SA	OT SA	TC EL	HR MD
PL OT		AE NI		TR LN		IR EA
IO AS	MO NL	AE NS	TE ZC	PE IO	EN AY	DG SR
NI OE		PE AL		AE UO		AE NT
LT GI	RI NE	ED SX	NA PE	RP TN	TA OE	RY SE

(Solution 124)

72 Birds

My friend asked me the ages of my three daughters.
I said: "If you multiply their ages it equals 90, and they are all under 15.
"If you add their ages then it equals the number of birds in that tree."
So my friend counted the birds in the tree, but he still did not know how old my children were!
How many birds were there in the tree?

(Solution 128)

73 Hexagons and Triangles

Which option below continues the above sequence?

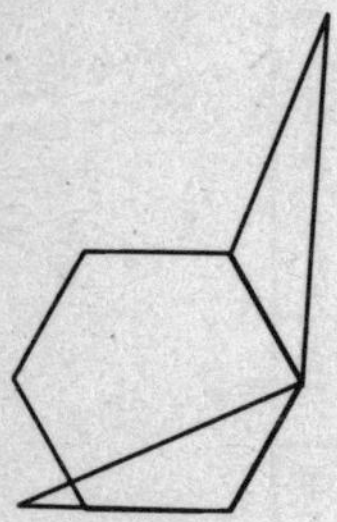

A

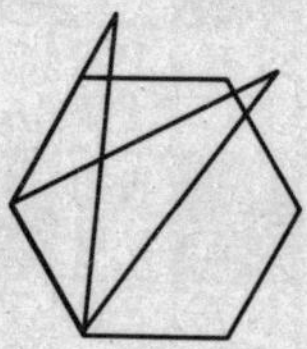

B

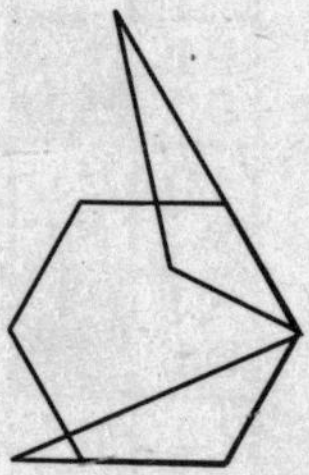

C

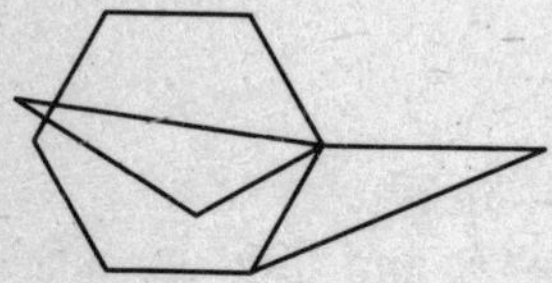

D

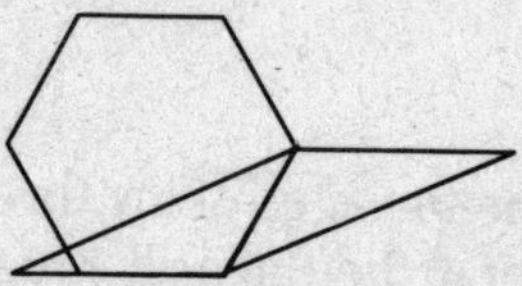

E

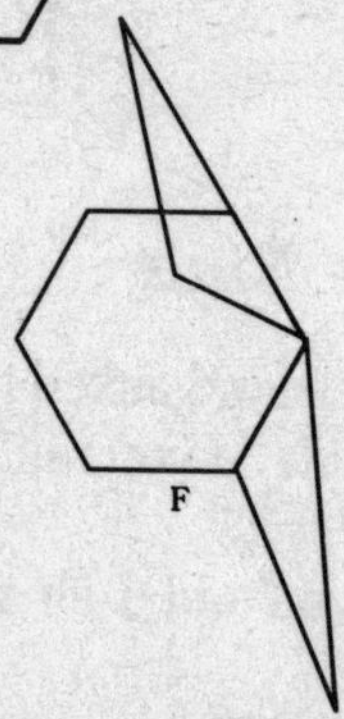

F

(Solution 132)

74 Decadice

With a pair of 10-sided dice, what are the odds of scoring at least 13 in one throw of the pair?

(Solution 137)

75 Hexagram

Solve the six anagrams of weapons and armour. Transfer the six arrowed letters to the key anagram boxes and solve this anagram to discover a key seventh term.

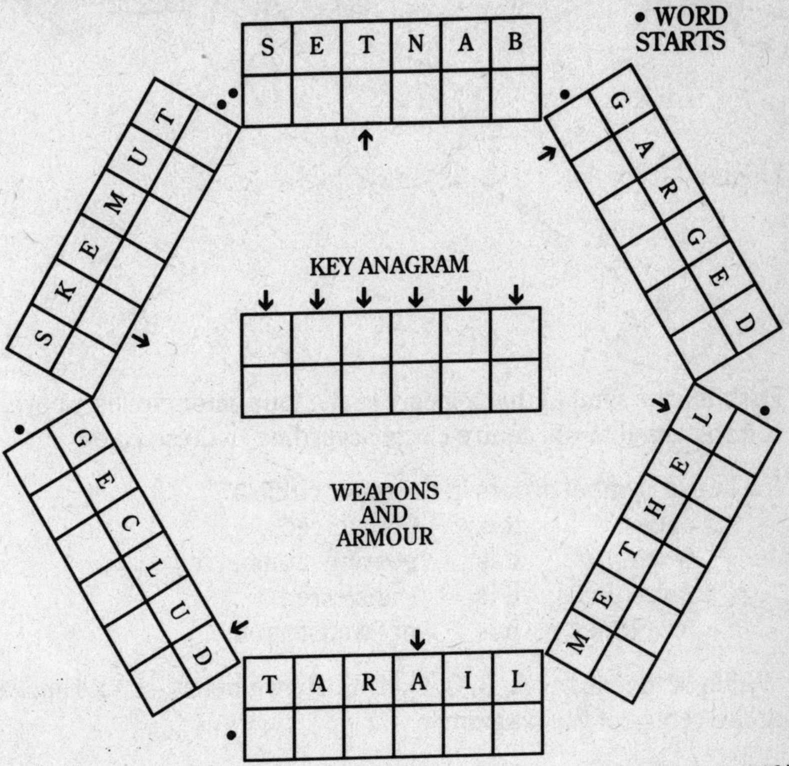

(Solution 140)

76 Symbols

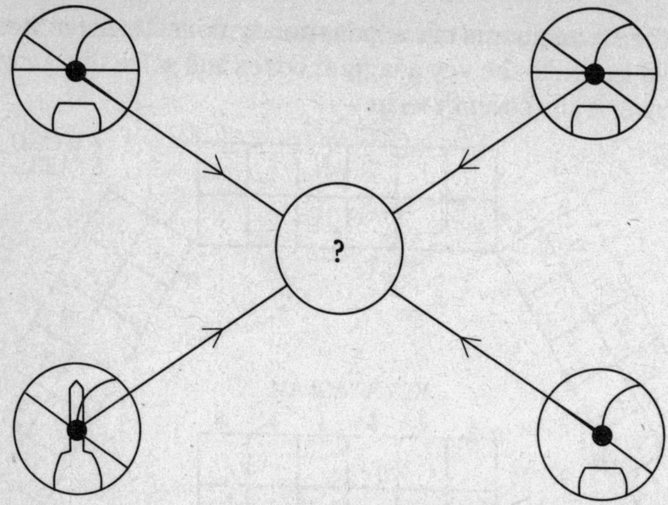

Each line or symbol that appears in the four outer circles, above, is transferred to the centre circle according to these rules:

If a line or symbol occurs in the outer circles:

once	it is	transferred
twice	it is	possibly transferred
three times	it is	transferred
four times	it is	not transferred

Which of the circles A, B, C, D, or E, shown below, should appear at the centre of the diagram?

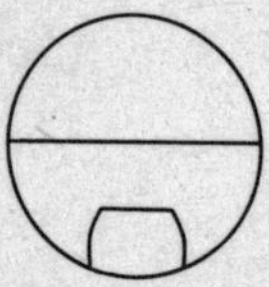
A

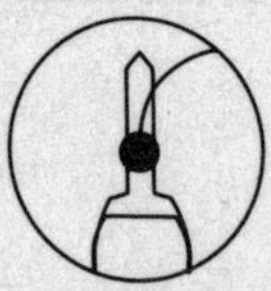
B

C

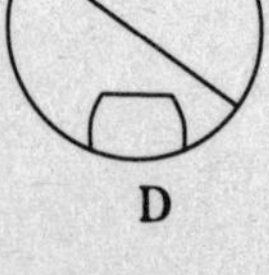
D

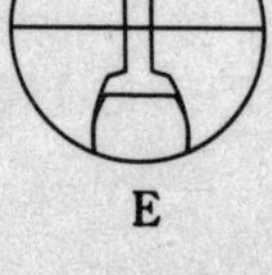
E

(Solution 144)

77 Odd One Out

Below are a number of car licence plates. Which is the odd one out?

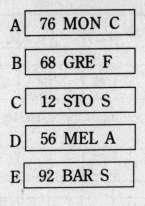

A	76 MON C
B	68 GRE F
C	12 STO S
D	56 MEL A
E	92 BAR S

(Solution 148)

78 Anagrammed Synonyms

In each of the following groups of three words, your task is to discover which two of the three words can be paired to form an anagram of one word that is a synonym of the word remaining. For example, LEG – MEEK – NET. The words LEG and NET are an anagram of GENTLE, which is a synonym of the remaining word MEEK.

1. LAP – APE – PLEA
2. SIMPER – POSE – ATONE
3. DIM – LIKE – ARE
4. SAY – NOT – MINE
5. TRADE – SIN – TAUT
6. CLUES – KISS – OAT
7. RED – COY – SEVER
8. UNDER – RID – NUB
9. ADD – GAUNT – ME
10. NO – RULER – CHARM

(Solution 152)

79 Bars

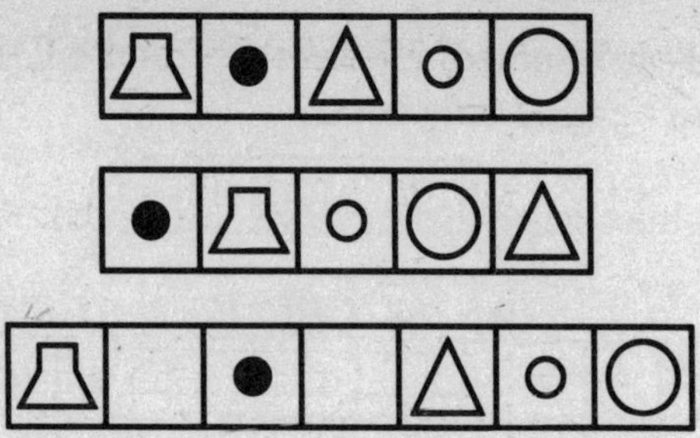

Which option below continues the above sequence?

A 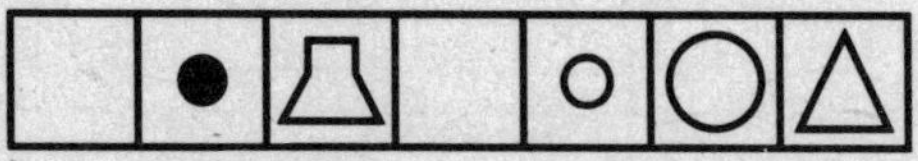

B 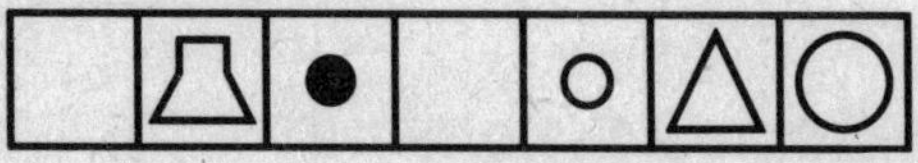

C 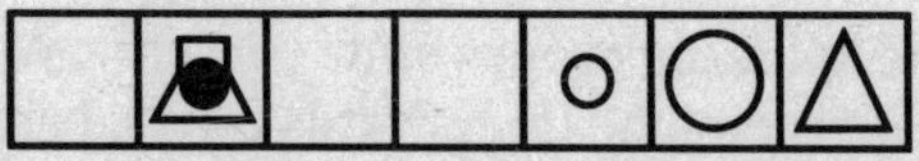

D 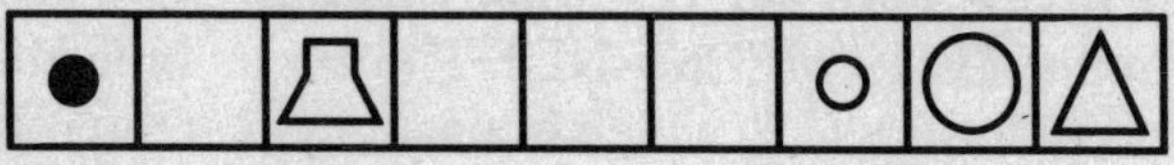

E 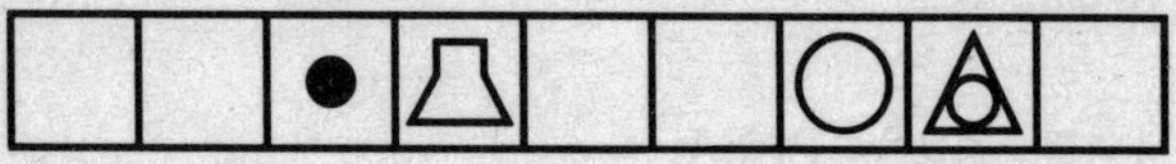

(Solution 156)

80 Palindromic

Rearrange these numbers to make the sequence in some way palindromic:

1, 3, 4, 9, 9, 12, 13, 14, 15, 16, 18

(Solution 160)

81 Cards

Select twelve cards, note the letters, and find a 12-letter word. Each card can be used only once.

Score the highest score that you can – the maximum is 160.

										(11)	(12)	(13)	(15)	
CARDS	2	3	4	5	6	7	8	9	10	J	Q	K	A	CARDS
♡	C	R	U	Y	B	X	V	H	D	V	T	I	N	♡
♧	S	Y	G	C	W	D	P	K	R	J	A	L	P	♧
♢	F	Z	O	L	G	Q	B	Q	M	W	O	T	A	♢
♤	S	U	E	Z	H	X	K	E	J	F	M	I	N	♤
SCORE	2	3	4	5	6	7	8	9	10	J	Q	K	A	SCORE
										(11)	(12)	(13)	(15)	

Example:

M	12
A	12
C	5
H	9
I	13
N	15
A	15
T	13
I	13
O	12
N	15
	134

(Solution 1)

82 Saying

This saying has had all of its vowels removed. The consonants are in their correct order but have been broken up into groups of four.

Replace the vowels and reconstitute the saying.

THST RNGT KFRM THWK
THRC HTKF RMTH PRND
THGV RNMN TTKF RMVR
YN

– GLMM SLW

(Solution 5)

83 Synonym Circles

Read clockwise to find two 8-letter synonyms. You have to find the starting point and provide the missing letters.

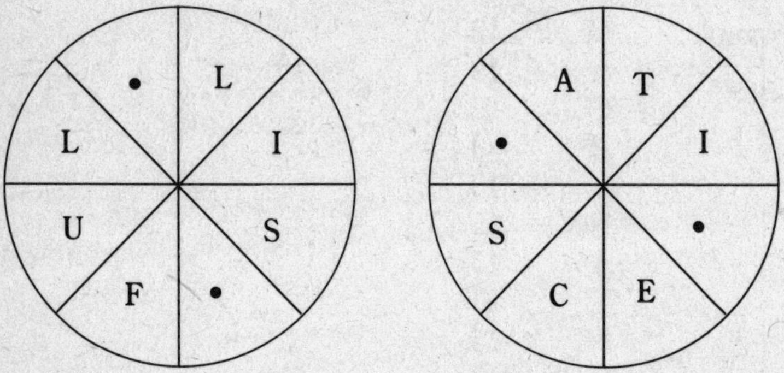

(Solution 9)

84 Nine Digits

The multiplication sum 51,249,876 × 3 uses the nine digits each, only once, producing the answer 153,749,628, which also uses the nine digits each, only once.

Can you find a multiplication sum using 6 as your multiplier that has the same property?

(Solution 13)

85 Grid

Each of the nine squares 1A to 3C should incorporate all the lines and symbols shown in the outer squares A, B, or C and 1, 2, or 3. Thus 2B should incorporate all the lines and symbols in 2 and B. One of the squares, 1A to 3C, is incorrect. Which one is it?

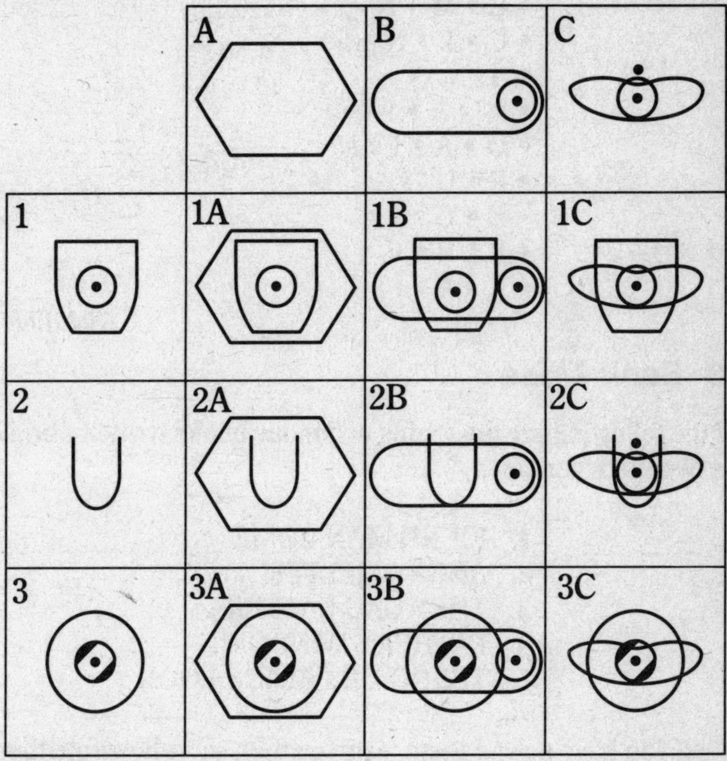

(Solution 17)

86 Alphametics

Replace the letters with numbers so that the total is correct:

```
   THE
   TEN
+  MEN
  ----
  MEET
```

(Solution 21)

87 Languages

Fill in the missing alternate letters to spell the names of nine languages. For example, • N • L • S • represents ENGLISH. Then rearrange the initial letters of each language to find a tenth language.

• E • M • N
• C • L • N • I •
• A •
• M • A • I •
• O • A • I • N
• R • U
• E • G • L •
• R • B • C
• E • A • I

(Solution 25)

88 Book Titles

All the following are anagrams of famous books written during the twentieth century:

1. FIEND MAN COME
2. ANGRY MELTER
3. THEY GAG BATTERS
4. FATHER'S WINDOW
5. TIRING DIM BLACK LOOK

When you have solved them, can you then say who wrote them?

(Solution 29)

89 Triangles Matrix

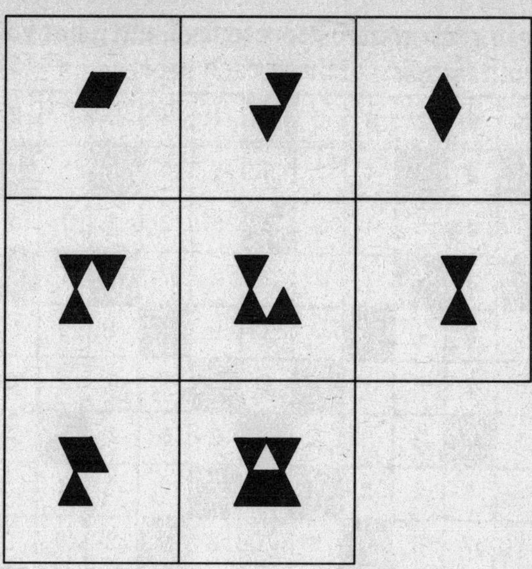

Find the missing tile from the choice below:

A

B

C

D

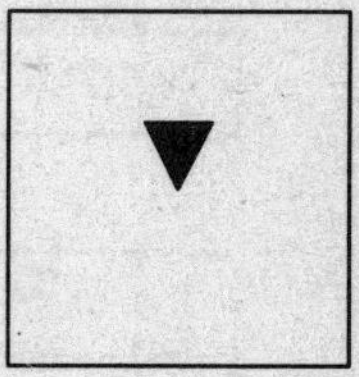

E

F

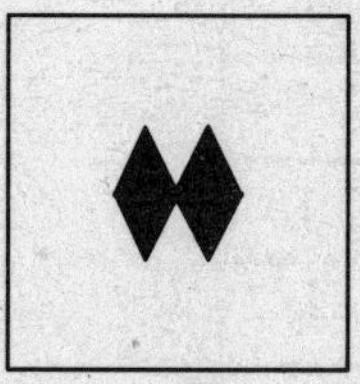

G

H

(Solution 33)

90 Alternative Crossword

The number in each square represents a letter, but you have to select one from a choice of three each time.

7	5	6	2	3	2		1	5	7	7	2	7
7		2		4	7	5	1	6		2		3
7	5	2	5	4	2		5	2	7	7	4	2
1		3		7	2	2	2	7		7		5
1	1	5	7		7	1	9		1	2	2	2
5	6	2	6	1		6		7	6	2	2	7
	1		3	5	4		2	3	2		4	
2	6	6	2	2		6		7	2	1	7	7
7	7	7	2		6	5	6		2	6	1	8
7		5		2	5	7	2	7		1		5
1	5	1	4	2	7		2	7	7	7	2	6
9		4		1	7	7	1	6		2		2
7	7	2	2	6	7		4	2	5	7	2	7

1	A B C
2	D E F
3	G H I
4	J K L
5	M N O
6	P Q R
7	S T U
8	V W X
9	Y Z –

(Solution 37)

91 Fore and Aft

Find a 3-letter word that completes all three words on the left and prefixes all three words on the right.

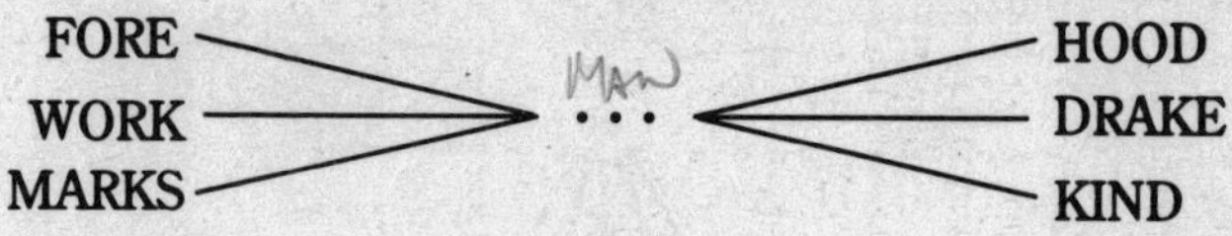

(Solution 38)

92 Odd One Out

Which is the odd one out?

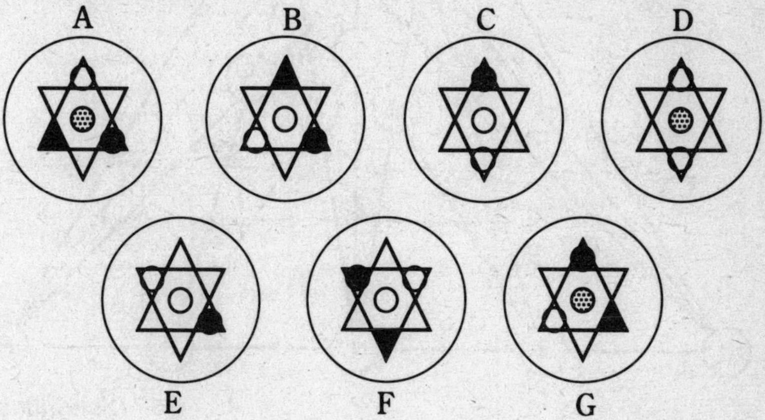

(Solution 44)

93 Sequence

What number comes next in this sequence?

12, 23, 35, 47, 511, 613, 717, 819, 923, 1029, ?

(Solution 49)

94 Network

Find the starting point and travel along the connecting lines in a continuous path to adjacent circles to spell out a 14-letter word. Every circle must be visited only once.

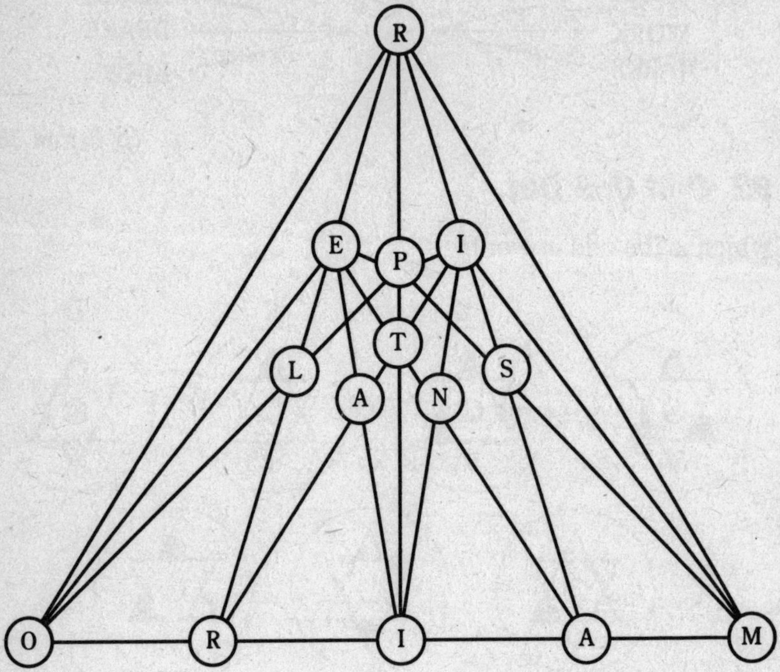

(Solution 53)

95 Odd One Out

Which is the odd one out?

A. Got
B. Car
C. Seals
D. Trips

(Solution 57)

96 Sequence

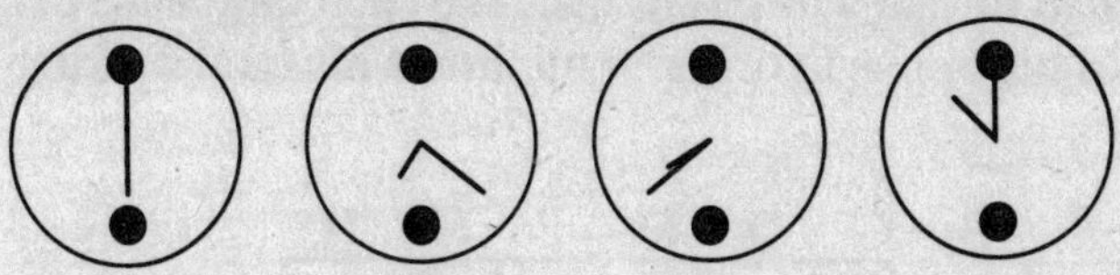

Which option below continues the sequence above?

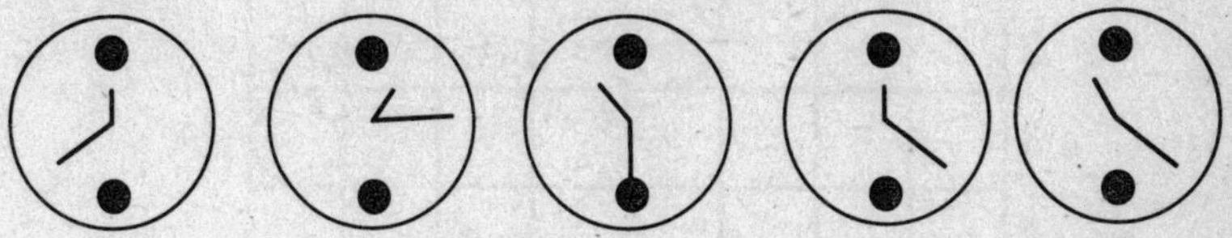

A B C D E

(Solution 61)

97 'D' Puzzle

Using the first and last letters already inserted, place the fifteen letters of the five words at the bottom anywhere in the grid to form five new 5-letter words reading across.

D				T
D				A
D				L
D				O
D				N

JEW
HIS
SIC
LAC
DIN

(Solution 65)

98 Fish Farm

A fish farmer had to visit a different fish lake each day. Where should he build his house in order to minimize his total walking distance?

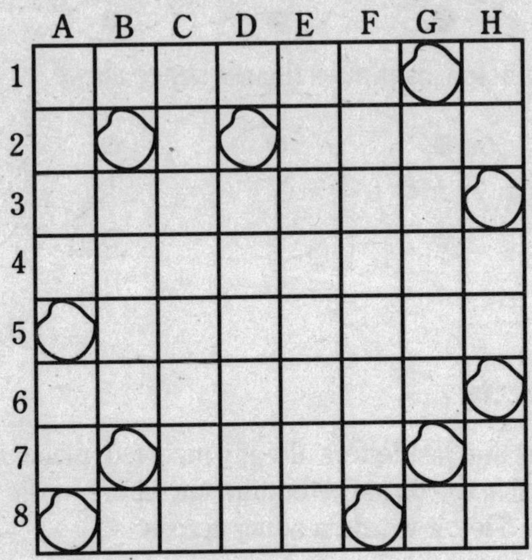

(Solution 69)

99 Magic Number Square

Insert the remaining numbers from 1 to 16 so that each horizontal, vertical, and corner-to-corner line totals 34.

			3
			12
15		9	

(Solution 73)

100 Trite Saying

Select the words in order to produce a trite saying.

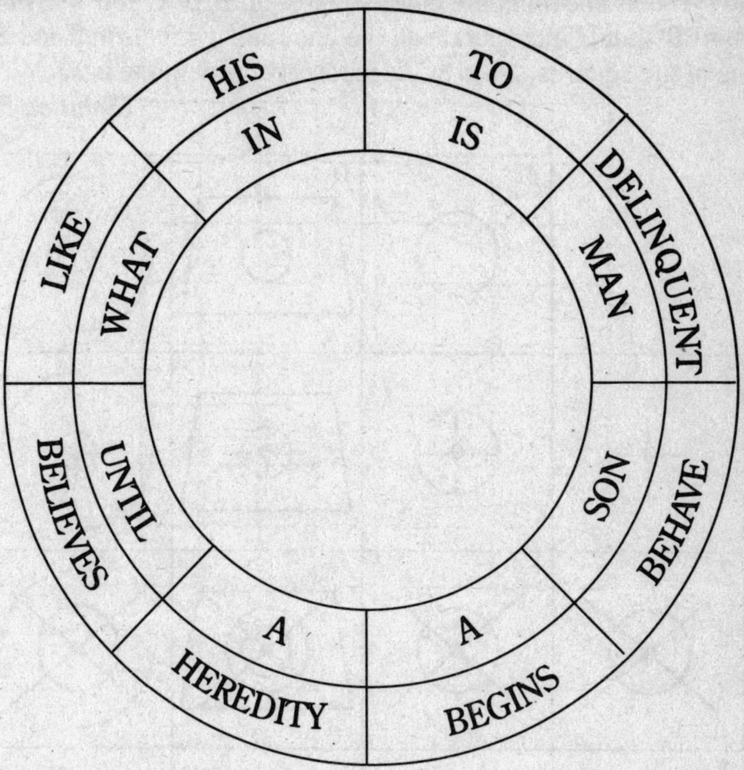

(Solution 77)

101 Cryptogram III

This is a straightforward cryptogram in which each letter of the quotation has been replaced by another.

IVAM UZ ZV HVHLAJB ZUKHAX PTEJLZT UY
UZ YST PTZY IJKT UQ YST FVBAC JY
FSUES YV PT PJC.

–J.J. KUAQT

(Solution 81)

102 Grid

Each of the nine squares 1A to 3C should incorporate all the lines and symbols shown in the outer squares A, B, or C and 1, 2, or 3. Thus 2B should incorporate all the lines and symbols in 2 and B. One of the squares, 1A to 3C, is incorrect. Which one is it?

(Solution 85)

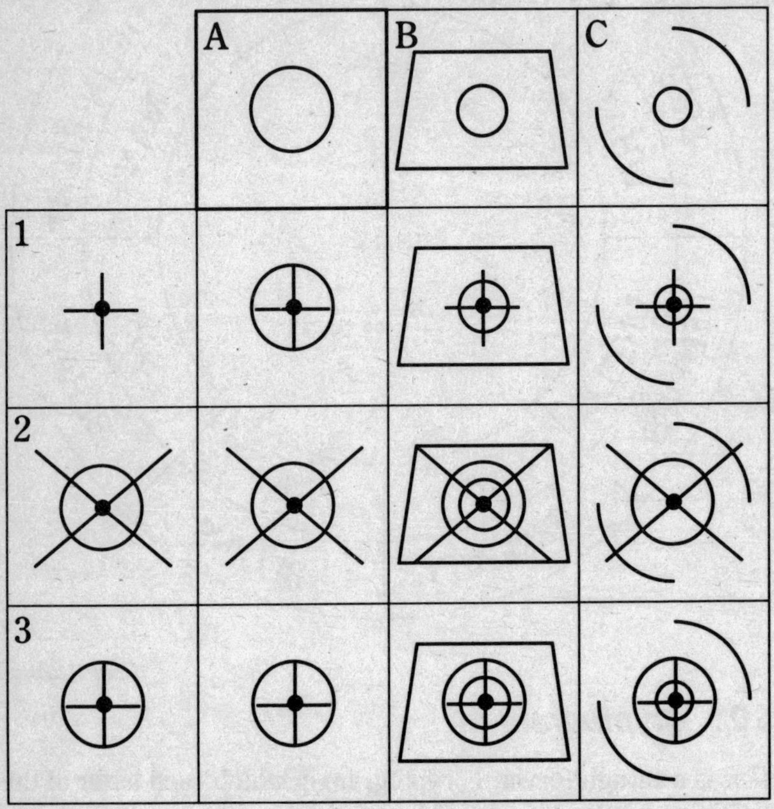

103 Anagram Theme

Arrange the sixteen words in pairs so that each pair is an anagram of another word. The eight words produced have a linking theme. For example, if the words TRY and CREASE appeared in the list they could be paired to form the word SECRETARY and the theme could be PROFESSIONS. (Words are not necessarily one from each column.)

AM	AMINE
BY	EMU
FARM	FAT
FINE	FORT
HE	RACK
RAG	RAIN
ROMP	SO
SWORE	TRACE

(Solution 89)

104 Analogy

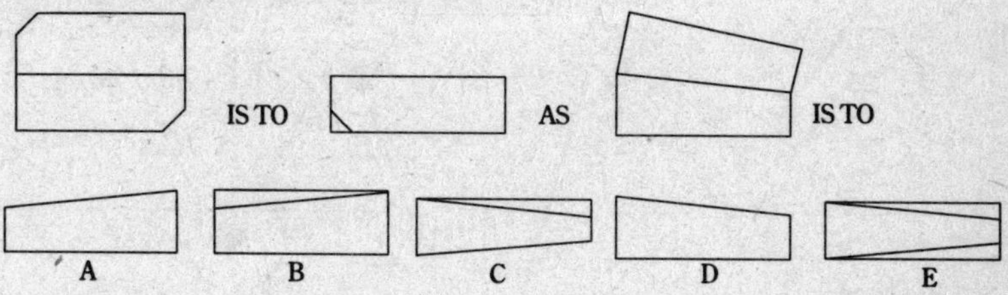

(Solution 92)

105 'Y' Puzzle

Find twenty-seven words that each contain at least one 'Y'. Move from letter to letter along the lines. Letters may be used more than once.

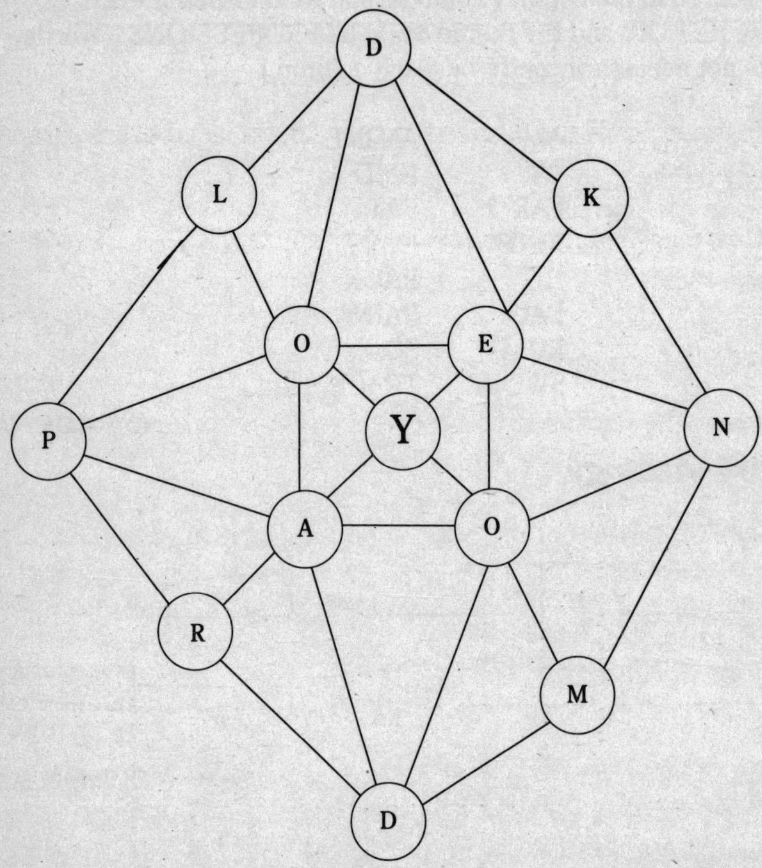

(Solution 97)

106 Rectangle

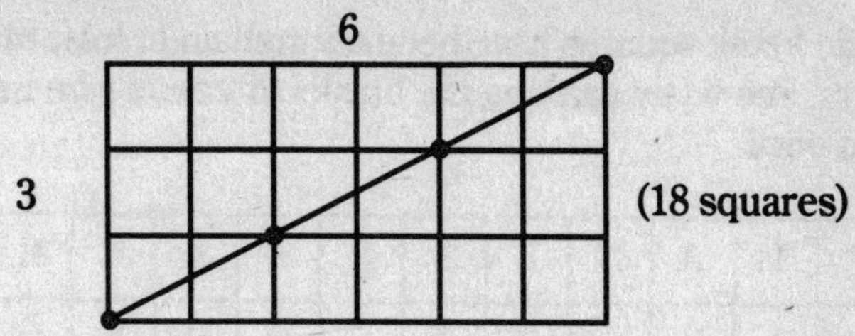

In the example the diagonal crosses four points that are corners of squares.

How many points will be crossed in a rectangle 36 × 24 (864 squares)?

(Solution 101)

107 Alphabet Clueless-Cross

Insert the remaining nineteen of the twenty-six letters of the alphabet to complete the crossword.

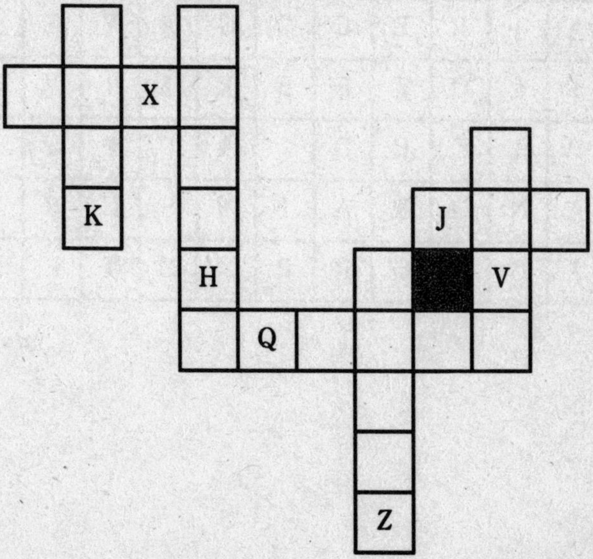

(Solution 105)

108 No Blanks

All the blank squares have been omitted and replaced with letters. See if you can find the blanks to form a symmetrical crossword.

P	L	A	N	E	T	S	F	A	T	H	E	R
U	A	R	O	R	O	T	O	R	N	O	V	A
F	R	I	D	A	Y	A	R	U	N	L	E	T
F	U	S	E	S	E	R	U	M	A	D	R	H
I	C	E	D	I	D	I	M	I	M	E	R	E
N	O	S	E	D	A	M	A	B	O	R	E	R
E	B	B	C	O	S	A	M	A	R	O	B	E
C	R	O	O	N	I	L	O	G	A	S	E	S
H	A	I	R	E	C	O	G	R	Y	E	L	P
A	I	L	O	Z	E	B	R	A	I	V	E	E
S	P	I	C	E	D	L	A	P	P	E	A	L
E	A	N	O	R	A	I	N	S	U	R	E	L
S	I	G	N	O	R	P	D	E	T	E	R	S

(Solution 109)

109 Logic

Logically, which circle fits the pattern?

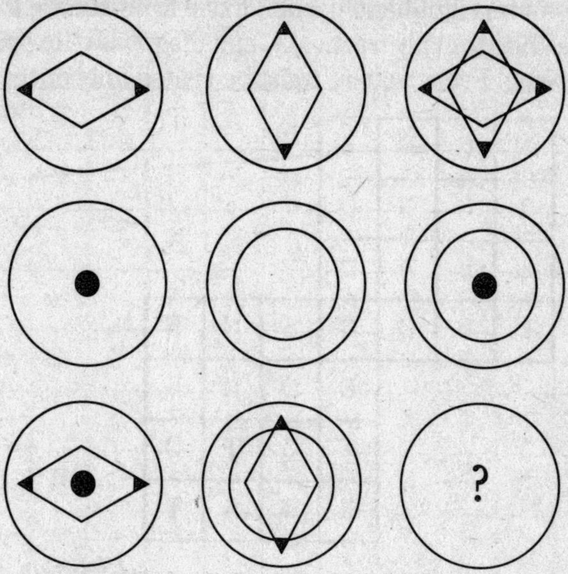

A

B

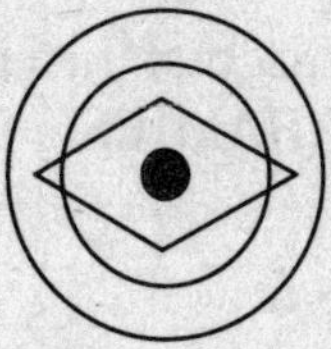

C

D

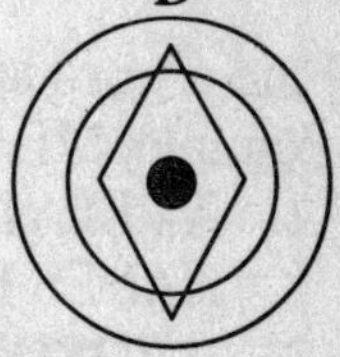

E

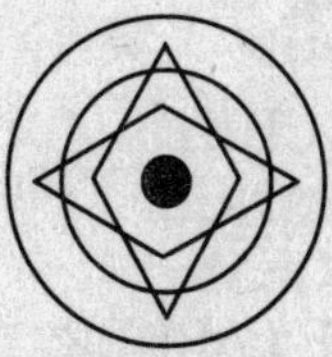

F

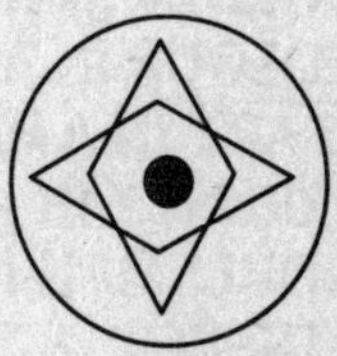

G

(Solution 112)

110 An Irish Proverb

Starting from the "N" in the top left-hand corner and ending with the "T" in the bottom right-hand corner, move from square to adjacent square (horizontally, vertically, and diagonally) to spell out an Irish proverb. Every square must be visited only once.

N	G	D	I			
T	O	N	D			
H	E	A	D			
H	E	O	D	S	N	E
			E	O	H	B
			T	O	T	O
			R	W	A	T

(Solution 117)

111 Containers

Find a word and its container for each of the clues below. For example, MEAT IN A RIVER = T(HAM)ES.

1. A RELATIVE IN A GLOVE
2. HADES IN THE ISLANDS
3. A BORDER IN A TOPIC
4. A COLOUR IN A SHIP
5. DEPART IN A HATCHET
6. CURRENCY IN A DANCE
7. A NOBLEMAN IN GEMS
8. AN INSECT IN THE LARDER
9. AT THAT TIME IN A CAPITAL
10. FOLD IN A STATE

(Solution 121)

112 Connections

Insert the numbers 0 – 9 in the circles, so that for any particular circle the sum of the numbers in the circles connected directly to it equals the value corresponding to the number in that circle, as given in the list.

Example: 1 = 14 (4 + 7 + 3)
4 = 8 (7 + 1)
7 = 5 (4 + 1)
3 = 1

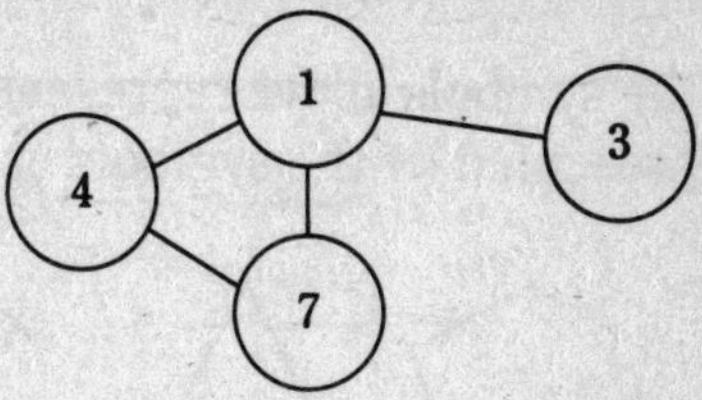

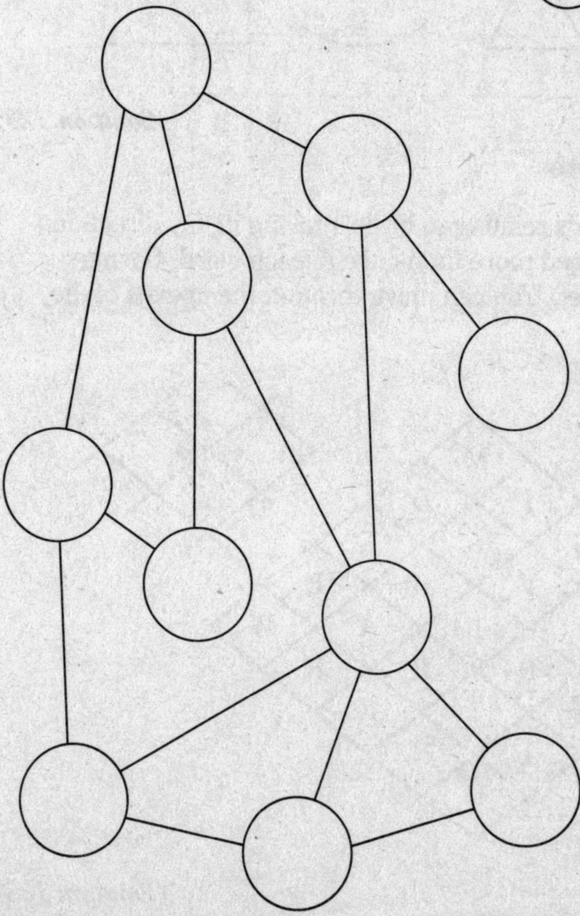

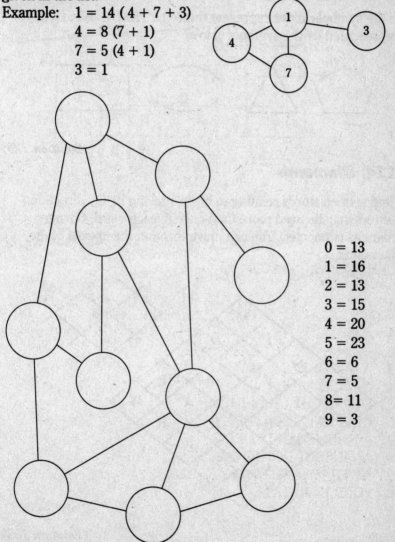

0 = 13
1 = 16
2 = 13
3 = 15
4 = 20
5 = 23
6 = 6
7 = 5
8= 11
9 = 3

(Solution 125)

113 Trade

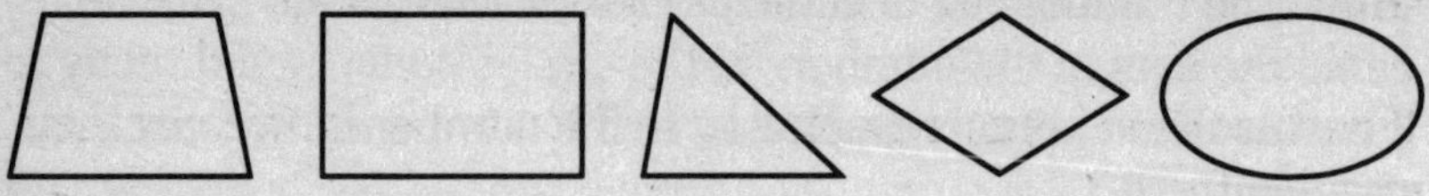

If the symbols above represent the word TRADE. What word is represented by the symbols below?

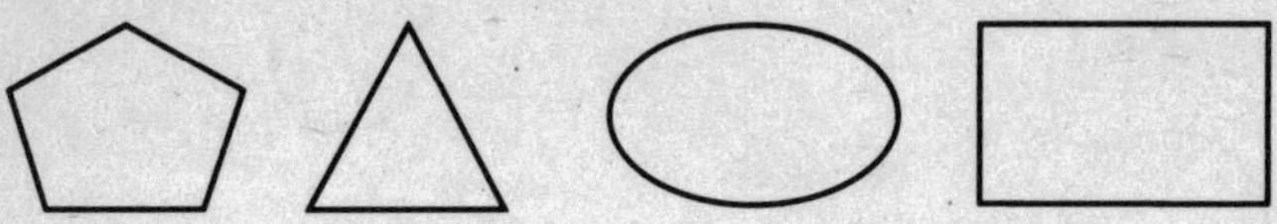

(Solution 129)

114 Diamonds

Find sixteen words relating to birds, moving in any direction. Letters may be used more than once in each word. Corners count as connected. You can move through the apexes of the diamonds:

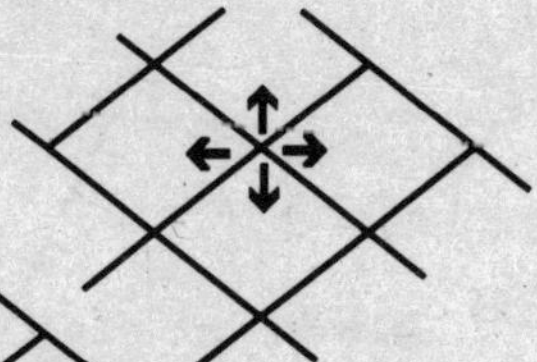

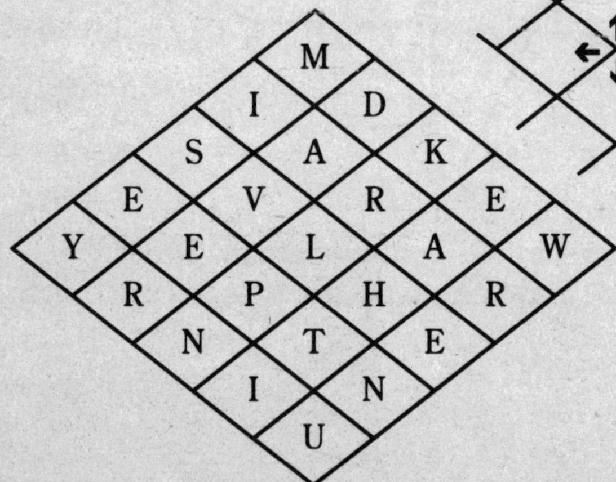

(Solution 133)

115 Cement

"How heavy is this bag of cement?" asked the builder.

"Five thousand pounds divided by half its own weight," said the merchant.

How much did the bag of cement weigh?

(Solution 136)

116 Words

Hostility
Intermezzo
Joyfully
Heifer
Fiddlesticks
Lockjaw

Logically, which word comes next?

Publisher
Racehorse
Tormentor
Galantine
Cantabile
Whimsical

(Solution 141)

117 Bracket Word

Place two letters in each pair of brackets so that they finish the word on the left and start the word on the right. Reading downwards in pairs, the letters in the brackets will spell out a 10-letter word.

SO	(• •)	AL
AR	(• •)	IN
BE	(• •)	D
T	(• •)	ON
ME	(• •)	L

(Solution 145)

118 Circles

Which of these fit into the blank circle to carry on a logical sequence?

A B C D E

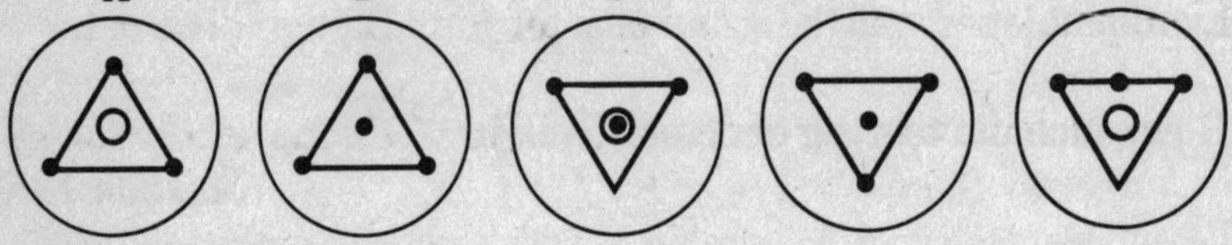

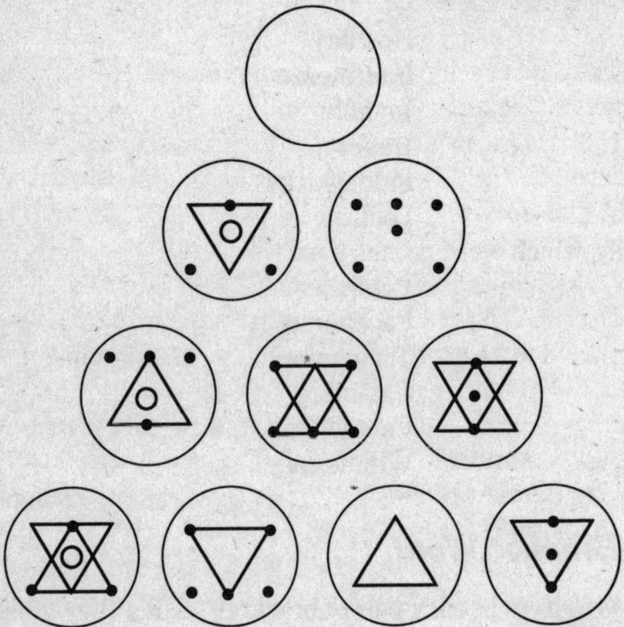

(Solution 149)

119 Roman Numerals

The year 2000 will have just two Roman numerals, MM. Which year in the previous 2000 had the most Roman numerals?

(Solution 153)

120 Porky Pies

How good are you at trivia? Each of the following presents three statements, one of which is a fabrication, the other two are true. Can you spot the untruth in each case?

1. a) Maloney was the name of actor John Barrymore's pet vulture.
   b) Raoulle was the barking dog in the 1978 movie *The Buddy Holly Story.*
   c) Herman was Maxim de Winter's pet cocker spaniel in the 1940 movie *Rebecca.*

2. a) The 31st president of the United States, Herbert Hoover, was a Quaker.
   b) John Edgar Hoover, head of the FBI, was twice married.
   c) Irwin H. "Ike" Hoover was the first chief usher at the White House.

3. a) Duke Ellington's real first name was Edmund.
   b) Dizzy Gillespie's real first name was Desmond.
   c) Jelly Roll Morton's real first name was Ferdinand.

4. a) Elvis Presley once recorded the song "I'll Take You Home Again, Kathleen".
   b) "I'm Forever Blowing Bubbles" was the theme song of the 1931 movie *Public Enemy.*
   c) "I Cried For You" was the song that Ginger Rogers sang to a photo of Mickey Rooney in the 1939 movie *Babes in Arms.*

5. a) In 1978, golfer Jack Nicklaus landed a 1,358-pound marlin, the biggest fish caught off Australia that year.
   b) Jockey Billy Pearson once won $64,000 on TV answering questions about art.
   c) Hurricane Mills was a heavyweight boxer who was once a member of the USA bobsled team.

(Solution 161)

121 The Hexagonal Circle

What should be the contents of the top hexagon?

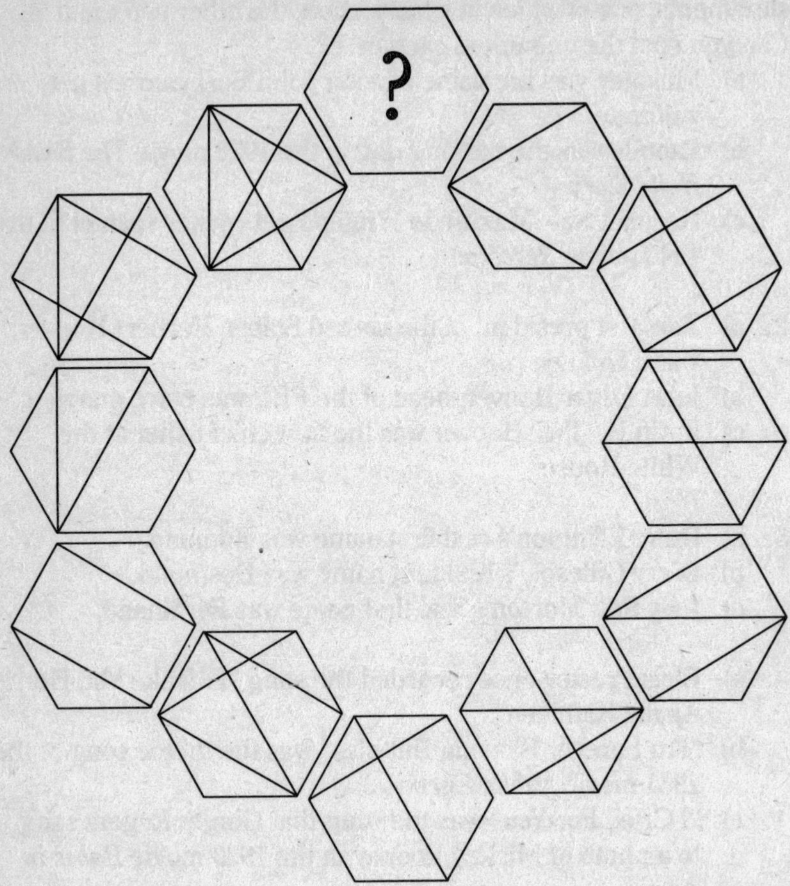

(Solution 2)

122 Logic

What number should follow next in this sequence to a definite rule?

4 – 6 – 6 – 6 – 4 – 2 – 4 – 8 – 2 – 1 – 8 – ?

(Solution 6)

123 Diamond

Find the longest word, moving to adjacent diamonds in any direction indicated in the diagram below.

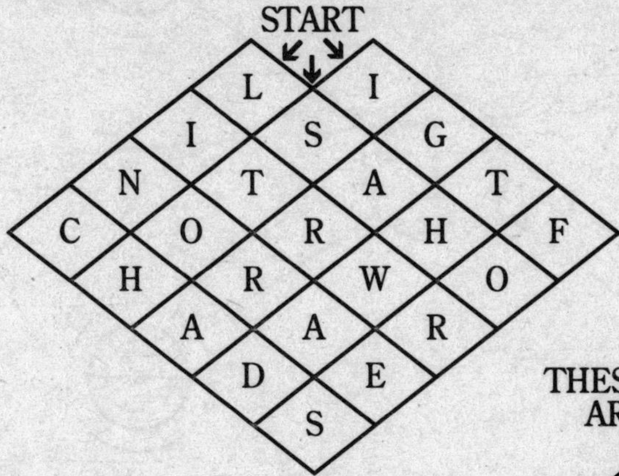

THESE DIRECTIONS
ARE ALLOWED

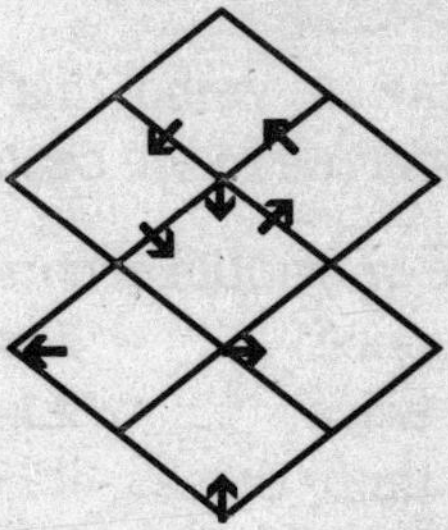

(Solution 10)

124 Common

What do these words have in common?

Rain
Mark
Land
Tine
Pore
Wait
Pain
Ales

(Solution 14)

125 Symbols

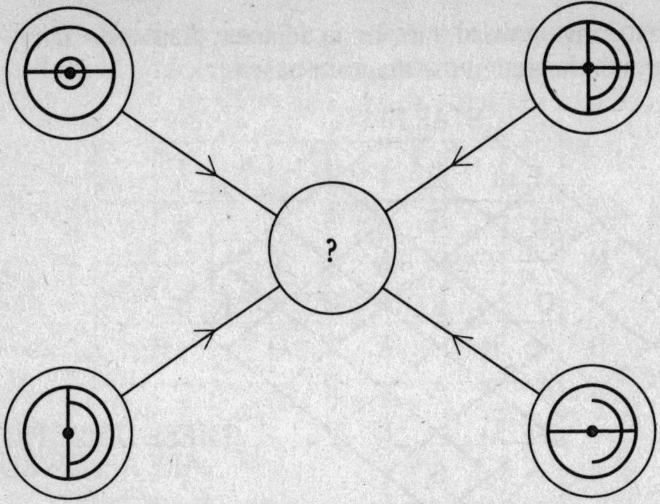

Each line or symbol that appears in the four outer circles, above, is transferred to the centre circle according to these rules:

If a line or symbol occurs in the outer circles:

once	it is	transferred
twice	it is	possibly transferred
three times	it is	transferred
four times	it is	not transferred

Which of the circles A, B, C, D, or E shown below should appear at the centre of the diagram?

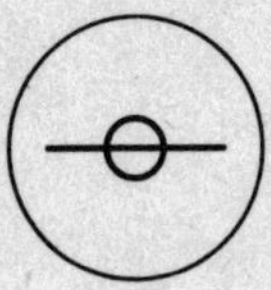
A

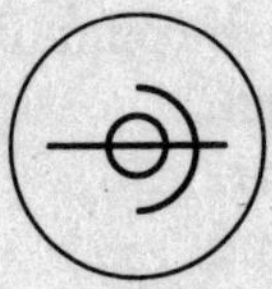
B

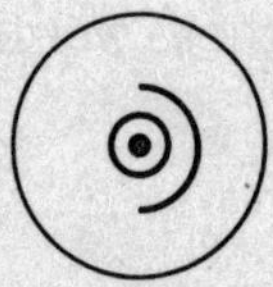
C

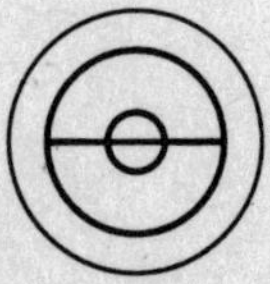
D

E

(Solution 18)

126 Division

Divide the grid into four equal parts, each of which is the same shape and contains the same sixteen letters, which can be arranged into a 16-letter word.

E	A	A	D	I	A	I	F
I	L	L	T	I	N	B	Y
F	I	N	T	D	I	E	G
B	T	I	G	Y	A	I	T
G	D	Y	E	I	A	I	I
N	I	B	F	T	D	A	I
Y	L	I	E	T	B	L	T
T	F	A	I	I	A	G	N

(Solution 24)

127 Sequence

What is the next number in this sequence?

199, 280, 344, 360, 396, ?

(Solution 26)

128 Synonyms

In each of the following, a number of synonyms of the keyword are shown. Take one letter from each of the synonyms to find a further synonym of the keyword. The letters appear in the correct order.

1. Keyword: HOMOGENEOUS
   Synonyms: Unvarying, Analogous, Kindred, Akin, Cognate
2. Keyword: PURITANICAL
   Synonyms: Narrow, Disapproving, Strict, Severe, Austere, Bigoted, Fanatical
3. Keyword: GARRULOUS
   Synonyms: Gossiping, Verbose, Talkative, Chatty, Loquacious, Gushing, Babbling
4. Keyword: GROOVE
   Synonyms: Furrow, Hollow, Gutter, Indentation, Trench
5. Keyword: PROPULSION
   Synonyms: Drive, Momentum, Pressure, Power, Thrust, Push, Impulse

(Solution 30)

129 Hexagonal Sequence

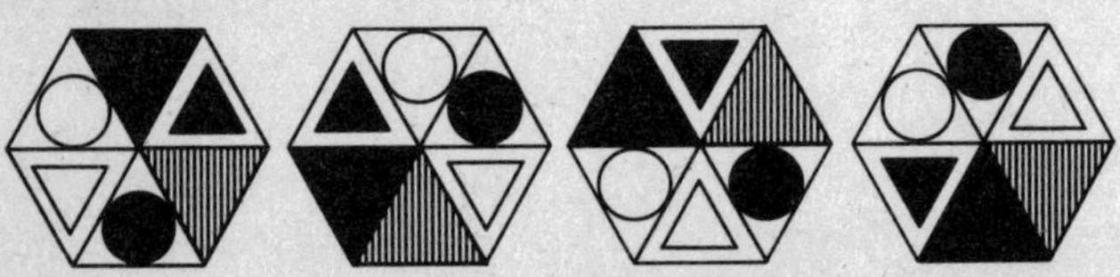

Which hexagon below continues the above sequence?

(Solution 34)

130 Word Power

Working from the top down, solve the clues and place the letters on the circles of the pyramid. Each answer is the previous answer rearranged, with one letter added. Clues are given in no particular order.

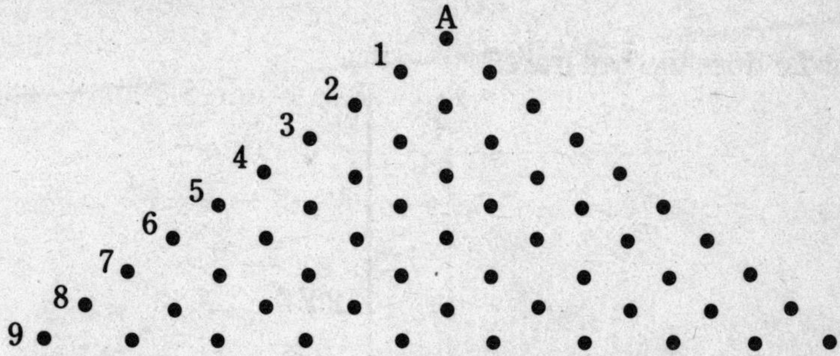

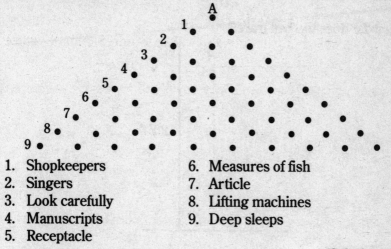

1. Shopkeepers
2. Singers
3. Look carefully
4. Manuscripts
5. Receptacle
6. Measures of fish
7. Article
8. Lifting machines
9. Deep sleeps

(Solution 39)

131 Odd One Out

Which is the odd one out?

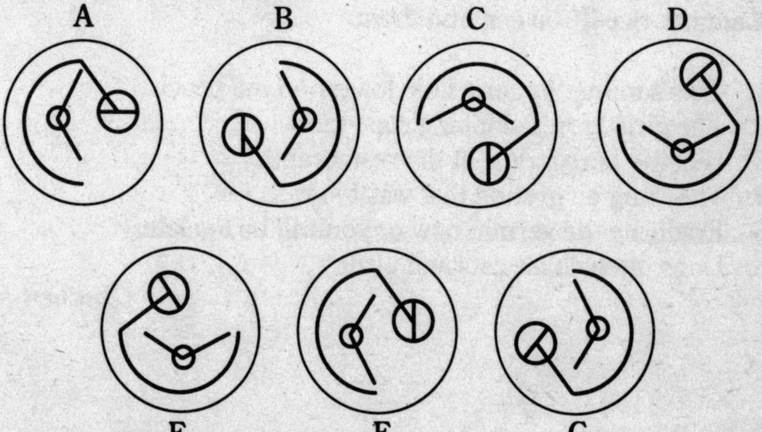

(Solution 42)

132 Ball

A ball is dropped to the ground from a height of twelve feet. It bounces up half of the original height, then falls back to the ground. It repeats this, always bouncing back half of the previous height.

How far does the ball travel?

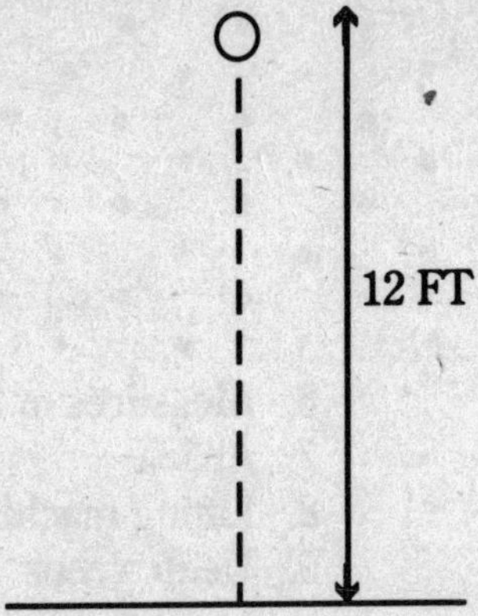

(Solution 46)

133 Hidden Fish

Hidden in the sentences are the names of five fish and one sea mammal. See if you can find them.

1. This summer linger a little longer on the beach.
2. The girls have a skipping rope race.
3. Will the bursar dine at the restaurant?
4. They dug on ground that was too wet.
5. Eradicate the vermin now or you will be too late.
6. Dogs often chase cats and birds.

(Solution 50)

134 Anagram Phrases

Each of the following is an anagram of a well-known phrase. For example:

SO NOTE HOLE = ON THE LOOSE

1. AH! LOVING FATE
2. SHOOT TENDER GREEN FLOWER AT GUESTS
3. TO NOTE FEET IN MINUS
4. HONE KEY OUR STRIP
5. USE DRAM OR FOE GO

(Solution 54)

135 Grid Logic

Insert the missing letters in the top left-hand corner square.

	TO	TO	FO	FO
OT	TT	TT	FT	FT
OT	TT	TT	FT	FT
OF	TF	TF	FF	FF
OF	TF	TF	FF	FF

(Solution 58)

136 Margana

If we presented you with the words MAR, AM and FAR and asked you to find the shortest English word that contained all the letters from which these words could be produced, we would expect you to come up with the word FARM.

Here is another list of words:

JOLT, ROUT, STAR, SIN

What is the shortest English word from which all these words can be produced?

(Solution 62)

137 Analogy

IS TO

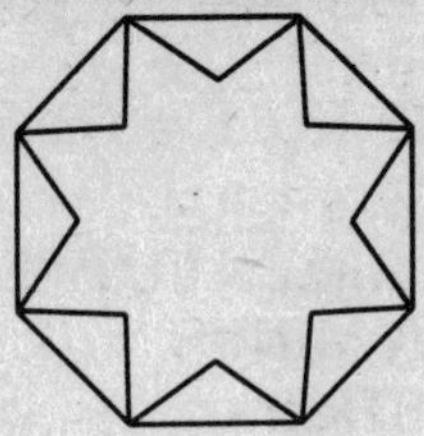

AS

IS TO

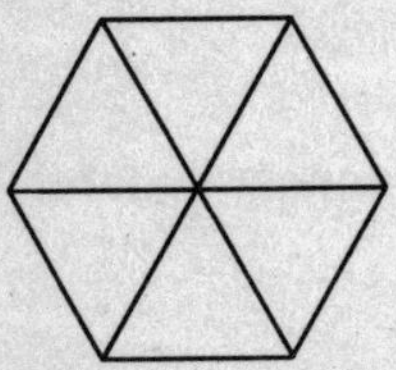

A

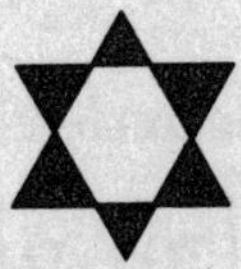

B

C

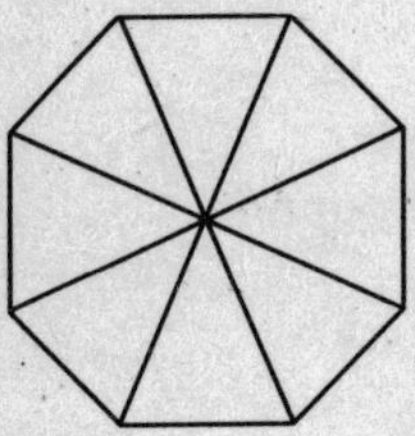

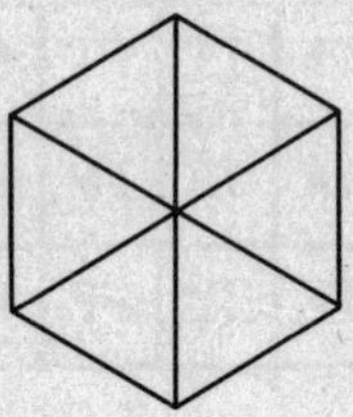

E

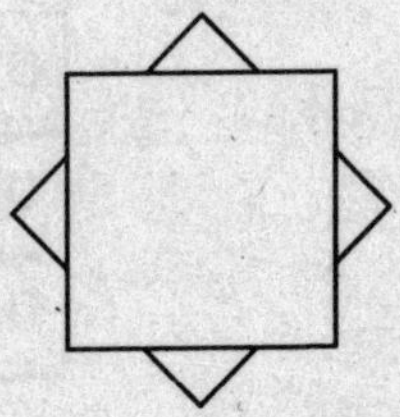

F

(Solution 66)

138 Four Letters

Each of these sets of four letters forms part of a longer word. Some of the words are hyphenated.

SHBO
YEBR
NGPL
GHFL
RKSM
EE-QU
TLEB
GSPR
HY-WA
GONL
CHHO
NWRI

(Solution 70)

139 Initials

What do these initials stand for? For example:

16 O in a P = 16 Ounces in a pound

6 – P on a P T
32 – P on a C
6 – S on a S
3 – F in a Y
1 – G T D A
3 – C in the F
13 – M in a L Y
12 – S on a D

(Solution 75)

140 Word Search

Find 31 NAUTICAL TERMS. Words run horizontally, vertically, or diagonally, but only in a straight line. Every letter is used at least once.

R	S	T	O	W	A	W	A	Y	R
E	E	O	S	A	L	V	O	E	E
T	O	R	N	A	D	O	G	D	T
A	S	P	O	R	T	G	I	K	A
W	R	E	N	H	E	T	H	C	W
K	A	D	W	L	S	C	R	O	H
A	T	O	T	E	T	E	E	L	S
E	B	O	H	E	W	E	R	W	E
R	O	C	K	E	T	E	P	O	R
B	A	R	N	A	C	L	E	R	F

(Solution 78)

141 Magic Prime Square

Using prime numbers only, complete the square so that each horizontal, vertical, and corner-to-corner line totals the same.

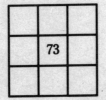

	73	

(Solution 82)

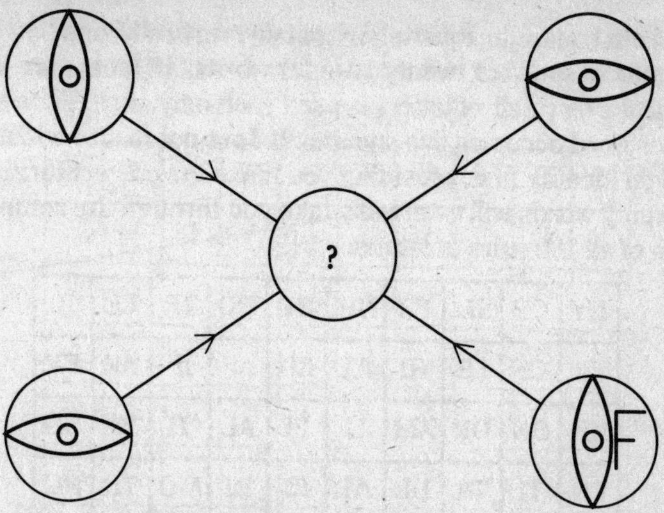

Each line or symbol that appears in the four outer circles, above, is transferred to the centre circle according to these rules:

If a line or symbol occurs in the outer circles:

once	it is	transferred
twice	it is	possibly transferred
three times	it is	transferred
four times	it is	not transferred

Which of the circles A, B, C, D, or E shown below should appear at the centre of the diagram?

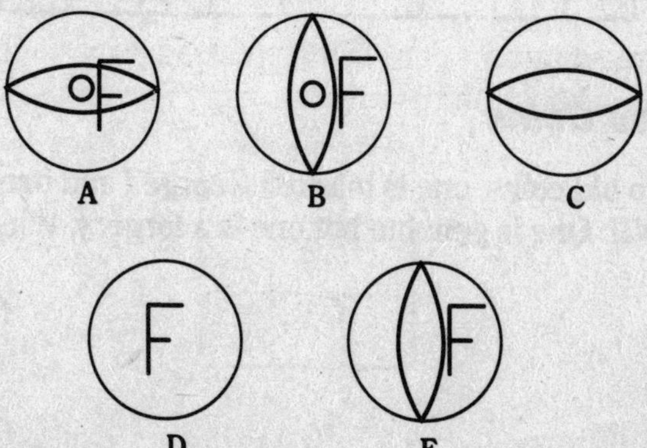

(Solution 86)

143 10-Letter Words Boggle

Work from square to square horizontally, vertically, and diagonally to spell out twenty 10-letter words. All letters are in pairs, and every pair of letters is used each only once. Thus each 10-letter word occupies five squares. It does not matter which word you identify first, providing you make the correct turnings. The twenty words will eventually take you through the complete pattern of all 100 pairs of letters.

HY	OP	IL	PH	HW	RT	WO	TR	LE	IL
PR	OS	LE	HI	AT	ED	AF	IP	AR	EV
UD	ON	DR	AM	LI	FI	AL	TI	VA	UD
EN	TI	TA	UL	AT	IC	BI	MO	TE	NG
NC	TI	EX	AL	IC	ST	LE	TO	AU	HI
IL	CO	AL	AC	JE	MA	ER	EV	ER	YT
IA	RY	RV	EO	AU	OV	RC	RI	TA	VE
IO	CU	FI	US	UL	SP	DE	AN	GE	ON
US	IT	CT	TF	IO	IC	UN	TI	TR	TI
TH	OU	GH	US	EX	HI	BI	ON	AJ	EC

(Solution 90)

144 Two Coins

I have two old coins, one is marked George I and one is marked Edward VII. One is genuine but one is a forgery. Which is the forgery?

(Solution 94)

145 Hexagons

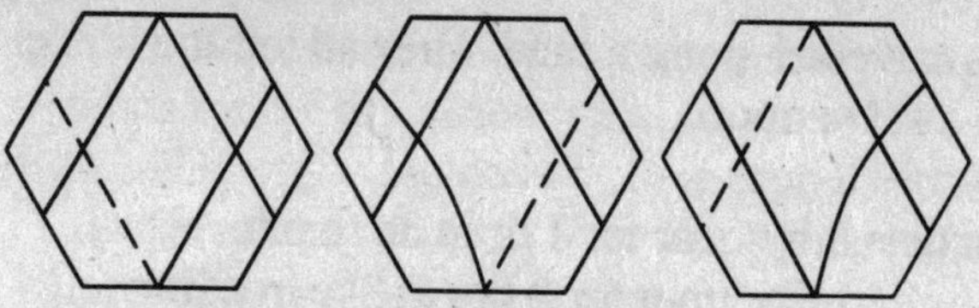

Which hexagon below continues the above sequence?

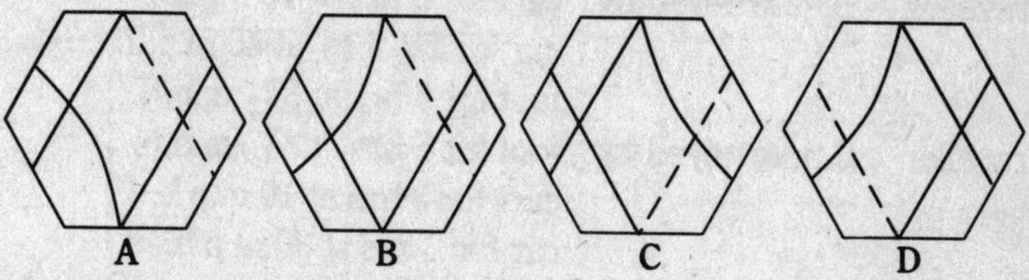

(Solution 98)

146 Star

Find the 12-letter word by going into all of the compartments, each only once.

(Solution 102)

147 Silent Order

Which 8-letter word links these words?

Knoll
Heifer
Indict
Knew
Doubt
Toast
Nascent
Knickers

(Solution 106)

148 Journey

Three hitchhikers travelled along a road. They all left the hostel at the same time – twelve noon.

Traveller	A journeyed by	car for 1 hr at 30 m.p.h.
		foot for 3 hrs at $3\frac{1}{3}$ m.p.h.
		cart for 4 hrs at 10 m.p.h.
Traveller	B journeyed by	cart for 2 hrs at 10 m.p.h.
		car for $1\frac{1}{2}$ hrs at 40 m.p.h.
		foot for 3 hrs at $3\frac{1}{3}$ m.p.h.
Traveller	C journeyed by	foot for 3 hrs at $3\frac{1}{3}$ m.p.h.
		cart for 3 hrs at 10 m.p.h.
		car for 2 hrs at 30 m.p.h.

Who overtook whom and at what time?

(Solution 111)

149 Magic Word Square

The answers to the five clues are all 5-letter words that, when placed correctly in the grid will form a magic square in which the five words can be read both horizontally and vertically.

Clues (in no particular order):
Rhythmical effects
Existing in particular place
In pieces
Short-necked giraffe-like animal
Watercourse

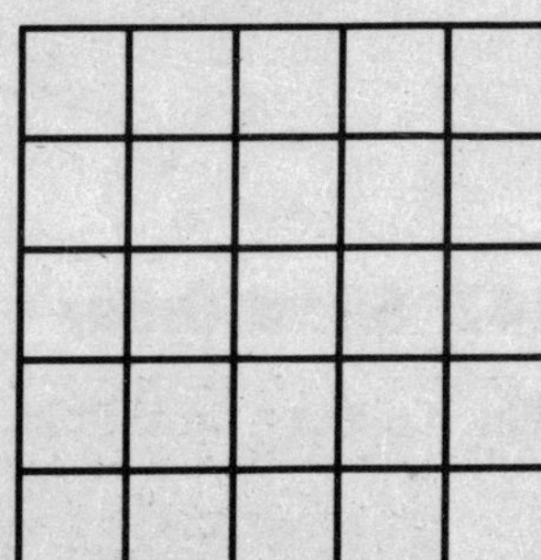

(Solution 114)

150 Sequence

Which option below carries on the above sequence?

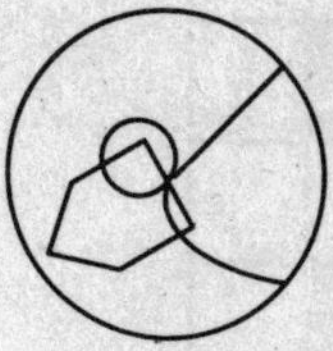

A

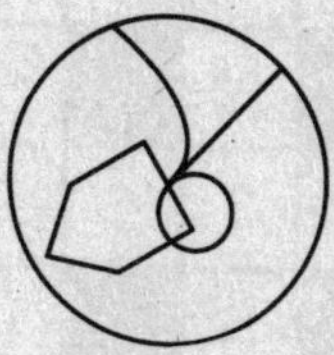

B

C

D

E

(Solution 118)

151 People

In a set of 100 people, 63 have a height of over 5′6″ and 75 have a weight of more than 140 pounds. What are the greatest and least possible numbers of people over 5′6″ and more than 140 pounds. Each person has at least one of these features.

(Solution 122)

152 Brain Strain

Insert numbers into the spaces so that the calculations are correct across and down. All numbers to be inserted are less than 10.

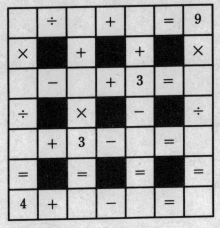

	÷		+		=	9
×		+		+		×
	−		+	3	=	
÷		×		−		÷
	+	3	−		=	
=		=		=		=
4	+		−		=	

(Solution 126)

153 Common

What do these words have in common?

Shadow
Rifles
Mugging
Tundra
Mural
Precaution
Emily
Boracic
Resort

(Solution 130)

154 Complete the Quotations

Each of the following is an anagram of one word. Solve the anagrams and then place the ten words into the correct quotations.

A. NOR I SHAME
B. CHEER SIR
C. O TIDY CRIME
D. MOTH PAN
E. PIN CASH
F. COVER ON SAINT
G. PRISES OPEN A TRAP
H. ROOT WORM
I. REACH IT CUTER
J. SEAL A PUP

1. It is far harder to kill a _____ than a reality."
   – *Virginia Woolf*
2. "_____ is often the busiest day of the week."
   – *Spanish Proverb*
3. "After all, the only proper intoxication is _____."
   – *Oscar Wilde*
4. "The _____ of bound books are like the flowers of the field."
   – *Hilaire Belloc*
5. "Gave up _____ for lent." – *F. Scott Fitzgerald*
6. "The excellence of a gift lies in its _____ rather than its value." – *Charles Dudley Warner*
7. "_____ obtains more with application than superiority without it." – *Baltasar Gracián*
8. "_____ is the beginning of abuse." – *Japanese Proverb*
9. "_____ is a sort of oratory of power by means of forms."
   – *Friedrich Nietzsche*
10. "He who likes _____ soon learns to climb."
    – *German Proverb*

(Solution 134)

155 A Long Time

Substitute numbers for letters in this multiplication problem. Each letter represents a different number from 1 to 9. There are two possible answers.

A × LONG = TIME

(Solution 138)

156 Shields Matrix

What symbol should logically appear on the bottom right-hand shield?

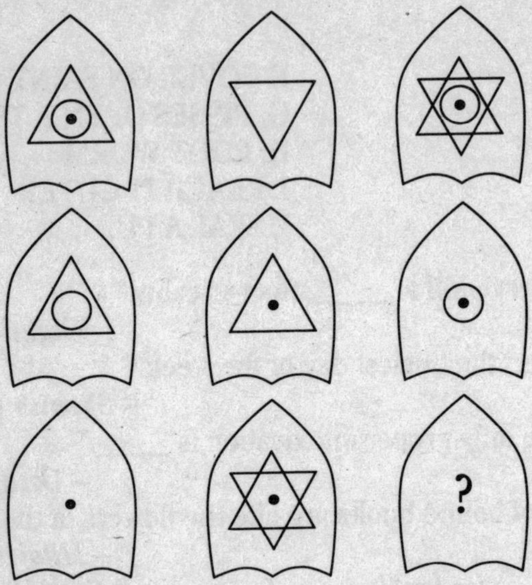

Choose from:

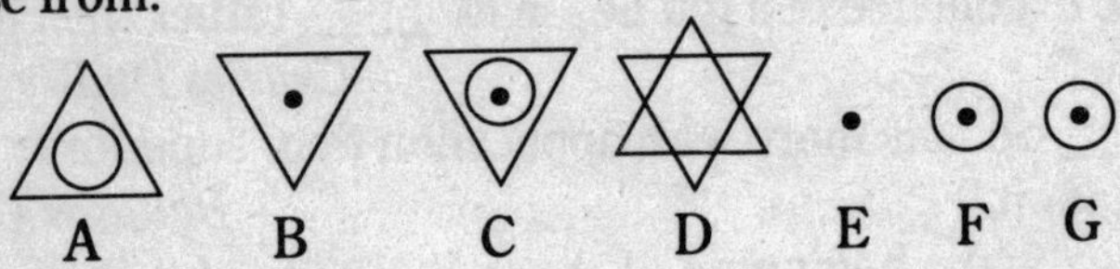

(Solution 142)

157 Animals

Hidden in the sentences are the names of five animals. See if you can find them.

1. Give the imp a large brandy.
2. You will soon age really quickly.
3. Watch out for he suspects trouble brewing.
4. Put the saucepan there on the table.
5. Drive a car a calculated distance.

(Solution 146)

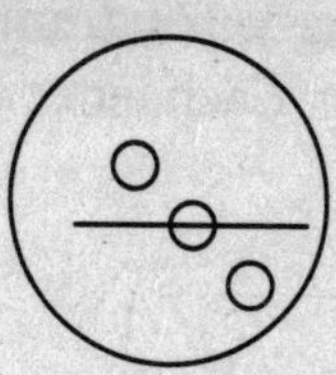

IS TO

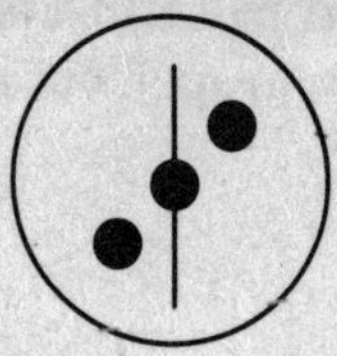

AS

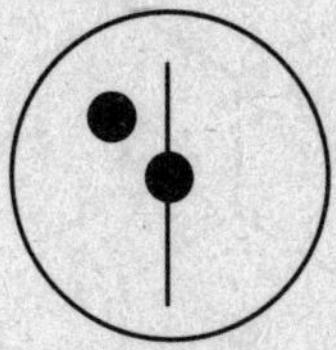

IS TO

?

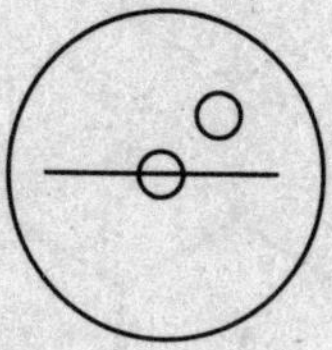

A

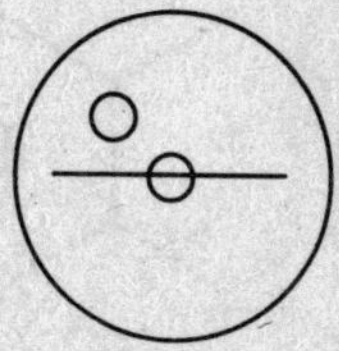

B

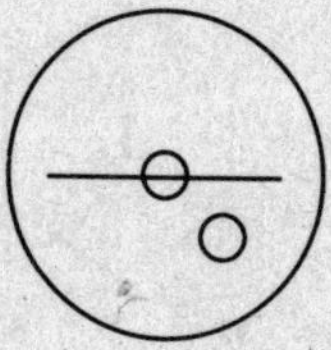

C

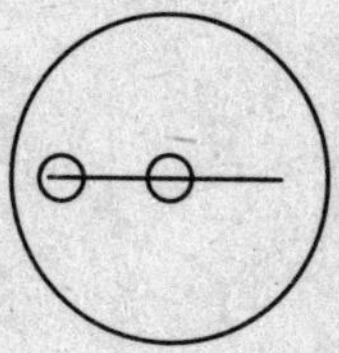

D

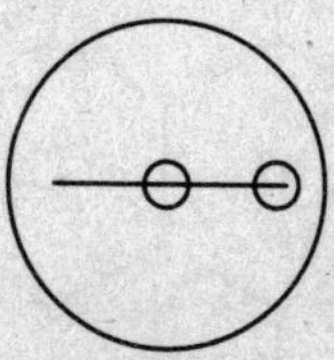

E

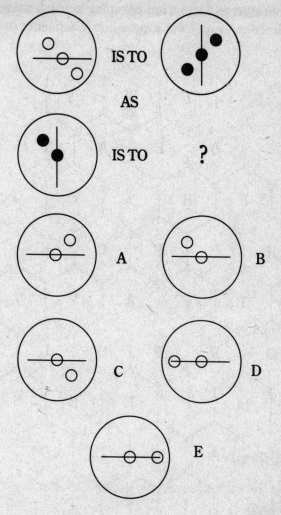

(Solution 150)

159 Honeycomb

Work from start to finish from adjoining letter to adjoining letter in any direction to spell out a quotation. Each letter is used only once.

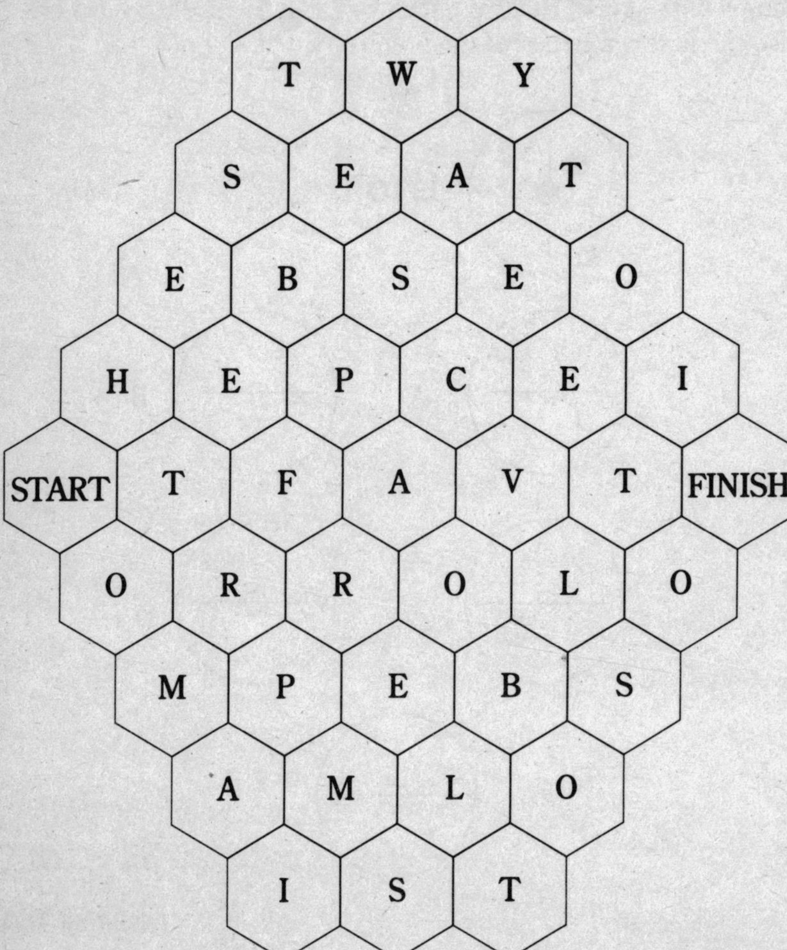

(Solution 154)

160 Word Cycle

Complete the twelve words below, so that the same two letters that end the first word also start the second word; the two letters that end the second word also start the third word; etc. To complete the cycle, the two letters that end the twelfth word are also the first two letters of the first word.

• • E E • •
• • N I • •
• • I G • •
• • S I • •
• • I G • •
• • L I • •
• • L L • •
• • C A • •
• • S T • •
• • T H • •
• • L U • •
• • T A • •

(Solution 157)

161 Analogy

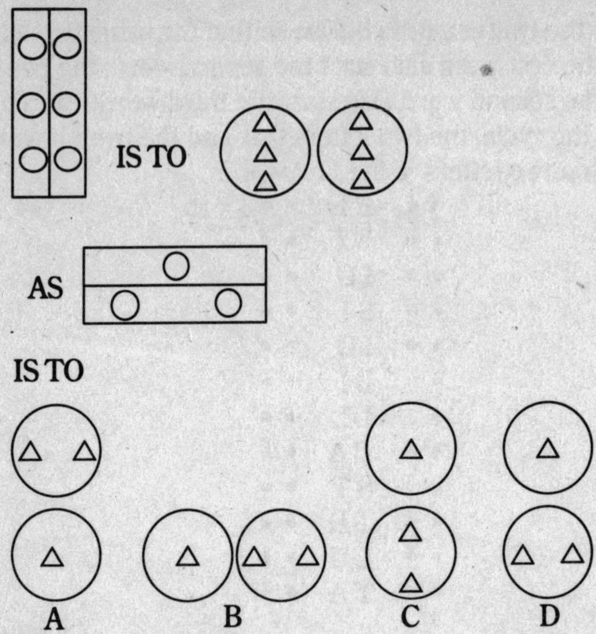

(Solution 158)

The Solutions

1 Cards

IMPLANTATION:

I	KH	13
M	QS	12
P	AC	15
L	KC	13
A	AD	15
N	AS	15
T	KD	13
A	QC	12
T	QH	12
I	KS	13
O	QD	12
N	AH	15
		160

(Question 81)

2 The Hexagonal Circle

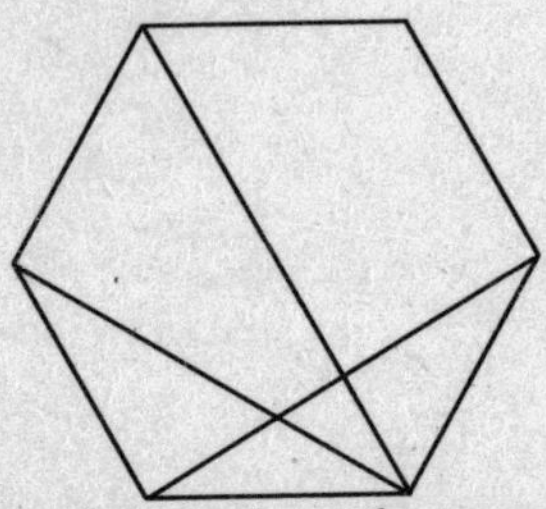

Start at the bottom hexagon and work upward. Every third hexagon in a straight line contains the contents of the two below it, but when two lines appear in the same position they cancel each other out.

(Question 121)

3 Knight's Saying

That man is great who can use the brains of others to carry out his work.

– by *Don Piatt*

(Question 1)

4 Triple Choice

1. (b)
2. (b)
3. (a)
4. (a)
5. (c)
6. (a)
7. (c)
8. (a)
9. (c)
10. (a)

(Question 41)

5 Saying

"The strong take from the weak, the rich take from the poor, and the government take from everyone." – *Glomm's Law*

(Question 82)

6 Logic

4:
Each number represents the number of letters in each word of the question.

(Question 122)

7 Centre Word

TEN:

ROTTEN	TENANT
BATTEN	TENDON
FATTEN	TENON

(Question 2)

8 Link Words

ATE

(Question 42)

9 Synonym Circles

Blissful
Ecstatic

(Question 83)

10 Diamond

Straightforward

(Question 123)

11 Pulleys

A to B gives a clockwise direction at a speed of 10, but B to C halves the speed and C to D reverses the direction, so E revolves counter-clockwise at a speed of 5.

(Question 3)

12 Horse Race

4 to 1 against:

No.	Odds	Stake to win £100	Returned £ (including stake)
1	2 to 1	33.33	100
2	3 to 1	25.00	100
3	4 to 1	20.00	100
4	5 to 1	16.67	100
5	4 to 1	20.00	100
		115.00	Total stake
		100.00	Pay out
		£15.00	Profit

$\frac{15}{100} = 15\%$

(Question 43)

13 Nine Digits

32,547,891 × 6 = 195,287,346

(Question 84)

14 Common

They are all endings of COUNTRIES:

bahRAIN
denMARK
finLAND
palesTINE
singaPORE
kuWAIT
sPAIN
wALES

(Question 124)

15 Poser

P	O	S	E	R
S	E	R	P	O
R	P	O	S	E
O	S	E	R	P
E	R	P	O	S

(Question 4)

16 Three Too Many

R	E	T	I	R	E	D
E		A		E		E
D	I	G	I	T	A	L
U		E		I		U
C	A	T	E	R	E	D
E		E		E		E
D	E	S	I	R	E	D

(Question 44)

17 Grid

1C.

(Question 85)

18 Symbols

B.

(Question 125)

19 Grid

1A.

(Question 5)

20 Symbols

B.

(Question 45)

21 Alphametics

$$\begin{array}{r} 490 \\ 407 \\ +\quad 107 \\ \hline 1004 \end{array}$$

(Question 86)

22 Cryptogram I

"Be bold. If you're going to make an error, make a doozy, and don't be afraid to hit the ball." – *Billie Jean King*

(Question 6)

23 Cryptogram II

Millions of words are written annually, purporting to tell how to beat the races, whereas the best possible advice on the subject is found in the three monosyllables: "DO NOT TRY." – *Dan Parker*

(Question 46)

24 Division

Indefatigability:

E	A	A	D	I	A	I	F
I	L	L	T	I	N	B	Y
F	I	N	T	D	I	E	G
B	T	I	G	Y	A	I	T
G	D	Y	E	I	A	I	I
N	I	B	F	T	D	A	I
Y	L	I	E	T	B	L	T
T	F	A	I	I	A	G	N

(Question 126)

25 Languages

German, Icelandic, Lao, Amharic, Romanian, Urdu, Bengali, Arabic, Nepali
Anagram: BULGARIAN.

(Question 87)

26 Sequence

477:
Square the middle digit each time and add this to the number.
For example:

$$3\dot{9}6 + 9^2\ (81) = 477$$

(Question 127)

27 Pentagon Figures

4:
$3 \times 9 \times 9 = 243$, or 3^5
$1 \times 2 \times 16 = 32$, or 2^5
$32 \times 8 \times 4 = 1024$, or 4^5

(Question 7)

28 Rectangle to Greek Cross

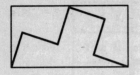

(Question 47)

29 Book Titles

1. *Of Mice and Men* (John Steinbeck)
2. *Elmer Gantry* (Sinclair Lewis)
3. *The Great Gatsby* (F. Scott Fitzgerald)
4. *The Winds of War* (Herman Wouk)
5. *To Kill a Mockingbird* (Harper Lee)

(Question 88)

30 Synonyms

1. Alike 2. Ascetic 3. Prating
4. Flute 5. Impetus

(Question 128)

31 Wot! No Vowels?

By, Slyly, Ply, Spy, Hymn, Tryst, Wry

(Question 8)

32 Motors

$$\frac{3}{10} \times \frac{2}{9} = \frac{6}{90} = \frac{1}{15}$$

Chances are 1 in 15.

(Question 48)

33 Triangles Matrix

C:
Looking both across and down, the contents of the third square are formed by combining the contents of the first two squares, except that where two triangles coincide in the same position in the first two squares, they are then cancelled out in the third square.

(Question 89)

34 Hexagonal Sequence

D:
The black segment moves 2 counterclockwise, 1 clockwise, etc.
The white circle moves 1 clockwise, 2 counterclockwise, etc.
The black circle moves 2 counterclockwise, 1 clockwise, etc.
The white triangle moves 2 counterclockwise, 1 clockwise, etc.
The black triangle moves 2 counterclockwise, 1 clockwise, etc.
The striped segment moves 1 clockwise, 2 counterclockwise, etc.

(Question 129)

35 Sequence

A.

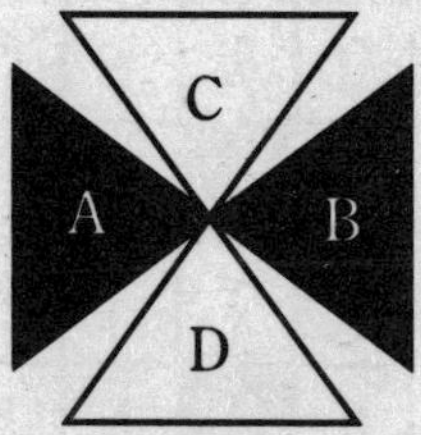

A moves 45° clockwise at each stage.
B moves 90° clockwise at each stage.
C moves 90° clockwise at each stage.
D moves 45° clockwise at each stage.
Note: In stage 3, D is hidden by B.

(Question 9)

36 Word Circles

Antonyms: Yielding, Stubborn
Synonyms: Haunting, Poignant

(Question 49)

37 Alternative Crossword

S	O	R	D	I	D		C	O	S	S	E	T
T		E		L	U	N	A	R		E		H
U	N	F	O	L	D		N	E	S	T	L	E
C		I		S	E	E	D	S		T		M
C	A	N	T		S	A	Y		C	E	D	E
O	P	E	R	A		R		T	R	E	E	S
	A		I	N	K		D	I	E		L	
E	R	R	E	D		P		S	E	C	T	S
S	T	U	D		P	O	P		D	R	A	W
S		M		D	O	T	E	S		A		O
A	M	B	L	E	S		D	U	S	T	E	R
Y		L		A	T	T	A	R		E		D
S	T	E	E	R	S		L	E	N	S	E	S

(Question 90)

38 Fore and Aft

MAN:

Foreman	Manhood
Workman	Mandrake
Marksman	Mankind

(Question 91)

39 Word Power

A

A N

C A N

S C A N

C R A N S

C R A N E S

T R A N C E S

C H A N T E R S

M E R C H A N T S

P A R C H M E N T S

(Question 130)

40 Children

To solve this problem use a Venn diagram:

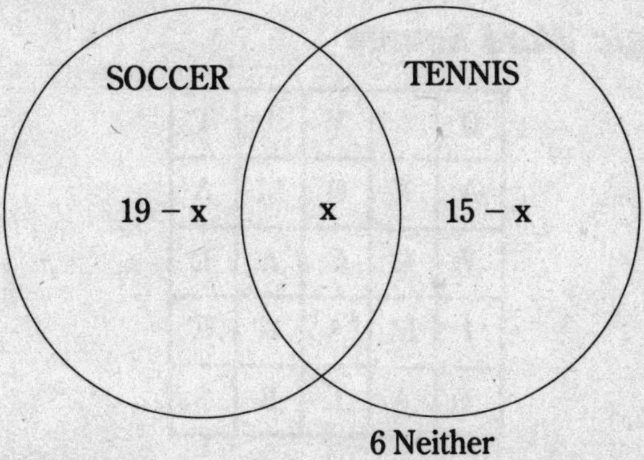

The area where the circles overlap indicates children who play both table tennis and soccer.

19 – x represents those who can play soccer but not table tennis.
15 – x represents those who can play table tennis but not soccer.

Now we have: $19 - x + x + 15 - x + 6 = 30$

$$40 - x = 30$$

$$x = 10$$

Ten children can play table tennis and soccer.

(Question 10)

41 Number Crunching Squares

160225:

$400^2 + 15^2$	$399^2 + 32^2$	$393^2 + 76^2$
$392^2 + 81^2$	$384^2 + 113^2$	$375^2 + 140^2$
$360^2 + 175^2$	$356^2 + 183^2$	$337^2 + 216^2$
$329^2 + 228^2$	$311^2 + 252^2$	$265^2 + 300^2$

(Question 50)

42 Odd One Out

D:
A is the same as C.
B is the same as F.
E is the same as G.

(Question 131)

43 Magic Word Square

D	A	V	I	T
A	R	O	M	A
V	O	C	A	L
I	M	A	G	E
T	A	L	E	S

(Question 11)

44 Odd One Out

D:
A is the same as G.
B is the same as F.
C is the same as E.

(Question 92)

45 Sequence

C:

There are three triangles that always have their bases on sides A, B, and C of the hexagon. The height of the three triangles increases by one quarter of the diameter of the hexagon at each stage.

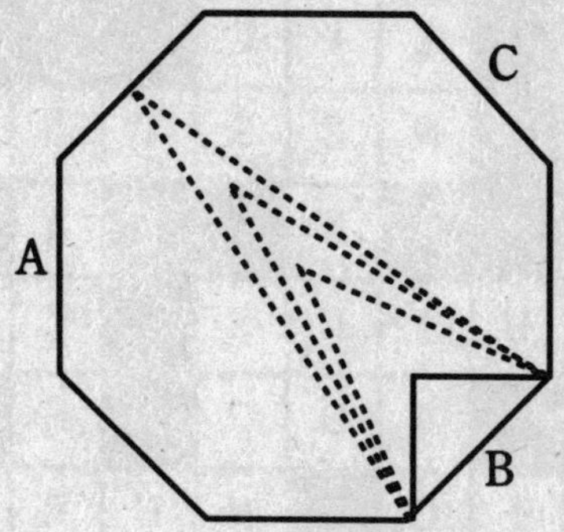

(Question 51)

46 Ball

36 feet:

$12 + 2\,(6 + 6/2 + 6/4 + 6/8 + 6/16 + 6/32 + ---)$

$= 12 + 2\,(12)$ ft $= 36$ ft.

(12 is equal to the series $6 + 6/2$, etc.)

(Question 132)

47 Magic '65'

20	11	13	4	17
6	24	7	23	5
22	18	1	14	10
2	9	25	8	21
15	3	19	16	12

(Question 12)

48 Do-It-Yourself Crossword

S	E	Q	U	E	S	T	R	A	T	E
P		U		A		A		P		A
E	X	I	S	T		P	R	E	S	S
L		E		E	V	E				E
L	I	T		N	E	S	T	L	E	S
		E			X			A		
M	I	N	U	T	E	S		T	I	C
O				A	D	O		E		L
P	A	N	I	C		N	U	R	S	E
E		E		I		I		A		A
S	P	E	C	T	A	C	U	L	A	R

(Question 52)

49 Sequence

1131:
Each number describes consecutive prime numbers:
12 = first prime number 2
23 = second prime number 3, etc.

The eleventh prime number is 31, or 1131.

(Question 93)

50 Hidden Fish

1. Merling
2. Groper
3. Sardine
4. Dugong
5. Minnow
6. Tench

(Question 133)

51 12 Letters

1. MUDDLE HEADED
2. HORROR STRUCK
3. BUTTER SCOTCH
4. BREATH TAKING

(Question 13)

52 Longest Word

Quatrefoils.

(Question 53)

53 Network

Proletarianism.

(Question 94)

54 Anagram Phrases

1. To have a fling
2. To let the grass grow under one's feet
3. Nine times out of ten
4. Keep your shirt on
5. For good measure

(Question 134)

55 Odd One Out

Stella Strong
In all the other name pairs the second word is the definition of the first:

Ethel	means	Noble.
Cyril	means	Lord.
Clive	means	Cliff.
Lloyd	means	Grey.

Stella actually means Star.

(Question 14)

56 Grid

3C.

(Question 54)

57 Odd One Out

D. Trips.

The others, if the preceding letter is included, form anagrams of an astrological feature:

A. Got = Goat (Capricorn)
B. Car = Crab (Cancer)
C. Seals = Scales (Libra)

(Question 95)

58 Grid Logic

OO = one across, one down.

TT, for example, represents two across, two down or three across, three down or two across, three down and vice versa.

(Question 135)

59 Grid

1B.

(Question 15)

60 The Paradox of the Unexpected Gift

1. The Greek philosopher Zeno suggested that in the last few seconds of Thursday you see someone approaching with the gift. "Here is the gift," he says and looks at his very precise watch. You claim that it's not unexpected for the reasons previously outlined. "But", says your friend "Thursday is ending and Friday is about to begin," and hands you the present at the precise instant of the change – the moment between Thursday and Friday.
2. You receive the gift outside working hours – surely this would be unexpected as you would have expected the presentation to be made in the office during working hours.
3. A colleague comes to your house on the Saturday or Sunday immediately prior to your last working week and presents you with the gift on one of the very two days you did not expect to receive it.
4. Five boxes are placed in the office. Four have weights precisely the same as the present and one contains the present. You are to pick one box each day when given the

word. The gift will, therefore, be unexpected – unless, of course, you haven't picked the correct box by Thursday (when the odds are even) or Friday (when the odds are a certainty).

5. On Monday a colleague asks, "Are you expecting to receive the gift today?" You say "No." Your colleague then gives you the gift.

(Question 55)

61 Sequence

E.

Starting at 6 o'clock the time advances 1 hour and 20 minutes at each stage:

6 o'clock, 7:20, 8:40, 10:00, 11:20.

(Question 96)

62 Margana

Journalist.

(Question 136)

63 D.I.Y. Diamond Crossword

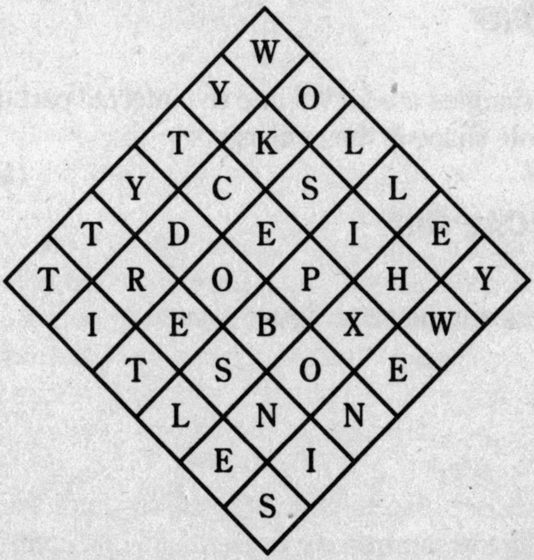

(Question 16)

64 Cross-Alphabet

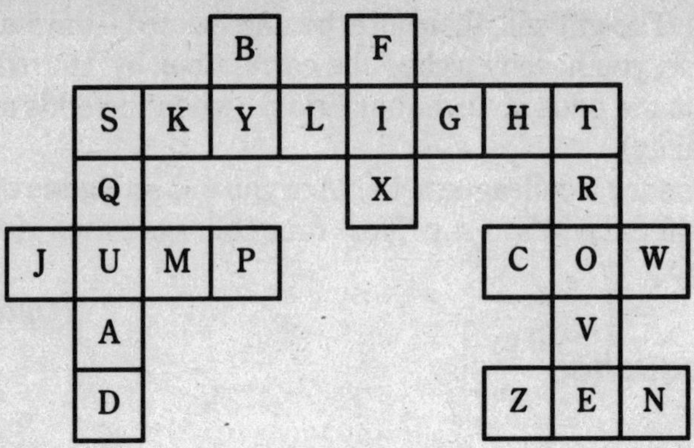

(Question 56)

65 "D" Puzzle

Didst
Dacha
Dwell
Disco
Djinn

(Question 97)

66 Analogy

A:
The outer triangles are folded into the internal part of the figure and the whole shape is then enlarged.

(Question 137)

67 Odd One Out

E:
All the others are the same figure rotated.

(Question 57)

68 Survey

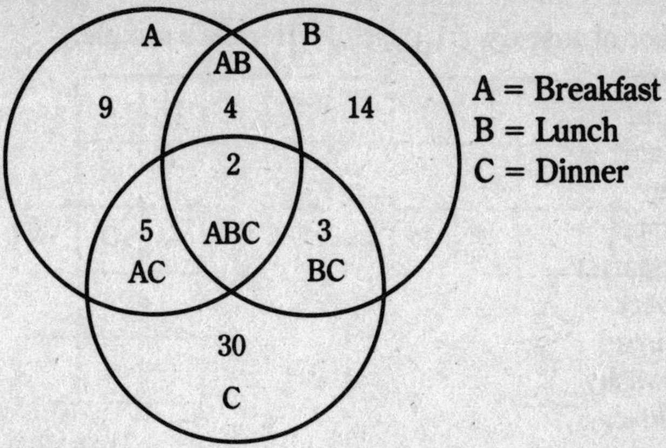

One meal eaten = 9 + 14 + 30 = 53.

(Question 17)

69 Fish Farm

The centre point between ten lakes north/south and ten lakes east/west.

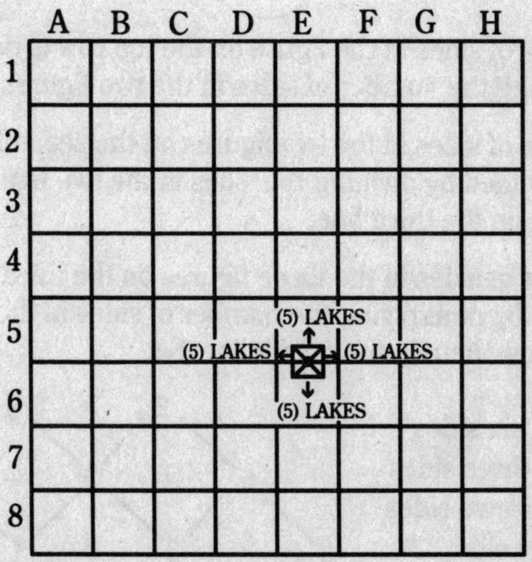

(Question 98)

70 Four Letters

A number of answers are possible. Here is a sample:
Washbowl
Eyebright
Gangplank
Highflier
Marksman
Three-quarter
Turtleback
Wingspread
Wishy-washy
Wagonload
Watchhouse
Wainwright

(Question 138)

71 Pyramid

The number of sides in the figure on the top row is determined by multiplying the number of sides in the two figures beneath it.

The number of sides in the two figures on the second line are each determined by dividing the sides in the two figures directly below them on the third line.

The number of sides in the three figures on the third line are determined by multiplying the number of sides in the two figures directly below them in the fourth line. So:

Hexagon = six sides
Triangle = three sides
Semicircle = two sides
Circle = one side

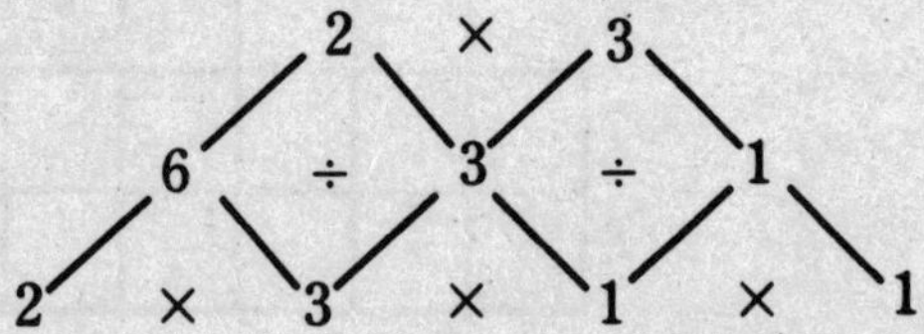

(Question 18)

72 Directional Crossword

1. Aggravate
2. Extortion
3. Neuralgia
4. Aerofoil
5. Liniment
6. Truffle
7. Element
8. Theme
9. Emerges
10. Sophism
11. Married
12. Dogs
13. Silos
14. Sum
15. Move
16. Eras
17. Sop

[1]A	[5]L	I	O	F	O	R	E	[4]A
[10]S	G	I	[13]S	G	O	[12]D	I	[7]E
O	E	G	N	I	E	G	L	L
P	[17]S	G	R	I	L	E	[15]M	F
H	O	A	R	A	M	O	U	F
I	P	R	R	E	V	E	[14]S	U
S	A	U	N	[16]E	M	A	N	R
[11]M	E	[8]T	H	E	M	[9]E	T	[6]T
[3]N	O	I	T	R	O	T	X	[2]E

(Question 58)

73 Magic Number Square

10	5	16	3
8	11	2	13
1	14	7	12
15	4	9	6

(Question 99)

74 Honeycomb

Marmalade	Margarine	Melba
Rice	Crab	Lamb
Gravy	Liver	Lard
Veal	Bran	Brawn
Beef	Egg	Gigot
Tart	Roll	Loaf

(Question 19)

75 Initials

6	Pockets on a pool table
32	Points on a compass
6	Sides on a snowflake
3	Feet in a yard
1	Good turn deserves another
3	Coins in the fountain
13	Months in a lunar year
12	Sides on a dodecahedron

(Question 139)

76 Lawns

$8845 = 66^2 + 67^2$

(Question 59)

77 Trite Saying

"Heredity is what a man believes in until his son begins to behave like a delinquent."

(Question 100)

78 Word Search

Bootlegger	Freshwater	Breakwater
Barnacle	Foreshore	Water
Shore	Fore	Stowaway
Torpedo	Port	Tornado
Rocket	Rope	Ketch
Row	Rowlock	Lock
Dog	Chest	Tide
Lee	Crew	Sleet
Wren	Bow	Tot
Tars	Salvo	Rock
Stow		

(Question 140)

79 Find a Word

Featherweight.

(Question 20)

80 Same Word

1. Noodle
2. Crock
3. Pitcher
4. Queue
5. Tern
6. Puncheon
7. Puck
8. Lurcher
9. Baste
10. Beagle

(Question 60)

81 Cryptogram III

"Golf is so popular simply because it is the best game in the world at which to be bad." – *A. A. Milne*

(Question 101)

82 Magic Word Square

103	79	37
7	73	139
109	67	43

(Question 141)

83 No Repeat Letters

Designator.

(Question 21)

84 The Train in the Tunnel

$(2.5 + 0.25) \times \frac{60}{75}$

= 2.2 minutes or 2 minutes 12 seconds.

(Question 61)

85 Grid

2C.

(Question 102)

86 Symbols

E.

(Question 142)

87 Symbols

A.

(Question 22)

88 Links Jigsaw Puzzle

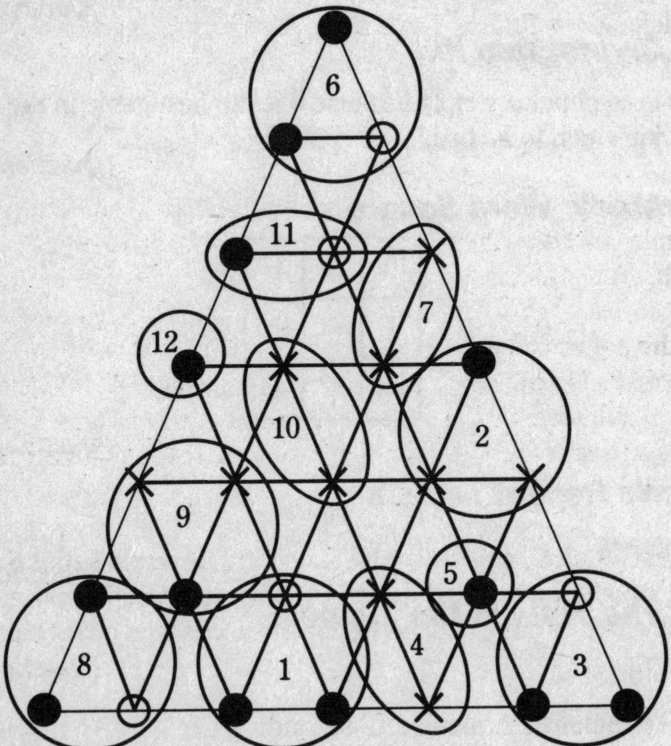

(Question 62)

89 Anagram Theme

All COMPUTER TERMS:

Interface (Fine Trace)
Program (Romp Rag)
Format (Fort Am)
Binary (By Rain)
Hacker (Rack He)
Mouse (So Emu)
Software (Swore Fat)
Mainframe (Amine Farm)

(Question 103)

90 10-Letter Words Boggle

Exultation, Dramatical, Affiliated, Worthwhile, Philosophy, Prudential, Conciliary, Curvaceous, Fictitious, Thoughtful, Auspicious, Exhibition, Trajection, Vegetarian, Undercover, Everything, Vaudeville, Tripartite, Automobile, Majestical.

(Question 143)

91 The Five Pennies

There are thirty-two different ways for the coin to fall as the first coin may fall either head or tails, as may the second, third, fourth, and fifth coins.

The thirty-two possible ways are:
A. Five heads (one way); B. Five tails (one way); C. Four heads and one tail (five ways); D. Four tails and one head (five ways); E. Three heads and two tails (ten ways); F. Three tails and two heads (ten ways).

Of these, A, B, C, and D (twelve ways) are favourable, but the other twenty ways, E and F, are not. The chances, therefore, are twelve chances out of thirty-two, or three chances out of eight.

(Question 23)

92 Analogy

D:
The top half is folded along the middle line on top of the bottom half.

(Question 104)

93 Plan in Works

A.
1. Man and boy
2. A pack of lies
3. In full cry
4. Go great guns
5. Out of joint
6. Cheek by jowl
7. Pipe down
8. Play safe
9. Lay hold of
10. Living doll

B.
1. Odds and ends
2. A tall order
3. To say the least
4. When the chips are down
5. Do or die
6. Hand in glove
7. At a push
8. Steal the show
9. Take by storm
10. On the wane

(Question 63)

94 Two Coins

George I. A coin would not be marked George I because at the time it was produced it would not be known whether there would be a George II. The first Elizabeth did not become Elizabeth I until the second Elizabeth became Queen. Similarly, Victoria is Queen Victoria and not Queen Victoria I.

(Question 144)

95 Piecemeal Quotation

"We would know mankind better if we were not so anxious to resemble one another." – *Goethe*

(Question 64)

96 Hexagon Logic

A =  B = 

Each straight row of four hexagons will then contain a circle, diamond, triangle, and ellipse.

(Question 24)

97 "Y" Puzzle

Key	Doyen	Monkey
Money	Day	Rayon
Dray	Ray	Aye
Pray	Prayed	Pay
Ploy	Donkey	Yard
Yon	Yen	Yap
Yeo	Keyed	Eye
Eyed	Yoyo	Monkeyed
Moneyed	Ployed	Yenned

(Question 105)

98 Hexagons

B:
The dotted line moves around each of the four positions in turn. Any dotted line becomes curved in the next option only.

(Question 145)

99 Links

1. ROW	6. SAIL
2. UP	7. HEAD
3. AND	8. SWORD
4. BOARD	9. OR
5. FOX	10. HELL

(Question 25)

100 Birds

1.	Wander	–	Gander
2.	Curled	–	Curlew
3.	Clover	–	Plover
4.	Muffin	–	Puffin
5.	Banner	–	Lanner
6.	Missed	–	Missel
7.	Beaver	–	Weaver
8.	Baffle	–	Yaffle
9.	Barbel	–	Barbet
10.	Canard	–	Canary

(Question 65)

101 Rectangle

13:

$6 \times 3 = \frac{6}{2} + 1 = 4$

$12 \times 8 = \frac{12}{3} + 1 = 5$

$12 \times 6 = \frac{12}{2} + 1 = 7$

$36 \times 24 = \frac{36}{3} + 1 = 13$

(Question 106)

102 Star

Dodecahedral.

(Question 146)

103 Pentagram

Foray
Decoy
Cadre
Corps
Truce
Key = PEACE

(Question 26)

104 Matrix

F:
This is a magic square of lines. The number of lines in each horizontal, vertical, and corner-to-corner line totals 15.

(Question 66)

105 Alphabet Clueless-Cross

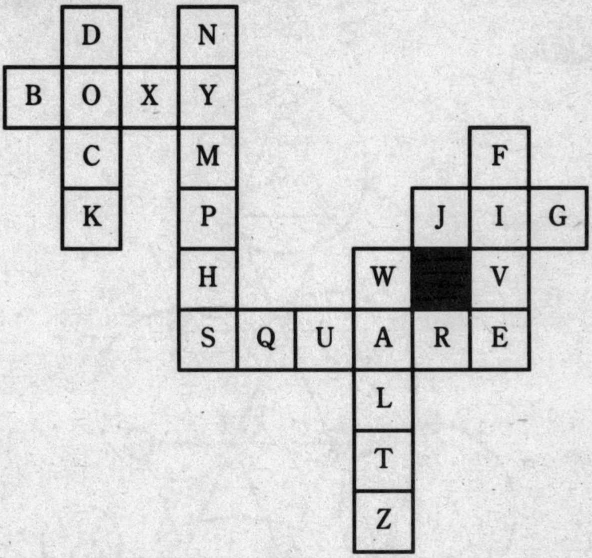

(Question 107)

106 Silent Order

Kickback:

K N O L L
H E I F E R
I N D I C T
K N E W
D O U B T
T O A S T
N A S C E N T
K N I C K E R S

Each word has a silent letter. Taken in order they spell KICKBACK.

(Question 147)

107 Three to Choose

1. (c)
2. (b)
3. (a)
4. (a)
5. (b)
6. (a)
7. (b)
8. (a)
9. (a)
10. (a)

(Question 27)

108 Links

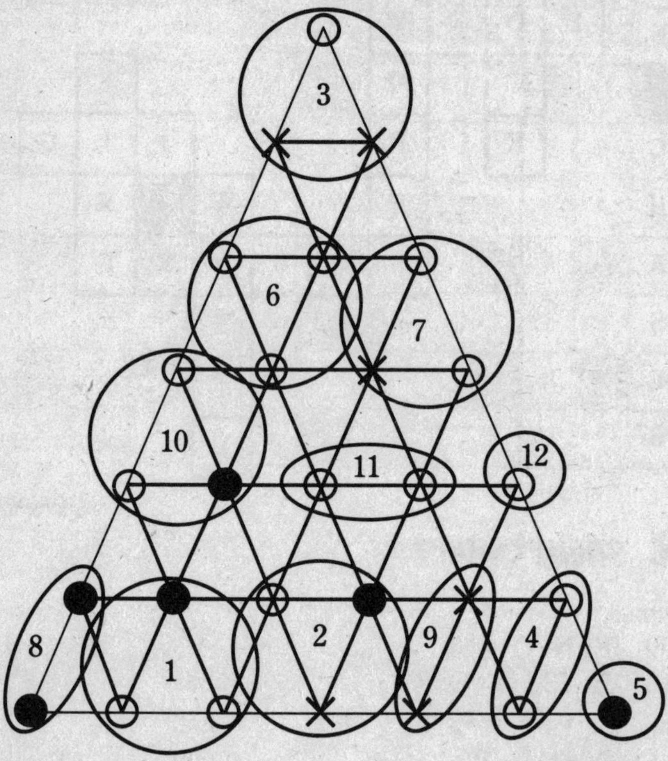

(Question 67)

109 No Blanks

P	L	A	N	E	T		F	A	T	H	E	R
U		R		R	O	T	O	R		O		A
F	R	I	D	A	Y		R	U	N	L	E	T
F		S		S	E	R	U	M		D		H
I	C	E	D		D	I	M		M	E	R	E
N	O	S	E	D		M		B	O	R	E	R
	B		C	O	S		M	A	R		B	
C	R	O	O	N		L		G	A	S	E	S
H	A	I	R		C	O	G		Y	E	L	P
A		L		Z	E	B	R	A		V		E
S	P	I	C	E	D		A	P	P	E	A	L
E		N		R	A	I	N	S		R		L
S	I	G	N	O	R		D	E	T	E	R	S

(Question 108)

110 Cricket Ground

	Hours	Reciprocal	Decimal
1 man	2	$\frac{1}{2}$	.500
1 man	3	$\frac{1}{3}$	.333
1 man	4	$\frac{1}{4}$	.250
1 man	5	$\frac{1}{5}$	.200
1 man	6	$\frac{1}{6}$	.167
			1.450

Take reciprocal again:

$$60\left(\frac{1\text{ hour}}{1.450}\right) = 41.4\text{ minutes.}$$

(Question 28)

111 Journey

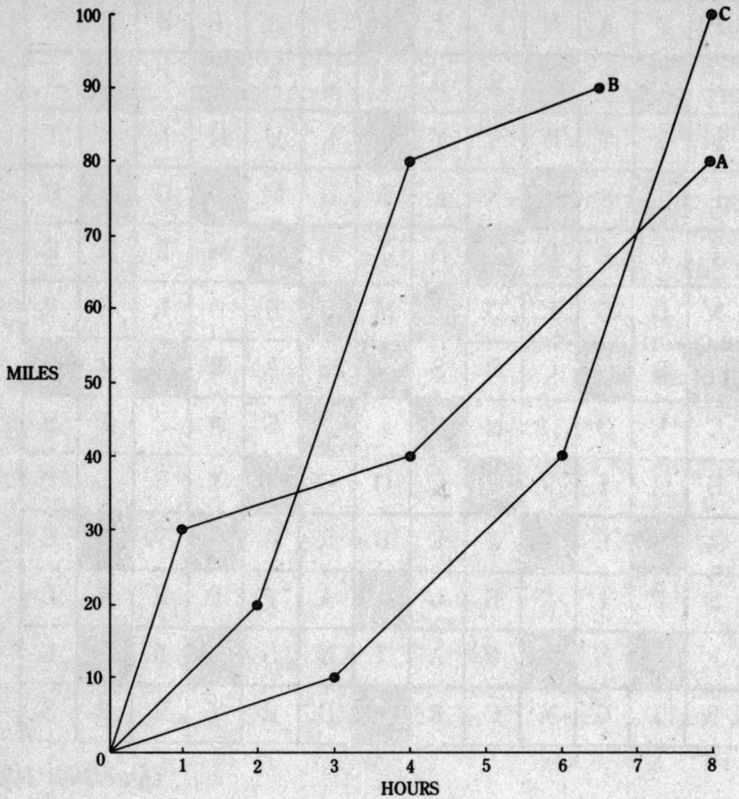

1. B overtook A at approximately 2:20.
2. C overtook A at approximately 7:00.

(Question 148)

112 Logic

A:

The contents of the first two circles in each row and column are combined to form the contents of the third circle.

(Question 109)

113 World Cup 1994

15070:
The goalkeeper and the captain can be ignored since they are in every selection. The problem then becomes how many sets of nine players out of eighteen players?

Also, countries can be written as:
twelve non-South American club players
six South American club players

The calculation then becomes:
Out of six South American — Out of twelve non-South American

Assume four South American

$$\frac{6 \times 5 \times 4 \times 3}{4 \times 3 \times 2 \times 1} \times \frac{12 \times 11 \times 10 \times 9 \times 8}{5 \times 4 \times 3 \times 2 \times 1}$$

$$= \frac{15}{1} \times \frac{792}{1} = 11880$$

Assume five South American

$$\frac{6 \times 5 \times 4 \times 3 \times 2}{5 \times 4 \times 3 \times 2 \times 1} \times \frac{12 \times 11 \times 10 \times 9}{4 \times 3 \times 2 \times 1}$$

$$= \frac{6}{1} \times \frac{495}{1} = 2970$$

Assume six South American

$$\frac{6 \times 5 \times 4 \times 3 \times 2 \times 1}{6 \times 5 \times 4 \times 3 \times 2 \times 1} \times \frac{12 \times 11 \times 10}{3 \times 2 \times 1}$$

$$= \frac{1}{1} \times \frac{220}{1} = 220$$

Total 15,070

(Question 68)

114 Magic Word Square

L	O	C	A	L
O	K	A	P	I
C	A	N	A	L
A	P	A	R	T
L	I	L	T	S

(Question 149)

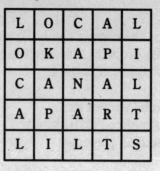

115 Word Circles

Synonyms: Despotic, Arrogant
Antonyms: Vivacity, Lethargy

(Question 29)

116 Pyramid Word

1. N
2. So
3. Has
4. Deft
5. Steer

15-letter word: SOFTHEARTEDNESS.

(Question 69)

117 An Irish Proverb

"Nodding the head does not row the boat."

(Question 110)

118 Sequence

C:

In each circle

 moves 45° clockwise

 moves 180° clockwise

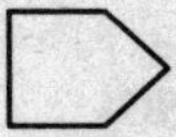 moves 225° clockwise

 moves 90° clockwise.

(Question 150)

119 Circles

Each pair of circles produces the circle above by carrying forward only those elements that are different. Similar elements are cancelled out.

For example:

D

Answer: 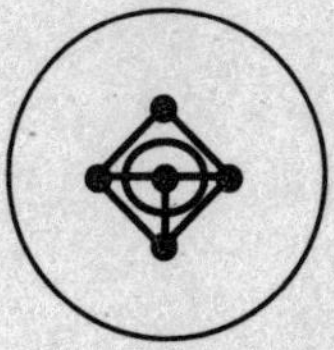

(Question 30)

120 Two Quick Teasers

1. By one third – three of anything, if increased by one third, becomes four.
2. 14,313: 13,000 + 1300 + 13

(Question 70)

121 Containers

1. G(aunt)let
2. Seyc(hell)es
3. T(hem)e
4. D(red)ger
5. C(leave)r
6. Fa(rand)ole
7. P(earl)s
8. P(ant)ry
9. A(then)s
10. Ken(tuck)y

(Question 111)

122 People

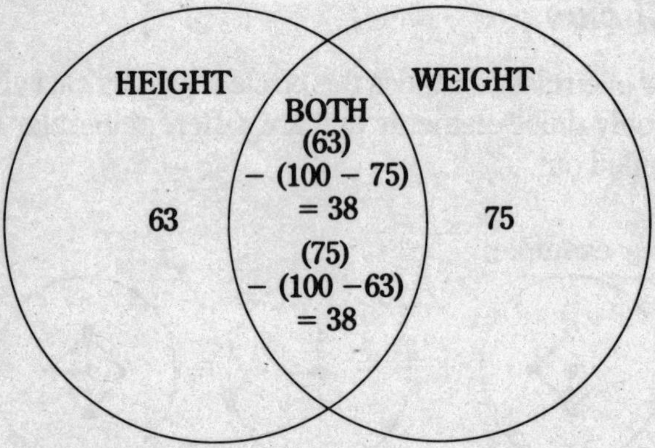

Use a Venn diagram to show detail:
Greatest = 63
Least = 38

(Question 151)

123 Eggs

$$\frac{6}{100} \times \frac{5}{99} = \frac{30}{9900} \text{ or } \frac{1}{330}$$

One chance in 330 or 329 to 1 against.

(Question 31)

124 Clueless Crossword

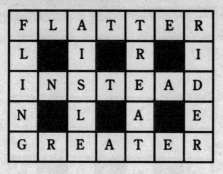

F	L	A	T	T	E	R
L		I		R		I
I	N	S	T	E	A	D
N		L		A		E
G	R	E	A	T	E	R

(Question 71)

125 Connections

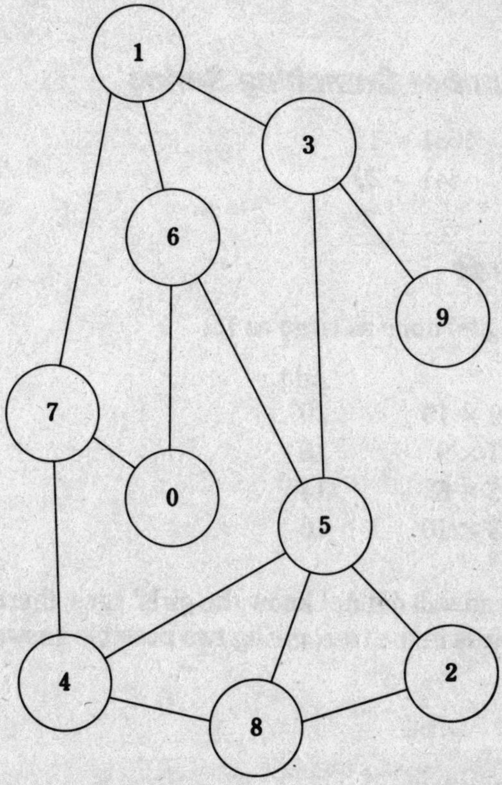

(Question 112)

126 Brain Strain

8	÷	2	+	5	=	9
×		+		+		×
2	−	1	+	3	=	4
÷		×		−		÷
4	+	3	−	1	=	6
=		=		=		=
4	+	9	−	7	=	6

(Question 152)

127 Number Crunching Series

1680: $1681 = 41^2$

$841 = 29^2$

(Question 32)

128 Birds

Factorizing 90 none as large as 15.

	Add
$90 = 1 \times 9 \times 10$	20
$90 = 2 \times 5 \times 9$	16
$90 = 3 \times 5 \times 6$	14
$90 = 3 \times 3 \times 10$	16

As my friend still did not know the girls' ages, there must have been 16 birds in the tree, giving two possible answers.

(Question 72)

129 Trade

Peer:

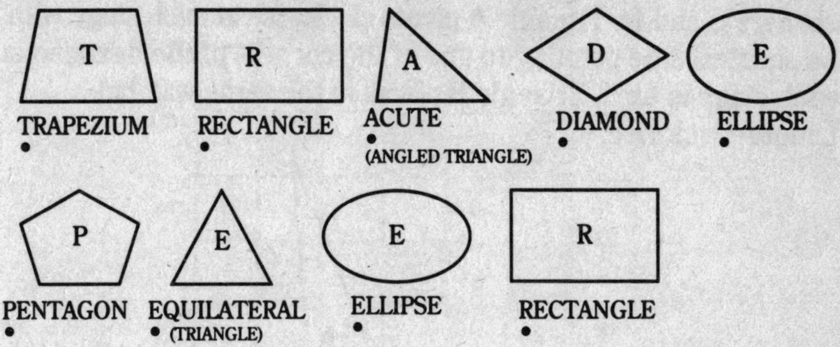

(Question 113)

130 Common

They all contain names of trees, flowers, or shrubs spelled backward.

Ash
Fir
Gum
Nut
Arum
Acer
Lime
Carob
Rose

(Question 153)

131 Pyramid

Instrumentalist.

(Question 33)

E:

There are two triangles, A and B, which remain pivoted on corners C and D. Triangle A pivots clockwise at each stage with its shortest side pointing to one of the corners of the hexagon at each stage in turn. Triangle B pivots in the same way but counterclockwise.

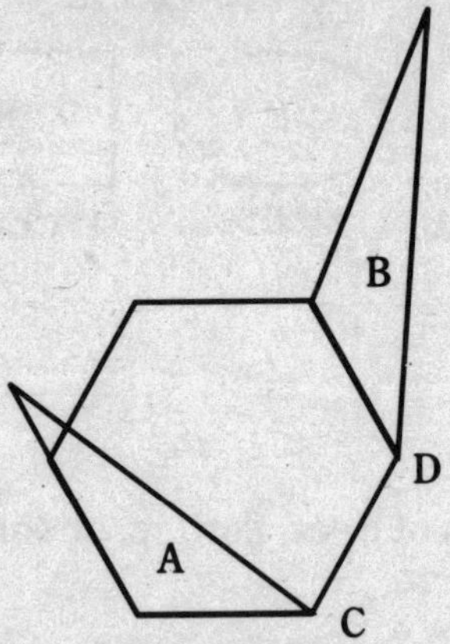

STAGE 1

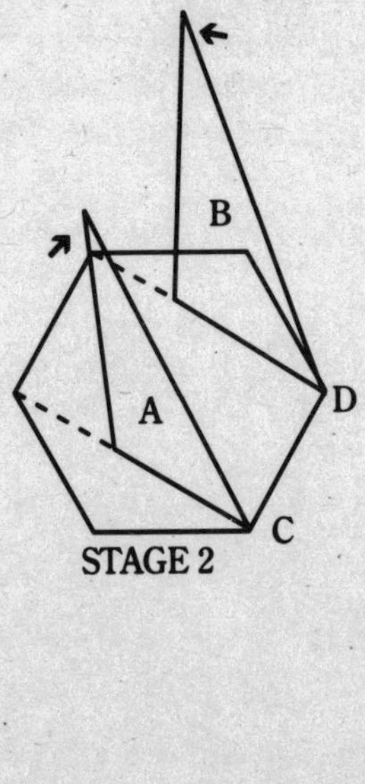

STAGE 2

(Question 73)

133 Diamonds

Mallard
Lark
Mavis
Drake
Tit
Tui
Kaka
Rhea
Hen
Raven
Wren
Pen
Pern
Reeve
Veery
Pipit

(Question 114)

134 Complete the Quotations

1 – D. Phantom
2 – H. Tomorrow
3 – F. Conversation
4 – A. Harmonies
5 – E. Spinach
6 – G. Appropriateness
7 – C. Mediocrity
8 – J. Applause
9 – I. Architecture
10 – B. Cherries

(Question 154)

135 Track Word

Incommensurable.

(Question 34)

136 Cement

$5000 \div x = 2x$
$5000 \div 50 = 100$ pounds

(Question 115)

137 Decidice

Lose

1-1	2-1	3-1	4-1	5-1	6-1	7-1	8-1	9-1	10-1
1-2	2-2	3-2	4-2	5-2	6-2	7-2	8-2	9-2	10-2
1-3	2-3	3-3	4-3	5-3	6-3	7-3	8-3	9-3	10-3
1-4	2-4	3-4	4-4	5-4	6-4	7-4	8-4	9-4	10-4
1-5	2-5	3-5	4-5	5-5	6-5	7-5	8-5	9-5	10-5
1-6	2-6	3-6	4-6	5-6	6-6	7-6	8-6	9-6	10-6
1-7	2-7	3-7	4-7	5-7	6-7	7-7	8-7	9-7	10-7
1-8	2-8	3-8	4-8	5-8	6-8	7-8	8-8	9-8	10-8
1-9	2-9	3-9	4-9	5-9	6-9	7-9	8-9	9-9	10-9
1-10	2-10	3-10	4-10	5-10	6-10	7-10	8-10	9-10	10-10

Win

Lose		Win
10		–
10		–
9		1
8		2
7		3
6		4
5		5
4		6
3		7
2		8
64	to	36

or 16 to 9 odds against.

(Question 74)

138 A Long Time

$4 \times 1738 = 6952$
$4 \times 1963 = 7852$

(Question 155)

139 Sequence

B:

The bottom symbol moves to middle and then to top in turn. That is, in Stage 1 the symbol  is at the bottom, in Stage 2 it is in the middle, and in Stage 3 at the top. Since that sequence is now complete, in Stage 4 it is the turn of symbol 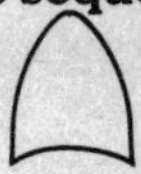 to move up in the same way.

(Question 35)

140 Hexagram

Basnet
Dagger
Helmet
Musket
Cudgel
Lariat
Key = SHIELD

(Question 75)

141 Words

Galantine:
Each word starts with the letter whose position in the alphabet coincides with the number of letters in the preceding word.

Lockjaw has seven letters, therefore, the next word starts with the seventh letter of the alphabet.

(Question 116)

142 Shields Matrix

D:
Looking both across and down, the contents of the third shield are formed by merging the contents of the first two shields, but matching symbols are cancelled out.

(Question 156)

143 Missing Number

4:

15 ÷ 12 = 1.25 (× 8) = 10

24 ÷ 16 = 1.5 (× 8) = 12

5 ÷ 10 = 0.5 (× 8) = 4

(Question 36)

144 Symbols

E.

(Question 76)

145 Bracket Word

Mechanical.

(Question 117)

146 Animals

1. Impala
2. Onager
3. Rhesus
4. Panther
5. Caracal

(Question 157)

147 Wot! No Vowels?

Crypt	Slyly	
Fly	Try	Fry
Dry	Pyx	Cry
Pry	Wynd	Sync
Lych	Fyrd	Ply
Shy	Wry	

(Question 37)

148 Odd One Out

The licence plates represent the year, followed by the first three letters of the city, followed by the first letter of the country of venues of Olympic Games of the twentieth century:

76 MON C	=	1976, Montreal, Canada
68 GRE F	=	1968, Grenoble, France
12 STO S	=	1912, Stockholm, Sweden
56 MEL A	=	1956, Melbourne, Australia
92 BAR S	=	1992, Barcelona, Spain

68 GRE F is the odd one out because it represents a winter Olympic Games; the others were all summer Olympic Games.

(Question 77)

149 Circles

C

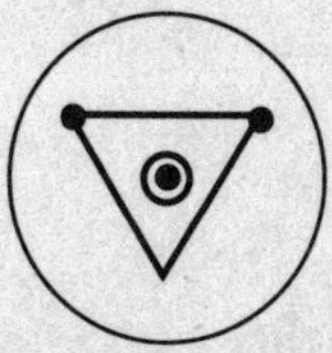

Each pair of circles produces the circle above it by carrying forward the elements, but similar elements are cancelled out. For example:

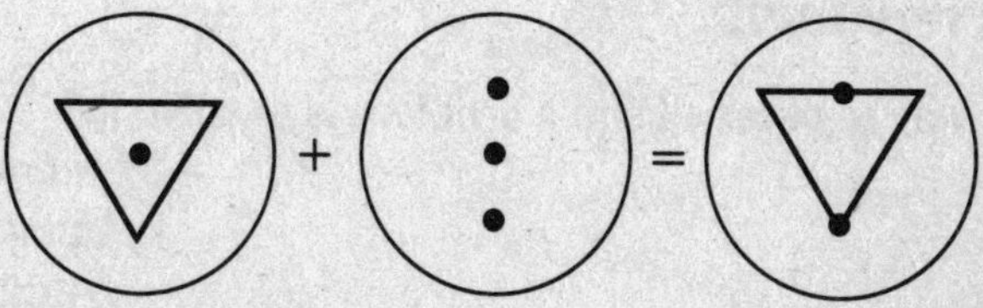

(Question 118)

150 Comparison

A.

(Question 158)

151 Consonants

1. Yardstick, Benchmark, Standard, Criterion
2. Recalcitrant, Obstinate, Wayward, Intractable
3. Enchant, Bewitch, Delight, Mesmerize
4. Locution, Articulation, Intonation, Accent
5. Allegory, Parable, Apologue, Fable
6. Guileful, Cunning, Underhand, Deceitful

(Question 38)

152 Anagrammed Synonyms

1. Plea – Appeal
2. Pose – Impersonate
3. Like – Admire
4. Say – Mention
5. Taut – Strained
6. Kiss – Osculate
7. Coy – Reserved
8. Rid – Unburden
9. Add – Augment
10. Ruler – Monarch

(Question 78)

153 Roman Numerals

1888 = MDCCCLXXXVIII

(Question 119)

154 Honeycomb

"The best way to escape from a problem is to solve it."

– Brendan Francis

(Question 159)

155 Grid

2C.

(Question 39)

156 Bars

C:
The symbols move as follows:

 one right, two left, one right, two left, etc.

 one left, one right, etc.

 two right, one left, two right, one left, etc.

 one left, two right, one left, two right, etc.

 one left, two right, one left, two right, etc.

(Question 79)

157 Word Cycle

Cheese, Senior, Origin, Insist, Stigma, Malice, Cellar, Arcane, Nestle, Lethal, Allude, Detach.

(Question 160)

158 Analogy

D:
The rectangle splits into two circles and the small circles become triangles.

(Question 161)

159 Analogy

B:
The diamond turns upside down (it appears the same both ways), the base of the rectangle moves down from the top point to the bottom point of the diamond. The small triangle rotates clockwise through 90°.

(Question 40)

160 Palindromic

Arrange the digits in this sequence:

16, 1, 12, 9, 14, 4, 18, 15, 13, 9, 3

Now convert the numbers into their corresponding letters in the alphabet:

P A L I N D R O M I C

(Question 80)

161 Porky Pies

1. (c) Maxim de Winter's pet cocker spaniel was named Jasper.
2. (b) John Edgar Hoover was a lifelong bachelor.
3. (b) Dizzy Gillespie's real first name was John.
4. (c) It was Judy Garland, not Ginger Rogers, who sang "I Cried For You".
5. (c) Hurricane Mills is a town north of Nashville.

(Question 120)

IQ
Firepower

1 Alphabet X-Word

Place the letters of the alphabet in the X-word to complete the words, using each letter only once.

A B C D E F G H I J K L M
N O P Q R S T U V W X Y Z

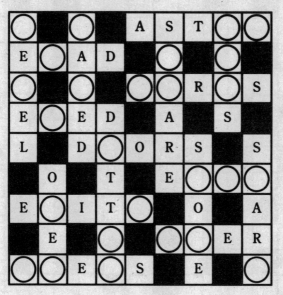

○	■	○	■	A	S	T	○	○
E	○	A	D	■	○	■	○	■
○	■	○	■	○	○	R	○	S
E	○	E	D	■	A	■	S	■
L	■	D	○	O	R	S	■	S
■	O	■	T	■	E	○	○	○
E	○	I	T	○	■	O	■	A
■	E	■	○	■	○	○	E	R
○	○	E	○	S	■	E	■	○

(Solution 4)

2 Bracket Word

Place two letters in each pair of brackets so that they finish the word on the left and start the word on the right. The letters in the brackets, read downwards in pairs, will spell out a 10-letter word.

S	(• •)	ID
RE	(• •)	D
DE	(• •)	IT
STO	(• •)	E
GO	(• •)	AS

(Solution 8)

3 Fivers

Place the 5-letter words in the grid to complete the crossword.

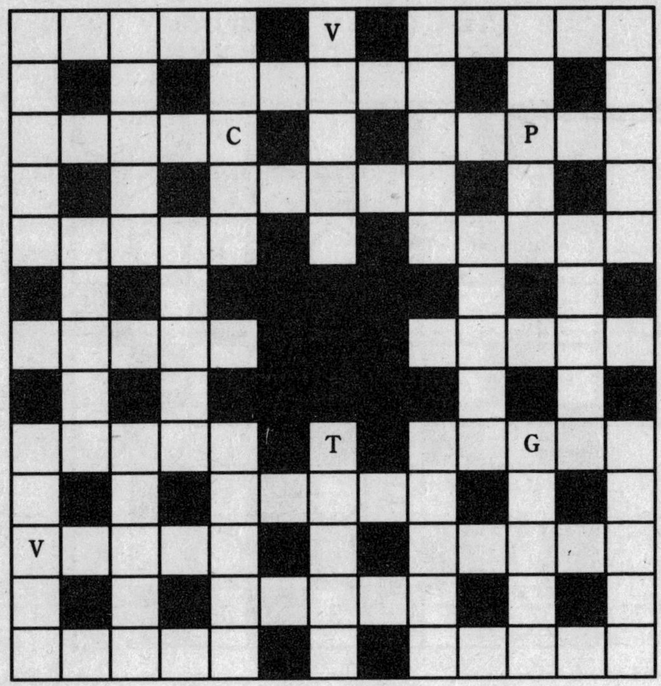

Across

Petal
Robot
Panic
Doted
Drape
Lanky
Unite
Elite
Sedan
Villa
Taped
Beget
Model
Irate
Deter
Roman
Toted
Pilot

Down

Piped
Tenet
Ready
Metes
Doped
Alone
Laden
Talon
Titan
Gamut
Evoke
Elope
Devil
Oxide
Lucid
Vital
Tuned
Beret

(Solution 13)

8 Orthographic Projection

Below are three views of the same object viewed from top, front, and right. Can you sketch the object being viewed?

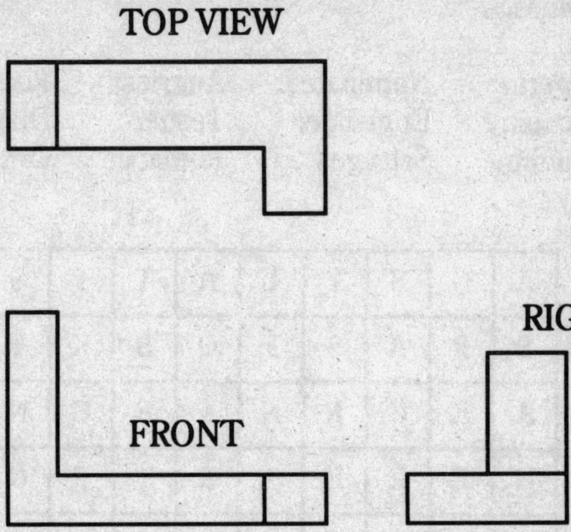

(Solution 32)

9 Quiz Team

A quiz team of six had to be selected from a group of eight men and eight women. How many different teams could be formed from this group, assuming that at least three women were in each team?

(Solution 36)

40 Anagrams

The thirteen words below are the anagrams of place names. Find these in the word square. They run in any direction, but only in straight lines.

Tangerine	Nominates	Angriest	Rechewing
Resoaping	Englander	Testier	Diagnose
Relanding	Salvages	Romance	Oration
Laity			

A	G	S	Y	L	A	T	I	S	A
S	R	A	S	E	O	S	K	I	T
A	E	G	R	N	I	E	C	N	O
N	E	E	E	I	R	T	R	G	S
D	N	V	I	N	A	S	E	A	E
I	W	S	G	G	T	E	M	P	N
E	I	A	N	R	N	I	O	O	N
G	C	L	A	A	O	R	N	R	I
O	H	O	T	D	Y	T	A	E	M
P	G	R	E	E	N	L	A	N	D

(Solution 40)

11 Pyramid Words

Complete each line of the pyramid with the help of the clues. Each line contains the letters of the word above it, in any order, plus one other letter.

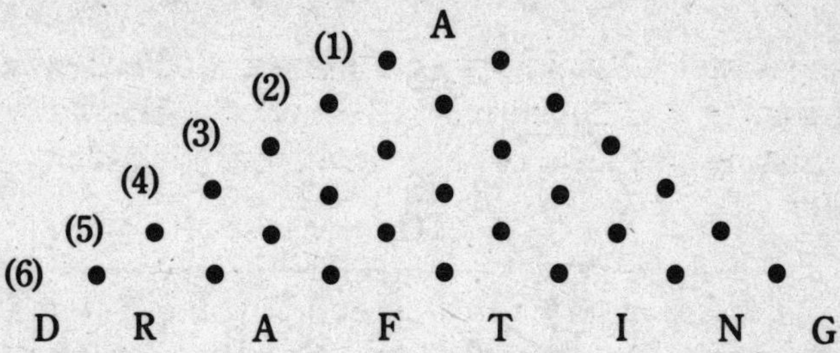

Clues

1. Preposition
2. Brown
3. Shout angrily
4. Vehicle
5. Degree of quality
6. Dealing in commodities

(Solution 48)

12 A Maze

In how many different ways can the word MAZE be read? Start at the central letter "M" and move to an adjoining letter up, down, backward, or forward, in and out in any direction.

(Solution 52)

13 Analogy

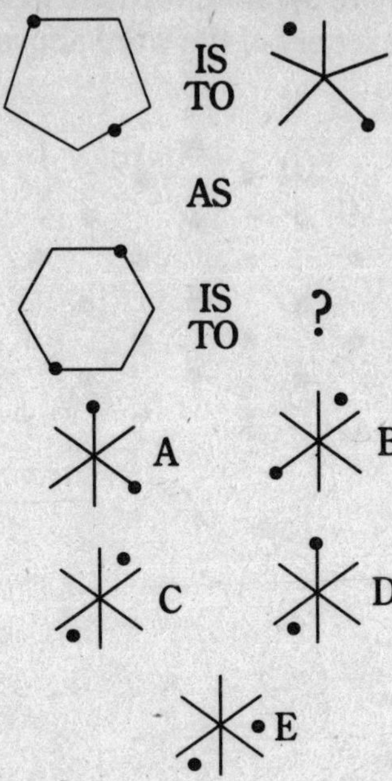

(Solution 56)

14 Tangled Antonym

Find two words that are antonyms, anagrams, and identical apart from the position of the two middle letters.

(Solution 60)

15 Six Fours

$$\frac{444 - 44}{4} = 100$$

Now find another way of arranging six 4's to equal 100 just by using any of the four mathematical symbols (+, −, ÷, ×), plus brackets and parentheses, but no decimals.

(Solution 64)

16 Rectangle Matrix

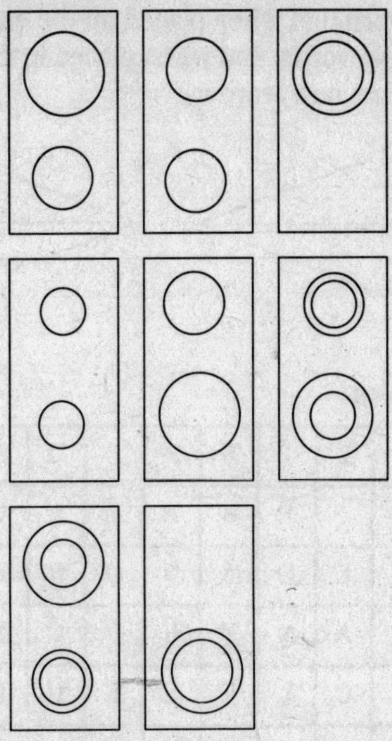

Look across each line and down each column and find the missing rectangle from the choices below.

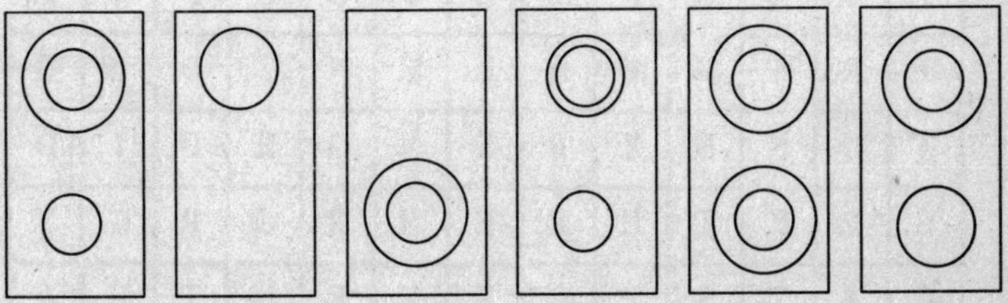

A B C D E F

(Solution 68)

17 Fore and Aft

Find a 3-letter word that when placed on the end of the first three words makes new words, and when placed in front of the last three words makes new words.

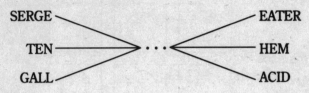

SERGE		EATER
TEN	. . .	HEM
GALL		ACID

(Solution 72)

18 No Blanks

A	P	O	L	I	S	H	E	D	A	I	S	Y
S	R	S	I	R	W	A	L	L	F	I	N	E
H	A	I	L	O	A	N	O	R	E	X	I	A
A	L	E	A	N	Y	F	P	C	R	A	C	K
C	I	R	C	L	E	E	E	U	R	E	K	A
K	N	S	P	E	D	U	D	R	E	A	M	R
K	E	D	G	E	N	D	S	E	T	U	D	E
I	S	W	R	R	M	A	T	S	O	F	E	E
T	R	A	U	M	A	L	U	N	T	O	L	D
T	U	N	N	Y	R	S	N	O	H	U	I	D
B	R	E	T	H	R	E	N	R	O	R	G	Y
C	A	T	S	P	O	T	E	E	N	T	H	A
S	L	E	E	T	W	I	L	I	G	H	T	K

Determine which squares should be blackened to make a symmetrical crossword.

(Solution 77)

19 Scale

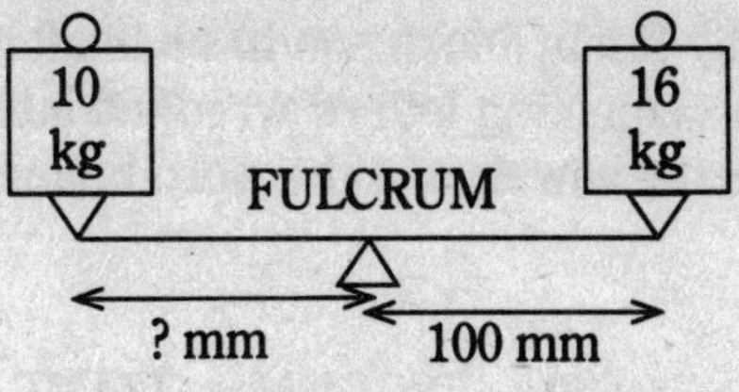

What distance from the fulcrum should the 10 kg weight be placed to make the scale balance?

(Solution 80)

20 Odd One Out

Which of these is the odd one out?

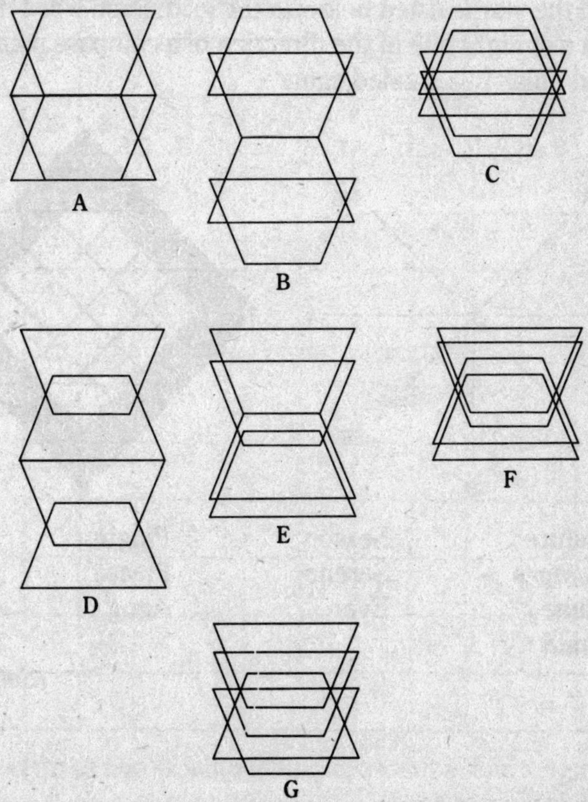

(Solution 84)

21 Restore the Vowels

This quotation by Emily Dickinson has had all its vowels removed and its remaining letters arranged into groups of five. Can you restore the vowels and the word boundaries to find the quotation?

YSKGR TQSTN SCCDN TLLYT NSWRT

HMWLD BVNTS.

(Solution 88)

22 Tight Squeeze

Place all the words listed below in the grid. Each word must travel in a straight line in the direction of a compass point and start and finish in a shaded square.

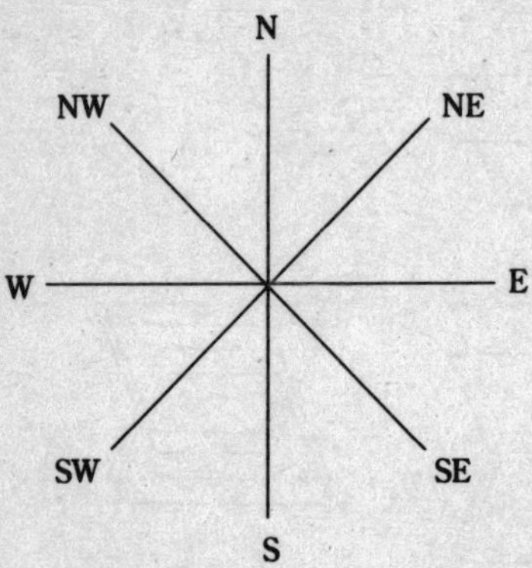

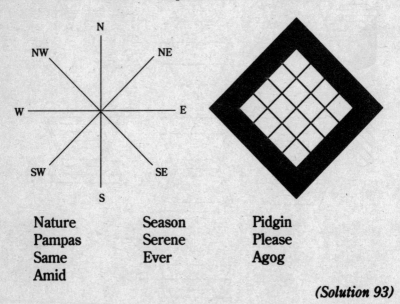

Nature	Season	Pidgin
Pampas	Serene	Please
Same	Ever	Agog
Amid		

(Solution 93)

23 Lateral Thinking

At first glance there appears to be no rhyme or reason to the way these numbers are distributed. But, of course, there is. What number is missing from the third circle?

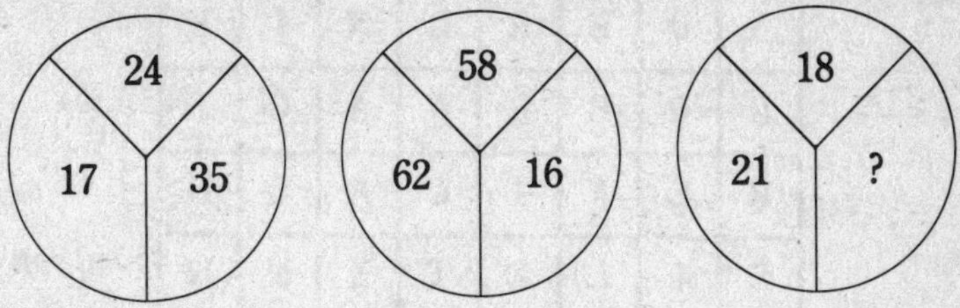

(Solution 96)

24 Circles

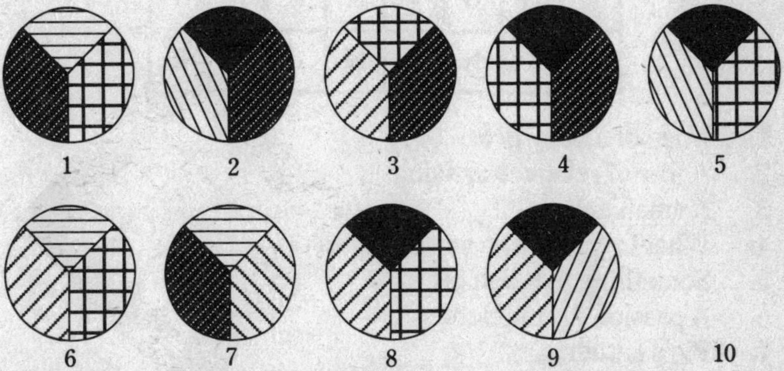

Which one of the following will complete the above set?

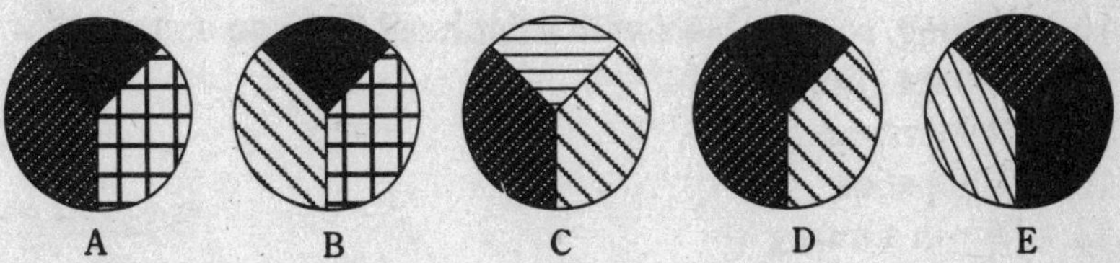

(Solution 100)

25 Daffynitions

Daffynitions are humorous definitions of everyday words. Can you find these? Words may run in any direction but only in straight lines.

A	D	E	R	D	N	I	K
R	P	B	R	A	A	C	I
R	E	P	I	C	A	D	D
E	I	L	E	T	X	N	N
S	C	A	T	A	E	I	E
T	E	A	R	S	R	W	Y
H	O	G	W	A	S	H	Y
A	I	N	A	M	O	G	E

1. Knee of a baby goat
2. A fear of relatives arriving
3. A small nail
4. What to take when you are tired
5. Something you fish off
6. A passion for omelettes
7. Pig's laundry
8. Skid stuff
9. Glum drops
10. A long, round object with a flat head that you aim at before hitting your thumb
11. A humbug
12. Chopstick
13. Air in a hurry

(Solution 104)

26 Knight

Using the knight's move as in chess, spell out the message. Start with "THE".

OUT	AT	HEAD LIGHT	MAY	TRAIN
OF	TUNNEL	TURN	THE	THE
LIGHT	TO	OF	ON-COMING	WELL
THE	AN	THE	BE	END

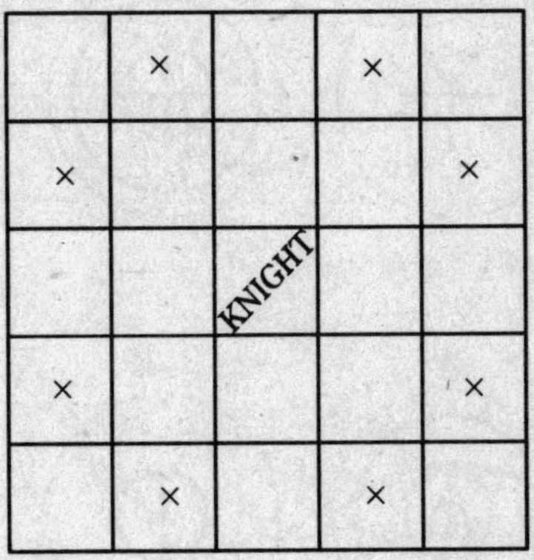

(Solution 108)

27 Age

Add to my age one-half, one-third, and three times three, six score plus ten the answer you will see.

How old am I?

(Solution 112)

Logically, which circle fits the pattern?

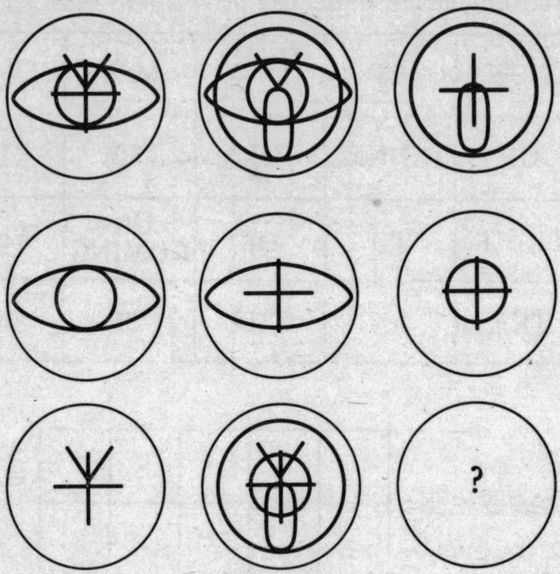

A B C

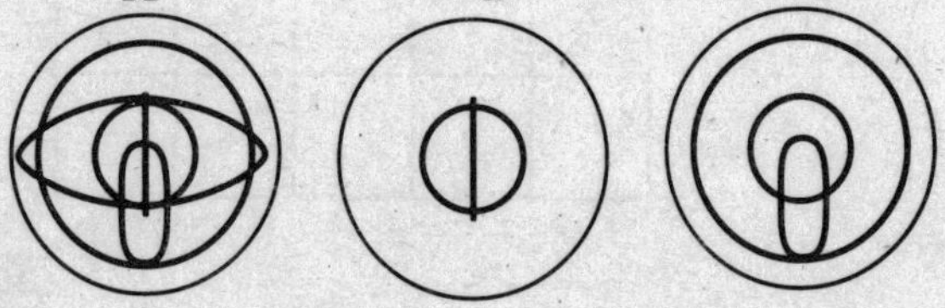

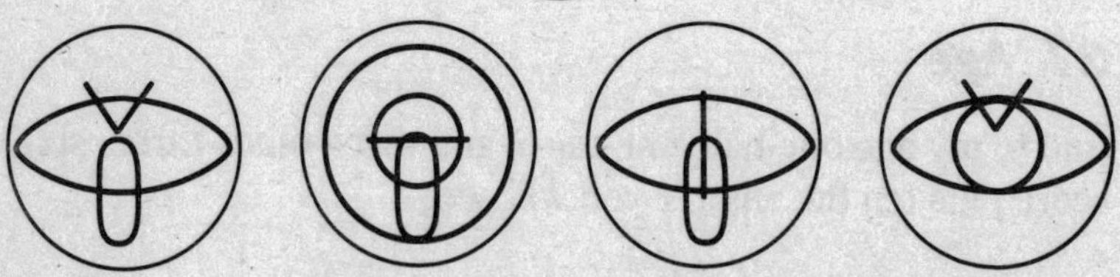

D E F G

(Solution 116)

29 No Repeat Letters

The grid contains twenty-five different letters of the alphabet. What is the longest word that can be found by starting anywhere and working from square to square horizontally, vertically, or diagonally and not repeating a letter?

K	W	M	V	J
P	A	B	E	X
L	Q	H	Y	O
U	F	R	T	N
S	C	D	I	G

(Solution 120)

30 Word Stack

Complete the pyramid with words reading across each line by using only the letters already placed. Each word is made up of the letters in the line above it, plus one more letter, which in each line is the letter provided.

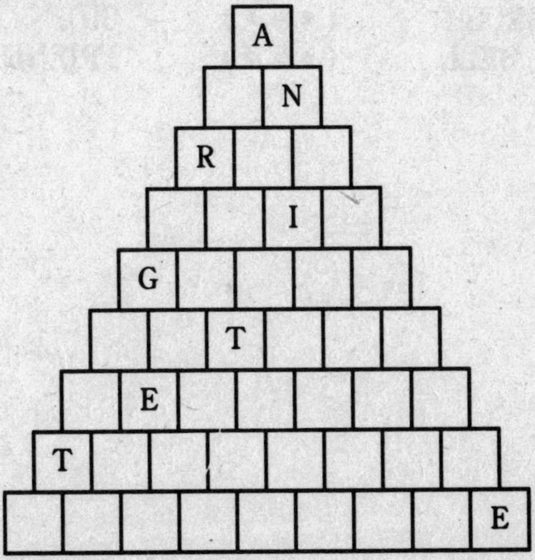

(Solution 124)

31 The Train in the Tunnel

A train moving at a speed of 75 m.p.h. enters a tunnel $2\frac{1}{4}$ miles long. The length of the train is $\frac{1}{4}$ mile. How long does it take for all of the train to pass through the tunnel from the moment the front enters to the moment the rear emerges?

(Solution 128)

32 Middle Words

In each of the following insert a word in the bracket that when tacked onto the end of the first word forms a new word, and when placed in front of the second word forms another word. For example: ARC (• • •) RING. Answer: HER – to form the words ARCHER and HERRING.

The number of dots indicates the number of letters in the word to be inserted. Some of the answer words may contain hyphens.

1. TAIL	(• • • • •)	WAY
2. FEED	(• • • • •)	BONE
3. DRY	(• • • • •)	YARD
4. CHAIR	(• • •)	KIND
5. BRUSH	(• • •)	SIDE
6. BELL	(• • •)	FRIEND

(Solution 132)

33 Diamond Matrix

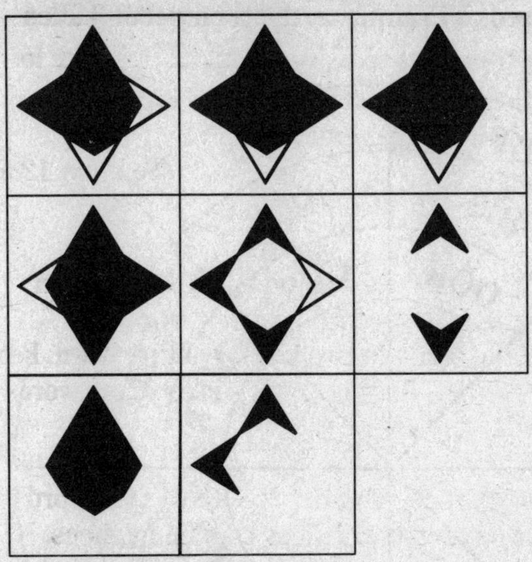

Look across each row and down each column to determine the missing tile from the choices below.

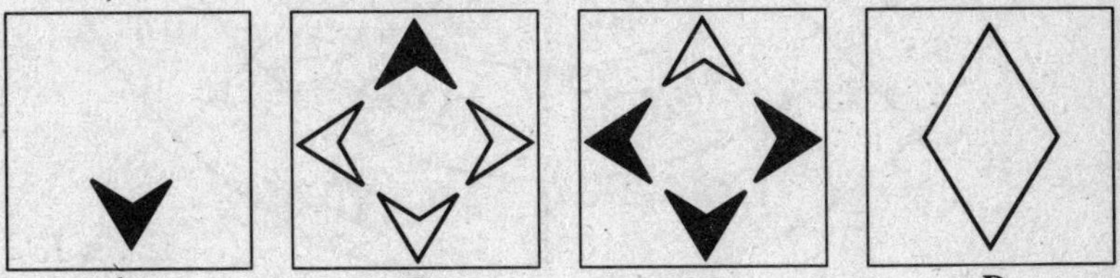

A B C D

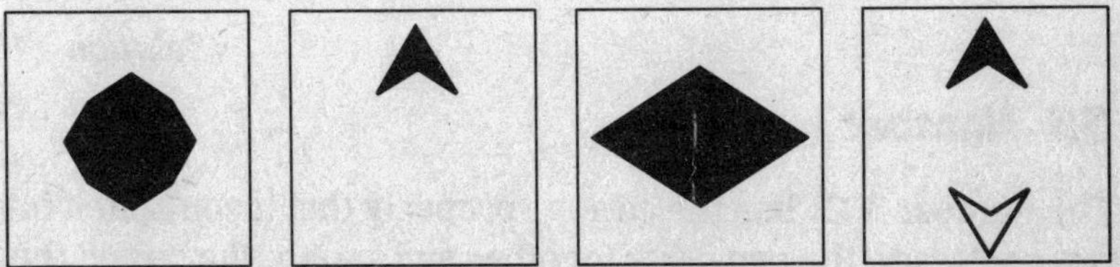

E F G H

(Solution 136)

34 Target Crossword

Find twelve 6-letter words by pairing up the twenty-four 3-letter bits.

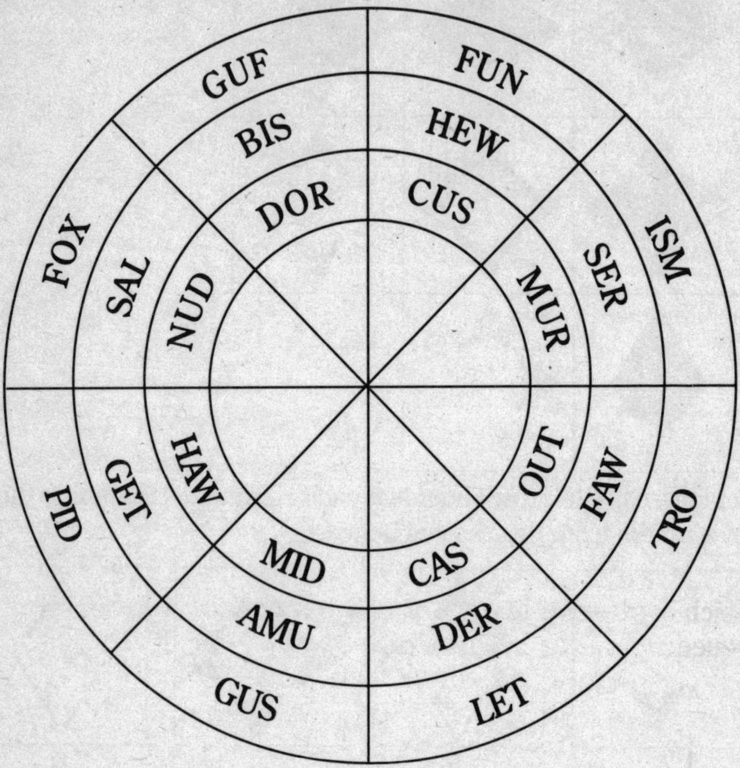

(Solution 140)

35 Number

The number 3025 has the curious property that if you split it into two parts, add the two parts together and square the result, the original number is produced.

$$30 + 25 = 55$$

$$55^2 = 3025$$

What are the only other 4-digit numbers with this property?

(Solution 143)

36 Circles

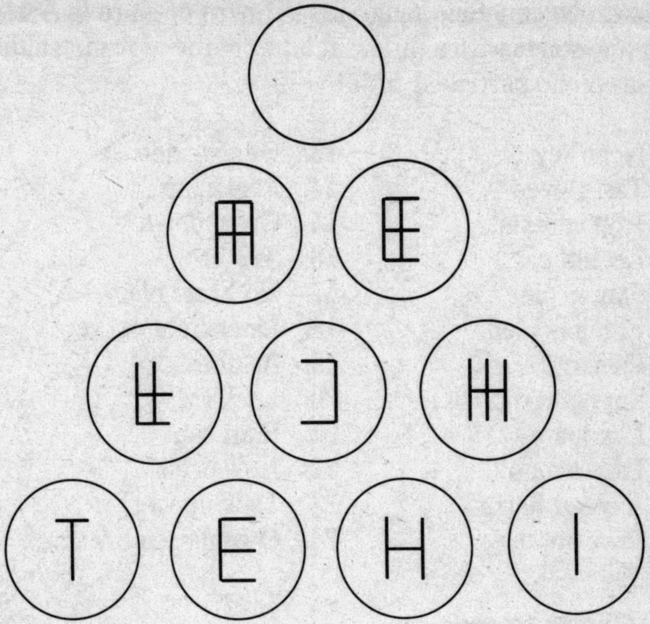

Which of these fits into the blank circle to carry on a logical sequence?

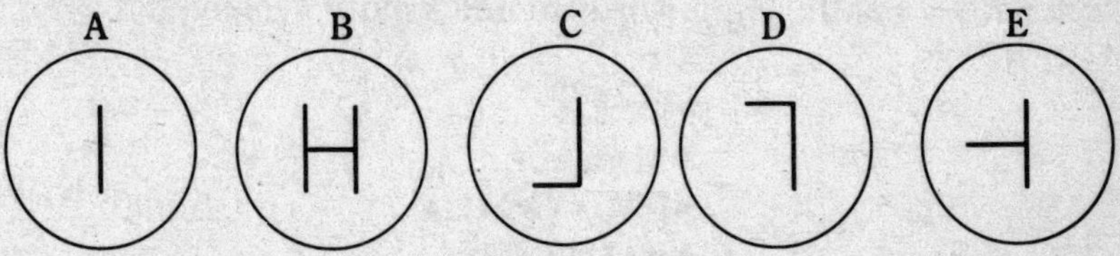

(Solution 148)

37 Anagrammed American Tour

Below are twenty-four anagrams of towns or cities in America. Each one starts with a different letter of the alphabet, although they are in no particular order.

1, Near key
2. Tan gloves
3. Hop reverts
4. Let hot car
5. Slay in pit
6. Freak is bled
7. Rave nut
8. Surf greed brick
9. Lair loam
10. Laze livens
11. A bleed harm
12. Jaws not me
13. Odd we ado
14. Real gang
15. Great down
16. Axe in
17. No I said plain
18. Lines hold nerve
19. As does
20. Luck rot
21. Rum soul
22. How print
23. Tack up wet
24. Owning ten

(Solution 153)

38 Great Words

Complete the words below, which are all synonyms of GREAT. Only alternate letters have been shown. Then rearrange the initial letters of the eight words to find a ninth synonym of GREAT.

•O•L•
•M•E•S•
•L•U•T•I•U•
•A•E•T•D
•L•R•O•S
•R•N•
•O•O•S•L
•U•U•T

(Solution 156)

39 Brain Strain

Insert the missing numbers so that the calculations are correct, both across and down. All numbers to be inserted are less than ten (there is no zero).

	−		÷		=	1
+		−		+		+
	×		÷	6	=	
÷		+		−		÷
	−	4	−		=	
=		=		=		=
2	×		−		=	

(Solution 44)

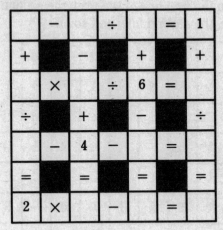

40 Einstein Rebus

What phrase is indicated below?

$$= mc^2$$

(Solution 3)

41 Word Power

The answer to each clue is a 9-letter word. The letters of each answer can all be found in the grid, although not necessarily in adjacent squares. In other words, the first letter of each answer is somewhere in the first line of the grid, the second letter is somewhere in the second line, and so on.

P	F	E	J	D	S	M	C	L
A	A	N	E	A	E	O	I	A
S	G	S	U	L	L	M	H	T
A	L	E	L	P	R	E	O	C
A	C	I	B	E	I	U	Y	S
R	T	R	B	I	M	S	R	N
O	T	A	O	I	I	A	O	A
E	A	U	N	T	T	C	T	N
S	E	T	E	E	K	N	E	Y

1. Ship's boat
2. Painter's support
3. Inheritance from father
4. Keen in thought
5. Chauffeur-driven car
6. To make famous
7. Hopeless
8. Cheer up
9. Bewitch

(Solution 7)

42 Three Too Many

Delete three of the four letters in each 4-letter square to complete the crossword.

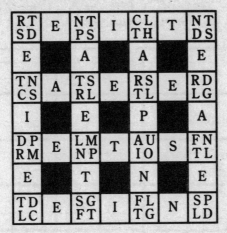

RT SD	E	NT PS	I	CL TH	T	NT DS
E		A		A		E
TN CS	A	TS RL	E	RS TL	E	RD LG
I		E		P		A
DP RM	E	LM NP	T	AU IO	S	FN TL
E		T		N		E
TD LC	E	SG FT	I	FL TG	N	SP LD

(Solution 11)

43 Dresses

The number of dresses owned by Yvonne is the same number owned by Lulu divided by the number owned by Irene.

Lulu has forty-two dresses and would own eight times as many as Irene if Lulu had fourteen more.

How many dresses does Yvonne have?

(Solution 15)

44 Squares

Divide the square into four equal segments. Each segment must contain one of each of the five symbols

+, ○, □, △, and ●

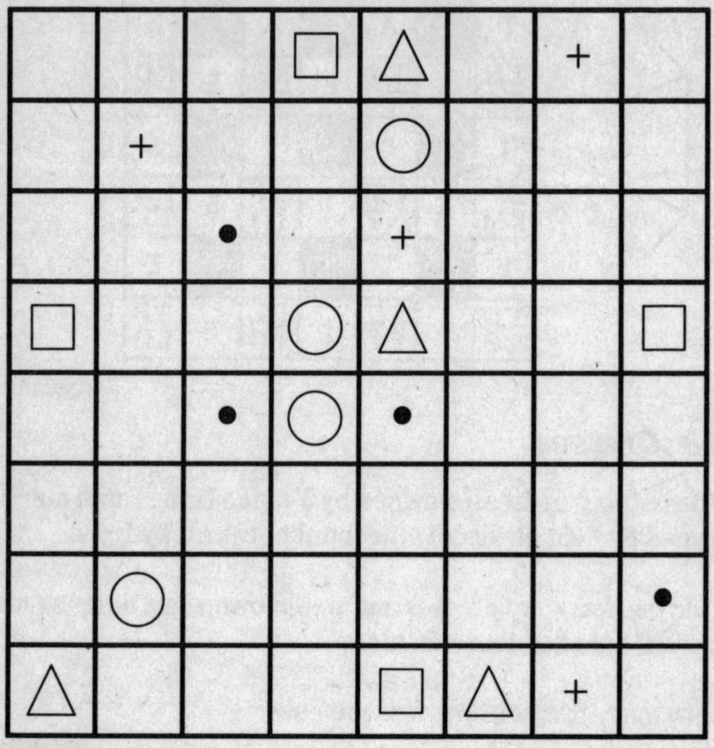

(Solution 19)

45 Sequence

7942, 6808, 5280, 1160, ?

What number comes next?

(Solution 23)

46 Octagon Words

Spiral clockwise around the octagons to find four words, two synonyms and two antonyms. You must provide the missing letters.

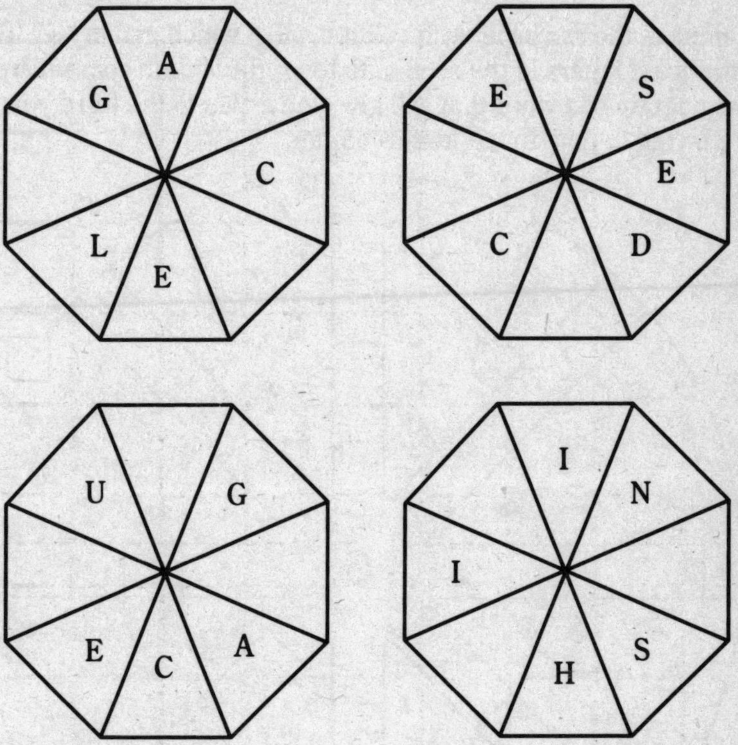

(Solution 27)

47 The Gallopers

The name given to this puzzle is the old fairground name for the roundabout ride on horses, now more familiarly known as the carousel.

Complete the words in each column, all of which end in "G". The scrambled letters in the section to the right of each column are an anagram of a word that will give you a clue to the word you are trying to find, to put in the column.

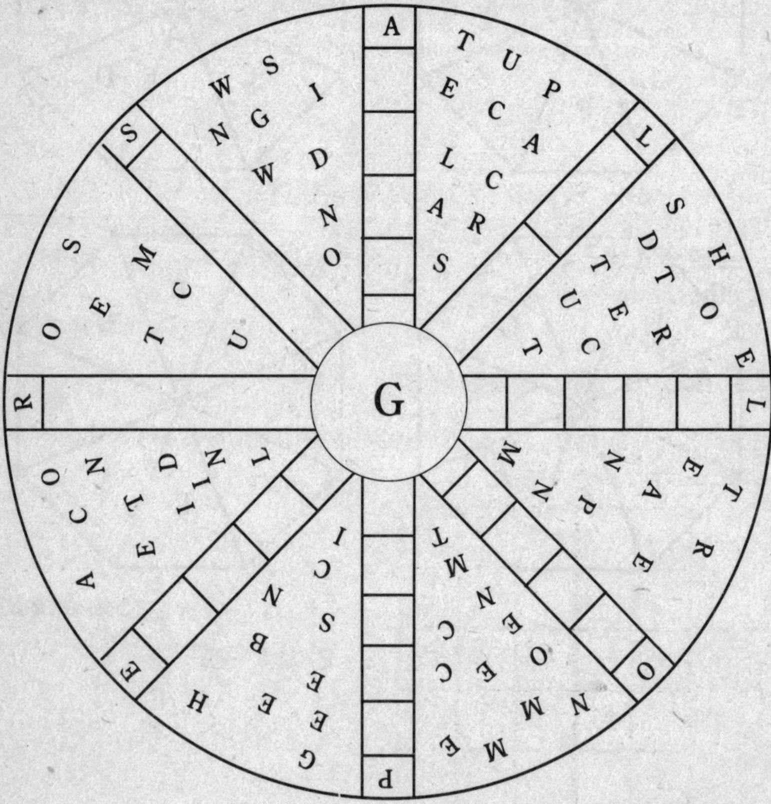

(Solution 31)

48 Greek Cross and Square

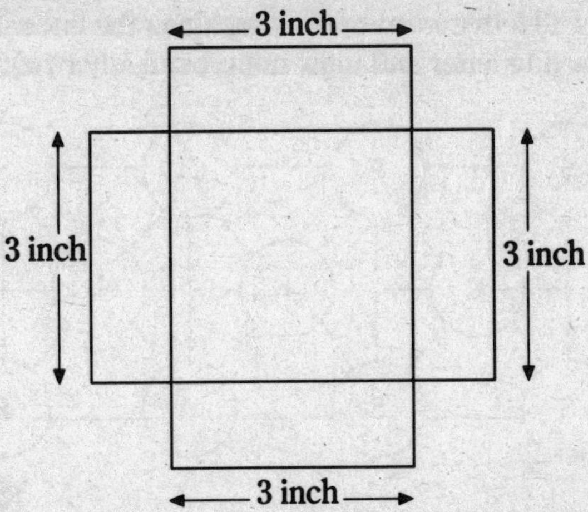

This is a 5-inch square with its corners removed. Divide the figure into five pieces to form a Greek Cross (a cross with all its sides equal) and an assembled square (pieces that can be put together to form a square).

(Solution 35)

49 Magic Word Square

Insert the letters in the grid to make five words that read the same down as across.

				T
			M	
		N		
	M			
T				

A	A	A	A	C
D	D	E	E	E
E	~~M~~	~~M~~	~~N~~	O
O	O	O	R	R
R	S	~~T~~	~~T~~	T

(Solution 39)

50 Find a Word

Trace out a 13-letter word by moving along the lines. You need to find the starting letter and must not cross a letter twice.

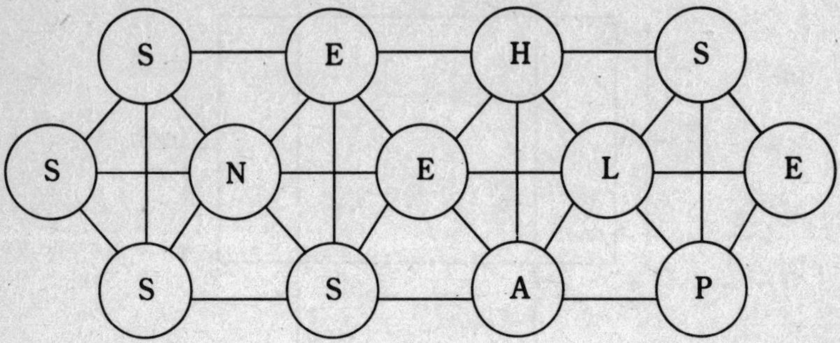

(Solution 43)

51 Cover-up

If I place a 6-inch square over a triangle I can cover three-quarters of the triangle. If I place the triangle over the square I can cover up to one-half of the square.

What is the area of the triangle?

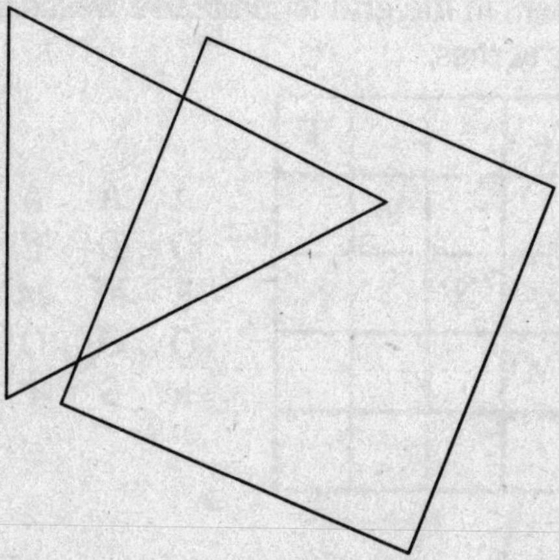

(Solution 47)

52 Links Jigsaw Puzzle

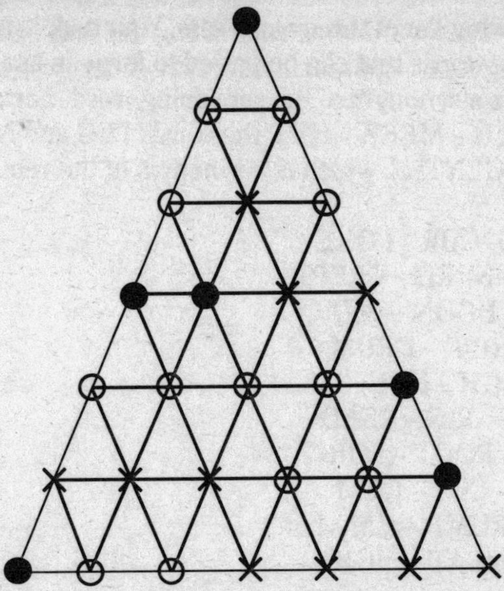

Place the twelve segment links over the triangular grid, above, in such a way that each link symbol is covered by exactly the same symbol. The connecting links must not be rotated.
Note: Not all of the connecting lines will be covered.

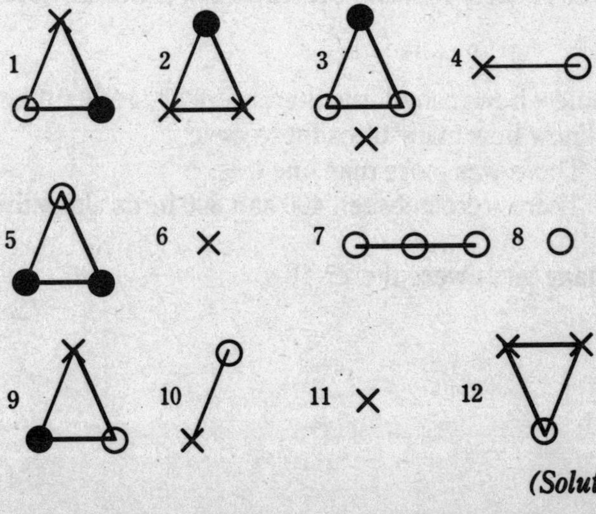

(Solution 51)

53 Anagrammed Synonyms

Study the following list of three word sets. Your task is to find the two of the three words that can be paired to form an anagram of one word that is a synonym of the remaining word. For example, in the group LEG – MEEK – NET, the words LEG and NET are an anagram of GENTLE, which is a synonym of the remaining word, MEEK.

1. SLUNG – AIR – LONE
2. PAST – NEED – CREPT
3. FINE – BOON – BET
4. ATE – RIPE – DRUM
5. SO – SIGH – HUG
6. STEER – RIG – READ
7. NICE – ROOT – POINT
8. SENT – CUT – GEM
9. FEE – RUMP – BALM
10. ART – NEAT – SIGHT

(Solution 55)

54 Forest

In this section of the forest there were a number of trees. Each tree had a number of birds in the branches. There were at least two birds in each tree, and each tree had the same number of birds.

If you knew how many birds there were altogether then you would know how many trees there were:

There was more than one tree.
There were between 400 and 800 birds altogether.

How many birds were there?

(Solution 59)

55 Inventions

Most people know that J. B. Dunlop invented the rubber tyre and that Sir Humphry Davy invented the safety lamp, but how many of us know, for example, that Walter Hunt was, in 1849, the inventor of the safety pin? See how many more of these inventions from between 1590 and 1895 you can work out. Only alternate letters are shown.

1.	1590	Zacharias Janssen	•O•P•U•D •I•R•S•O•E
2.	1643	Evangelista Torricelli	•A•O•E•E•
3.	1656	Christiaan Huygens	•E•D•L•M •L•C•
4.	1758	John Dollond	•C•R•M•T•C •E•S
5.	1775	David Bushnell	•U•M•R•N•
6.	1780	Samuel Harrison	•T•E• •E•
7.	1786	John Fitch	•T•A•B•A•
8.	1792	William Murdoch	•L•U•I•A•I•G •A•
9.	1796	Aloys Senefelder	•I•H•G•A•H•
10.	1804	William Congreve	•O•I• – •U•L •O•K•T
11.	1810	Frederick Koenig	•R•N•I•G •R•S•
12.	1821	Michael Faraday	•L•C•R•C •O•O•
13.	1824	Joseph Aspdin	•O•T•A•D •E•E•T
14.	1839	James Nasmyth	•T•A• •A•M•R
15.	1846	Richard M. Hoe	•O•A•Y •R•N•I•G •R•S•
16.	1855	J. E. Lundström	•A•E•Y •A•C•E•
17.	1858	Charles and William Marsh	•A•V•S•E•
18.	1877	Emile Berliner	•I•R•P•O•E
19.	1889	C. G. De Laval	•T•A• •U•B•N•
20.	1895	Charles Frederick Cross	•A•O•

(Solution 63)

56 Connections

Insert the numbers 0 – 10 in the circles below, so that for any particular circle the sum of the numbers in the circles connected directly to it equals the value corresponding to the number in that circle, as given in the list.

Example:

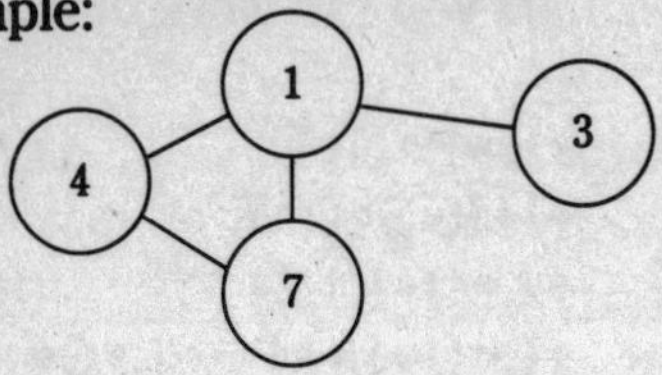

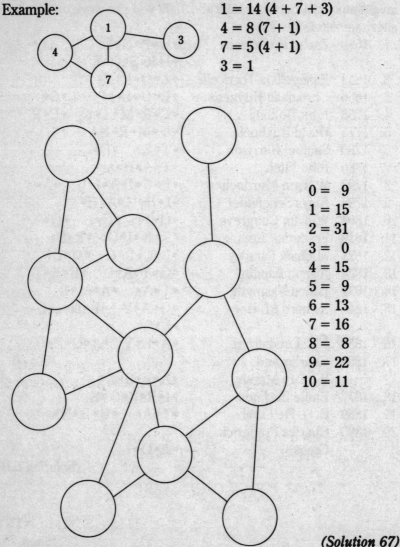

1 = 14 (4 + 7 + 3)
4 = 8 (7 + 1)
7 = 5 (4 + 1)
3 = 1

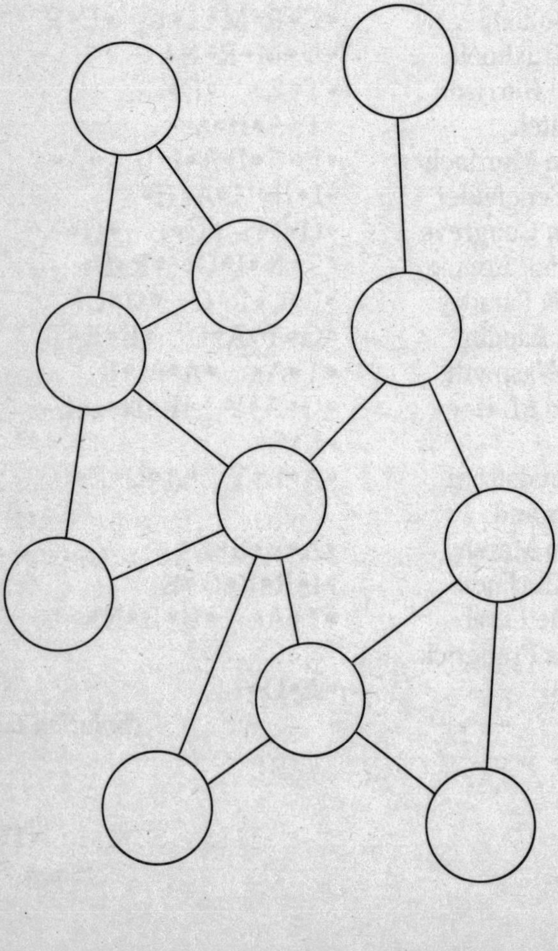

0 = 9
1 = 15
2 = 31
3 = 0
4 = 15
5 = 9
6 = 13
7 = 16
8 = 8
9 = 22
10 = 11

(Solution 67)

57 Circle Jigsaw Puzzle

Assemble the nine pieces to form the circle below:

(Solution 71)

58 Saying

This saying has had all of its vowels removed. The consonants are in their correct order but have been broken up into groups of four.

Replace the vowels and reconstitute the saying.

WHVR LRNS TCNT RLTH
WTHR WLLH VDST RYDT
HLST SFTP CFCN VRST
N

TLLR SCMM NTRY

(Solution 75)

59 Honeycomb

Move from honeycomb cell to honeycomb cell in any direction to spell out the names of fifteen types of fruit. You may move horizontally, vertically, or diagonally, and letters may be used more than once in each word.

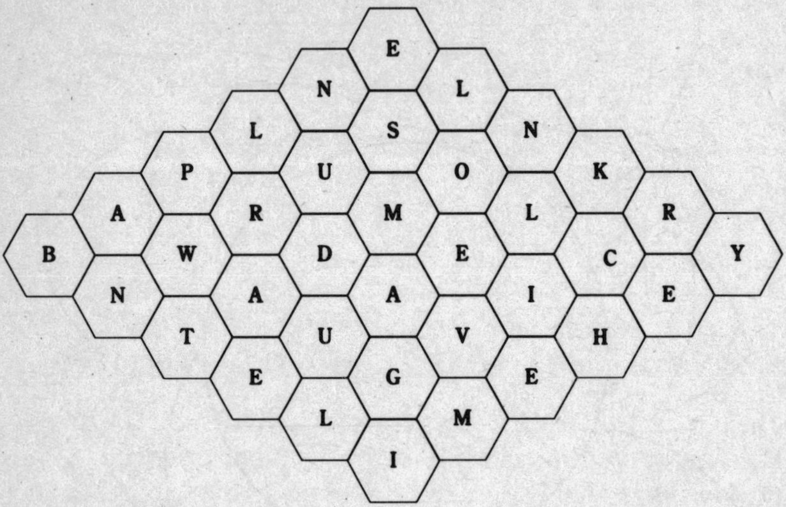

(Solution 79)

60 Clueless Crossword

Delete three of the four letters in each box to form a normal crossword grid.

PJ TS	CH UR	OA IN	TU GP	PB IL	OE LN	GE SR
OA TN		RM NK		RI LE		RE XT
RI UA	AP NE	GD PI	NT ER	EA IB	OE SA	SE RW
NA RS		EN LO		ZR EV		AE FP
TW EN	XI AR	XY NR	DA IE	DS EL	RS OE	NP TE

(Solution 83)

61 One-Armed Bandit

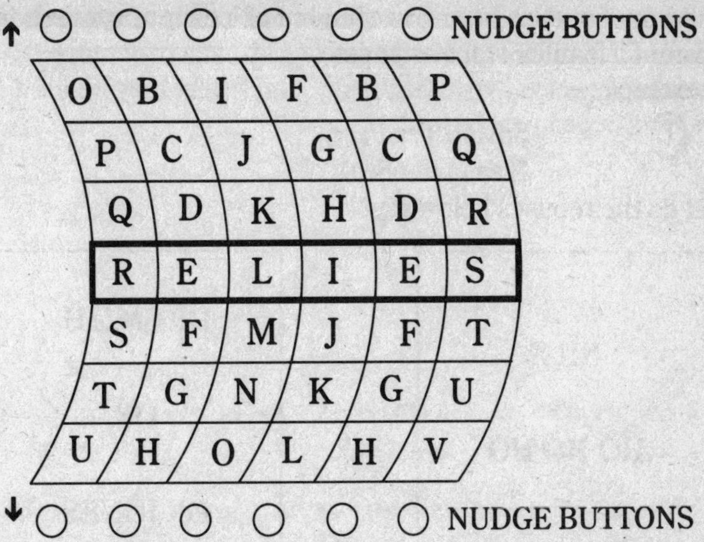

The one-armed bandit has produced a 6-letter word. You may keep one of the letters in "RELIES". The others must be produced by nudging 1, 2, or 3 spaces up or down, as required, to produce another 6-letter word.
Clue: Parts of the body.

(Solution 87)

62 Rebuses

One form of a rebus is an arrangement of letters or symbols to represent a familiar word or phrase.
For example:

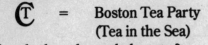

 = Boston Tea Party (Tea in the Sea)

What do the rebuses below say?

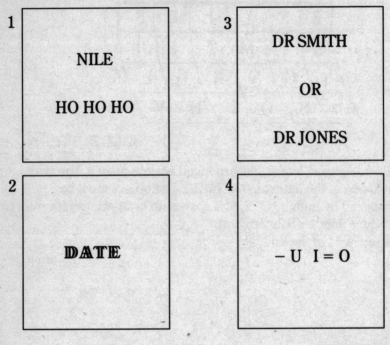

1

NILE

HO HO HO

2

DATE

3

DR SMITH

OR

DR JONES

4

– U I = O

(Solution 91)

63 Synonyms

In each of the following a number of synonyms of the keyword are shown. Take one letter from each of the synonyms to find a further synonym of the keyword. The letters appear in the correct order.

1. Keyword: GHOST
   Synonyms: Phantasm, Phantom, Apparition, Umbra, Wraith, Spectre

2. Keyword: SUIT
   Synonyms: Accord, Confirm, Harmonize, Correspond, Cohere, Agree, Tally

3. Keyword: ORDER
   Synonyms: Course, Sequence, Progression, Chain, Succession, String

4. Keyword: FRAGMENT
   Synonyms: Smidgen, Spot, Syllable, Speck, Scrap, Crumb, Particle, Mite

5. Keyword: BRIM
   Synonyms: Selvage, Brink, Periphery, Fringe, Perimeter.

(Solution 95)

64 Magic Square Jigsaw Puzzle

Insert the pieces so that each horizontal, vertical, and corner-to-corner line totals 260.

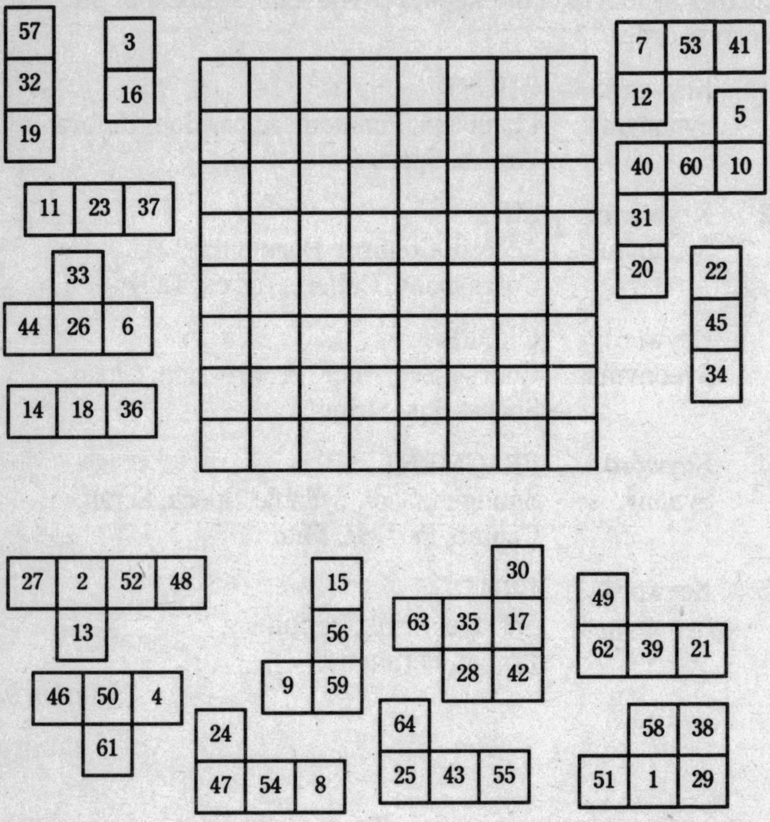

(Solution 99)

65 Analogy

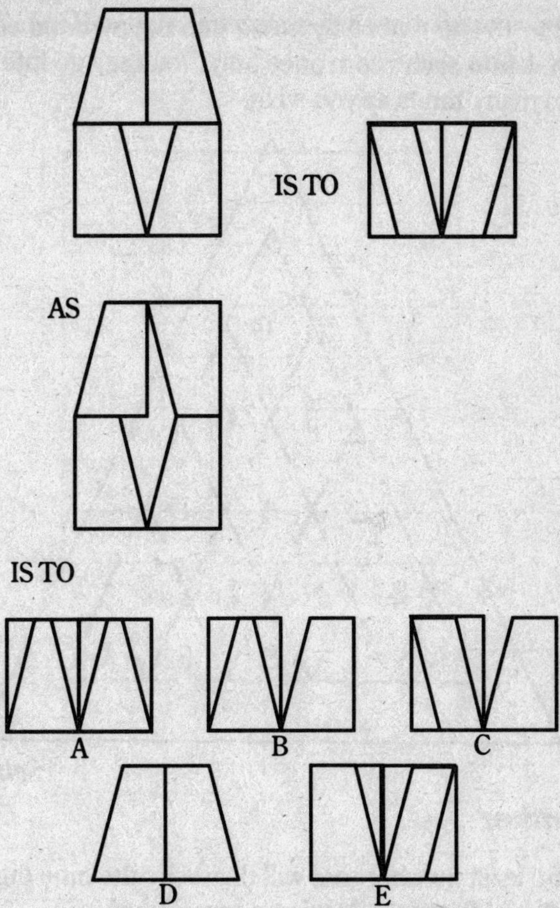

(Solution 103)

66 Pyramid

Spell out the 15-letter word by going into the pyramid one room at a time. Go into each room once only. You may go into the passage as many times as you wish.

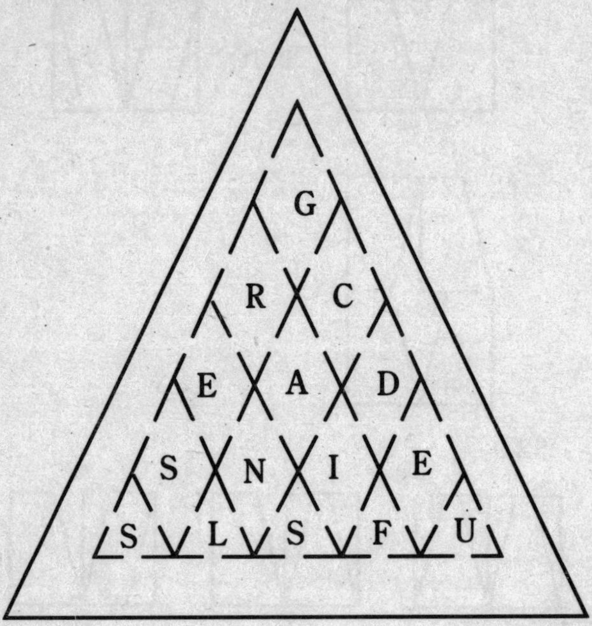

(Solution 107)

67 Number

What is the least number that will divide by the nine digits 1, 2, 3, 4, 5, 6, 7, 8, and 9 without leaving a remainder?

(Solution 111)

68 Odd One Out

Which is the odd one out?

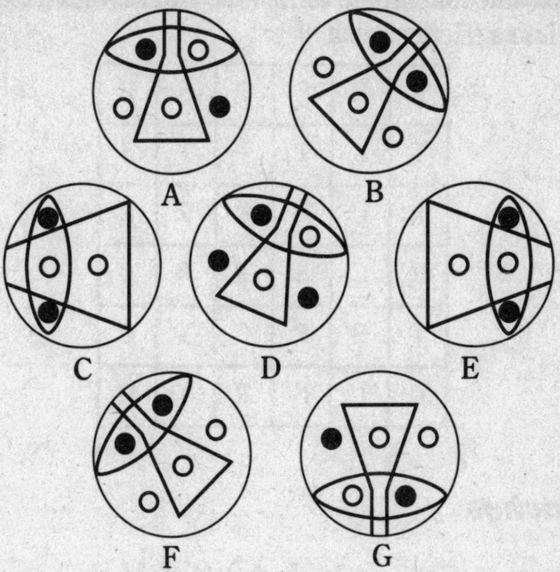

(Solution 115)

69 Pyramid Word

Solve the five clues, place the five words in the pyramid, then rearrange all fifteen letters to find a 15-letter word.

Clues:

1. Chemical symbol for iodine
2. Third person singular
3. Cunning
4. Unmixed
5. Sturdy

(Solution 119)

70 Division

Divide the grid into four equal parts, each of which should be the same shape and contain the same nine letters, which can be arranged into a 9-letter word.

R	R	E	C	S	U
T	U	T	T	T	S
R	U	U	R	R	E
R	C	S	T	R	U
T	S	E	C	T	C
U	U	E	R	T	U

(Solution 123)

71 Matches

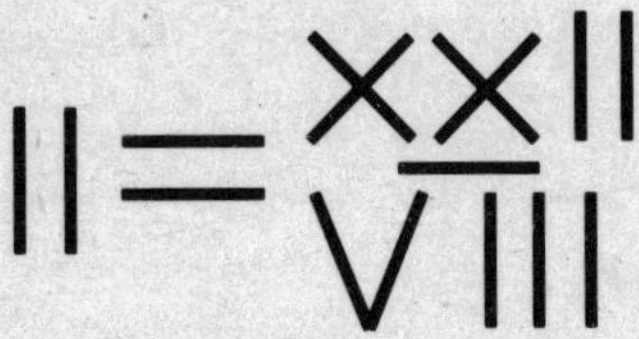

Move one match to make this correct.

(Solution 127)

72 Common Words

What do these words have in common?

Bar
Joy
Kin
Mar
Sal
Land
Gent

(Solution 131)

73 The Hexagon Cross

Can you draw the contents of the empty hexagon, second from the right?

(Solution 135)

74 Alphabet Clueless Cross

Insert the twenty-six letters of the alphabet to complete the crossword.

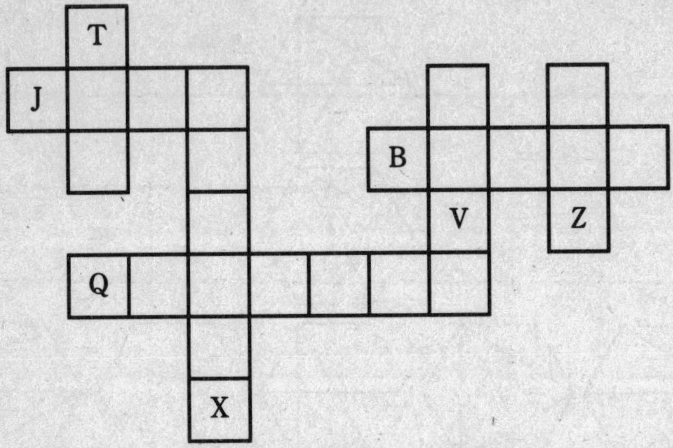

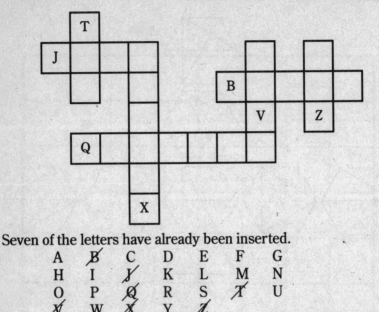

Seven of the letters have already been inserted.

A ~~B~~ C D E F G
H I ~~J~~ K L M N
O P ~~Q~~ R S ~~T~~ U
~~V~~ W ~~X~~ Y ~~Z~~

(Solution 139)

75 Children's Party

There are 100 children at a party.

60 eat jelly
23 eat pudding
62 eat cake
8 eat jelly and pudding
45 eat jelly and cake
5 eat pudding and cake
2 eat jelly, pudding and cake.

1. How many eat only one item?
2. How many eat none of these items?

(Solution 144)

76 Squares

Divide the square into four equal segments. Each segment must contain the five symbols (one of each)

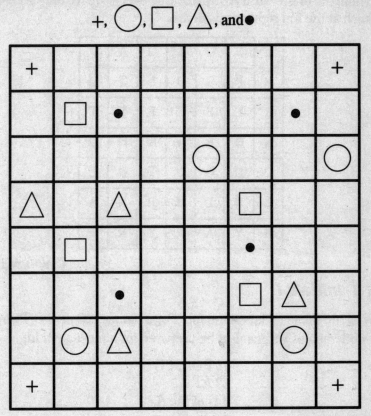

+, ○, □, △, and ●

+							+
	□	●				●	
				○			○
△		△			□		
	□				●		
		●			□	△	
	○	△				○	
+							+

(Solution 147)

77 The Absurd Puzzle

Start at the central square and work from square to square horizontally, vertically, and diagonally to spell out seven synonyms of the word ABSURD. Use every square only once and finish at the top right-hand square.

T	S	O	I	O	A	D	→
E	P	S	O	L	T	M	
R	E	P	H	F	Y	T	
S	O	R	*	N	O	D	
C	U	O	O	Y	D	E	
Z	R	L	H	B	N	A	
A	Y	A	R	E	R	I	

(Solution 151)

78 Initials I

What do these initials stand for? For example, 2G of V = Two Gentlemen of Verona. But be prepared for almost anything!

16 P in a CG
32 AT
4 H of the A
6 S to a H
7 S in the BD
4 of a K in P
90 D in a Q
3 PC of L
40 Y for a R A
8 S of A

(Solution 155)

79 Analogy Test

All the analogies below are either synonyms or antonyms. You must correctly place the twenty-four words provided at the bottom into the twelve analogies.

For example: 1. Fond is to ____ as hard is to ____.
2. Tired is to ____ as loud is to ____.
Correctly place the words: fresh, firm, soft, devoted.

Answer: 1. Fond is to devoted as hard is to firm. (synonyms)
2. Tired is to fresh as loud is to soft. (antonyms)

1. Sharp is to ____ as dilate is to ____.
2. Constrict is to ____ as selvage is to ____
3. Hue is to ____ as hag is to ____.
4. Forte is to ____ as avow is to ____.
5. Law is to ____ as digit is to ____.
6. Sere is to ____ as copious is to ____.
7. Caveat is to ____ as tergiversate is to ____.
8. Cataract is to ____ as decry is to ____.
9. Fogy is to ____ as bathetic is to ____.
10. Bayou is to ____ as sapid is to ____.
11. Atrophy is to ____ as stolid is to ____.
12. Roily is to ____ as articulate is to ____.

Correctly place the words:
Slough, Limpid, Witch, Contract, Integer, Monition, Desert, Amelioration, Mossback, Controvert, Blunt, Wet, Appreciate, Disintegrate, Musty, Tone, Concentrate, Scanty, Trickle, Incompetence, Responsive, Canon, Periphery, Savoury.

(Solution 160)

80 Enclosed Letters

The letters S-Q-U-A-R-E are enclosed by a square in which only the letters S-Q-U-A-R-E appear. Which other letters can be enclosed by another figure whose name they can be arranged to spell out, and so that no other letters appear in that figure?

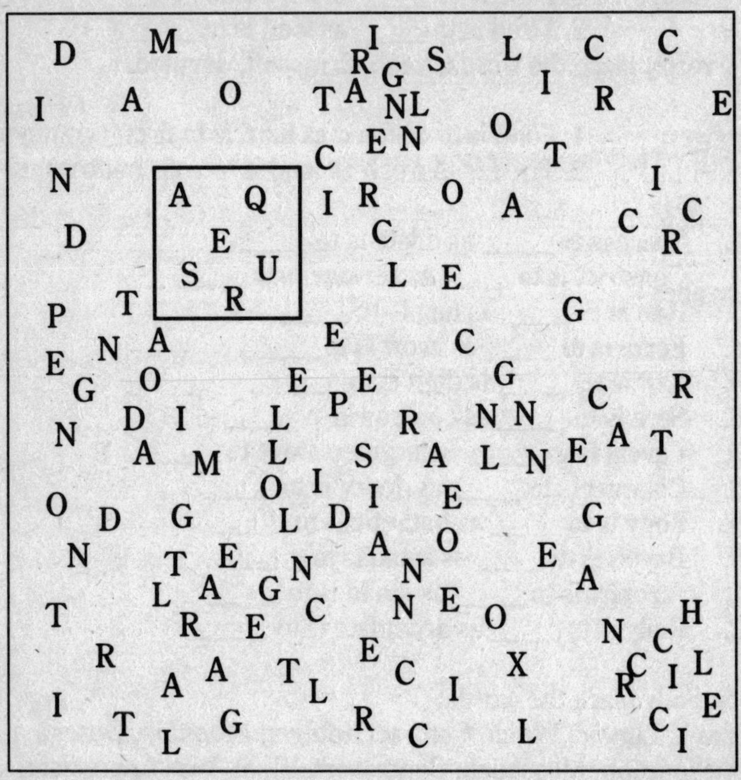

(Solution 2)

81 Hidden Birds

Find the names of four birds hidden in the sentences.

1. A message from all aardvarks, "Ants are in abundance."
2. Most rich people give to charity organizations.
3. Hear the drums and pipers play in the new year.
4. First one chatterbox, then another chatterbox.

(Solution 6)

82 Twelve Letters

Find four 12-letter words. The first half is inside the star; the second half is outside the star. Some answers may contain hyphens.

Clue: Would have been useful in Rome!

1 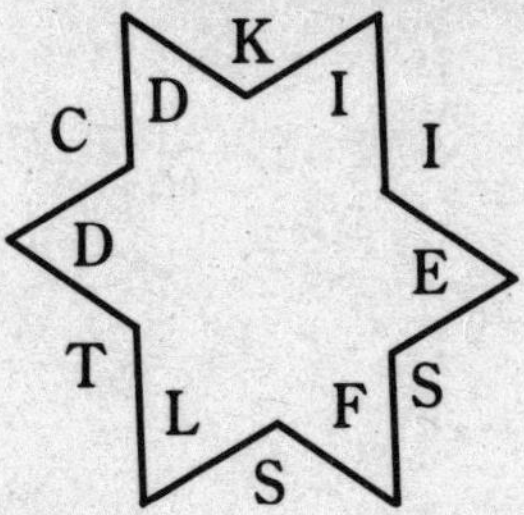

Clue: No upstairs!

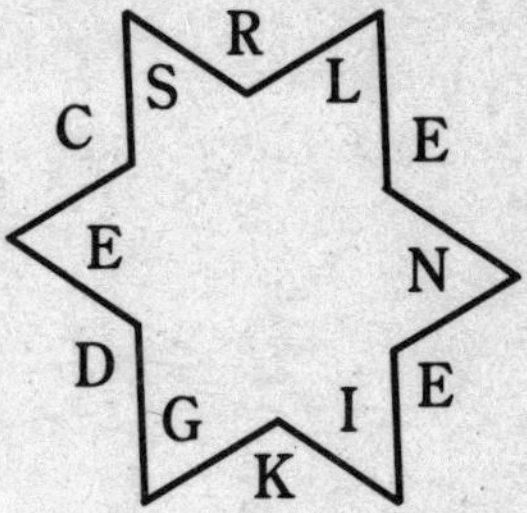 2

3 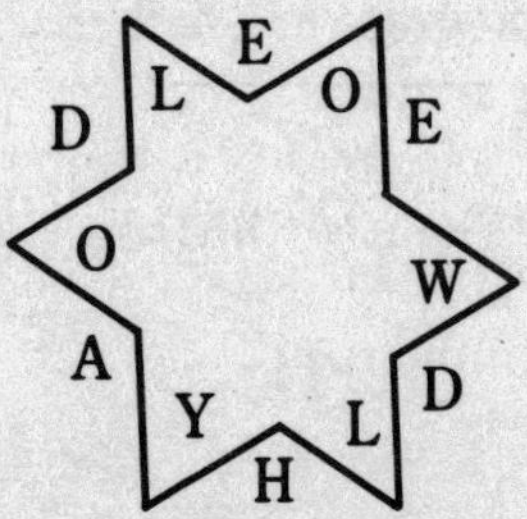

Clue: Sheep like!

 4

Clue: Sell the land!

(Solution 10)

83 Clock

The end of a minute hand of a clock moves through 8.4 inches in 36 minutes.

Find the length of the minute hand.

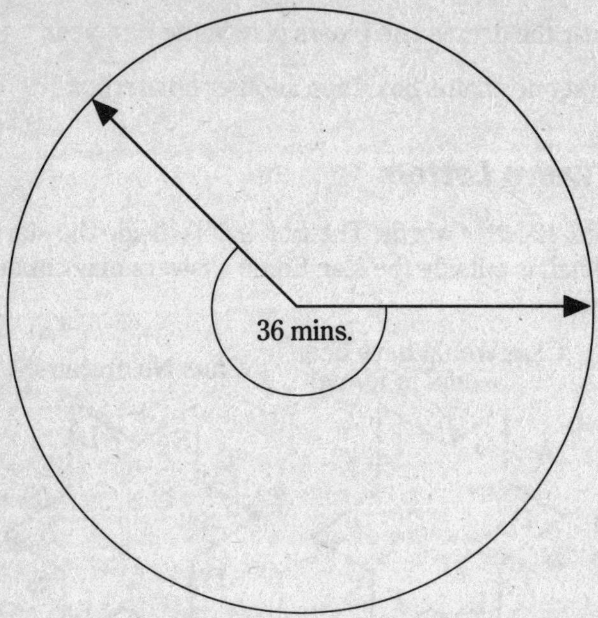

(Solution 14)

84 Cryptogram

This is a straight substitution cryptogram in which each letter of the alphabet has been replaced by another.

MZY FPJBFNHI SXZYIJFEJ ZN VMJ

VPHVM TBX QJ YMJX VMJPJ'L

XZ MJIG RX VPHVM

– LZGMZTIJL (ZJFRGHL PJC)

(Solution 18)

85 Sequence

Which option carries on the sequence?

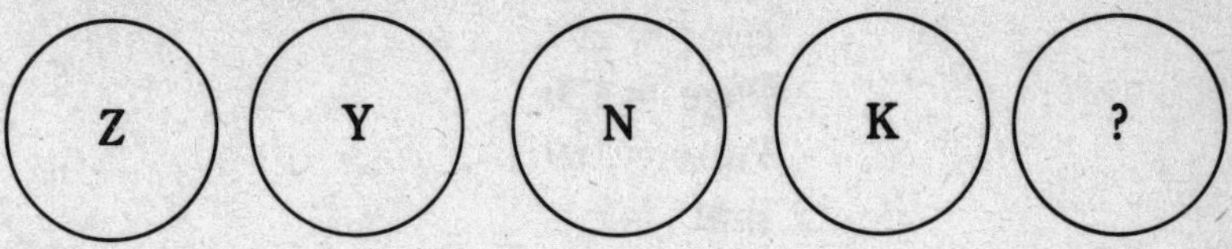

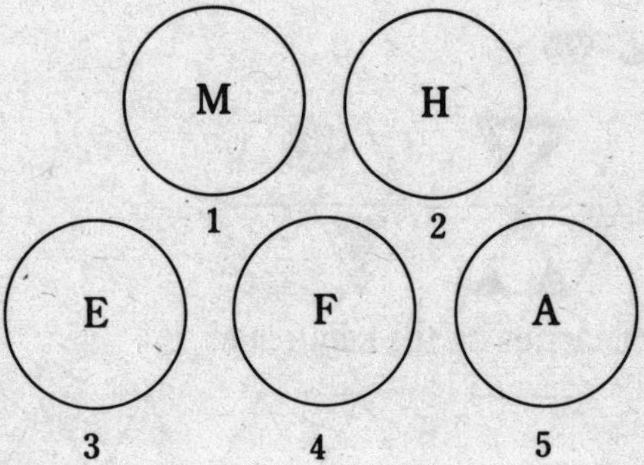

(Solution 22)

86 Anagram Theme

Arrange the fourteen words in pairs so that each pair is an anagram of another word or name. The seven words produced have a linking theme. For example, if the words TRY and CREASE appeared in the list, they could be paired to form SECRETARY and the theme could be professions.

Ale	Nail
As	Plop
Beg	Pole
Best	Rein
Day	Some
Do	Tier
Err	Top

(Solution 26)

87 Elementary Mathematics

What is the value of brat?

Coin = 76
Hear = 20
Rage = 120
Pure = 169
Brat = ?

(Solution 30)

88 Hexagons

Which option carries on the sequence?

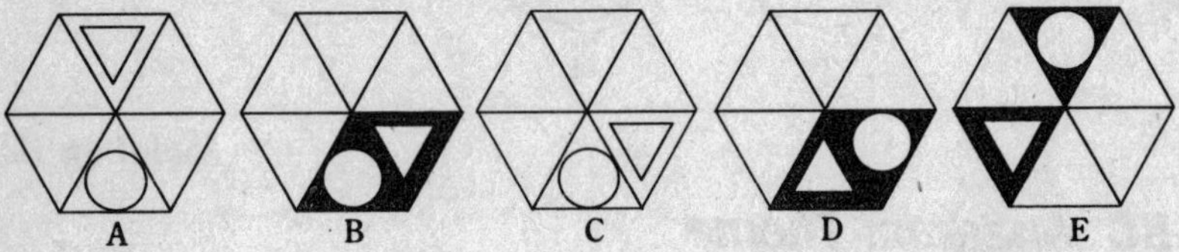

(Solution 34)

89 Front

Which word can be placed in front of these words to make new words?

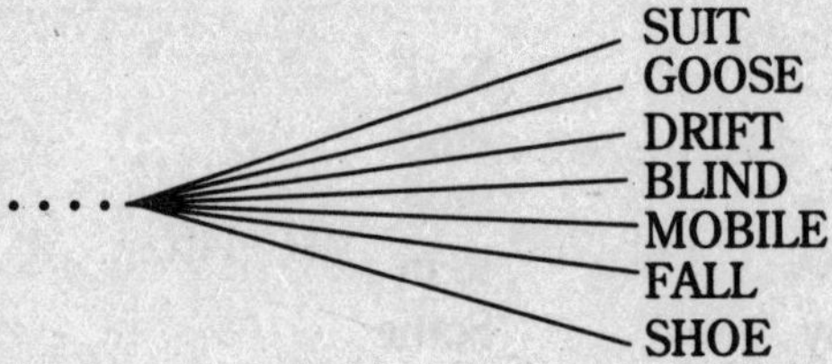

(Solution 38)

90 Middle Letters

These letter groupings are found in the middle of certain words. Some are hyphenated. Find the words.

1. KETYSP
2. ICDE
3. CISSI
4. SEZF
5. EUPM
6. DYPI
7. NEYSP
8. KEYP
9. APFR
10. HSTR

(Solution 42)

91 Circles

What number should go into (?) ?

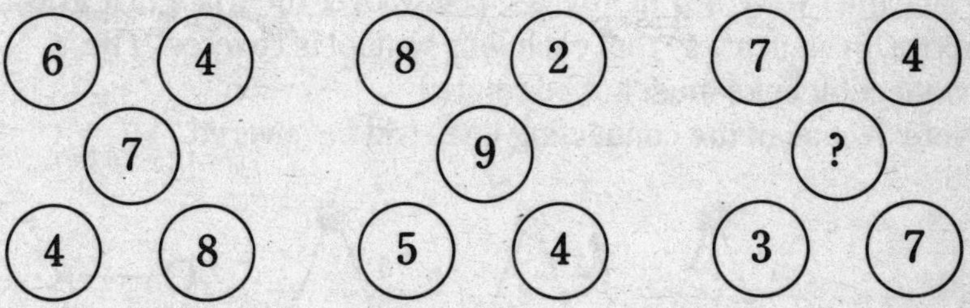

(Solution 46)

92 Sequence

What comes next in this sequence?

145, 230, 315, 400, 445

(Solution 50)

93 Links Jigsaw Puzzle

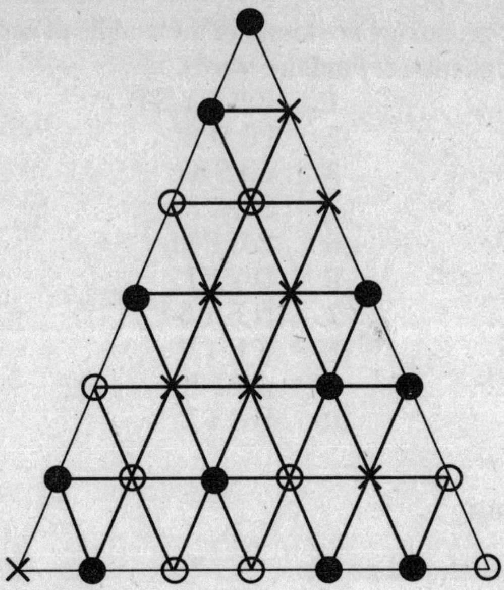

Place the twelve segment links, below, over the triangular grid, above, in such a way that each link symbol is covered. The connecting links must not be rotated.
Note: Not all of the connecting lines will be covered.

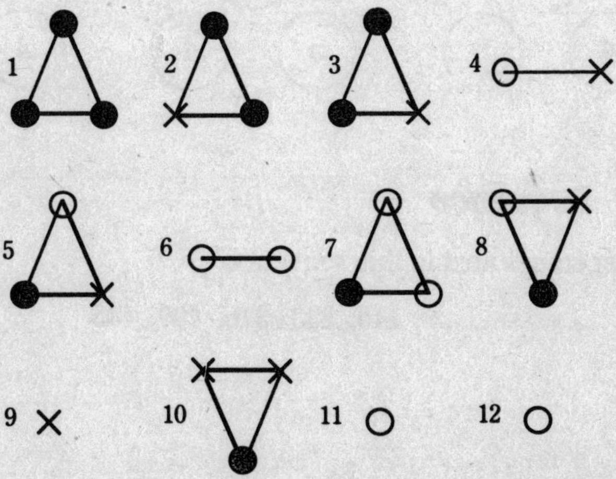

(Solution 54)

94 Side by Side

The answers to each pair of clues are two words that appear side by side in *Webster's Collegiate Dictionary* (tenth edition).

For example, A. A remedy for all ills – Panacea
B. Dash or flamboyance – Panache

1. A. A round building
   B. A person not of noble birth
2. A. Crafty
   B. An instrument for boring holes
3. A. Injurious to reputation
   B. Capable of preserving prudent silence
4. A. High seriousness
   B. To move toward something
5. A. Refer to
   B. A trusted teacher or guide
6. A. Resembling leather
   B. An Old World herb
7. A. A full suit of armour
   B. A complete view
8. A. Slyly derogatory
   B. To smell by inhalation through the nose
9. A. A state of agitated confusion
   B. A woodwind instrument
10. A. A story with a compact and pointed plot
    B. Something new or unusual

(Solution 58)

95 No Repeat Letters

The grid below contains twenty-five different letters of the alphabet. What is the longest word that can be found by starting anywhere and working from square to square horizontally, vertically, or diagonally and not repeating a letter?

B	M	S	E	X
P	A	I	H	O
L	J	V	N	G
C	F	Q	D	Y
K	U	R	T	W

(Solution 62)

96 Saying

Place the letters on the right in the grid to complete the saying.

➔		O		O	T		A	ABB
		K	A		O			DDF
	Y	O			S	E		LLL
		I		W	I		L	LNN
		E		O		E		NRT
	H	E		Y	O			TTU
	E		V	E	-	-	-	UUW

(Solution 66)

97 Eight Sticks

Arrange the eight sticks to form three squares of the same size. Four of the sticks are twice as long as the other four.

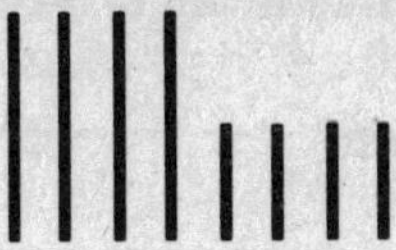

(Solution 70)

98 Wordsearch

Find twenty-two occupations. Words can be found horizontally, vertically, and diagonally, forward and backward, but only in straight lines. Letters can be used more than once but only once in each word. Only three letters are not used and they also form a word.

H	T	I	M	S	R	E	V	L	I	S
E	E	C	H	E	M	I	S	T	H	T
A	A	I	L	A	R	T	X	E	R	O
D	M	N	E	M	A	T	E	E	R	C
M	S	A	C	A	V	P	A	E	E	K
A	T	H	T	N	F	S	H	L	T	B
S	E	C	U	A	U	C	L	U	S	R
T	R	E	R	R	A	I	T	P	I	O
E	E	M	E	E	S	O	I	Y	O	K
R	E	R	R	T	R	H	P	T	B	E
R	E	P	E	E	W	S	D	A	O	R

(Solution 74)

99 Wager

A man bets $30 and wins back his original wager plus $60. He spends one-third on a present for his wife, $10 for a taxi ride, and 10% of the remainder as a tip for the taxi driver.

How much does he have left?

(Solution 78)

100 Squares

Divide the square into four equal segments. Each segment must contain the five symbols (one of each)

+, ○, □, △, and ●

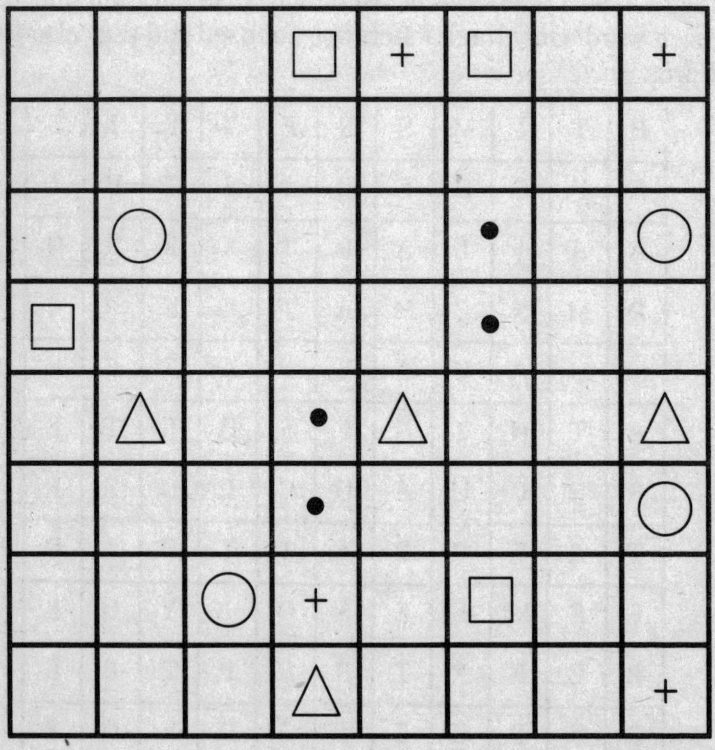

(Solution 82)

101 Margana

If we presented you with the words MAR, AM, and FAR and asked you to find the shortest English word that contained all the letters from which these words could be produced, we would expect you to come up with the word FARM.

Here is a further list of words:

SHADY, CRY, RUSH, RAIL

What is the shortest word from which all these words can be produced?

(Solution 86)

102 Thirty Bits

Arrange the thirty small words into ten long words, using three bits per word. One answer is a proper noun.

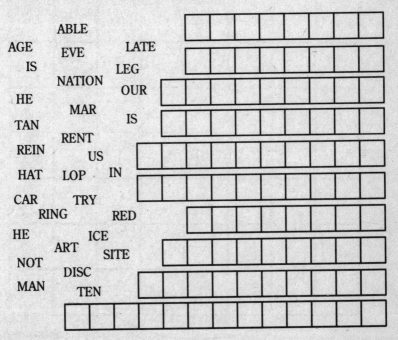

ABLE
AGE
EVE
LATE
IS
LEG
NATION
OUR
HE
MAR
TAN
IS
RENT
REIN
US
HAT
LOP
IN
CAR
TRY
RING
RED
HE
ICE
ART
SITE
NOT
DISC
MAN
TEN

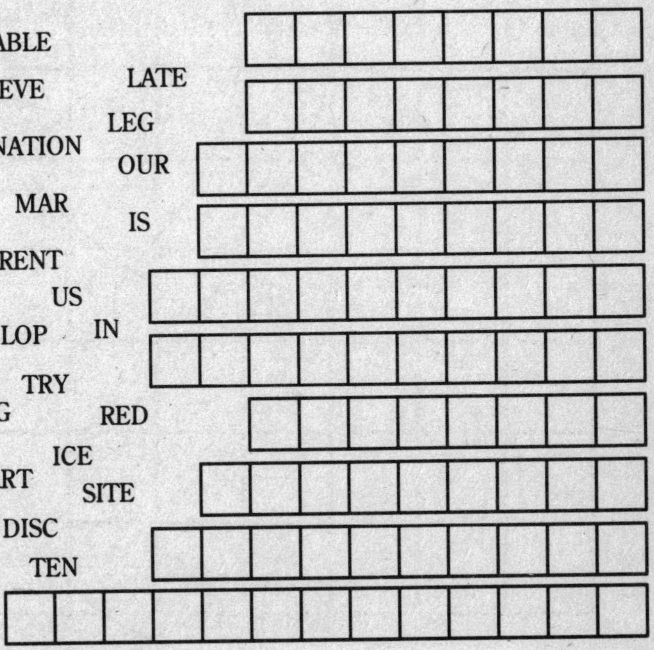

(Solution 90)

103 Five Fractions

$$\frac{13485}{2697} = 5$$

Can you find five other ways to arrange the digits 1, 2, 3, 4, 5, 6, 7, 8, and 9 using each only once to form a single fraction that equals five?

(Solution 94)

104 Track Word

Work around the track to find a 15-letter word. You have to provide the missing letters and find the starting point. The word might appear reading clockwise or counter-clockwise, and the overlapping letter appears twice.

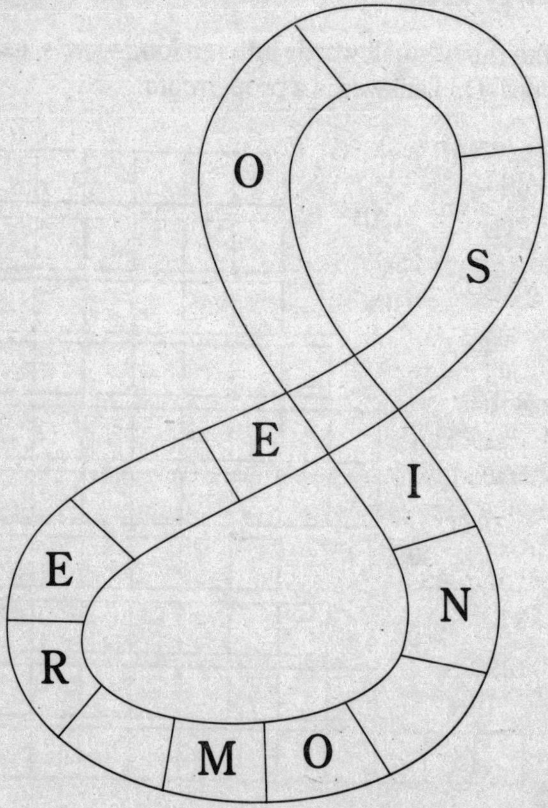

(Solution 98)

105 Star

Find the 12-letter word by going into all the compartments, visiting each compartment only once.

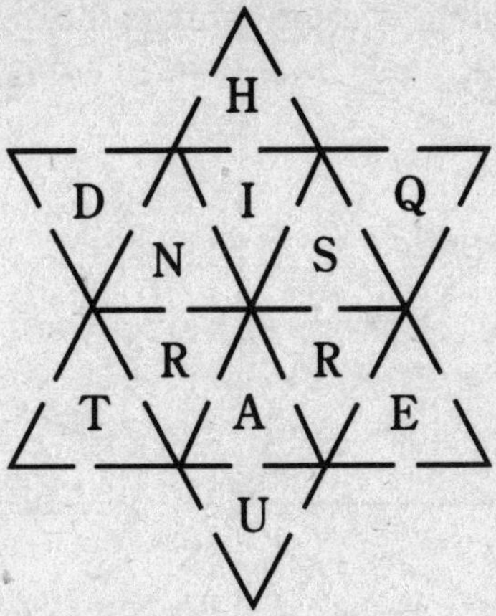

(Solution 102)

106 Common Clues

What do all the answers to the following clues have in common?

1. A Short crowbar
2. A British soldier
3. A Milksop
4. A Venture excursion
5. A Male goat
6. Crystallized sugar
7. A Wheeled platform for a television camera
8. A Circular current
9. To Torment repeatedly
10. A Pool of money

(Solution 106)

107 Quotation

Starting with BORE, find a quotation by Henny Youngman.

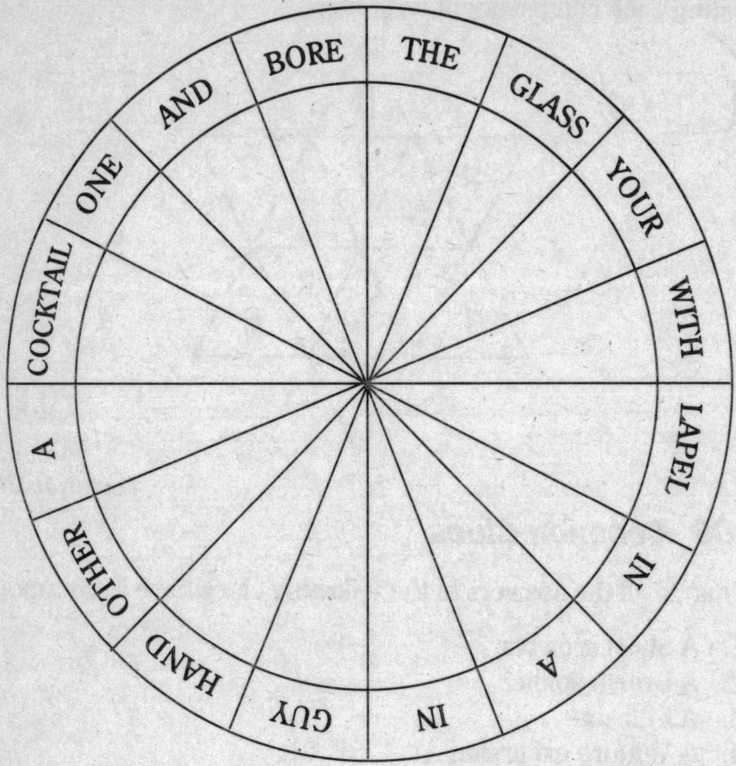

(Solution 110)

108 Letters

The four letters R-A-C-E are placed in a row at random. What is the probability that an English word is formed?

(Solution 114)

109 Sequence

Which option carries on the sequence?

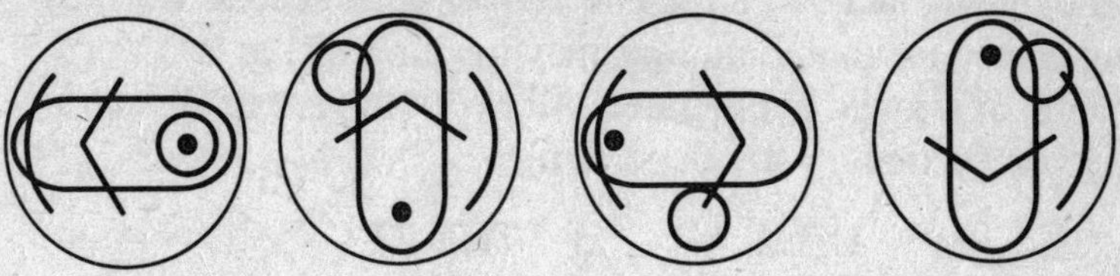

?

A B C

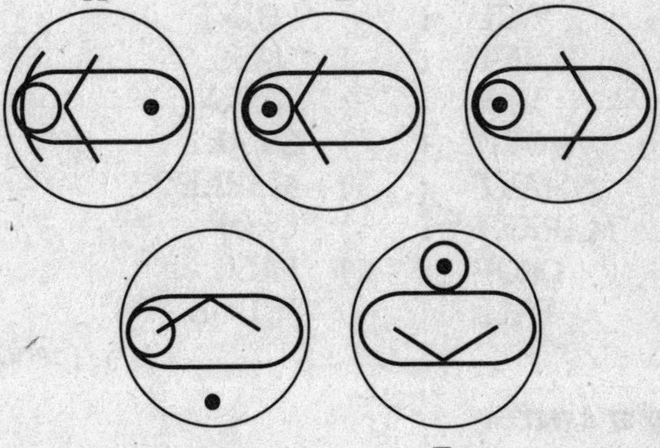

D E

(Solution 118)

110 Work It Out

What number is missing from the third triangle?

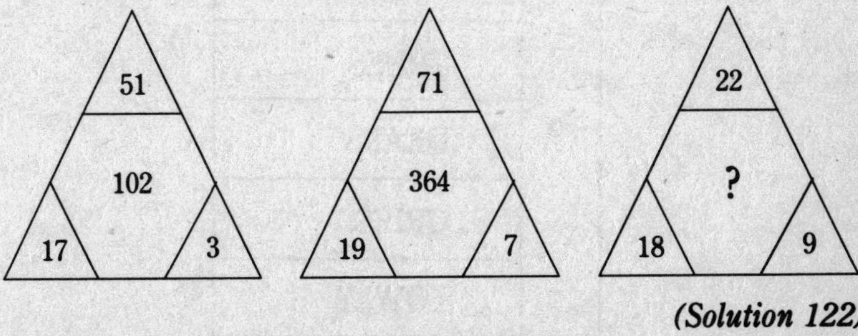

(Solution 122)

111 Links

Insert the missing words so that a link is made with the first word by being tacked on the end and with the second word by being placed in front. Solutions may be one-word or two-word answers, or may be hyphenated. All words appear in *Webster's Collegiate Dictionary* (tenth edition).

OPEN	( )	TICKET
TICKET	( )	BOY
BOY	( )	CAR
CAR	( )	TAIL
TAIL	( )	POINT
POINT	( )	DAY
DAY	( )	WORN
WORN	( )	SMART
SMART	( )	MARKET
MARKET	( )	CROP
CROP	( )	FALL
FALL	( )	JUDGE

(Solution 126)

112 Add a Letter

Find a letter to replace "?", that, when added to each of the 5-letter sets and rearranged, will form five 6-letter words that are names of colours.

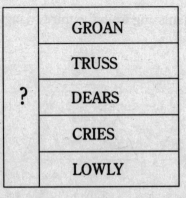

?	GROAN
	TRUSS
	DEARS
	CRIES
	LOWLY

(Solution 130)

113 Network

Find the starting point and travel along the connecting lines in a continuous path to adjacent circles to spell out a 14-letter word. Every circle must be visited only once.

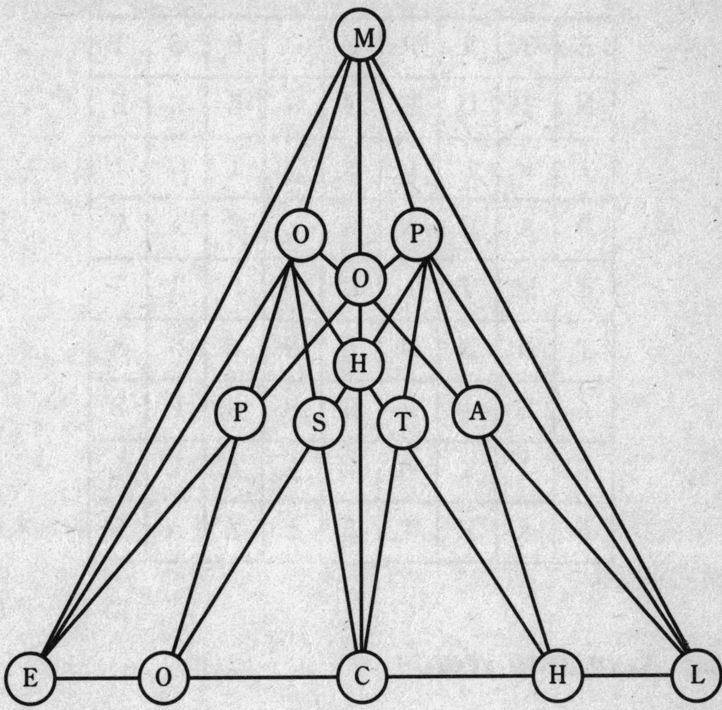

(Solution 133)

114 Apples

A farmer told his farm manager to pack 896,809 apples into as few sacks as possible. Each sack had to have the same number of apples, and he had to use more than one sack.

How many sacks did he use?

(Solution 138)

115 Jumble

Commencing always with the middle letter "U" spell out eight 11-letter words moving in any direction. Each letter can be used only once.

E	T	E	R	E	D	S	S	T
N	T	U	E	S	S	E	L	E
I	R	L	L	E	N	T	O	I
D	A	C	N	S	L	R	A	V
E	M	T	L	U	N	P	I	T
T	A	R	N	P	N	R	N	A
A	G	I	M	H	B	S	P	B
R	I	T	O	L	L	A	E	L
E	R	E	T	S	E	K	A	E

(Solution 142)

116 Kangaroo Words

A kangaroo word is one that contains a synonym within it, for example, CALUMNIES = LIES or ILLUMINATED = LIT. Now find the kangaroo words within the words below. All letters of the synonyms appear in the correct order.

Catacomb	Chariot
Instructor	Pasteurized
Masculine	Fatigue
Hurries	Exhilaration
Deliberate	Latest
Chocolate	Destruction
Facetiousness	Encourage

(Solution 146)

117 Comparison

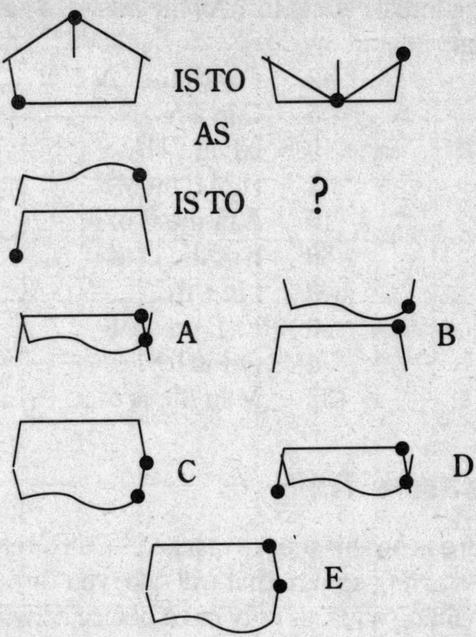

(Solution 150)

118 Panvolic Homophones

Homophones are words that are spelled differently but sound the same, such as son and sun. Panvolic homophones are pairs of homophones that contain all five vowels in each part.
For example, ADIEU – ADO.

Can you find another pair?

(Solution 154)

119 All American

What do the initials stand for? All the answers have American connections.

2	P with the LN of R
5	C in a N
5	GL in CNA
4	H of P on MR
10	A in the B of R
50	S of the D of I
9	I in a BG
90	FBB on a BF
4	of J is ID
435	M in the H of R

(Solution 158)

120 Treasure Trail

The treasure is on the square marked "T". To reach it you have to find the starting square that will take you through every one of the 35 remaining squares only once before arriving at the treasure.

"1S" means one square south; "4E" means four squares east.

5E 1S	4E 3S	2W 4S	2S 2W	3W 4S	1S 2W
5E 1N	2E 4S	1S 3E	1S 1W	4W 1N	2W 1S
3E 2S	1S 1W	2S 3E	1N 3W	3S 4W	2N 1W
3N 1E	3E 2S	2S 1W	T	2W 2S	1W 1S
5E 1S	1W 2N	4N 1E	2N 1E	1N 2W	3N 4W
1N 2E	1E 5N	2N 1W	1E 2N	1W 2N	1W 4N

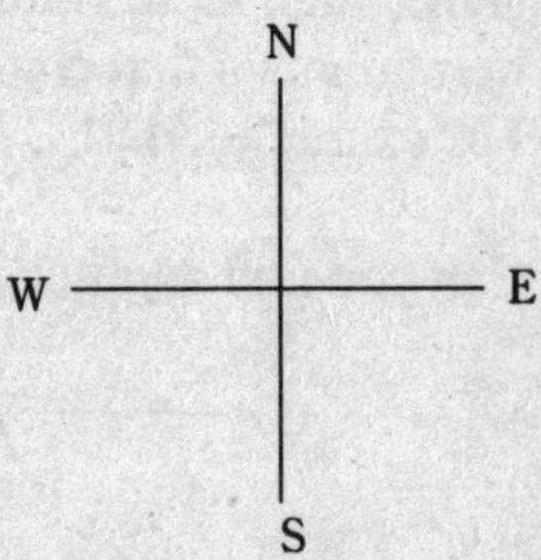

(Solution 1)

121 Alphametics

Replace the letters with numbers.

```
   T H E
   T E N
 + M E N
 -------
 M E E T
```

(Solution 5)

122 Missing Letters

Fill in the missing letters to find ten words for types of food.

• R • C • N • E • U
• L • N • U • T • E
• A • E • O • N •
• R • N • I • A • E
• A • C • A • I • E
• C • N • T • E •
• O • G • N • O • A
• A • E • K • A • T
• A • L • A • E • L •
• E • P • R • I • T

(Solution 9)

123 Express Train

An express train takes three seconds to enter a tunnel one kilometre long. If it is travelling at 120 km per hour, how long will it take to pass through the tunnel?

(Solution 12)

124 Squares

Divide the square into four equal segments. Each segment must contain the five symbols (one of each)

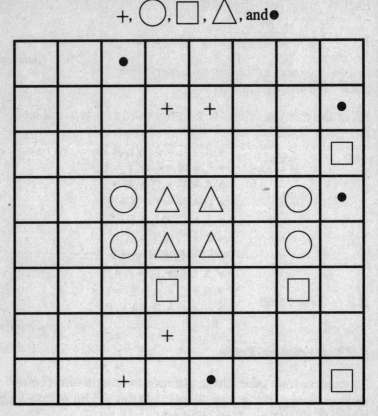

+, ○, □, △, and ●

		●					
			+	+			●
							□
		○	△	△		○	●
		○	△	△		○	
			□			□	
			+				
		+		●			□

(Solution 17)

125 Odd One Out

Which is the odd one out?

Primula
Foxglove
Geranium
Lupine
Delphinium
Salvia

(Solution 20)

126 Cryptograms

The following are straightforward substitution cryptograms where each letter of the alphabet has been replaced by another. Each cryptogram is in a different code.

1. YX'V PJC VWMAA VXCR ZPG WMJ, PJC

   EYMJX ACMR ZPG WMJHYJN.

   – JCYA MGWVXGPJE

2. L HJQCGC BLIP IPG GSVGKIJQKN JQC

   IPG PDVG DO TGLQZ JTHG ID YGG

   GMADVG. LI BJY IPG OLAYI ILUG L

   PJC GRGA TGGQ JTADJC.

   – KPJAHGY HLQCTGAZP

(Solution 25)

127 Squares

The square of 11,826 is 139,854,276, which is the lowest square number to use the digits 1 – 9 only once. What is the highest square number to use the digits 1 – 9 only once?

(Solution 29)

128 Behind

Which word goes behind these words to form new words?

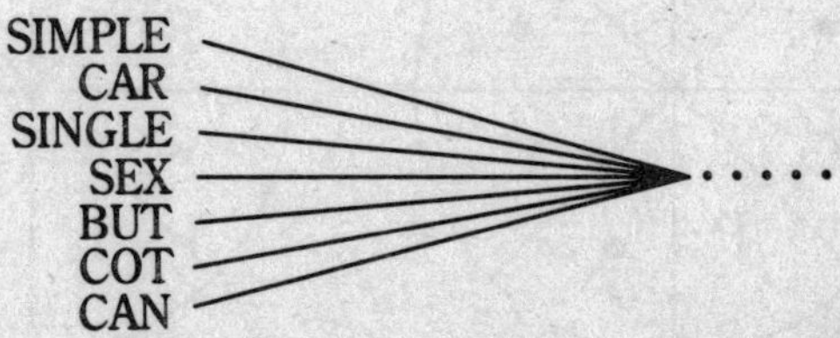

(Solution 33)

129 Going Around in Circles

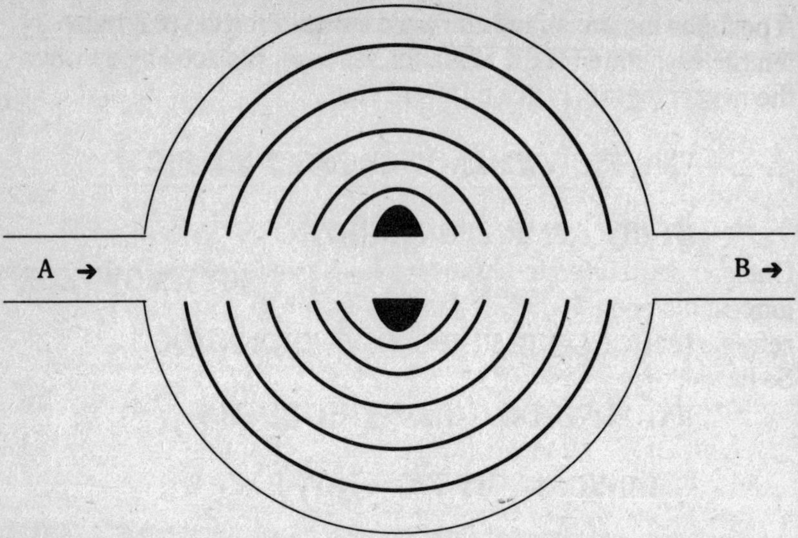

A man walks from point A to point B by walking around every one of the six circular paths. How many different routes are there by which he is able to do this? He does not go over any part of the route twice but does, of course, arrive at the same point more than once on his travels.

(Solution 37)

130 Synonym Circles

Move clockwise to find two 8-letter words that are synonyms. You must find the starting point and provide the missing letters.

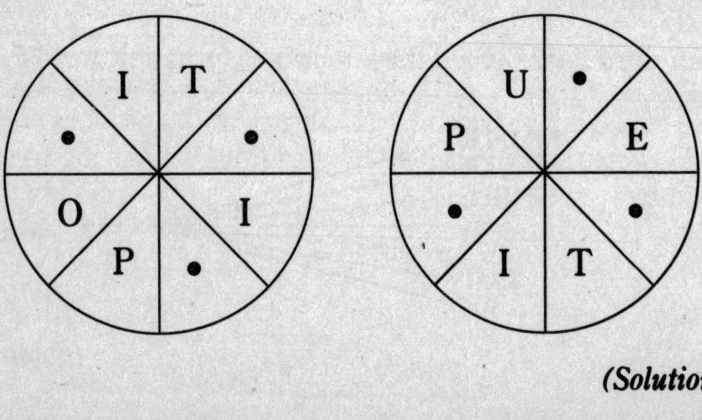

(Solution 41)

131 Postman

A postman had to deliver all his letters in one road that had only ten houses, numbered 1 to 10. Each house was 100 steps from the next.

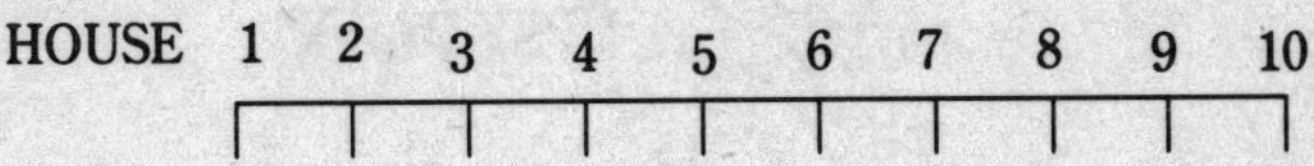

One day he decided to visit every house once, yet walk the longest distance. He wanted to finish at no. 6, where he had refreshments.

So he walked	1 to 10	9
	10 to 2	8
	2 to 9	7
	9 to 3	6
	3 to 8	5
	8 to 4	4
	4 to 7	3
	7 to 5	2
	5 to 6	1
		$45 \times 100 = 4500$ steps

How could he have walked further, still finishing at no. 6, and visiting each house only once?

(Solution 45)

132 The Gramophone Record

A gramophone record is twelve inches in diameter. It has a 4.75-inch middle and a 0.25-inch outer border. The remaining seven inches of playing surface has an average of 100 grooves to the inch. How far does the needle travel during the playing time of one side?

(Solution 49)

133 Rebuses

One form of a rebus is an arrangement of letters or symbols to represent a familiar word or phrase, for example:

e
e
s

UPSY DAISY

What do these rebuses represent?

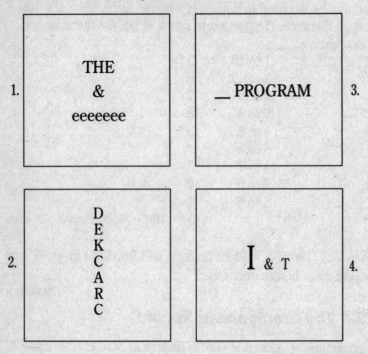

1.

THE
&
eeeeeee

3.

_ PROGRAM

2.

D
E
K
C
A
R
C

4.

I & T

(Solution 53)

134 Concentration

A B C D E F G H

What letter is three to the right of the letter two to the left of the letter three to the left of the letter immediately to the right of the letter three to the right of the letter immediately to the left of the letter "E"?

(Solution 57)

135 Magic Word Square

The answers to the five clues are all 5-letter words that when placed correctly in the grid will form a magic word square where the same five words can be read horizontally and vertically.

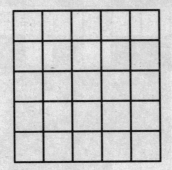

Clues (in no particular order):
Poetry
Impelled
Black bird
Open
Come into

(Solution 61)

136 Categorize

Arrange these fifteen words into five groups of three synonyms each.

Greasy	Limp	Apogee
Nought	Dictator	Despot
Pinnacle	Zenith	Oily
Flaccid	Unctuous	Cipher
Flabby	Zero	Tyrant

(Solution 65)

137 Cross-Alphabet

Insert each of the twenty-six letters of the alphabet into the grid only once to form a crossword.

Clues (in no particular order):
Grasp suddenly
Placed side by side
Song of praise
With haste
Cap with tassel
Solemn promise

(Solution 69)

138 Do-It-Yourself Crossword

Place the letters in the grid to make a crossword. Twelve letters have been placed already.

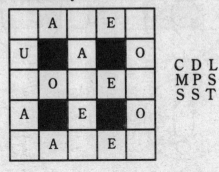

	A		E	
U	■	A	■	O
	O		E	
A	■	E	■	O
	A		E	

C D L
M P S
S S T

(Solution 73)

139 Daughter

My age and the age of my daughter are the same if the digits of one are reversed. A year ago I was twice as old as my daughter.

How old am I, and how old is my daughter?

(Solution 76)

140 Word Cycle

Complete the ten words below so that two letters are common to each word. That is, the same two letters that end the first word also start the second word, and the two letters that end the second word also start the third word, and so on. To complete the cycle, the two letters that end the tenth word are also the first two letters of the first word.

••EL••	••GI••
••SS••	••RU••
••IX••	••RI••
••ON••	••BU••
••IC••	••VI••

(Solution 81)

Analogy

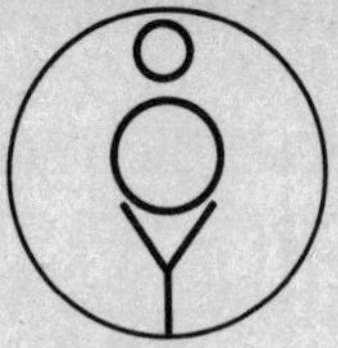

IS TO

AS

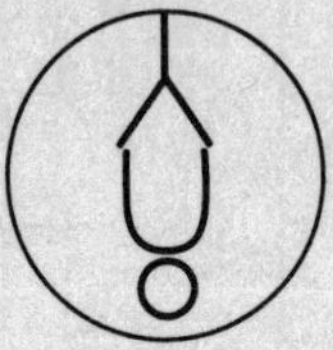

IS TO

?

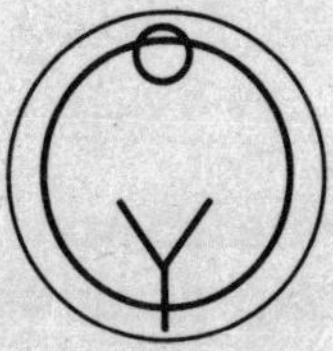

A

B

C

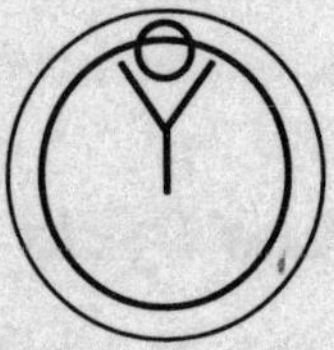

D

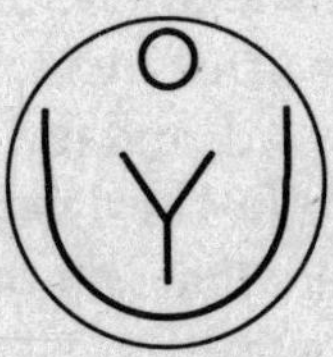

E

(Solution 85)

142 Pyramid Quotation

"One joy scatters a hundred griefs."

Using each of the twenty-eight letters of the above Chinese proverb only once, complete the pyramid with one 1-letter, one 2-letter, one 3-letter, one 4-letter, one 5-letter, one 6-letter, and one 7-letter word. Clues are given, but in no particular order.

Clues:
Thick stiff paper
To such an extent
Gluttonous
Anything enjoyable
The chemical symbol for sulphur
Caretaker
Broad piece of any thin material

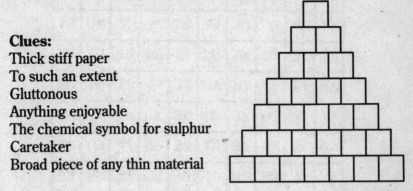

(Solution 89)

143 Too

If "too" is pronounced "too" and "two" is also pronounced "too", how should you pronounce the second day of the week?

(Solution 92)

144 Links

Which word links all of these words together?

Psychology
Pleasure
Lisle
Island
Aesop
Benign
Aeroplane

(Solution 97)

145 Twenty 10-Letter Words

AN	TE	CE	DE	DI	DU	AL	DI	SA	OI
NT	ME	OY	NT	IN	VI	IM	LE	PP	NT
UI	EM	PL	TI	AN	PL	AC	AB	EF	RT
RC	TO	US	AT	QU	HY	RT	WO	FO	LE
CI	EN	ED	CE	RE	MO	AL	TE	NO	SS
CY	PE	DI	SH	OR	NI	AN	DE	DE	HY
AN	EX	IP	TH	AU	GL	WF	LI	NT	DR
TT	CE	CO	LL	ED	NE	AL	NQ	UE	AT
AD	MI	EN	PR	AT	ER	GG	PP	ED	OV
TY	SI	OP	ON	TI	ES	SU	LY	SU	ER

Work from square to square horizontally, vertically, and diagonally to spell out twenty 10-letter words in pairs of letters. It does not matter which word you identify first. If you make the correct turnings you will eventually travel through the whole pattern of 200 letters.

(Solution 101)

146 Taps

A sluice tap empties a swimming pool in 7 hrs. A second tap empties the same swimming pool in 9 hrs. How long would it take to empty the pool if both sluice taps are opened together?

(Solution 105)

147 Enigmagram

Solve the four anagrams of types of boats. Transfer the arrowed letters and solve the fifth anagram.

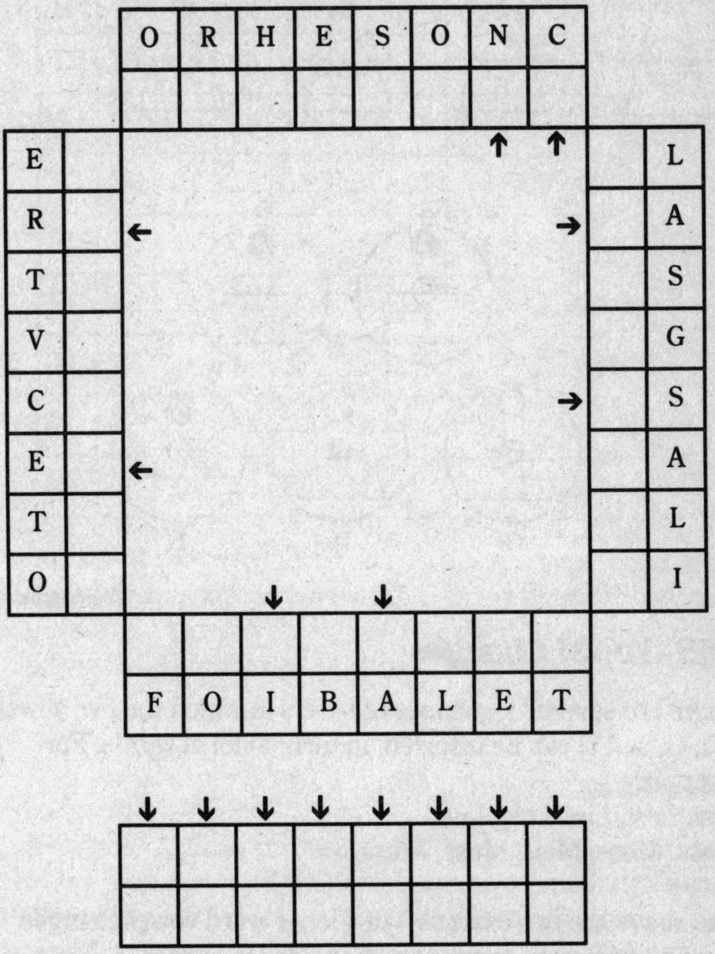

(Solution 109)

148 Sequence

Which option carries on the sequence?

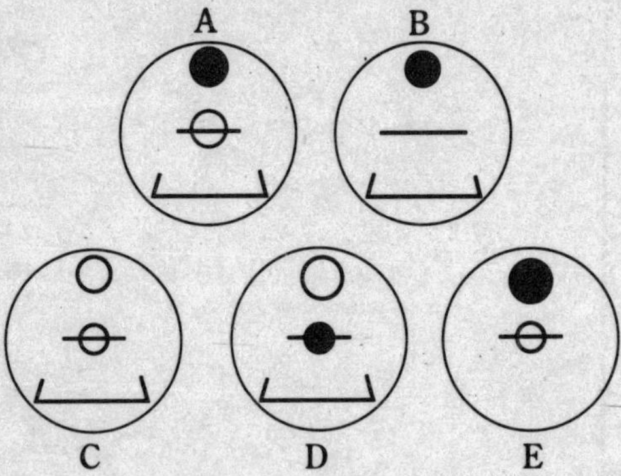

(Solution 113)

149 Vowel Changes

There are several sequences of letters in which the five vowels A, E, I, O, and U can be inserted, in turn, to form words. For example:
Last, Lest, List, Lost, Lust
Mass, Mess, Miss, Moss, Muss.

The above are two examples of 4-letter word vowel changes. Can you find two more examples using *7-letter* words?

(Solution 117)

150 Cryptograms

The following are straightforward substitution cryptograms where each letter of the alphabet has been replaced by another. Each is in a different code.

1. PJC YX DZ GVKKXE PDVQBHPJY, PYO

   JXA EIPA ZXNQ HXNJAQZ HPJ CX

   GXQ ZXN, PYO EIPA ZXN HPJ CX

   GXQ ZXNQ HXNJAQZ.

   – RXIJ G. OVJJVCZ

2. PJC LHJ AQRZ YPMGHIC LHDCB H

   LHFPGQRS.

   – HJUGCA FHYDBPJ

(Solution 121)

151 Tall Story

"I had a good catch the other day," said Sid. "A prize pike." "How much did it weigh?" asked Jim. "800 pounds divided by half its own weight," boasted Sid.

How much did the pike allegedly weigh?

(Solution 125)

152 Alternative Crossword

In the upper grid, the crossword letters have been replaced by numbers. Select the correct letter for each number from the three alternatives given, and enter the letter into the grid opposite to make a crossword.

7	2	1	7	■	2	1	1	7
4	■	7	5	6	2	7	■	3
3	7	■	5	1	8	■	7	5
7	1	6	■	4	■	5	6	2
■	4	3	8	1	1	4	2	■
2	2	5	■	1	■	2	1	1
1	7	■	1	2	7	■	2	5
7	■	5	7	7	2	7	■	5
1	6	2	7	■	5	5	7	2

1	A B C
2	D E F
3	G H I
4	J K L
5	M N O
6	P Q R
7	S T U
8	V W X
9	Y Z -

(Solution 134)

153 Trusty Truism

Spell out the trusty truism by placing the letters in the blank squares.

	H		G		A
	S	I			R
O		N	O		B
		H	S	I	
E		O	F		H
		E		C	

B D E E

E F N N

O R S S S

T T T W

(Solution 137)

154 Synchronized Synonyms

Each grid contains the letters of eight 8-letter words. Each word in grid 1 has a synonym in grid 2, and the letters of each of the eight pairs of synonyms are in exactly the same position in each grid. All letters are in the correct order and each letter is used only once. Clues to each pair of synonyms are given, in no particular order. For example, the answers to the clue "Merriment" are the words "Hilarity" in grid 1 and "Laughter" in grid 2.

GRID 1

M	L	C	I	D	R	A	O
C	D	H	O	U	S	E	V
O	T	O	E	S	R	M	A
B	I	T	L	I	C	L	P
N	O	A	A	N	O	L	E
A	A	N	I	R	C	T	H
I	T	T	E	U	Z	I	E
E	T	S	O	D	E	N	Y

GRID 2

P	P	G	R	S	C	C	R
P	H	L	O	O	O	E	A
A	P	O	S	D	R	G	M
I	I	P	P	A	S	N	I
T	U	I	A	L	I	U	G
A	G	A	A	H	R	T	A
I	T	L	T	N	T	T	E
G	E	G	O	E	E	N	R

Clues:

Consider	Merriment
Settle	Appealing
Disconnected	Avaricious
Squandered	Locale

(Solution 129)

155 Missing

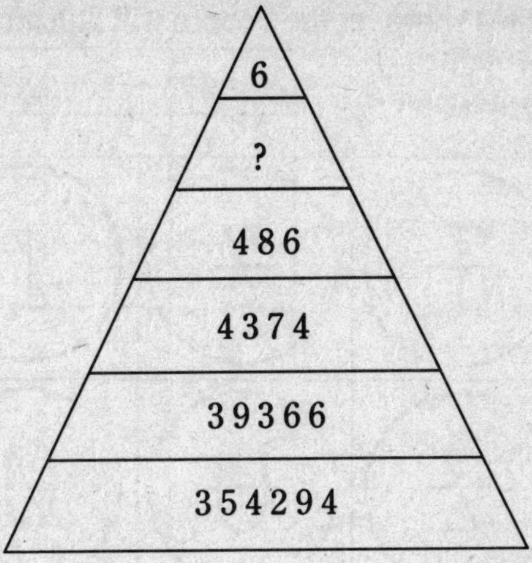

Find the missing number.

(Solution 141)

156 Magic Prime

Place the numbers 1 – 25 to form a magic square where each horizontal, vertical, and diagonal line totals 65. The prime numbers 2, 3, 5, 7, 11, 13, 17, 19, and 23 should be placed in the shaded squares only.

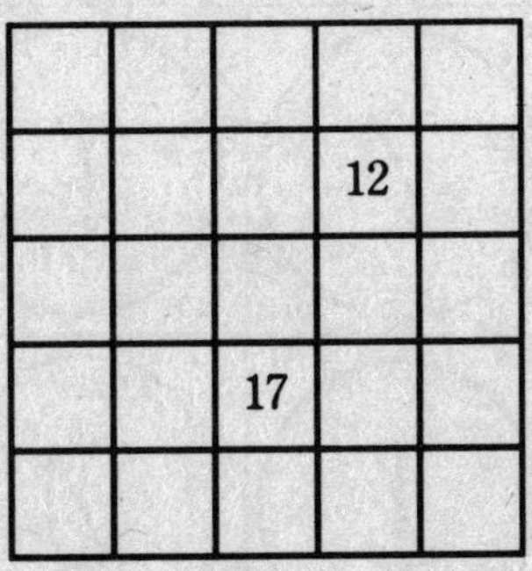

(Solution 145)

157 Logic

Which of the tiles shown at the bottom will fit logically into the missing space?

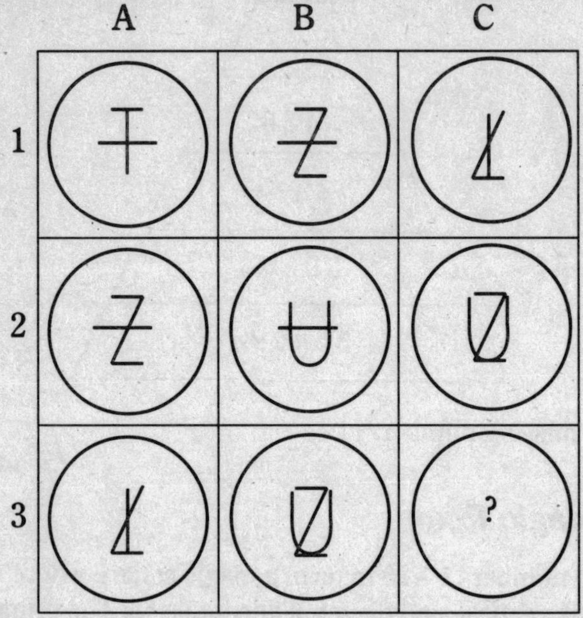

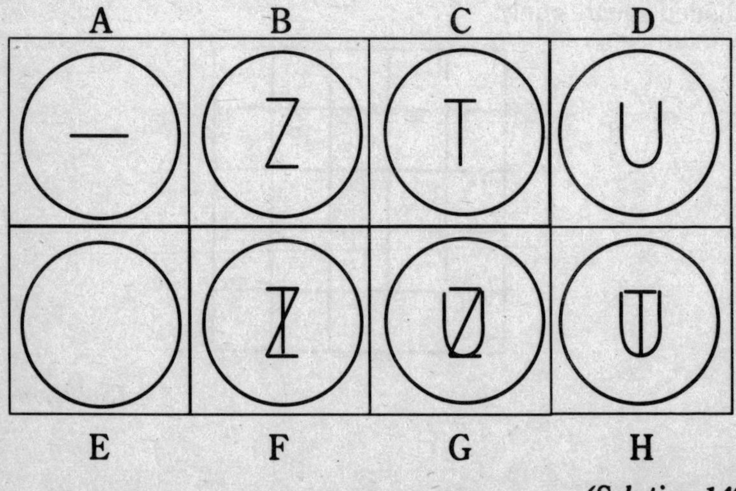

(Solution 149)

158 Letters

What letter comes next in this sequence?

A B D O P Q

(Solution 152)

159 Word Circle

NE: FOGD
SE: UREO
SW: WEEP
NW: RILO

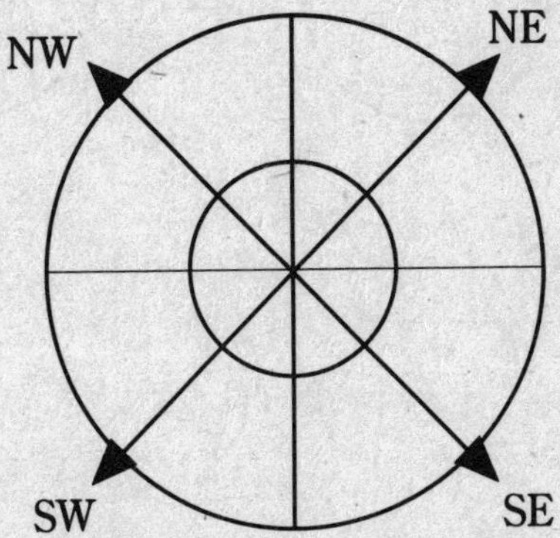

Place the letters in the correct sectors in each quadrant to obtain two 8-letter words, one reading clockwise and the other counter-clockwise. The two words are antonyms.

(Solution 157)

160 Analogy

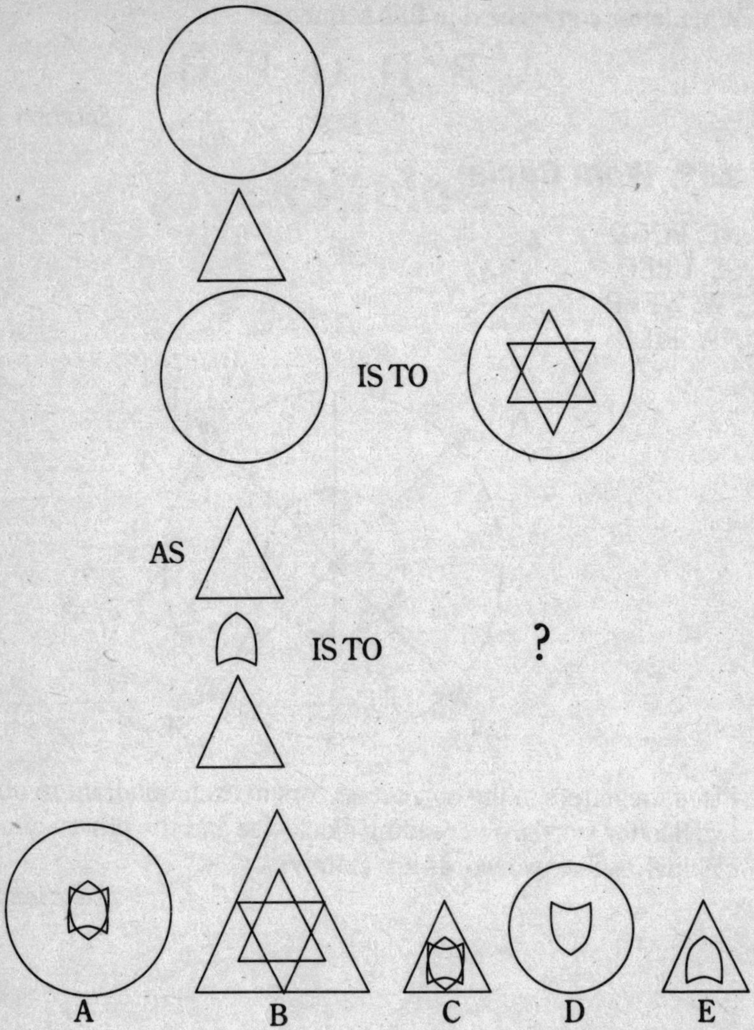

(Solution 159)

The Solutions

ure Trail

sit the squares in the following order:

22	13	18	10	3	26
25	30	1	27	21	23
5	11	28	24	7	2
12	34	16	T	32	14
19	4	9	6	15	29
8	17	33	31	35	20

(Question 120)

2 Enclosed Letters

Rectangle:

(Question 80)

3 Einstein Rebus

Loss of energy.

(Question 40)

4 Alphabet X-Word

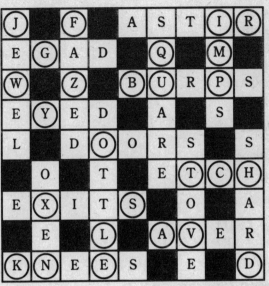

J	■	F	■	A	S	T	I	R
E	G	A	D	■	Q	■	M	■
W	■	Z	■	B	U	R	P	S
E	Y	E	D	■	A	■	S	■
L	■	D	O	O	R	S	■	S
■	O	■	T	■	E	T	C	H
E	X	I	T	S	■	O	■	A
■	E	■	L	■	A	V	E	R
K	N	E	E	S	■	E	■	D

(Question 1)

5 Alphametics

$$
\begin{array}{r}
490 \\
407 \\
+\ 107 \\
\hline
1004
\end{array}
$$

(Question 121)

6 Hidden Birds

1. Mallard
2. Ostrich
3. Sandpiper
4. Stonechat

(Question 81)

7 Word Power

1. Jollyboat
2. Maulstick
3. Patrimony
4. Sagacious
5. Limousine
6. Celebrate
7. Desperate
8. Enhearten
9. Fascinate

(Question 41)

8 Bracket Word

Academical:

S	(AC)	ID
RE	(AD)	D
DE	(EM)	IT
STO	(IC)	E
GO	(AL)	AS

(Question 2)

9 Missing Letters

Fricandeau
Blanquette
Macedoine
Frangipane
Saccharine
Schnitzel
Gorgonzola
Sauerkraut
Tagliatelle
Peppermint

(Question 122)

10 Twelve Letters

1. Fiddlesticks
2. Singledecker
3. Woolly-headed
4. Market-garden

(Question 82)

11 Three Too Many

D	E	P	I	C	T	S
E	■	A	■	A	■	E
C	A	T	E	R	E	D
I	■	E	■	P	■	A
D	E	N	T	I	S	T
E	■	T	■	N	■	E
D	E	S	I	G	N	S

(Question 42)

12 Express Train

$$\frac{120}{60} = 2 \text{ km per min.}$$

or 1 km per 30 sec.
Plus time to pass given point = 3 sec.
Total 33 seconds

(Question 123)

13 Fivers

P	E	T	A	L		V		M	O	D	E	L
I		E		U	N	I	T	E		O		A
P	A	N	I	C		T		T	A	P	E	D
E		E		I	R	A	T	E		E		E
D	O	T	E	D		L		S	E	D	A	N
	X		V						L		L	
P	I	L	O	T				R	O	B	O	T
	D		K						P		N	
D	E	T	E	R		T		B	E	G	E	T
E		A		E	L	I	T	E		A		U
V	I	L	L	A		T		R	O	M	A	N
I		O		D	R	A	P	E		U		E
L	A	N	K	Y		N		T	O	T	E	D

(Question 3)

14 Clock

$$\text{Hand movement} = \frac{36 \text{ mins}}{60 \text{ mins}} \times 360° = 216°$$

$$\text{Circumference} = \frac{360°}{216°} \times 8.4 = 14''$$

$$\text{Radius} = \frac{14''}{2 \times 3.1416 \; (\pi)} = 2.23''$$

(Question 83)

15 Dresses

Let x = dresses owned by Yvonne.

$$\text{Then } x = \frac{\text{Lulu}}{\text{Irene}}$$

$$x = \frac{42}{\text{Irene}}$$

$$\text{Then} \quad 42 + 14 = 8 \times \text{Irene}$$

$$\text{Irene} = 7$$

$$x = \frac{42}{7} = 6$$

Yvonne owns six dresses.

(Question 43)

16 Equation

By adding one stroke to the first plus sign you get $545 + 5 = 550$

(Question 4)

17 Squares

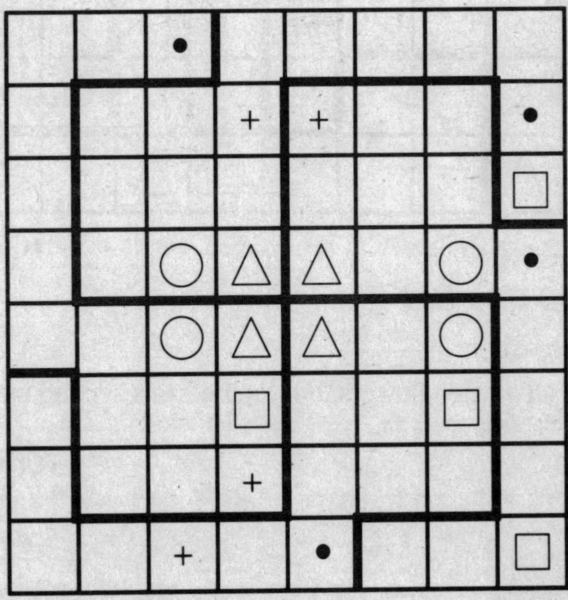

(Question 124)

18 Cryptogram

"How dreadful knowledge of the truth can be when there's no help in truth."

_ *Sophocles, Oedipus Rex*

(Question 84)

19 Squares

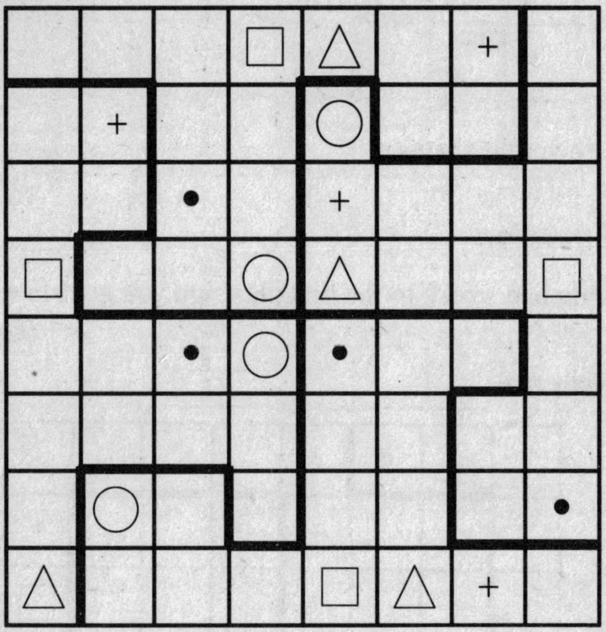

(Question 44)

20 Odd One Out

Lupine.
They are all garden flowers, but lupine has a second meaning – Wolf-like.

(Question 125)

21 Squares

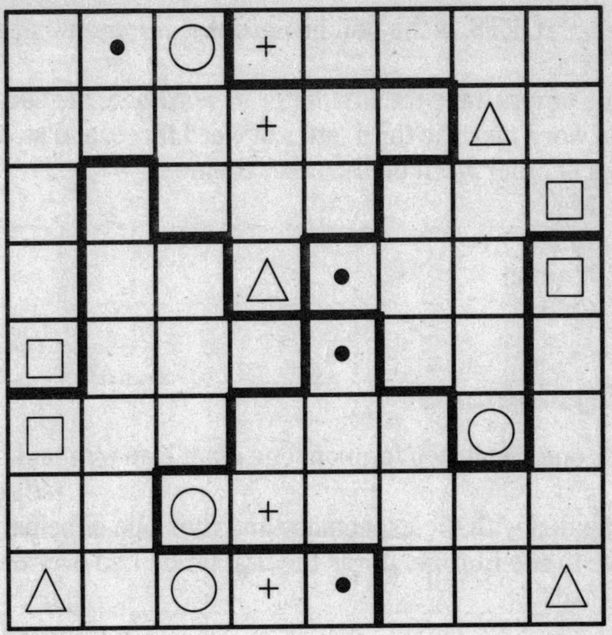

(Question 5)

22 Sequence

2. H:
Letters composed of 3 strokes in alphabetical order

A F (H) (K) (N) (Y) (Z)

(Question 85)

23 Sequence

160:
74 × 92, 60 × 88, 58 × 20, 16 × 10

(Question 45)

24 Groups

Group 4, SPORTS, is the odd group out.

In all the others, take the first letter of word one, the second letter of word two, the third letter of word three, and so on to spell out another word on the same theme:

1. Maine
2. Kenya
3. Mambo
5. Cairo

(Question 6)

25 Cryptograms

1. "It's one small step for man, one giant leap for mankind."
– Neil Armstrong
2. "I landed with the expectancy and the hope of being able to see Europe. It was the first time I had ever been abroad."
– Charles Lindbergh
(Question 126)

26 Anagram Theme

The theme is breeds of dogs.

Samoyed	(Day Some)
Papillon	(Nail Plop)
Beagle	(Beg Ale)
Pointer	(Top Rein)
Poodle	(Pole Do)
Basset	(Best As)
Terrier	(Tier Err)

(Question 86)

27 Octagon Words

Synonyms: Decrease, Diminish
Antonyms: Gauchely, Graceful

(Question 46)

28 Columns of Figures

D:
The smallest number is dropped each time and the remaining numbers appear top to bottom, then bottom to top alternately.

(Question 7)

29 Squares

923,187,456: the square of 30,384.

(Question 127)

30 Elementary Mathematics

120:
Add the atomic numbers of the elements represented by the letters comprising the two halves of the words.

Co	= Cobalt	27	76
In	= Indium	49	
He	= Helium	2	20
Ar	= Argon	18	
Ra	= Radium	88	120
Ge	= Germanium	32	
Pu	= Plutonium	94	169
Re	= Rhenium	75	
Br	= Bromine	35	120
At	= Astatine	85	

(Question 87)

31 The Gallopers

Amazing	(Spectacular)
Long	(Outstretched)
Lasting	(Permanent)
Opening	(Commencement)
Praying	(Beseeching)
Ebbing	(Declination)
Rig	(Costume)
Sag	(Downswing)

(Question 47)

32 Orthographic Projection

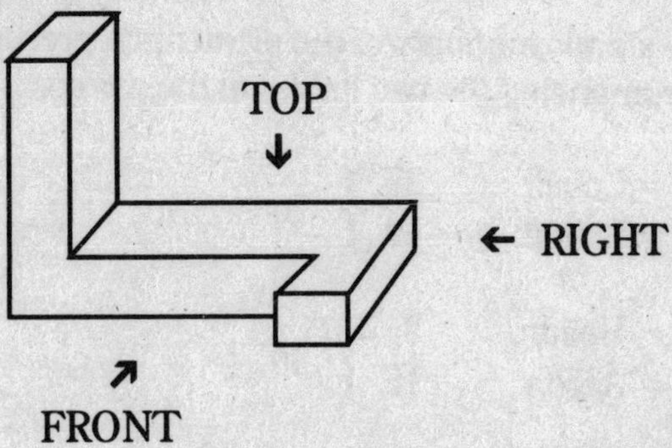

(Question 8)

33 Behind

TON:
Simpleton
Carton
Singleton
Sexton
Button
Cotton
Canton

(Question 128)

34 Hexagons

B:
The circle moves three spaces each stage (i.e., it alternates between top and bottom) and is black on a white background then white on a black background in turn.

The triangle moves two spaces counterclockwise at each turn and alternates between black on white and white on black.

(Question 88)

35 Greek Cross and Square

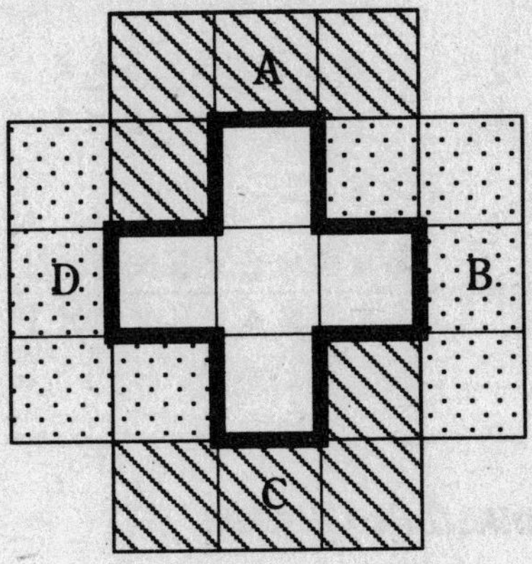

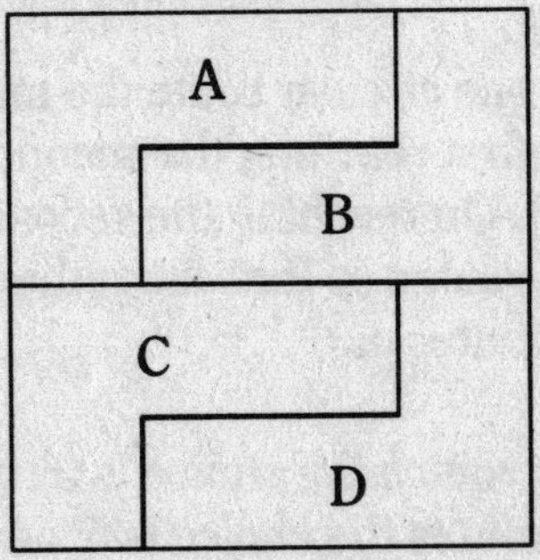

(Question 48)

36 Quiz Team

	Men (8)	Women (8)	
Assume 3 women	$\frac{8 \times 7 \times 6}{3 \times 2 \times 1}$	$\frac{8 \times 7 \times 6}{3 \times 2 \times 1}$	$56 \times 56 = 3136$
Assume 4 women	$\frac{8 \times 7}{2 \times 1}$	$\frac{8 \times 7 \times 6 \times 5}{4 \times 3 \times 2 \times 1}$	$28 \times 70 = 1960$
Assume 5 women	$\frac{8}{1}$	$\frac{8 \times 7 \times 6 \times 5 \times 4}{5 \times 4 \times 3 \times 2 \times 1}$	$8 \times 56 = 448$
Assume 6 women	no men	$\frac{8 \times 7 \times 6 \times 5 \times 4 \times 3}{6 \times 5 \times 4 \times 3 \times 2 \times 1}$	$28 = 28$
			5572

(Question 9)

37 Going Around in Circles

46,656, which is 6^6:
If there was only one circular route the man could continue in three ways when first reaching the second intersection (left, right, or forward). On reaching the second intersection he has the choice of two routes so that altogether there would be six (3×2) possible routes or 6^1.

With two circular routes the choice is 6^2, and so on. Therefore, with six circular routes the choice is 6^6 or 46,656.

(Question 129)

38 Front

Snow.

(Question 89)

39 Magic Word Square

C	A	D	E	T
A	R	O	M	A
D	O	N	O	R
E	M	O	T	E
T	A	R	E	S

(Question 49)

40 Anagrams

Argentine
Singapore
Leningrad
Italy
Minnesota
Greenland
Las Vegas
Tangiers
Trieste
Cremona
Greenwich
San Diego
Ontario

(Question 10)

41 Synonym Circles

Impolite
Impudent

(Question 130)

42 Middle Letters

1. Lickety-split
2. Manic-depressive
3. Narcissistic
4. Laissez-faire
5. One-upmanship
6. Higgledy-piggledy
7. Money-spinner
8. Monkey-puzzle
9. Leapfrog
10. High-strung

(Question 90)

43 Find a Word

Shapelessness.

(Question 50)

44 Brain Strain

5	−	3	÷	2	=	1
+	■	−	■	+	■	+
9	×	2	÷	6	=	3
÷	■	+	■	−	■	÷
7	−	4	−	2	=	1
=	■	=	■	=	■	=
2	×	5	−	6	=	4

(Question 39)

45 Postman

5 to 10	5	
10 to 1	9	
1 to 9	8	
9 to 2	7	
2 to 8	6	
8 to 3	5	
3 to 7	4	
7 to 4	3	
4 to 6	2	Total 49 × 100 = 4900 steps

(Question 131)

46 Circles

7:
$6 \times 4 = 24 \div 8 = 3 + 4 = 7$
$8 \times 2 = 16 \div 4 = 4 + 5 = 9$
$7 \times 4 = 28 \div 7 = 4 + 3 = 7$

(Question 91)

47 Cover-up

The maximum overlaps in each case have the same area, so three-quarters of the triangle equals one-half the square. The area of the triangle is therefore 24 square inches.

(Question 51)

48 Pyramid Words

```
                A
        (1)   A   T
      (2)   T   A   N
    (3)   R   A   N   T
  (4)   T   R   A   I   N
 (5)  R   A   T   I   N   G
(6) T   R   A   D   I   N   G
  D   R   A   F   T   I   N   G
```

(Question 11)

49 The Gramophone Record

3 1/2 inches:
It travels in a straight line across the disk.

(Question 132)

50 Sequence

530:
The numbers are all times of day with the dots missing and 45 minutes added each time.
1:45, 2:30, 3:15, 4:00, 4:45, 5:30

(Question 92)

51 Links Jigsaw Puzzle

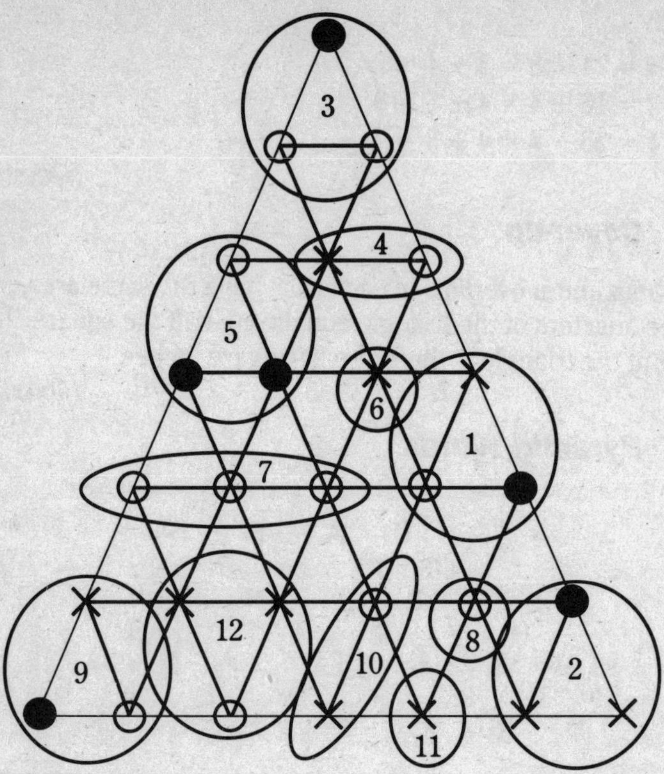

(Question 52)

52 A Maze

28.

(Question 12)

53 Rebuses

1. The Andes
2. Cracked up
3. Space program
4. The long and short of it

(Question 133)

54 Links Jigsaw Puzzle

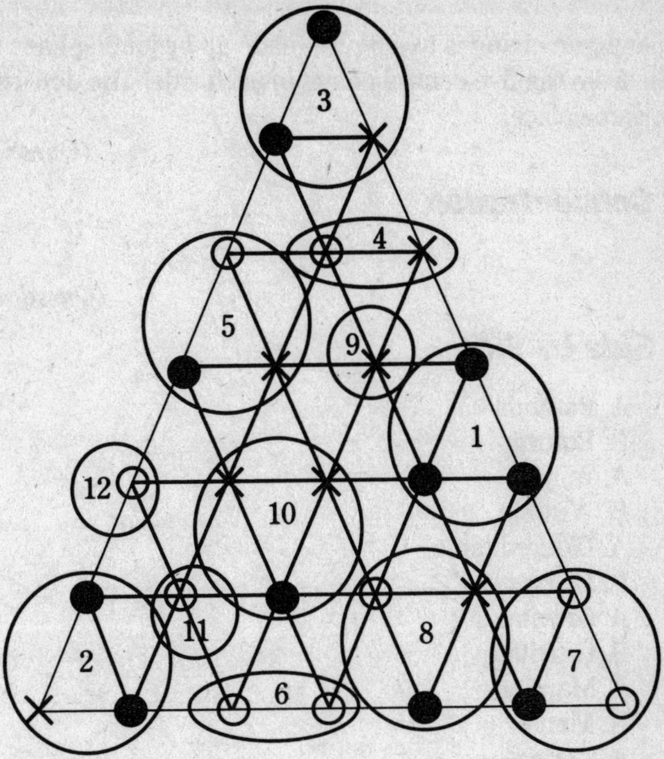

(Question 93)

55 Anagrammed Synonyms

1. Lone – Singular
2. Past – Precedent
3. Boon – Benefit
4. Ripe – Matured
5. Sigh – Sough
6. Read – Register
7. Root – Inception
8. Cut – Segment
9. Balm – Perfume
10. Neat – Straight

(Question 53)

56 Analogy

C:

The pentagon changes to a figure made up by joining lines to the middle from the five central points of each side. The dots remain in the same place.

(Question 13)

57 Concentration

F.

(Question 134)

58 Side by Side

1. A. Rotunda
   B. Roturier
2. A. Wily
   B. Wimble
3. A. Discreditable
   B. Discreet
4. A. Gravitas
   B. Gravitate
5. A. Mention
   B. Mentor
6. A. Coriaceous
   B. Coriander
7. A. Panoply
   B. Panorama
8. A. Snide
   B. Sniff
9. A. Fluster
   B. Flute
10. A. Novella
    B. Novelty

(Question 94)

59 Forest

Assume 600 birds. That could be 20 trees with 30 birds or 30 trees with 20 birds, so all numbers that factorize are eliminated because the results would be ambiguous.

That leaves prime numbers. Assume 523. That would be 1 tree with 523 birds or 523 trees with 1 bird, which is not allowable.

That only leaves a prime number squared. There is only one between 400 and 800, which is 529. The square root of 529 is 23.

So, there are 23 trees, each with 23 birds.

(Question 54)

60 Tangled Antonym

Untied United.

(Question 14)

61 Magic Word Square

D	R	O	V	E
R	A	V	E	N
O	V	E	R	T
V	E	R	S	E
E	N	T	E	R

(Question 135)

62 No Repeat Letters

Flamingoes.

(Question 95)

63 Inventions

1. Compound Microscope
2. Barometer
3. Pendulum Clock
4. Achromatic Lens
5. Submarine
6. Steel Pen
7. Steamboat
8. Illuminating Gas
9. Lithography
10. Solid-Fuel Rocket
11. Printing Press
12. Electric Motor
13. Portland Cement
14. Steam Hammer
15. Rotary Printing Press
16. Safety Matches
17. Harvester
18. Microphone
19. Steam Turbine
20. Rayon

(*Authors' note:* obviously some of these claimed inventions are contentious, but all came from recognized and reliable sources!)

(Question 55)

64 Six Fours

$4 \times [(4 \times 4) + 4 + 4] + 4$

(Question 15)

65 Categorize

Unctuous – Oily – Greasy
Zero – Cipher – Nought
Zenith – Apogee – Pinnacle
Dictator – Despot – Tyrant
Flaccid – Flabby – Limp

(Question 136)

66 Saying

"Do not talk about yourself. It will be done when you leave."

– *Wilson Mizner*

(Question 96)

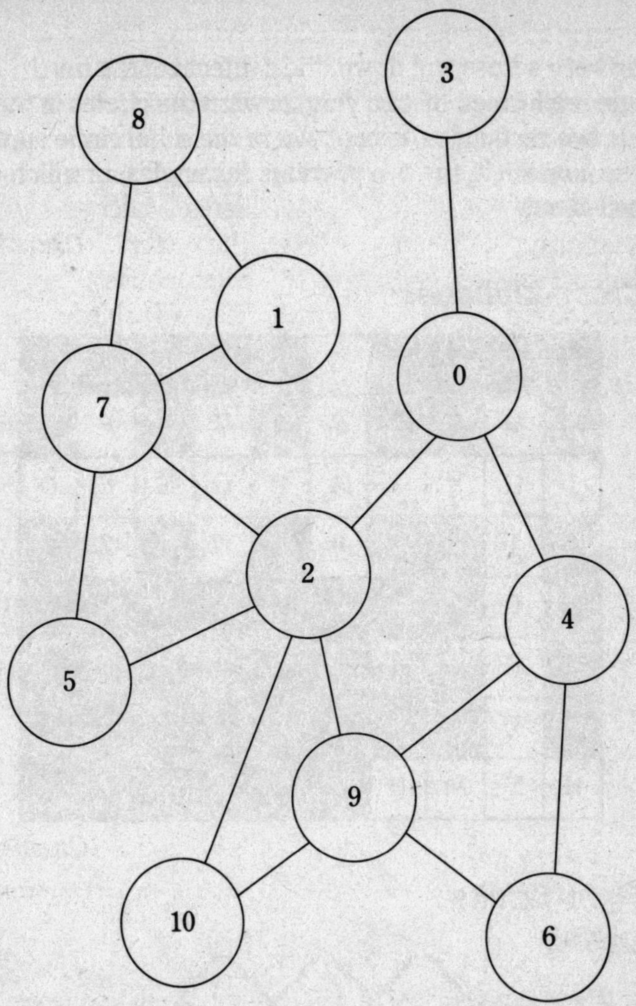

(Question 56)

68 Rectangle Matrix

E:
Looking both across and down, the contents of the third rectangle are formed by carrying forward the circles in the previous two rectangles, except where the same circle appears in the same position in the two previous rectangles, in which case it is cancelled out.

(Question 16)

69 Cross-Alphabet

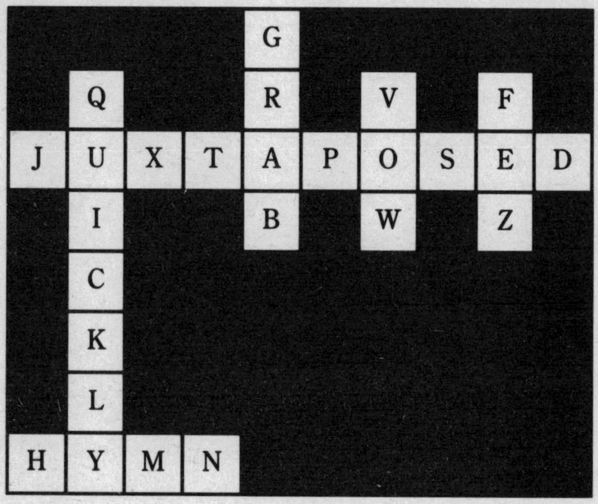

(Question 137)

70 Eight Sticks

(Question 97)

71 Circles Jigsaw Puzzle

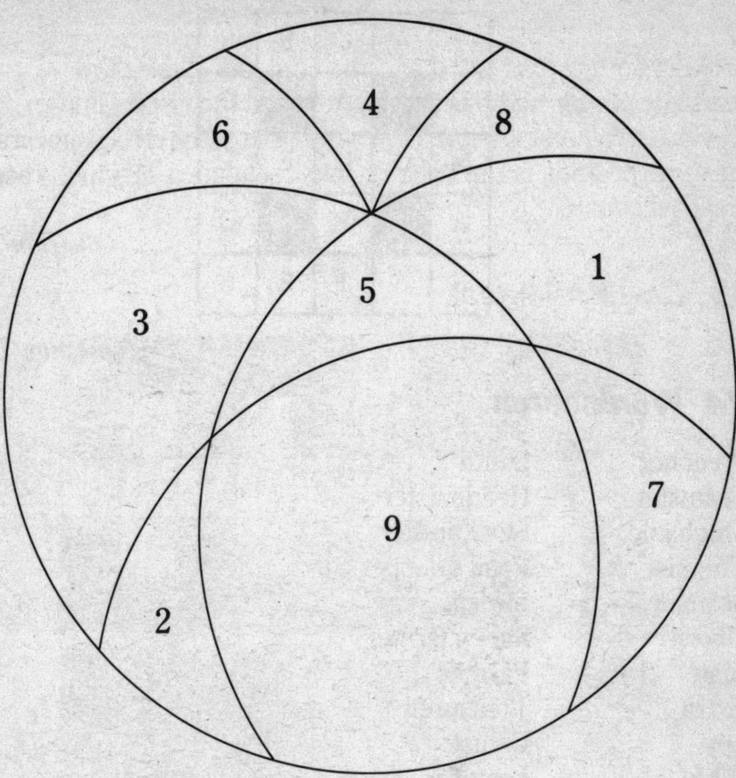

(Question 57)

72 Fore and Aft

ANT:

Sergeant	Anteater
Tenant	Anthem
Gallant	Antacid

(Question 17)

73 Do-It-Yourself Crossword

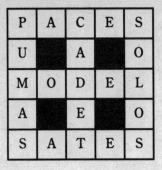

P	A	C	E	S
U	■	A	■	O
M	O	D	E	L
A	■	E	■	O
S	A	T	E	S

(Question 138)

74 Wordsearch

Preacher	Smith
Teamster	Headmaster
Mechanic	Stockbroker
Chemist	Road sweeper
Seaman	Sweep
Oboist	Sheep farmer
Mate	Farmer
Extra	Treasurer
Spy	Cellist
Whip	Lecturer
Silversmith	Tutor

Unused letters: VET

(Question 98)

75 Saying

"Whoever learns to control the weather will have destroyed the last safe topic of conversation."

– *Teller's Commentary*

(Question 58)

76 Daughter

I am 73, she is 37.

(Question 139)

77 No Blanks

■	P	O	L	I	S	H	E	D	■	■	S	■
■	R	■	I	■	W	■	L	■	F	■	N	■
H	A	I	L	■	A	N	O	R	E	X	I	A
■	L	■	A	■	Y	■	P	■	R	■	C	■
C	I	R	C	L	E	■	E	U	R	E	K	A
■	N	■	■	■	D	U	D	■	E	■	■	■
K	E	D	G	E	■	■	■	E	T	U	D	E
■	■	■	R	■	M	A	T	■	■	■	E	■
T	R	A	U	M	A	■	U	N	T	O	L	D
■	U	■	N	■	R	■	N	■	H	■	I	■
B	R	E	T	H	R	E	N	■	O	R	G	Y
■	A	■	S	■	O	■	E	■	N	■	H	■
■	L	■	■	T	W	I	L	I	G	H	T	■

(Question 18)

78 Wager

$45.

(Question 99)

79 Honeycomb

Date	Lemon	Ugli
Prune	Melon	Lime
Plum	Olive	Lichee
Pawpaw	Damson	Cherry
Banana	Guava	Sloe

(Question 59)

80 Scale

160mm:

$$16 \times 100 = 1600$$

$$\frac{1600}{10} = 160$$

(Question 19)

81 Word Cycle

Shelve, Vessel, Elixir, Ironic, Icicle, Legion, Onrush, Shrine, Nebula, Lavish.

(Question 140)

82 Squares

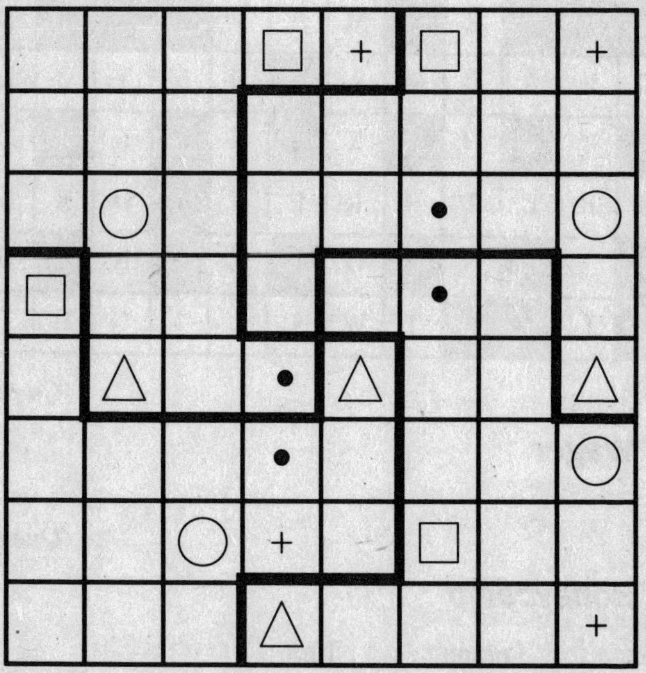

(Question 100)

83 Clueless Crossword

S	H	I	P	P	E	R
T		N		E		E
R	E	D	R	E	S	S
A		E		V		E
W	A	X	I	E	S	T

(Question 60)

84 Odd One Out

G:
Each figure is made up of four trapezoids, two of them thus:

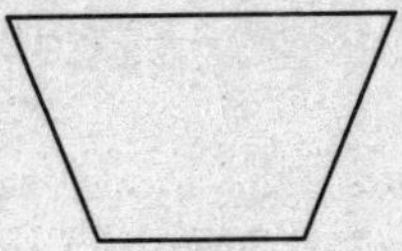

and two:

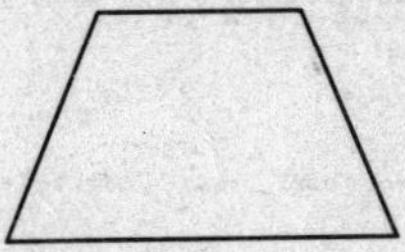

But G has three of one and one of the opposite.

(Question 20)

85 Analogy

A:
The small circle moves 180°.
The letter Y moves 180°.
The larger circle becomes a large "U", reversed in A.

(Question 141)

86 Margana

Hydraulics.

(Question 101)

87 One-Armed Bandit

Thighs.

(Question 61)

88 Restore the Vowels

"You ask great questions accidentally. To answer them would be events."

(Question 21)

89 Pyramid Quotation

S, So, Fun, Card, Sheet, Greedy, Janitor.

(Question 142)

90 Thirty Bits

Artistry, Inherent, Redevelop, Manhattan, Martensite, Discourage, Ushering, Legislate, Noticeable, Reincarnation.

(Question 102)

91 Rebuses

1. Nylon hose
2. Double date
3. Witch doctor
4. Without you I am nothing

(Question 62)

92 Too

Monday.

(Question 143)

93 Tight Squeeze

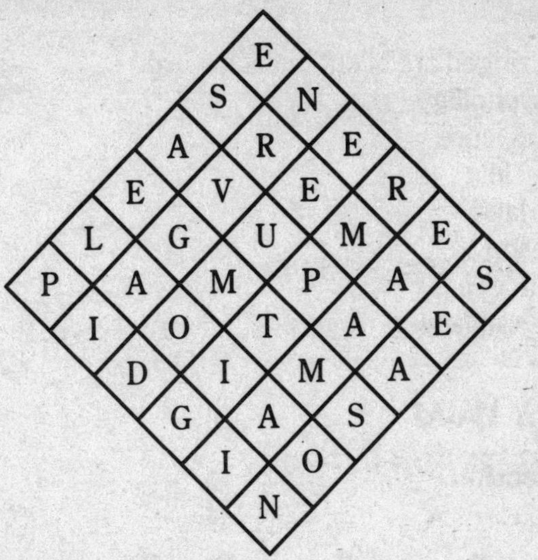

Or rotations of the same grid.

(Question 22)

94 Five Fractions

13845/2769, 14865/2973, 18645/3729, 14685/2937, 14835/2967.

(Question 103)

95 Synonyms

1. Spirit
2. Comport
3. Series
4. Molecule
5. Skirt

(Question 63)

96 Lateral Thinking

49:

The three numbers in the same position in each triangle total 100

24 + 58 + 18 = 100

17 + 62 + 21 = 100

35 + 16 + 49 = 100

(Question 23)

97 Links

PASSAGE:
The letters ringed are silent in each word.

Ⓟ sychology
Ple ⓐ sure
Li ⓢ le
I ⓢ land
Ⓐ esop
Beni ⓖ n
A ⓔ roplane

(Question 144)

98 Track Word

Incomprehension.

(Question 104)

99 Magic Square Jigzaw Puzzle

7	53	41	27	2	52	48	30
12	58	38	24	13	63	35	17
51	1	29	47	54	8	28	42
64	14	18	36	57	11	23	37
25	43	55	5	32	46	50	4
22	40	60	10	19	33	61	15
45	31	3	49	44	26	6	56
34	20	16	62	39	21	9	59

(Question 64)

100 Circles

D:
There are five different segment designs.

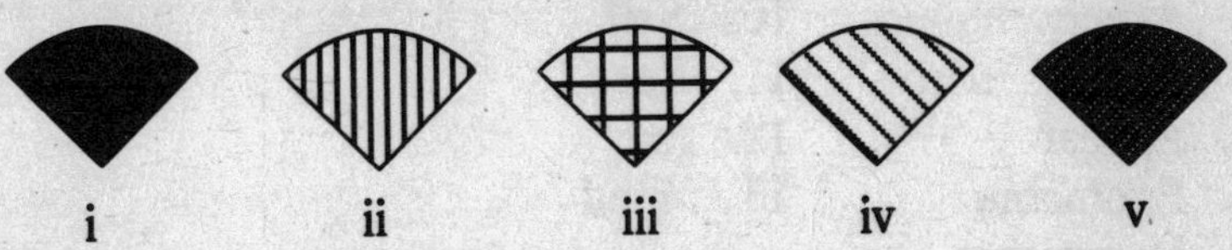

D is the final combination needed to complete every possible grouping in threes of the five segments:
i.e., ii iii v, i ii v, iii iv v, i iii v, i ii iii, ii iii iv, ii iv v, i iii iv, i ii iv, and finally the missing grouping, i iv v.

(Question 24)

101 Twenty 10-Letter Words

Expediency, Circuitous, Employment, Antecedent, Individual, Implacable, Disappoint, Effortless, Noteworthy, Antiquated, Ceremonial, Delinquent, Dehydrated, Oversupply, Suggestion, Propensity, Admittance, Collateral, Newfangled, Authorship.

(Question 145)

102 Star

Hindquarters.

(Question 105)

103 Analogy

C:
The top half is folded over onto the bottom half.

(Question 65)

104 Daffynitions

1.	Kidney	8.	Ice
2.	Kindred	9.	Tears
3.	Attack	10.	Nail
4.	Arrest	11.	Bee
5.	Appear	12.	Axe
6.	Egomania	13.	Wind
7.	Hogwash		

(Question 25)

105 Taps

$$7 = \frac{1}{7} = .1429$$

$$9 = \frac{1}{9} = \underline{.1111}$$

$$.2540$$

$$= \frac{1}{.2540} = 3.937 \text{ hrs}$$

(Question 146)

106 Common Clues

They are all informal names:

1.	Jimmy or Jemmy	6.	Candy
2.	Tommy	7.	Dolly
3.	Molly	8.	Eddy
4.	Sally	9.	Harry
5.	Billy	10.	Kitty

(Question 106)

107 Pyramid

Disgracefulness.

(Question 66)

108 Knight

"The light at the end of the tunnel may well turn out to be the headlight of an oncoming train."

(Question 26)

109 Enigmagram

Schooner
Galliass
Lifeboat
Corvette
Fifth anagram: Fireboat.

(Question 147)

110 Quotation

"Bore: A guy with a cocktail glass in one hand and your lapel in the other."

(Question 107)

111 Number

2520 ($5 \times 7 \times 8 \times 9$)

(Question 67)

112 Age

66:
Let x = my age

then, $x + \frac{1}{2}x + \frac{1}{3}x + 9 = 130$

$1\frac{5}{6}x = 121$

Multiply by 6: $11x = 726$
$x = 66$

(Question 27)

113 Sequence

A:
The black dot gets larger.
The circle gets smaller.
The central horizontal line gets smaller.
The triangular piece gets smaller.

(Question 148)

114 Letters

1 in 6.
There are four – acre, acer, race, care – in the twenty-four possible arrangements:

$$\frac{4}{24} \text{ or } \frac{1}{6}$$

(Question 108)

115 Odd One Out

D:
A is the same as G
B is the same as F
C is the same as E

(Question 68)

116 Matrix

C:

Add the first column to the second column to obtain the third column, but similar symbols cancel each other out.

(Question 28)

117 Vowel Changes

Blander, Blender, Blinder, Blonder, Blunder.
Patting, Petting, Pitting, Potting, Putting.

(Question 149)

118 Sequence

A:

 moves counterclockwise 135°

 moves clockwise 90°

 moves 90°

 moves 180°

 moves clockwise 90°

(Question 109)

119 Pyramid Word

I, Is, Sly, Pure, Stout
15-letter anagram: Superstitiously.

(Question 69)

120 No Repeat Letters

Labyrinth.

(Question29)

121 Cryptograms

1. "And so my fellow Americans, ask not what your country can do for you, ask what you can do for your country."

   – John F. Kennedy

2. "One man with courage makes a majority."

   – Andrew Jackson

(Question 150)

122 Work It Out

36:
(51 − 17) × 3 = 102
(71 − 19) × 7 = 364
(22 − 18) × 9 = 36

(Question 110)

123 Division

Structure.

R	R	E	C	S	U
T	U	T	T	T	S
R	U	U	R	R	E
R	C	S	T	R	U
T	S	E	C	T	C
U	U	E	R	T	U

(Question 70)

124 Word Stack

A, An, Ran, Rain, Grain, Rating, Tearing, Treating, Integrate.

(Question 30)

125 Tall Story

40 pounds: 800 ÷ 20 = 40

(Question 151)

126 Links

Season, Office, Scout, Coat, End, Man, Care, Out, Money, Share, Land, Line.

(Question 111)

127 Matches

$$\overline{\mathrm{II}} = \frac{\mathrm{XXII}}{\mathrm{VII}}$$

pi = $\frac{22}{7}$

Also, any trivial solution, for example,

$$\mathrm{I} \neq \frac{\mathrm{XXII}}{\mathrm{VII}}$$

Where $\neq$ is the unequal sign.

(Question 71)

128 The Train in the Tunnel

Two minutes:
$(2.25 + 0.25) \times \frac{60}{75}$

(Question 31)

129 Synchronized Synonyms

Consider :	Ruminate, Cogitate
Settle :	Colonize, Populate
Disconnected :	Detached, Separate
Squandered :	Misspent, Prodigal
Merriment :	Hilarity, Laughter
Appealing :	Adorable, Charming
Avaricious :	Covetous, Grasping
Locale :	Location, Position

(Question 154)

130 Add a Letter

E:
Orange
Russet
Reseda
Cerise
Yellow

(Question 112)

131 Common Words

They are all names of animals with the letter E omitted:

Bear
Joey
Kine
Mare
Seal
Eland
Genet

(Question 72)

132 Middle Words

1. Gate	4. Man
2. Back	5. Off
3. Dock	6. Boy

(Question 32)

133 Network

Ophthalmoscope.

(Question 113)

134 Alternative Crossword

S	E	A	T		D	A	B	S
L		T	O	P	E	S		H
I	S		M	A	W		T	O
T	A	P		L		O	R	E
	L	I	V	A	B	L	E	
D	E	N		C		D	A	B
A	S		B	E	T		D	O
T		M	U	S	E	S		N
A	P	E	S		N	O	S	E

(Question 152)

135 The Hexagon Cross

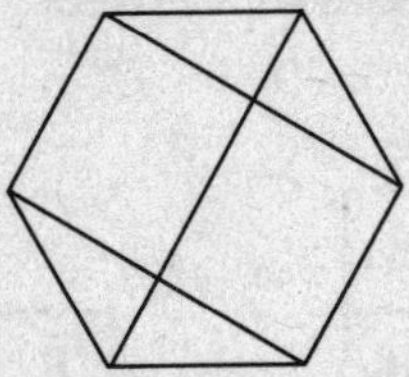

Converging on the central hexagon north, south, east, and west, the contents of the central hexagon are formed by merging the contents of the two previous hexagons. Where two lines appear in the same position they cancel each other out.

(Question 73)

136 Diamond Matrix

F:
The third tile of each row and each column is formed by merging the contents of the first two tiles, but only when the portions are identical. When a black portion and a white portion occur in the same place, they cancel each other out.

(Question 33)

137 Trusty Truisms

"The grass is brown on both sides of the fence."

– *Radar's Fundamental Truth.*

(Question 153)

138 Apples

896,809 is the result of multiplying two prime numbers together: 947 × 947

So the answer is 947 sacks.

(Question 114)

139 Alphabet Clueless-Cross

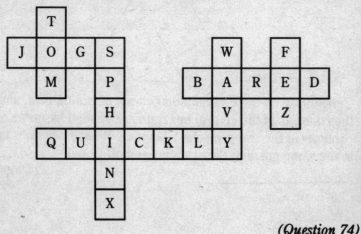

	T									
J	O	G	S				W		F	
	M		P			B	A	R	E	D
			H				V		Z	
	Q	U	I	C	K	L	Y			
			N							
			X							

(Question 74)

140 Target Crossword

Guffaw
Hawser
Fungus
Dorsal
Cashew
Bistro
Cuspid
Amulet
Outfox
Nudism
Murder
Midget

(Question 34)

141 Missing

54:
Each number is multiplied by 9.

(Question 155)

142 Jumble

Unprintable
Unspeakable
Upholsterer
Unmitigated
Ultramarine
Uncluttered
Uselessness
Ultraviolet

(Question 115)

143 Number

2025:
$20 + 25 = 45$
$45^2 = 2025$

9801:
$98 + 01 = 99$
$99^2 = 9801$

(Question 35)

144 Children's Party

To solve this problem we use a Venn diagram.

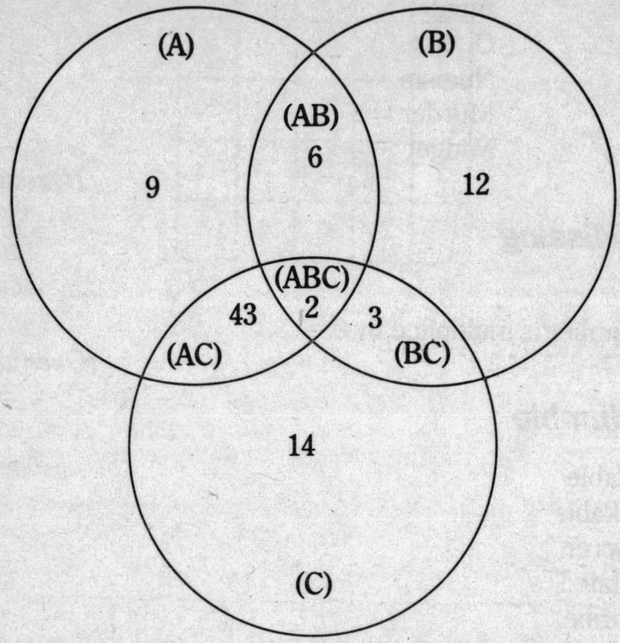

A = Jelly
B = Pudding
C = Cake
AC = Jelly/Cake
BC = Pudding/Cake
AB = Jelly/Pudding
ABC = Jelly/Pudding/Cake

Jelly	9 + 6 + 2 + 43 = 60
Pudding	12 + 6 + 2 + 3 = 23
Cake	14 + 43 + 3 + 2 = 62
Jelly/Pudding	6 + 2 = 8
Jelly/Cake	43 + 2 = 45
Pudding/Cake	3 + 2 = 5
Jelly/Pudding/Cake	2 = 2

Answer:

1. 9 + 12 + 14 = 35 eat only one item.
2. 9 + 6 + 12 + 43 + 2 + 3 + 14= 89
   100 − 89 = 11 eat none.

(Question 75)

145 Magic Prime

15	2	9	18	21
8	16	25	12	4
22	14	3	6	20
1	10	17	24	13
19	23	11	5	7

(Question 156)

146 Kangaroo Words

Tomb, Tutor, Male, Hies, Debate, Cocoa, Fun, Cart, Pure, Fag, Elation, Last, Ruin, Urge.

(Question 116)

147 Squares

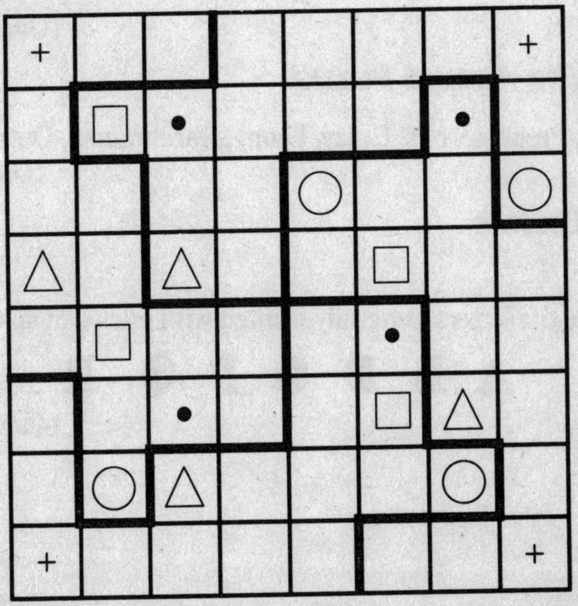

(Question 76)

148 Circles

C:
Each pair of circles produces the circle above, but similar symbols are not carried up.

(Question 36)

149 Logic

H:
Looking both across and down, the circled contents of the third tile are formed by carrying forward the symbols in the previous two tiles, except where the same line appears in the same position in the two previous tiles, in which case it is canceled out.

(Question 157)

150 Comparison

A:
The top half folds down and the dot in the bottom left moves to the top right.

(Question 117)

151 The Absurd Puzzle

Foolish, Preposterous, Crazy, Loony, Harebrained, Dotty, Mad.

(Question 77)

152 Letters

R:
They are the letters generally printed with enclosed spaces:

A B D O P Q R

(Question 158)

153 Anagrammed American Tour

1. Kearney
2. Galveston
3. Shreveport
4. Charlotte
5. Ypsilanti
6. Bakersfield
7. Ventura
8. Fredericksburg
9. Amarillo
10. Zanesville
11. Marblehead
12. Jamestown
13. Deadwood
14. La Grange
15. Edgartown
16. Xenia
17. Indianapolis
18. Hendersonville
19. Odessa
20. Turlock
21. Romulus
22. Winthrop
23. Pawtucket
24. Newington

(Question 37)

154 Panvolic Homophones

Gorilla – Guerrilla.

(Question 118)

155 Initials I

16 pawns in a chess game
32 adult teeth
4 horsemen of the apocalypse
6 sides to a hexagon
7 stars in the Big Dipper
4 of a kind in poker
90 degrees in a quadrant
3 primary colours of light
40 years for a ruby anniversary
8 states of Australia

(Question 78)

156 Great Words

Noble, Immense, Illustrious, Talented, Glorious, Grand, Colossal, August.
Anagram: GIGANTIC

(Question 38)

157 Word Circle

Epilogue, Foreword.

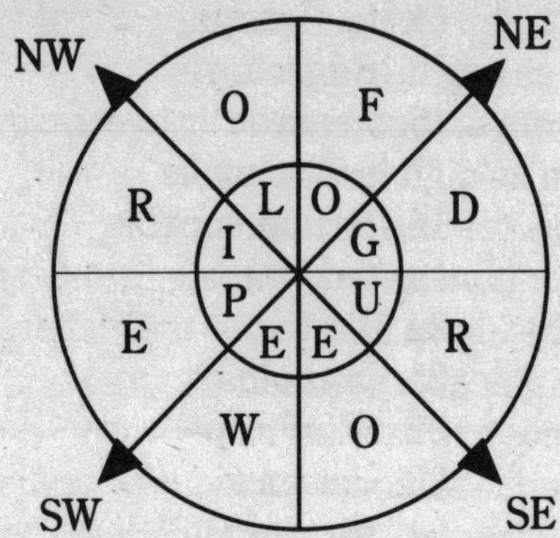

(Question 159)

158 All American

2 presidents with the last name of Roosevelt
5 cents in a nickel
5 great lakes in central North America
4 heads of presidents on Mount Rushmore
10 amendments in the Bill of Rights
50 signers of the Declaration of Independence
9 innings in a ball game
90 feet between bases on a baseball field
4 July is Independence Day
435 members in the House of Representatives

(Question 119)

159 Analogy

C:
The middle figure is superimposed on itself rotated 90° and goes inside one of the two figures above and below it.

(Question 160)

160 Analogy Test

1. Sharp is to blunt as dilate is to contract.
2. Constrict is to concentrate as selvage is to periphery.
3. Hue is to tone as hag is to witch.
4. Forte is to incompetence as avow is to controvert.
5. Law is to canon as digit is to integer.
6. Sere is to wet as copious is to scanty.
7. Caveat is to monition as tergiversate is to desert.
8. Cataract is to trickle as decry is to appreciate.
9. Fogy is to mossback as bathetic is to musty.
10. Bayou is to slough as sapid is to savoury.
11. Atrophy is to amelioration as stolid is to responsive.
12. Roily is to limpid as articulate is to disintegrate.

(Question 79)